TAMING

THE

SHARKS

Series on Law, Politics, and Society
Christopher P. Banks, Editor

TAMING
THE
SHARKS

Towards a Cure for the
High-Cost Credit Market

CHRISTOPHER L. PETERSON

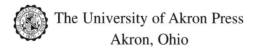

The University of Akron Press
Akron, Ohio

Manufactured in the United States of America
First edition 2004

08 07 06 05 04 5 4 3 2 1

Library of Congress Cataloging-in-Publication Data

Peterson, Christopher L.
  Taming the sharks : towards a cure for the high-cost credit market / Christopher L. Peterson.
    p. cm. — (Series on law, politics, and society)
  Includes bibliographical references and index.
  ISBN 1-931968-09-8 (cloth : alk. paper)
  1. Consumer credit. I. Title. II. Series.
  HG3755.P437 2004
  332.7'43—dc22   2004001503

The paper used in this publication meets the minimum requirements of American
National Standard for Information Sciences—Permanence of Paper for Printed Library
Materials, ANSI Z39.48—1984. ∞

Text Design by Charles Sutherland

For Margaret P. Battin and Tera J. Peterson

CONTENTS

TABLES

Acknowledgments

My first thanks must go to Professor Margaret Battin to whom this book is respectfully dedicated. It simply would never have occurred to me to write this or any other book without her cheerful example, intuitive questions, and timely encouragement. Next I gratefully acknowledge generous financial assistance from a Mariner S. Eccles Research Fellowship in Political Economy. Special thanks to Professors John Flynn, Leslie Francis, Bonnie Mitchell, and Linda Smith, all of whom stoically commented on early chapter drafts. Many friends and mentors have favored me with helpful ideas, support, inspiration, and kindness. In particular, I wish to thank the Honorable Wade Brorby, Quang Dang, Virginia Evans, Jason Hancock, Julie Hill, Ryan Hoglund, Margaret Kelly, Eric Luna, the Honorable Michael McConnell, Ed Mierzwinski, and Jen Scott. Thanks to Christopher Banks, Amy Petersen, Michael Carley and everyone else at the University of Akron Press for their patience and confidence in this project. I also wish to thank the anonymous reviewers of the manuscript for their time and effort.

I am blessed with a large and happy family including all the Millers, Sonny, Cora, Christian, Richard, and Guido—each of whom helped make this book possible. To my brother Ed, I am particularly thankful for his example and friendship. To my parents, Robert and Margaret, I am grateful for everything I have and am. Finally, my wife, Tera, is heroically patient, astonishingly wise, and funny too. Although this book is also dedicated to her, it is slight thanks for her innumerable hours of reading, editing, and encouragement. To her is due my last measure of gratitude—a debt I hope to have the honor of repaying for the remainder of my years.

CHAPTER 1

Debt Fever: An Introduction to High-Cost Consumer Credit

If you advance money to any poor man amongst my people, you shall not act like a money lender: you must not exact interest from him. If you take your neighbor's cloak in pawn, you shall return it to him by sunset, because it is his only covering. It is the cloak in which he wraps his body; in what else can he sleep? If he appeals to me, I will listen, for I am full of compassion.

—*Exodus* 22:25–7

A LEADING AND ACCLAIMED BUSINESS historian said of credit that, "free market long-term rates of interest for any industrial nation, properly charted, provide a sort of fever chart of the economic and political health of that nation."[1] In general, mainstream America has enjoyed historically low interest rates for over a decade, suggesting a robust economy and a responsive democracy. Our consumer credit system facilitates access to shelter, transportation, education, and many other goods and services both necessary and desirable in modern life. A family home bought over time with an inexpensive fixed-rate mortgage is a mainstay of the American dream, creating stability in extended families, neighborhoods, and entire communities. In financing a car, a worker can exchange a financial obligation for the priceless freedom to travel where and when she chooses. Borrowing in order to finance an education is an irreproachable investment in one's future. For these reasons and others we should all be proud that affordable credit is available to so many Americans.

Nevertheless, we must also remember that nations are made of groups within groups and ultimately of individuals. To say a nation has an interest rate fever is only to make a generalized claim about particular people, each with names and stories, and each of whom more or less contributes to the truth of the statement. A nation infected with a fever is so called because many people pay high prices for the use of money, people like Leticia Ortega, a computer store cashier in San Antonio, Texas. Short on cash, Ortega was facing termination of her past due telephone and electrical utilities. With her next paycheck still two weeks away, she saw an advertisement for a short-term loan in the *Thrifty Nickel*, a weekly local classified listing newsletter. The advertiser, National Money Service, Inc., offered a two-week $300 loan for a charge of $90. Despairing for some other solution to her shortfall, Ortega borrowed the money. But after two weeks had passed she was no closer to financial solvency than before. Unable to pay the entire $390 due, National Money Service "rolled over" the loan by withdrawing $90 directly from Ortega's checking account. Because Ortega was living paycheck to paycheck, with no surplus income available to retire the $300 debt, she continued to pay the $90 every two weeks for nearly a year. Eventually she paid $1,800—a substantial portion of her yearly income—but still owed all of the original debt. The annual interest rate of Ortega's loan was just under a feverish 800 percent.[2]

Even "healthy" nations have always had individuals who pay feverish prices for the use of money. The governments, corporations, banks, and wealthy individuals of our society have in general successfully immunized themselves from high interest rates through sound monetary policy, well-considered government regulation, and, most importantly, by harnessing competitive market forces. But for America's working class, and for America's increasingly vulnerable lower-middle-class, the analogy between health and credit prices begins to suggest a different medical chart. This book argues the high-cost consumer credit often extended to this group is best seen as *a persistent low grade infection*, sometimes more and sometimes less noticed by elites, but always burning the vulnerable.

Americans in all demographic categories are borrowing more relative to their disposable income than ever before. In fact, for the first time in American history, our collective debts have exceeded our collective disposable income. As Table 1.1 shows, debt burden as a percentage of disposable income has grown steadily throughout the latter twentieth century. From a modest 31.9 percent of disposable personal income in 1949, outstanding debt grew to 71.9 percent by 1979. By the mid-1990s debt represented 91.9 percent of personal disposable income. And, despite rapid growth in stocks and productivity in the latter 1990s, by the turn of the century Americans had more debt than disposable income. Thus, as the Economic Policy Institute explained, "[a]t the aggregate level, debt is a more important feature of the household economy than at any time in modern history."[3]

TABLE 1.1

Aggregate household debt as a percentage of personal disposable income, 1949–99

1949	1967	1973	1979	1989	1995	1999
31.9%	66.9%	65.2%	71.9%	84.6%	91.9%	103.0%

Source: Economic Policy Institute, The State of Working America 2000/2001[4]

For most Americans this increasing debt has been benign. The purchased use of money—credit—is a valuable commodity for na-

tions, corporations, and households alike. As one scholar has explained, "consumer credit is about much more than instant gratification. It is also about discipline, hard work, and the channeling
of one's productivity toward durable consumer goods."[5] For affluent Americans it is safe to say the increasing debt load of the past
two decades may be ascribed to comparatively well-considered obligations purchased at tolerably low interest rates for mostly good
reasons. Moreover, the stock market boom and dramatically rising
productivity of American workers in the 1990s was kind to America's more affluent citizens, offsetting the impact of rising debts.
Despite the burst technology bubble and currently slower growth,
for the relatively affluent middle class on up, America has a strong
economy and bright prospects.

But for less well-off Americans, the ever-rising proportion of
disposable income dedicated to outstanding debt hints at a darker
future. At the end of the twentieth century a new and distressing
trend of spreading financial infection has emerged—an interest
rate fever for which a growing number of working-class and lower-
middle-class Americans have scant resistance. With approximately 90 percent of all stocks and bonds owned by the wealthiest
10 percent of American society, the stock market boom of the
1990s scarcely benefitted our most vulnerable groups.[6] According
to the most recently published federal survey of consumer finances, approximately 12.6 percent of all American families have
annual incomes of $10,000 or less. Of these families—including
families with household heads at ages close to or in retirement—
less than two percent have invested in mutual funds, less than four
percent own any stocks at all, and no statistically significant number own bonds.[7] Table 1.2 explains that while vulnerable families'
assets grew, their debts grew faster. The result was that the least
wealthy 40 percent of American households saw a dramatic decline in their net worth despite the growing economy. Thus, as
one scholarly work puts it, "the real story of the 1990s was not the

stock market boom, but the debt explosion."[8] Or, in the more re-strained—and portentous—words of Federal Reserve Board Chairman Alan Greenspan, "families with low-to-moderate incomes and minorities did not appear to fully benefit from the highly favorable economic developments of the mid-1990s."[9]

TABLE 1.2

Average assets and liabilities of the least wealthy 40 percent of American households (constant 1998 dollars)

	Stocks*	All other assets	Total debt	Net worth
1983	$ 400	$16,800	$12,500	$4,700
1992	800	19,100	17,600	2,300
1995	1,100	20,600	20,700	1,000
1998	1,700	23,800	24,400	1,100

*All direct and indirect stock holdings
Source: Economic Policy Institute Analysis of Survey of Consumer Finance Data

At the same time net worth has declined, low to moderate income Americans have also experienced stagnation or a decline in the real value of their wages. Between 1973 and 1999, the median weekly wage in the United States fell 12 percent from $502 to $442. Although the real value of median weekly wages recovered slightly in the mid- to late 1990s, it still has not recovered to its 1988 level. In the words of Federal Reserve Board researchers," mean incomes for all education groups in 1998 were lower than they had been in 1989." For families headed by a worker with no high school degree, real income declined *even* in the rapid growth years between 1995 and 1998.[10]

Unsurprisingly, key indicators of financial instability have increased in proportion to declining real wages and net worth. For instance, the 1990s saw significant increases in the number of households with debt service payments equal to more than 40 percent of household income—an important indicator of financial hardship caused by over-indebtedness. Perhaps more ominous is a startling increase in the number of lower-middle-income families who were late in paying bills over the past decade. Of families with annual incomes between $25,000 and $49,999, in 1989 only 4.8 percent were late sixty days or more in paying at least one bill. By 1998 this figure nearly doubled to close to one family in ten.[11]

While working poor families saw increased debt load and decreased earning power, their access to traditional banking services has also decreased. Prefacing a major market shift in the financial servicing of America's working poor, the number of families without a bank account increased by 77 percent between 1977 and 1989.[12] Many of the key pressures keeping working poor families out of banks and savings associations remained, and perhaps increased, in the 1990s growth economy. A Federal Reserve Board report shows that while most banking fees paid by solvent customers remained static, those fees commonly charged to consumers in financial trouble grew dramatically in the late 1990s. Stop payment orders, overdraft charges, not sufficient funds fees, and below minimum balance fees—all acutely felt by families experiencing income shocks—grew much faster than inflation in the last decade. For instance, bank and savings association overdraft charges grew 17 and 23 percent respectively between 1994 and 1999 alone. Not sufficient funds check fees and stop payment order prices both rose about 15 percent in this five year period. And bank fees charged to customers whose savings account balances dipped below minimum requirements grew by a surprising 31.3 percent.[13] At the turn of the century, the best estimates suggest 13 to 15 percent of all American families are "unbanked"—"nearly double the proportion in England."[14] Of families without checking accounts, 86.2 percent had annual incomes less than $25,000 and 44.7 percent had annual incomes less than $10,000. About 57 percent of these families were non-white or Hispanic. Currently, over 20 million Americans have no access to mainstream banking services.[15]

Observing these trends, many have begun to ask this question: If working poor and lower-middle-class families have, over the past two decades, borrowed more, but banked with traditional first-tier lenders less, with whom are they doing business? A short survey of recent headlines begins to answer this question:

- "Short-term Loan Firms Prospering: Critics Say High Interest Rates, Easy Terms Have Led to Exploitation of Working Poor"
- "Easy Money: Subprime Lenders Make a Killing Catering to Poorer Americans. Now Wall Street Is Getting in on the Act"
- "Payday Lenders Face Fiery Criticism: Consumer Advocates Say Federal Law Allows Institutions to Operate Like Loan Sharks"
- "Time to Restore Loansharking Laws"
- "Borrowing Trouble: How Can Legislators Not Be Offended By Payday-Advance Business that Charge Outrageous Fees to Cash Strapped Consumers?"
- "How High Can the Finance Companies Go? With Interest Rates, the Sky Is the Limit"
- "Banking on a Costly Alternative: Low Earners Turn to Check Cashing Stores"
- "Wolf At the Door: Vulnerable Need Protection Against Predatory Lenders"
- "Shark Attacks: An Encounter with Predatory Lenders Can Leave You Without Your Money—Or Your Home"
- "Feeding Off the Bottom"
- "Little Loans Come at Staggering Cost"
- "New Lenders with Huge Fees Thrive on Workers With Debts"
- "It Was Illegal When It Was Loansharking"[16]

Unfortunately, hard data on financial service providers that cater to the working poor is notoriously sparse.[17] Nevertheless, upon examining the growth and business practices, as well as the stories associated with many second-tier lenders, the answer becomes clear. Working poor families have turned to a looseknit patchwork of businesses, including small moneylending firms, multinational consumer credit corporations, high-rate credit card issuers, mortgage loan companies, payday loan/check-cashing outlets, automobile title loan companies, rent-to-own furnishing stores, and pawnshops, to serve their financial needs. Although this industry has a wide variety of practices, norms, and agendas, the one unifying characteristic possessed by all is that they sell credit at relatively high cost.

WHAT IS HIGH-COST CREDIT?

The personal finance industry catering to high-risk, low-income borrowers defies easy description. A variety of names are associated with this industry including alternative finance lenders, subprime lenders, specialty lenders, small loan lenders, fringe bankers, predatory lenders, and sometimes loansharks. In the eighteenth and nineteenth centuries the word "usury" contextually linked the group together—given widespread interest-rate caps which drew a rough line between socially acceptable and unacceptable credit. Originally the word "usury" came from the Latin noun *usura* which referred to the "use" of anything; "hence, usury was the price paid for the use of money."[18] But as moderately priced consumer credit sold to the middle class became entrenched in the twentieth century, the legal as well as cultural lines distinguishing usurious credit eroded. For some "usury" refers to an unfair loan. Others use the word to describe an illegal loan without hinting at any concurrent moral condemnation. The word can also refer to the body of law regulating the amount of interest charged. It may also refer to a particular statutory limitation in a particular jurisdiction. Sometimes usury refers not to an entire loan, but only to the amount of interest that exceeds the legal rate. Courts have disagreed whether non-interest charges are included for purposes of calculating usury law violations. Often it is not clear from the context which meaning the authors intend. At the beginning of the twenty-first century the word "usury" has become something of an inconveniently ambiguous anachronism.

A more useful reference increasingly used in both federal and state law is the simple description "high cost."[19] The essential difference between mainstream creditors and "alternative finance lenders" is relatively expensive prices. Moreover, "high cost," unlike usury, is a fluid enough concept to readily include both interest and non-interest charges, such as origination fees, brokerage fees, processing fees, application fees, credit insurance premiums, appraisal fees, refinancing charges, late payment penalties, early payment penalties, and dozens of other creditor inventions which tend to obscure the true cost of a loan. Admittedly, at what point credit should be considered high cost is open to debate. Some would say all consumer credit has high costs, in comparison to commercial loans, while others would argue no loan has a high cost if the borrower willingly agrees to it. We can save this argument for another day. For the purposes of this book, it is not necessary to discuss at length at what particular point a loan should be considered "high cost." Certainly, an 800 percent annual percentage rate ("APR") "payday" loan qualifies. A 6.7 percent APR thirty-year fixed-rate mortgage with low points and fair contractual terms does not. Whether a 29 percent APR revolving credit card contract qualifies as high cost is an open question. For our purposes, the term is one of convenience aimed at describing the upper end of consumer credit usually extended to the poor and those with risky credit records. Nevertheless, a more detailed picture of high-cost credit can come from examining a selection of some prominent high-cost credit arrangements and lenders.

"Only Until Payday"—Deferred Deposit Lenders

Perhaps the archetypal high-cost creditor is the payday lender. While the industry prefers the term "deferred deposit lender," companies within the industry are also known as check cashers, check lenders, deferred presentment lenders, post-dated check lenders, sale-lease-back companies, and payday advance companies. Payday lenders trace their American origins to the "five for six" salary lenders prevalent at the end of the nineteenth century. Customers of these early salary lenders would often borrow five dollars on Monday and in exchange pay six dollars on Friday or Saturday. Contrary to popular Hollywood imagery of extortionate mafia lenders, the term "loanshark" actually evolved in large Eastern cities some time after the Civil War to describe specifically these early salary lenders.[20] The term did not come to describe the mafia until at least the 1930s. Today's payday lenders provide nearly identical loans as our first loansharks, only now lenders have the added security of holding the debtor's personal check.

In a typical contemporary transaction, a customer might borrow $100 by writing a check made out to the creditor for $117.50. The date written on the check reflects the due date of the loan. Typically, a loan is for two weeks. Thus, two weeks after obtaining the post-dated check, the creditor will collect by depositing the check. Lenders verify the debtor's identity by asking for documents or identification such as a drivers license, recent pay stubs, bank statements, car registration, or telephone bills. Most lenders will telephone the borrower's human resource manager or boss to verify employment. Virtually all lenders require the names, addresses, and telephone numbers of close family and friends in the event the borrower skips town. Payday lenders decide whether to issue a loan on the spot without obtaining a credit report. Both parties are aware the checking account does not have sufficient funds to cover the check when it is signed. After the paperwork is complete, the debtor walks away with $100 in cash or a check drawn on the lender's account. When the two weeks are up, the debtor can redeem the check with cash or a money order, permit the check to be deposited, or attempt to renew the loan by paying another fee. If the borrower cannot pay off the loan, the obligation continues to accrue $17.50 in interest every two weeks. Although the initial $17.50 fee represents only 17.5 percent of the loan amount, the annual percentage rate of the transaction is around 456 percent.[21] In comparison, the average reported interest rates of mafia lenders in New York City during the 1960s was a relatively inexpensive 250 percent.[22]

Surprising to some, a 456 percent APR loan is not unusual. Because the federal government does not collect data on payday lender interest rates, there are no firm nationwide statistics showing payday loan prices. However, studies by state agencies, consumer advocates, and academics regularly suggest *average* payday loan annual percentage rates are roughly between 391 and 550 percent. In the quick cash, no credit check, easy money, storefront credit shops that line America's strip malls, loans with quadruple-digit annual percentage rates are common. For example, while an Indiana Department of Financial Institutions survey found the average Indiana payday loan interest rate was 498.75 percent, one company offered a $100 loan at a $20 charge per day—a staggering 7,300 percent APR loan. North Carolina consumers purchase about 63 percent of their payday loans at annual interest rates between 406.08 percent and 805.15 percent. Payday lenders in Salt Lake City charge an average rate of 528.49 percent. A consumer advocate coalition study surveying lenders in nineteen states and the District of Columbia found an average payday loan interest rate of 474 percent.[23]

Moreover, these calculations of average interest rates severely underestimate the true prices of payday loans. Payday creditors typically charge other unexpected fees in the course of a normal loan. For example, insufficient funds fees applied to normal bounced checks also apply to payday loan checks. Usually both the payday lender as well as the debtor's bank or credit union will charge the debtor separate fees for bouncing a loan check. Some lenders will require debtors to give two separate checks for one loan so when the debtor defaults, the lender can collect two insufficient funds fees. These insufficient funds fees can be as expensive as the interest on any given payday loan. Some creditors will charge an insufficient funds fee every time they attempt to deposit the original loan check, usually once every two weeks. For example, if a lender charges a $25 insufficient funds fee on a $100 loan carried for a typical six months, the contract will oblige the debtor to pay an additional $300 above and beyond the disclosed interest rate.

However, insufficient funds fees are hardly the only culprit. Hidden fees are limited only by the lender's imagination. For example, Check City, a Utah payday lender, includes in its boilerplate contract a $75 per hour "collection fee" for time expended collecting a loan. The contract is silent on how much time the creditor may take. And, to help ensure the lender can pocket this independent fee, the contract states, "I authorize Check City . . . , at any time on or after the due date of my loan or payroll advance, to initiate a charge to any checking account of mine, by electronic funds transfer or otherwise, for the unpaid amount of my loan, including interest, all costs and expenses of collection (including attorneys fees) and late and returned check charges."[24]

Many states have usury laws limiting interest to around 36 percent annually. In these states the payday lending business is conducted by evading interest-rate caps. Such evasion is easier and more common than it sounds. Currently, one common loophole involves "charter renting." Payday lenders interpret federal banking law to exempt nationally chartered banks from state interest-rate caps. Payday loan companies form relationships with federal banks where the payday lender solicits, manages, and issues each loan, but ostensibly uses the federal bank's funds in exchange for a per-loan fee. The result is that payday lenders often operate with impunity even in states where popularly elected legislatures have passed outright bans on payday lending.[25] For example, the New York state legislature has limited interest rates to no more than 25 percent annually. Still, payday lenders linked to out-of-state banks have attempted to offer payday loans within the state. A chagrined New York Banking Department superintendent recently complained "banks that choose to offer this type of loan product at exorbitant interest rates are blatantly abusing [federal] authority. These types of actions, when judged in the court of public opinion, can lead to a groundswell of outrage resulting in reputational harm and safety and soundness problems."[26] But despite this and similar complaints around the country, payday lenders attached to even the most insignificant of federal banks remain free to charge whatever interest rates they choose.

Payday lenders defend their products by pointing out their loans are intended only to help consumers deal with short-term cash shortfalls. They argue it is not fair to quote annual percentage rates for loans which only last for one or two weeks. However, what empirical data is available shows payday loans are often in reality medium- or long-term obligations. For example, North Carolina regulators counted the total number of payday loan transactions of given customers at a given company in a year. About 87 percent of borrowers would roll over any given loan at least one time with any given lender. Not counting debtors who borrowed from multiple locations, 38.3 percent of customers renewed their payday loans more than ten times. About 14 percent of borrowers renewed their payday loans with the same lender more than nineteen times per year. Illinois regulators found payday loan customers "who were borrowing continuously for over a year on their original loan." Indiana also found approximately 77 percent of payday loans are rollovers of existing loans. Consumer advocates have found the average customer borrows 10.19 payday loans per year, with some debtors borrowing many more times. In fact, one debtor renewed 66 times in order to pay off a single payday loan—approximately a two-and-one-half year debt—assuming a typical two-week renewal cycle. Even an industry-funded study found about 40 percent of payday loan borrowers rolled over more than five loans in the preceding twelve months, including about 20 percent of all borrowers who renewed existing loans nine times or more.[27]

Trouble comes for many debtors after they borrow and they realize how difficult repayment can be on a limited income and paycheck-to-paycheck standard of living. A government study indicates "the average customer is usually a woman in her middle thirties earning just over $24,000 a year. She usually rents her home and once she becomes a customer of a short-term loan company she usually remains a customer for *at least* six months."[28] Similarly, an informal Florida survey found the typical payday debtor is a twenty-eight-year-old white female who earns between $14,500 and $20,000 per year working in the service or health care industries.[29] For such debtors, payday loans may become a trap they cannot escape without missing rent, utilities, car payments, or food expenditures. These loans can create a biweekly cycle of income and expenses leaving only enough surplus income to pay the most recent accrual in interest and fees. In the words of the Illinois Department of Financial Institutions:

> Industry members who have testified at . . . public Illinois Senate hearings have referred to their customers as average citizens who encounter unexpected financial hardships. What they have failed to mention was that the financial strains placed on consumers were rarely short-lived. Customers playing catch-up with their expenses do not have the ability to overcome unexpected financial hardships because

their budgets are usually limited. The high expenses of a short term loan depletes the customer's ability to catch-up, therefore making the customer "captive" to the lender.[30]

A leading consumer advocate report goes one step farther saying, "[t]hese loans are designed to keep consumers in perpetual debt."[31]

While industry representatives dispute such claims, Janet Delaney from Alabama might not. She is employed as a hospital food-service worker, making around $16,000 a year. When she needed $200 to cover impending bills she turned to a local payday lender. The business loaned Delaney her shortfall for a $38 fee. But when her next payday rolled around, she still didn't have enough money to cover the check. Instead she rolled over her loan for an additional $38. A University of Alabama law student who eventually highlighted Delaney's plight explained, "[a] year later, she had paid $1,220 in fees and still owed $200. Over a twelve-month period, Ms. Delaney paid 610 percent interest, returning to the payday lender thirty-two times and borrowing from two other payday lenders just to make the fee payments."[32]

Many states have responded by passing laws which prohibit lenders from "rolling over" payday loans. State legislators hope these laws will prevent the abuses associated with long-term payday loan debt. However, these restrictions have proven even easier to evade than traditional interest-rate caps. Despite a Utah rule prohibiting rollovers beyond twelve weeks, the author of one study recorded a "refreshingly candid" conversation with a young female cashier at a Salt Lake City check lender. "Brandy" explained "[w]e have them paying for sometimes two or three years. . . . They just have to keep on paying. They will, like, pay for the loan two or three times and still owe the loan."[33] Rollover prohibitions are difficult to enforce, because lenders can structure the transaction to allow the debtor to pay off the old loan with proceeds from a "new loan."[34] Also, nothing prevents debtors from taking out another payday loan at a different location.

In addition to high prices on longer term payday loans, many have observed a systemic pattern of questionable business practices and state law violations in the payday lending industry. For example, in 718 payday lender inspections conducted over a three-year period, North Carolina Banking officials found 8,911 violations of simple state consumer-protection rules.[35] Moreover, many commentators have complained payday lenders manipulate the criminal justice system to help collect debts. Ambiguous fraudulent check laws and theft statutes in many states allow payday lenders to threaten criminal prosecution for writing "bad" checks.

> Payday lenders in Ohio, for example, sue under the "Civil Damages for Crime Victim" statute . . . which provides triple damages to victims of theft offenses, including bad checks. Inspection of court records in Dayton Municipal Courts Division over eight months in 1999 found 381 actions by five payday lenders. Defaulting customers were charged triple damages, 10 percent interest on the damages, and court costs. The total dollar amount for the judgments from all 381 cases was $285,406. In 60 percent of the cases, wages were garnished.[36]

Similarly, a Texas regulator testified that in only one year, payday lenders filed 13,000 criminal charges against their customers in one Dallas precinct. Of course, payday lenders know perfectly well debtors are signing checks which cannot clear when written—a cash shortage is the whole premise of payday loans. But even in states which prohibit criminal justice action, a hollow threat of prosecution by a county attorney can provide enough leverage and fear to accomplish the same objective. It goes without saying traditional creditors such as banks, credit unions, and savings and loan associations, unlike payday lenders, cannot use the criminal justice system to collect their bad debts.[37]

Fueled by these and other remarkably profitable trade practices, the payday lending industry has exploded. Although the business of selling short-term credit at high prices has an old pedigree, the relatively young version of securing debt with personal checks has grown exponentially in the past two decades. In North Carolina, payday lending outlets roughly quadrupled in four years, growing from 307 in 1997 to 1,204 in 2000. Payday lending outlets quintupled in Salt Lake City between 1994 and 2000. Wyoming payday lenders tripled between 1996 and 1997. Iowa's payday lenders increased from eight to sixty-four in two years. Colorado officials have estimated payday lenders have grown to make up 20 percent of that state's licensed lenders. One Wisconsin consumer advocate observes, "[t]he payday lenders are moving in by the day here. . . . We're watching it happen."[38] An explanation for this growth is not difficult to find. By one estimate in the late 1980s, opening a payday lending outlet required an initial investment as small as $65,000 and could create before-tax returns of $117,000 in a single year.[39] The Tennessee Department of Financial Institutions "reported to its state legislature that licensed payday lenders earned over 30 percent return on investment in the first nine months of legal operation."[40] One economics professor estimates check cashing/lending operations earn ten to twenty times higher return on equity than traditional banks.[41] Summarizing this trend, John D. Hawke, U.S. Comptroller of the Currency, recently pointed out "there are now more payday loan offices in California than McDonald's and Burger King restaurants."[42]

Neither does this astounding growth appear to be slackening off. A recent trade association convention drew standing-room-only crowds for those interested in converting other businesses into payday loan outlets. This continuing growth will inevitably affect our culture and change the assumptions we hold about financial services. For example, in Louisiana, a company called Mr. Payroll has teamed up with Circle K convenience stores to sell payday check loans alongside fountain drinks, gasoline, and Twinkies. Not to be outdone, Utah regulators have issued a payday loan license to Atlantis Burger, allowing debtors to purchase triple-digit-interest-rate loans while stopping off for a hamburger. Some predict payday loans will soon be offered through ATM terminals. Finally, the Illinois Department of Financial Institutions warns the payday loan market may grow an additional 600 percent in the coming decade.[43]

The Venerable "Hock Shop"

Pawnbrokers are the veterans in the high-cost credit market. For a variety of reasons, some not related to credit, pawnbrokers have faced a continuing struggle to improve their public image dating back thousands of years.[44] First, fairly or not, pawnbrokers are associated with stolen goods. Many jurisdictions require identification and thumbprinting of pawnshop customers to discourage resale of stolen property. Similarly, pawnshop gun sales, sometimes in questionable compliance with federal gun control laws, do not help reputation-building efforts.[45] Pawnshops have also often been associated with gambling, as well as adult bookstores, strip clubs, and liquor stores. Pawnbrokers in close proximity to casinos tend to do brisk and steady business by financing gambling binges and reselling pawned merchandise to winners. One Massachusetts pawnbroker describes regularly taking out ads saying "Lose to the bookies? Come see us!"[46] A surprisingly common municipal squabble involves local planning commissions or city councils harassing pawnbrokers with restrictive zoning ordinances.[47]

But most important of all, critics accuse pawnbrokers of using credit to profit from the misfortunes of the impoverished. Usually consumers seeking pawn credit are highly cash-constrained. A recent survey indicated 69 percent of pawnshop customers had been more than 60 days late in paying some bills during the previous year. 70 percent had been contacted by a debt collection agency. And "16 percent had their wages garnished within the previous two to three years for a purpose other than child support," according to one researcher.[48] One pawnbroker, owner of the Happy Hocker in Cleveland, Ohio, estimates that at least 80 percent of his customers do not have bank accounts.[49] Almost all pawn debtors lack the credit history and real property security to obtain cheaper credit from banks or credit unions. In the words of the CEO and founder of Cash America, Inc., the nation's largest pawnshop chain, "I could take my customers and put them on a bus and drive them down to a bank and the bank would laugh at them. That's why they're my customers."[50]

Although some pawnshop customers only shop at pawnshops for negotiable prices on second-hand consumer goods, loaning money is the backbone of most pawn operations. Typical pawn loans are very simple transactions where the creditor provides a fixed-term loan to a customer who leaves a personal item in the possession of the lender as collateral. After the customer repays all the required interest and fees, the lender will return the security to the borrower. The majority of customers return and reclaim their goods. Veteran pawnbrokers estimate 45 out of 50 borrowers will eventually succeed in redeeming their security. A leading scholar on pawn credit comparably estimates 10 to 30 percent of borrowers default on their pawn loans. Pawnbrokers' interest rates vary with the regulations of different states and localities. In states with unregulated markets, pawnshop interest rates average around 240 percent APR. But in states with active interest-rate regulation, such as Oregon, charges can reach as low as 40 percent annually. Nevertheless, in Texas, which boasts more pawnshops than any other state and also regulates pawn charges, the average annual rate is around 200 percent. Although no national data is available,

Cash America, with 420 shops in eighteen states around the country, extends pawn credit at an estimated aggregate average annual interest rate of 205.3 percent.[51]

One positive feature of pawn credit is its tendency to be naturally short-term and terminal. Unlike payday loans where consumers often are forced to repay their loans over relatively long periods, a defaulting pawn debtor simply forfeits the personal item left with the pawnbroker as collateral. On the other hand, pawn customers do not have access to the goods which secure their loans. When a customer pawns a television set or diamond ring this may not be serious. However, the most secure loans are those where the customer cannot get by without the collateral. "I've seen people take their dentures out of their mouths before," explains Steve Anderson, manager of ACME Pawn in Colorado Springs, Colorado. "One guy took his gold tooth out of his mouth and we took that."[52]

Often the only items a working-class family owns which will obtain the necessary credit are tools. This can leave carpenters, auto mechanics, and other self-employed and journeymen workers without the means to conduct their trades. For instance, the Wichita, Kansas economy relies heavily on manufacturing of airplane parts. When the market for air travel dried up following the September 11, 2001 World Trade Center and Pentagon terrorist attacks, local pawnbrokers reported an "onslaught" of machinist tools from laid off aerospace workers.[53] Unfortunately, many workers have difficulty finding employment again since they must pay back their loan, plus a stiff premium, before reclaiming their tools. Undoubtably, this phenomenon is nothing new and has caused untold misery for thousands of years. Thus, the biblical injunction in Exodus exhorting, "if you take your neighbor's cloak in pawn, you shall return it to him by sunset, because it is his only covering. It is the cloak in which he wraps his body; in what else can he sleep?" While few contemporary Americans pawn clothing, the profit motive which spawned the ancient dictum is not lost on Wall Street. In the twenty days following the September 11, 2001 terrorist attacks the Dow Jones Industrial Average lost 8 percent, the NASDAQ lost 12 percent, but Cash America saw the price of its publically traded stock jump 8 percent in the opposite direction as traders clamored for opportunities to weather the impending downturn. A headline on one daily business newspaper offered the financial advice: "Get Into the Pawnbrokers for Hard Times Ahead."[54]

Although the bursting of the American technology bubble undoubtably gave pawnbrokers a shot in the arm, the industry has been growing steadily for the past twenty years. Low-to-moderate income consumers have lost access to banks and credit unions since the late seventies, so they have naturally moved to pawnshops for their financial needs. Moreover, pawnbrokers themselves explain widespread overextension of lower-middle-class debtors has forced increasing numbers to turn to a formerly unthinkable source of credit to overcome income shocks and unexpected expenses. "Our business is at an all-time high," explains Tony Mills, owner of Big Time Pawn in Tulsa, Oklahoma. "There are a lot of people in serious debt . . . and then, if they lose their jobs . . . they are bringing in things to get quick cash." In the 1980s alone, the number of pawnshops nationwide *more than doubled*. Although the greatest number of pawnshops per capita are in the southern and mountain states, some northeastern and far west states have experienced dramatic pawnshop growth as well. For example, Pennsylvania saw a 130 percent increase in pawnshop licenses between 1980 and 1991. While pawnshops grew slightly less quickly in the 1990s than in the 1980s, the explanation given by most pawnbrokers is not particularly heartening—competition from payday lenders.[55]

Rent-to-Own Resurgent

Another important player in the high-cost consumer credit market issues credit akin to pawn loans. Rent-to-own lenders lease appliances, furniture, electronic equipment, and occasionally jewelry for weekly payments. If a customer successfully makes payments for a specified duration of time, the rent-to-own store transfers ownership of the item to its customer. Rent-to-own contracts vary from around fifty to one hundred and fifty weeks with seventy-eight weeks being the norm. More expensive items usually rent for longer periods. Typically, customers can return an item at any time, ending the arrangement. Rent-to-own purchase prices are usually two or three times the retail value of the good. Moreover, because a significant portion of rent-to-own merchandise has been used previously and then repossessed, the actual depreciated value of the items is much less than normal retail value. Contracts also typically provide for a number of ancillary charges such as late payment fees, rental contract reinstatement fees, and rental property retrieval fees. Rent-to-own firms also sell renter's insurance plans which prevent the firm from suing the customer if an item is lost or stolen. But, unlike normal insurance, the lost item is not replaced. A "vast majority" of customers sign up for these protection plans. About 95 percent of customers borrowing from Rent-A-Center, which in 1993 controlled 25 percent of the 2.3 billion dollar U.S. market, purchased such insurance, generating 29 million dollars of revenue.[56]

The industry vociferously maintains rent-to-own contracts are not loans. In support of this notion, the industry has consistently claimed only 25 to 30 percent of transactions result in purchases. However, according to the most comprehensive study available, conducted by the Federal Trade Commission, about 67 percent of rent-to-own customers intend to purchase the merchandise, 8 percent were unsure of their intentions, and only 25 percent intend to rent items for a short while and then return them. Moreover, FTC data indicates rent-to-own transactions more closely resemble loans than leases since "70 percent of rent-to-own merchandise was purchased by the customer." Thus, while rent-to-own dealers describe the transaction as a traditional lease with a bonus of ownership provided as an incentive to renew, in reality the transaction is more like a chattel-secured installment loan with high interest and foreclosure rates.[57] Nevertheless, the rent-to-own industry has aggressively lobbied state legislatures around the country to avoid regulation under consumer credit laws. In the past fifteen years, forty-six states have passed industry supported legislation treating rent-to-own transactions as leases over the objections of consumer advocates. The industry has also pressured Congress for separate lenient treatment. Hiring some of the nation's most expensive lobbyists, the rent-to-own industry hopes to wipe out state laws by passing a relatively weak federal bill posing as consumer protection. Even in a Congress focused on alleviating an impending recession following the September 11 terrorist attacks, rent-to-own lobbyists were still hard at work trying to pass legislation to preempt laws in New Jersey, Minnesota, Wisconsin, and Vermont, which still treat rent-to-own business as a credit transaction.[58] Rent-to-own stores have a strong social incentive to avoid characterizing their contracts as loans since, when viewed as credit, rent-to-own contracts are typically one- to three-year loans with annual interest rates ranging between 70 percent and 360 percent. Most commentators estimate the national average rent-to-own APR is somewhere around 100 percent.[59]

The rent-to-own industry commonly practices aggressive and direct marketing tactics. The comments of Gerald Defiore, a former store manager from Spartanburg, South Carolina provides insight on one of many marketing tactics:

> You would brochure the projects one week before the [welfare] checks came out so you already had that seed planted in their mind. . . . Then the day the checks came out, you'd go back and knock on doors and fill out the work forms there. Corporate was in on it, the stores were in on it. These people didn't stand a chance.[60]

Comparably, the Rent-A-Center headquarters in Wichita, Kansas uses the six references required to open a rent-to-own agreement for marketing purposes. Individual stores only contact two of the references in determining whether to rent to the customer, using the other four references as marketing contacts to send mailings to. Thus, entire extended families are targeted by advertisements with opening lines like, "Wouldn't you rather watch a big screen TV than the one you have now?"[61]

Rent-to-own stores usually emphasize courteous treatment of prospective customers. One industry CEO said that the rent-to-own industry "treats them [customers] like kings and queens." Employees of one firm "are required to greet customers, preferably by name, within ten seconds of their entrance and to conduct payment disputes out of earshot of other renters. Stores are also encouraged to keep fresh coffee brewing."[62] However, rent-to-own contracts require substantial collection efforts. Stores will generally contact renters/borrowers a day or two after a missed payment. Personal visits to the homes of debtors are standard practice after as few as three days of arrears. Stores generally repossess items after a week of delay. The collection process has traditionally been vulnerable to abuse and misbehavior. A small but significant percent of rent-to-own repossessions are completed by breaking in to the customers' homes. The contracts of one leading rent-to-own company includes a boilerplate provision which attempts to sanction entry into the customer's residence even when the customer is not home. The Federal Trade Commission estimates about 7,000 of these break-in repossessions occur each year. One Nebraska rent-to-own customer mistakenly shot and killed a repossession agent, believing the man was a burglar.[63] "Employees handling repossessions have been known to bring along members of a feared motorcycle gang as well as to vandalize customer's homes, extract sexual favors from strapped customers and even, in one instance, force a late payer to do involuntary labor." Particularly infamous are so-called "couch payments," or extracting sexual favors at the homes of renters in lieu of repossession or cash payment. The Rent-A-Center CEO

> acknowledges that abuses such as couch payments occurred in the past and "are probably going on today." There are simply "more control problems" in a business where the activity takes place out of the store, he says. But the company stresses that such abuses are "few and far between" and not "in any way condoned by Rent-A-Center."

However, one reporter interviewed twenty-eight former store managers of Rent-A-Center—six admitted the practice occurred in their areas.[64]

Like payday lenders and pawnshops, rent-to-own operations have grown quickly in the past two decades. Fortune Magazine recently listed Rent-A-Center, the nation's largest chain with 2,400 stores nationwide, as one of the 100 fastest growing companies in the United States. In one year Rent-A-Center pulled in $1.7 billion dollars in revenue. Moreover, the highly profitable industry has undergone substantial consolidation with Rent-A-Center and the next largest chain, Rent-Way, owning more than half of the market. Both of these companies roughly doubled in size in 1998 alone. Since 1982 the number of rent-to-own outlets nationwide grew from around 2,000 to approximately 8,000 at the turn of the century. Thus, our nation's rent-to-own stores have quadrupled in only twenty years.[65]

Car Titles and the "Repo-Man"

There are many different ways to use automobiles as collateral for credit. The most obvious is borrowing the purchase price of a new or used car. Traditionally, car buyers arrange their own financing through a bank or credit union. However, car dealers often help buyers avoid the trouble of arranging their own financing by partnering with lenders to offer financing packages to approved customers. In the high-cost credit market, car dealers catering to buyers with problematic credit histories often hold car loans themselves, allowing them to repossess at will and then quickly resell the car. These lenders draw customers in need of transportation with promises such as "good credit, bad credit, no problem," "no credit check," "no hassles," "no money down," and perhaps more surreptitiously, "low introductory rate."

Cars and trucks are also used to secure credit not related to the purchase of the vehicle. Car title lenders or auto-pawnbrokers loan money to cash seeking consumers who own their cars. Some lenders require the borrower to turn over the car, which is then stored on a fenced lot until repayment. But, the great majority of non-purchase price auto lenders simply hold the car title—and a copy of the keys. The latter strategy is more common because it allows customers to borrow on what may be their only significant asset without losing access to convenient transportation. Typically, car title loans contracts provide that the debtor relinquishes ownership of the car upon a single missed payment.

There is a broad range of interest rates on high-cost car loans. Mainstream bank or credit union car-purchase loans fluctuate in the neighborhood of 10 percent APR, depending on the length of the loan and whether the car is new or used. But borrowers with problematic credit histories typically pay two or three times as much. Average car title and auto-pawn loans cost between 200 percent and 300 percent APR, but can reach as high as 900 percent.[66] Like payday lenders, car title lenders use creative charades to evade state interest-rate caps, where they exist. For example, some companies claim they are buying cars from the customer and then selling them back at a higher price. One journalist notes, "[t]hey have trouble, however, explaining why the customer continues to drive the car he just sold."[67] Moreover, like other high-cost creditors, car lenders often use contracts with stiff penalties for late payment, repossession, bounced checks, and more. While interest rates tend to be less for car-secured credit than unsecured credit, such as payday loans, interest rates alone often do not represent the true price debtors pay. Some car title lenders thrive less on the interest rates they charge than upon repossessing cars. Jeanette Greco's story is not unusual. When Greco's husband died his estate became tied up in court. The New Port Richey, Florida woman needed cash to pay her son's tuition, so she decided to take out a title loan on the almost-new car her deceased husband had given her as a present. The lender required Greco to turn over the title to the $30,000 specially-ordered Dodge Stealth in exchange for her $1,000 loan. After making faithful payments on what turned out to be a 500 percent APR secured loan for several months, Greco's father suffered a heart attack in Puerto Rico. Greco missed several of her weekly payments when she traveled to Puerto Rico to take care of him. When she returned the car was gone, along with all of the family Christmas presents she had been storing in the trunk. While she never saw the Christmas presents or her car again, court records indicate the car was sold at auction for $3,500. The lender did not even rebate auction proceeds in excess of the Greco's remaining debt. Despondent about her options, Greco observed, "lawyers cost twice as much as what you pawned the car for."[68]

Title loan contracts often allow repossession after only one day of arrears. Even in states which require the repossessing lenders to rebate the excess value of the car beyond the outstanding debt, lenders may quickly sell the car at less than its fair value rather than find a buyer willing to pay a fair price for the car. Repossessing creditors also have a strong financial incentive to "sell" the car at less than its market value to a subsidiary holding company or to an individual in a financial relationship with the lender. Cloaked by a nonexistent transaction, the creditor can claim no proceeds are left over to rebate to the debtor, when in reality the creditor keeps both full repayment of the loan and the collateral. In states where there is no rebate requirement, or where the requirement is not vigorously enforced, creditors simply resell repossessed cars at fair market value and keep all of the proceeds. Many car title lenders also have car dealer licenses. Regardless, some lenders loan to title debtors who are *likely* to default, in order to find creative ways to capture the value of the car.

Unsurprisingly, many car title debtors become desperate to avoid repossession. Like all car owners, car title debtors use their vehicles as transportation to and from their jobs, to drive their children to school, or to visit sick family members. Many car title debtors face unemployment if their car is repossessed. When Debra Lusan, a working mother from St. Louis, fell behind on daycare payments for her two children, she took out a $600 title loan. After paying $900, she had long since lost track of how much the title lender claimed she owed, but she still kept on paying. "I just want to get my title back," she explained.[69] Many car title debtors undergo privation, sacrificing food expenditures, utility payments, and health care treatment, rather than lose access to transportation.

Another problem with high-cost automobile credit comes from the rapid depreciation in the value of cars. When consumers purchase new cars with reasonably priced financing, the car is likely to provide reliable transportation long after the loan is repaid. But where working-poor consumers buy used cars with high-priced credit, the loan often outlives the car. Accidents and breakdowns can make cars functionally worthless while the buyer still owes thousands of dollars borrowed at high rates. Because few working-poor families can manage two car payments, the buyer is left without reliable personal transportation.

Equity Predators: The Market for High-Cost Home and Mobile Home Credit

The market for home loans has increasingly become the subject of a widespread national debate over wealth inequality, racism, and exploitation of the elderly. For most families, home ownership is the key to long-term financial stability. Many commentators believe relative disparity in home ownership is essential to understanding contemporary American racial inequality. For example, at the height of the 1990s growth economy, approximately 71 percent of whites were homeowners compared to only 44 percent of blacks.[70] Moreover, a longstanding dispute exists over whether mortgage lenders discriminate, either intentionally or unintentionally, against minority loan applicants. Because homes are so important and costly, most American families spend their lives attempting to pay off home mortgages. The federal government has provided valuable tax incentives and subsidies to encourage and facilitate this process. State and local governments have also attempted to aggressively regulate the market for home-secured loans, often leading to conflict over which level of government is the appropriate source of homeowner protection.

In the last five years this mortgage lending debate has focused on the subprime market and particularly upon home-secured loans consumer advocates describe as "predatory." Lenders classify debtors based on their credit histories into categories ranging from "A" to "D." Prime loans are those extended to customers with "A" credit histories. The subprime market services borrowers with "A-," "B," "C," and even "D" credit histories. The government-sponsored enterprises Fannie Mae and Freddie Mac purchase most prime mortgage loans from lenders who originate the loans. These two companies either hold conventional prime loans themselves or bundle and resell them as securities to Wall Street investors. Although recently Fannie Mae and Freddie Mac have began purchasing some A- loans, in general, both have strict underwriting

standards and pay similar prices for all the loans they purchase.
This, along with front-end competition for borrowers, stabilizes
the prices prime-market lenders charge. Subprime lenders, however, resell their loans to many different places and often will hold
and service the loans themselves. As an industry insider explains,
"[t]hat means subprime originators have much more leeway when
it comes to setting rates and underwriting standards. As a result,
rates, fees, and program guidelines vary drastically depending on
which broker or lender a consumer visits."[71]

The boundaries between legitimate sub-prime loans and predatory mortgages are difficult to draw. California-based Ameriquest
Mortgage Co., one of the nation's leading subprime lenders, exemplifies the conundrum. While Ameriquest has donated gener-
ously to consumer education funds and other charitable causes, its
credit record is perhaps even more checkered than its customers'.
In 1996 Ameriquest paid four million dollars to settle a lawsuit
brought by the Department of Justice which claimed its brokers
charged higher fees to women, seniors, and minorities than to
young white males. In 2000, the community activist group
ACORN filed a complaint with the Federal Trade Commission alleging the company consistently misleads its customers about the
true costs of interest rates and fees. Recently, company detractors
stormed an Ameriquest branch location. While employees hid in
a back office behind a locked door, the protestors marched around
chanting "people over profits" and "no more loan sharks." To un-
derscore the point, one protestor wore a shark costume.[72]

Apologists argue these attacks are undeserved and point to
Ameriquest as a relatively progressive leader in the subprime market. For instance, after the ACORN protests Ameriquest adopted
a ten-city pilot program which provides home ownership counseling to potential borrowers. The company would even counsel potential customers to shop around for the best deal.[73] But consumer
advocates remain skeptical. So too does Ward Adams from An-

chorage, Alaska. Last year Adams, an out-of-work carpenter and a veteran, fell behind on his bills and was looking for some way out. Ameriquest offered to pay off his credit card debts if he would agree to refinance his family home with them. Ameriquest mailed all of the necessary documents, which Adams admits he did not understand. An Ameriquest representative who claimed to have lived in Anchorage for eighteen years "would call me up and we'd [small talk] like he was my best friend over the phone. He was calling me constantly, sometimes just to [chat]." Adams was ready to sign the contract, but thought twice when he realized the representative "didn't know any of the crossroads or anything about Anchorage." Adams talked to some real estate friends and a nonprofit consumer debtor counseling service, both of whom admonished him not to sign. The Ameriquest loan would have nearly doubled the interest rate of Adams' federally subsidized 7 percent Veterans Administration loan. His mortgage payment would have increased about $350 a month. "How am I going to pay that? There would be no way," Adams explained his shock, "It was spooky. . . . I was down to the wire—all I had to do was sign the paperwork and send it back."[74]

While Ward Adams may have narrowly avoided losing his home, horror stories of those not so lucky have come to permeate the nation's newsprint media and policy rhetoric. For example, in 1990, 71-year-old Lula Mae Rosser owned the small Atlanta home where she had lived for forty years. She agreed to a $12,500 loan at 16.9 percent APR to finance the repair of her decaying roof. Over the next decade the same lender, Better Homes Co., refinanced the loan two additional times, eventually driving the amount owed up to $30,000. A disabled former housekeeper, Rosser lived on her $463-a-month social security income. After the final refinancing, the monthly payments amounted to $365— almost 80 percent of Rosser's monthly income. Traditional prime lenders avoid lending to families with income-to-payment ratios greater than 28 percent. Inexplicably, the loan application forms incorrectly listed Rosser's income at $664 per month. By January of 2002, she had declared bankruptcy to at least temporarily prevent Bank One, who had purchased the debt second hand from Better Homes, from foreclosing on her only shelter.[75]

Although there is no bright line determining when a subprime loan becomes a "predatory" loan, most agree the distinction turns not only on contract terms but also on the borrower's circumstances. A high interest rate loan might provide a young dual-income family with a needed opportunity, but the same loan could be a devastating financial blow to an elderly widow, such as Rosser, with a fixed social security income. Still, there are many loans and practices which almost all impartial observers agree are predatory. Federal Reserve Board Governor Edward Gramlich has labeled as "predatory" lending to borrowers who have no ability to repay the debt, inducing a borrower to refinance a loan repeatedly, and concealing the true nature of the contract from an unsuspecting or unsophisticated borrower. Other suspect practices include packing loans with excessive single premium credit life insurance, negative amortization, unnecessarily high balloon payments and prepayment penalties, refinancing low-cost or subsidized home loans, inflated appraisal and credit report fees, yield spread premiums, mandatory binding arbitration clauses, and marketing practices targeted by race or age rather than credit history. What victims of predatory lending do not understand until too late is that in a typical high-cost home loan transaction the interest rate is often a relatively unimportant factor in the true price of the loan. The heart of much criticism over high-cost home-secured lending is that many lenders seek to capture home equity rather than a return on their investments.[76]

For instance, multiple refinances—or "flips"—offer high-cost home lenders an unparalleled opportunity to strip homeowners of home equity. At each new refinancing the lender collects another round of points and other miscellaneous closing charges, almost always including a new credit insurance policy. When a borrower falls behind on payments, many high-cost home lenders will use the situation to flip the loan. The lender might explain, "we see you have been late on your most recent payment. If you could use some extra cash right now, why not refinance your loan and take advantage of our temporary low introductory interest rate." The sales agent never mentions that refinancing triggers a prepayment penalty and other charges costing thousands of dollars. Because cash-strapped delinquent borrowers are eager to cooperate in order to prevent additional late payment penalties or foreclosure proceedings, they are easy fodder for sales staff paid on commission. Because these charges do not come out of the borrower's pocket, debtors often do not understand the true cost. Rather, the charges are added on to the total amount the borrower owes on the home. Or—put a different way—these charges are deducted from the equity the borrower has built up in the home over time. Predatory lenders commonly include a small amount of cash as proceeds from the new loan to help encourage borrowers to sign. The unsuspecting but satisfied borrower walks away with a few hundred dollars in his pocket and no idea he has just been taken for thousands. After only a few flips, borrowers can loose a lifetime investment in home equity, never having realized the true consequences of their contracts. A borrower may have spent hundreds of thousands of dollars on the home, but when it comes time to sell—or when foreclosure proceedings begin—the borrower owns nothing.

High-cost manufactured home credit poses special problems for vulnerable debtors. Manufactured home loan interest rates are generally two or three percentage points higher than conventional home loans for borrowers with comparable credit histories. Moreover, the value of manufactured homes tends to depreciate, more like an automobile than conventional housing. But unlike car loans, which typically last no more than five years, manufactured home mortgages last fifteen, twenty, or even thirty years. Also, manufactured home buyers tend to lease rather than buy plots for their homes, leaving any appreciated value in the real estate itself for the landlord. Soon after the contract is signed, many borrowers find their manufactured home is worth nowhere near as much as they owe. The homeowner becomes trapped not only in the loan, but also within a manufactured home park. Because it typically costs around $7,500 to move a "mobile" home even a short distance, park owners can dramatically increase plot rental fees or require expensive lot improvement charges after a homeowner has moved in. Manufactured homeowners have a median household income of only $23,000 per year and an average age of 52.7 years. Typically, they live check-to-check lifestyles, forcing them to accept monthly rent increases since they cannot afford the one-time up front cost of moving their homes. Manufactured homeowners may alternatively seek refinancing to relocate, subjecting them to another round of points and probably a prepayment penalty, all of which leave them even deeper in debt.[77]

Furthermore, recent investigations and studies have exposed widespread fraud, inflated pricing, and a variety of other unscrupulous practices throughout the manufactured home finance market. One study analyzed more than 400 manufactured home consumer complaints filed with the Texas Attorney General. The study found sales staff commonly falsify loan application information in order to qualify eager buyers who cannot realistically afford homes. Alternatively, many dealers will lend the borrower nearly all of the down payment, which is then incorporated into the home loan. These practices lead to high default rates. But, because many lenders are affiliated with home manufacturers, they share an interest in high sales volume as well as economies of scale in repossession proceedings. Moreover, if a debtor tries to assert her rights in court, the lender may hamstring the borrower's legal position by claiming the borrower committed fraud against the lender. These dealer practices drive responsible lenders out of the manufactured home finance market and secondary market since these lenders cannot accurately measure the quality of their investments. Moreover, because manufactured home buyers are usually locked into a contract before their home is delivered, dealers have little incentive to carefully install the home—leading to substandard housing. Many manufactured home buyers complain their homes are never set up properly, lack specially ordered features, or are even different models than those displayed by the dealer. And, if a borrower refuses to accept the delivered home, dealers sometimes retaliate by reporting or threatening to report the borrower to credit bureaus. Many manufactured home lenders and dealers conduct scrupulous businesses. But with approximately 8 percent of the United States population residing in around 9 million manufactured homes, unfair manufactured home lending is a surprisingly large and neglected problem.[78]

The market for subprime and manufactured home mortgages grew rapidly in the 1990s. Federal Reserve Board researchers explain that between 1993 and 1998 "subprime and manufactured home lenders' share of conventional purchase mortgages extended to lower income and minority borrowers tripled (quadrupled in the case of Hispanic borrowers) . . . reaching levels of one-fifth to one-third." In the same five-year period the annual shipments of manufactured homes grew about 47 percent, as compared to annual increase of only 24 percent in conventional site-built homes. While this increase is in part due to growing variety in manufactured housing styles and amenities, it is also due to a growing proportion of the American population groping for financial solutions for lives on the edge of solvency. For instance, African Americans are increasingly turning to manufactured homes instead of conventional homes. Between 1993 and 1998 the proportion of African Americans applying for home purchase mortgages from manufactured home lenders rather than conventional home lenders more than doubled from 20 percent to 42 percent.[79] No data exists which casts light on the proportion of subprime and manufactured home loans fairly considered predatory. However, if interest rates and other credit charges do provide a fever chart of economic health, recent trends both in the home mortgage market as well as the market for other forms of high-cost credit suggest a significant threat for many vulnerable Americans.

THE SYMPTOMS OF DEBT FEVER

High-cost debt can have a devastating impact on the lives of debtors and their families. While the consumer credit industry in general accounts for nearly 87 percent of debt listed in bankruptcy, no reliable data estimates what proportion originates from alternative finance lenders.[80] Generally the more disposable income is spent on debt, the greater a household's chances of bankruptcy are. Therefore, it is not surprising that bankruptcy has grown in step with increases in consumer debt.[81] Bankruptcy is intended by law as a last-resort method of discharging unpayable debts. It is also intended to give debtors a fresh start to allow them to continue to function as productive members of society.[82] However, a great deal of stigma and moral judgment are attached to declaring bankruptcy. It is the legal and moral equivalent of declaring oneself a financial failure, and undoubtably shatters the self image of many who take the option. As the nation's leading bankruptcy scholar explains, "everyone wants to be a success in the American competition for prosperity; bankruptcy singles out those who did not make it. . . . We should be haunted by questions of why so many Americans are losers in the great financial game of life."[83]

Similarly, home foreclosures associated with high-cost mortgage credit can tear families and communities apart. One congressional representative persuasively explained, "[i]f owning a home is the American dream, then the threat of losing that home is the American nightmare. . . . The human costs of mortgage is startling. A family's life savings and a major part of its earnings, understandably, is often tied up in its home. For many, losing their home is an event from which they will never recover."[84] Foreclosure uproots the social links between people. Children are usually forced to change schools. Commuting to and from places of employment often becomes more challenging. New living arrangements are almost always less convenient, healthy, safe, and emotionally satisfying. Many families are forced to bounce from home to home of families and friends until a new job or apartment can be found. Because home ownership defines "social personhood," home foreclosure destroys the self image and social embedding of families. In the worst cases, new living arrangements are found only in a homeless shelter, in a family car, or on the street.[85] Statistics for the causes and numbers of homelessness are notoriously difficult to establish, but few see that problem as independent of home foreclosure, and foreclosure is certainly not independent of high-cost lending. What we do know is that increases in home foreclosure have tracked the "explosive" growth of the high-cost lending market. U.S. Census Bureau data shows that in the past twenty years, the number of home foreclosures has increased by more than 384 percent—almost *quadrupling*—despite two decades of fast aggregate economic growth.[86]

However, defaulting high-cost debtors do not always face events that culminate in a single crisis point such as foreclosure or bankruptcy. For many the collection process and worry over the impending risk of these more cataclysmic events are the sources of great suffering. One study asked debtors in default on mortgage payments how they felt when they realized they had missed a payment and could not make it up. The nearly universal response was shock and fear. Some of the typical answers were: "I panicked, cried." "We worry sick about it. It scares us to death." "Well, it was a shock . . . I went a bit berserk really. . . ." "I felt ill, I remember the shock. I thought 'where the hell are we going to find the money from'?"[87] These concerns are mirrored in dramatic increases in the number of support and therapy groups dedicated to helping those living in debt. For example, Debtors Anonymous, a support and therapy system based on Alcoholics Anonymous, first appeared in 1968 in New York. By 1998, twenty separate weekly Debtors Anonymous meetings were listed in the Washington, D.C. area alone. As the high-cost credit industry has exploded so too has Debtors Anonymous, which now lists at least 500 therapy groups in the United States, as well as additional groups in thirteen other countries.[88]

In high-cost lending, where default is dealt with as a matter of course, the tactics used by creditors are often aggressive and the stakes for debtors high. Often creditors use pressure collection techniques which involve frequent calls, demand letters, threats, manipulation, and intimidation. Moreover, federal legislation regulating debt collection has a relatively narrow scope, in addition to enforcement problems. But its chief drawback is that it only covers third-party debt collection agencies. This creates a significant incentive for lenders to collect debts themselves rather than selling the debt at a reduced price to secondhand collectors. Thus, in the high-cost credit market, it is common practice to keep collection activities "in house." In an industry where profit revolves around how much money can be collected, rather than predictions of credit risk, the incentive to use high-pressure tactics, regardless of the consequences for debtors' personal lives, is difficult to control. Checks on abuse, either through government-sponsored rules or the good intentions of well-meaning creditors, tend not to overcome this incentive. A culture of disregard for debtors' emotions and suspicion of debtors' motivations can gradually build up in even well-meaning high-cost credit organizations.

High-cost creditors focus on pressuring customers into paying, regardless of the consequences payment might bring. The *Con-*

sumer Credit Collector, a monthly newsletter published for debt collectors and often distributed by credit companies to their employees, reflects industry standards in the collection process. The cover page article of one issue entitled: "Pressure As a Collection Tool: Turn Up the Heat to Get Paid," quotes a typical collector who is having trouble "turning up the heat." "My manager says I'm too nice to our debtors and don't know how to get tough when I need to. Actually, I could become much more forceful in my collecting, but I never know when the time is right." The article goes on to explain what "pressure" in the high-cost credit industry means:

> You must convince your customer that you have taken a personal interest in this account and that you won't be satisfied until the delinquency is remedied. Your customer must realize that this balance is the most important account you have. Once the debtor has accepted these two points, you have applied the necessary pressure that will enable you to get paid.[89]

No room is left for the possibility that debtors simply cannot pay. The culture instead classifies any attempt by the debtor to take this position as merely making "excuses." Another article in the same issue entitled, "Set Deadlines to Create Urgency," is illustrative:

> It is important for collectors to set deadlines when collecting. Deadlines stress to debtors the urgency of the situation and your seriousness in collecting the account. A deadline also forces debtors to search for sources of repayment immediately and not delay further. . . . every conversation with a debtor should include some type of deadline.[90]

The stresses associated with high-cost debt often lead to serious emotional and psychological trauma. A whole range of depressive symptoms are part of the normal cycle for those in credit trouble, including sleeplessness, anxiety, aggression, frequent crying, increased alcohol intake, and weight loss. Moreover, "[d]efault debtors blame themselves rather than society for the circumstances they find themselves in, and attribute these circumstances to bad luck rather than any structural aspect of society." In the words of one debtor, "I feel I've let them [the creditors] down, I feel guilty about that; my reliability is not there." Even debtors who do not blame themselves are still controlled by their fear that others will make harsh judgements against them. Borrowers in credit trouble rarely discuss their financial problems with others. The senses of shame and embarrassment, combined with decreasing financial ability to maintain a normal social life, cause debtors to retreat into social isolation from both friends and family. This retreat deprives them of normal means of emotional coping and support that allow individuals to deal with life problems, thus magnifying the emotional crisis.[91] A debtor persuasively explains in her own words:

> [Collection Agents] talked to me as if I were a child, not letting me speak. They didn't speak about facts, only me as a person—me as a bad person. One told me that people collecting welfare paid them more monthly than I was offering to pay. I was neither on welfare, collecting unemployment, nor employed, but it made no impression on them. They asked why I didn't have a job, what had I been doing about it. They insinuated that there was something definitely wrong with me, and they wanted to know what it was. Shame and hopelessness set in. They called a lot, never allowing much peace between their verbal batterings. The collection agency switched me from one representative to another, so no history, rapport or empathy could develop. They were just doing their job.

There is no debtors prison but after a few of these relentless, harassing phone calls I wished there were. Maybe then I could escape the verbal and psychological abuse. I didn't discuss the problems with my friends, because their disdain would be too demoralizing. The fear, shame and pressure from others, and especially myself, was paralyzing.

It was a nightmarish descent into debtor's hell. I already know I was a social misfit because I no longer had a credit card, but now I had to experience degrading humiliation because I couldn't pay my monthly minimum. So what could I do? Commit suicide? Declare bankruptcy? Leave town and change my name, leaving no forwarding phone number? . . . When I was younger and saw old newsreels of people jumping to their death because of the 1929 stock market crash, I couldn't believe it. "Just for money?" I wondered. But now I understand it.[92]

Many of the symptoms associated with debt trouble, including anxiety, feelings of helplessness, aloneness, self-contempt, anger, and terror, are also counted by medical, psychological, and legal professionals as risk factors for suicide.[93] Debtors have even been know to sell their organs on the transplant black market to pay off their debts. But in the high stakes collection of second-tier debts, mortal danger does not come merely from debtors themselves. For example, Henry James Hubbard III borrowed $300 from Georgia Auto Pawn in Macon, Georgia. Although the loan was secured by the title to Hubbard's car, Georgia Auto Pawn nevertheless charged interest and fees amounting to about 300 percent APR. About five months later Mr. Hubbard fell behind on his payments. When a collection agent came to repossess the car, Hubbard understandably protested. When both men drew guns, the collection agent shot Hubbard three times while his wife looked on. In court, a medical examiner testified that based upon the angle of Hubbard's wounds, he died from a bullet to the chest suffered while lying on his back.[94]

THE DEBT FEVER IMMUNE SYSTEM: FREE MARKETS

While clearly horror stories such as Mr. Hubbard's do not represent typical high-cost debtor experiences, hearing the tragic stories of high-cost debtors and observing recent credit trends, it is easy to wonder what has gone wrong? These stories and data do not easily cohere with the traditional liberal economic world view which today permeates our policy-making, legal jurisprudence, and economic theorizing. Rooted in the ideas of Adam Smith, Jeremy Bentham, and other Enlightenment thinkers, the default American explanation of market behavior leaves little room for these relatively unclean stories of contemporary high-cost debt. In our default worldview every individual, abstracted as *homo economicus*—the economic man—makes self-interested decisions which collectively create the best possible policy outcomes we can reasonably expect. Adam Smith described the phenomenon of self-interested individual decisions creating collective welfare as "an invisible hand" guiding the allocation of resources to an optimal outcome. Smith's description lies at the heart of the American presumption against government interference in individual market decision-making. Traditional economic reasoning suggests free market forces should act as a sort of natural defense mechanism, or immune system, against feverish credit prices.

This persuasive and elegant account of market decision-making imbues the public relations, legal advocacy, and government lobbying of the high-cost credit industry. High-cost lenders rely on arguments about the beneficial effects of their products, the inevitability of a high-cost credit supply, and the patronizing motives of government regulation. For instance, subprime mortgage lenders argue their home loans give low-income borrowers a chance to enter mainstream society which they would otherwise never possess. To their credit, home ownership rates have shown impressive gains despite the vast increase in home foreclosures. Similarly, payday lenders explain their loans help families navigate short-term financial crises. They insist it is arrogant for legislators to presume they know which loans are in a borrower's best interests better than the borrower herself. One North Carolina payday lender persuasively explains:

"Thank you for being here," "Thank God you were here for me when I needed you." These are very common quotes heard in my lobbies. I'm sure it's easy for you to sit in your office and tell your readers how "bad" payday lenders are. We offer a service, plain and simple. . . . Our customers like our service. If they didn't, they wouldn't use us, plain and simple.[95]

Indeed, who are legislators to tell a struggling mother she should not borrow money to feed her children, pay her rent, or purchase costly prescription medication? Lenders and their supporters accuse their detractors of clinging to archaic Puritan debt phobia to the disadvantage of real people with real needs.

Many high-cost creditors and industry groups report favorable customer satisfaction. High-cost creditors argue payday loan rollovers, repeat pawning, widespread rent-to-own growth, and reiterate home and manufactured home refinancing are all evidence of—not desperation-based borrowing—but contentment. In this view, high-cost debtors, like all consumers, vote with their feet. High-cost creditors merely respond by supplying legitimate services to this natural demand. Moreover, high-cost lenders emphasize that their customers often have no other credit choices. Regulation which impedes this natural market function will only dry up a necessary and beneficial market. If markets persist despite the regulation, the costs of regulation are passed on to borrowers in increased prices which hurt consumers more than no regulation at all. Lenders assert most consumers would prefer a lower price to added regulatory protection. High-cost lenders argue their services are inevitable, explaining that if government regulation shuts down our current high-cost lenders, a black market will rise from their ashes. Lenders argue the same services will be provided, but consumers would pay an additional premium to insure illegal lenders against the risk of getting caught. Moreover, an unregulated black market would attract lenders specializing in corruption, fraud, and violence.

Much of the controversy over high-cost lending exists because of our well-founded faith in the simple free market principles which ground these compelling creditor arguments. To be sure, free market competition, along with a strong democracy, has been the backbone of American economic and political success in the twentieth century. But as many economists, sociologists, political scientists, journalists, judges, and legislators have recognized, these market principles have not always produced for us the optimal outcomes Adam Smith's allegory of the invisible hand has led us to hope for. This book attempts to reconcile traditional microeconomic reasoning with an interest rate fever chart that suggests many Americans are suffering. This book also examines the way the state interacts with the high-cost credit market, hoping to distill lessons which might help us better close the gap between our traditional economic predictions and reality. This book hopes to help us move towards a cure for our feverish high-cost credit market.

CHAPTER 2

The Short Story of the Long History of High-Cost Credit Policy

HIGH-COST CONSUMER CREDIT IS older than money. Recent trends showing growth in the high-cost credit market might mislead us into believing attendant social problems are a new phenomenon. Nothing could be further from the truth. The practice of exchanging things of value in return for the obligation of future repayment is one of humanity's most useful and, paradoxically, dangerous social inventions. The history of credit in general, and of high-cost credit in particular, dates back to the beginning of recorded history, with the notion of interest evolving thousands of years before coined currency.[1] So too do social and government policies designed to temper the consequences of high-cost debt predate money. Thus, in searching for a cure to the high-cost credit market, we must begin with a basic understanding of the medications administered to the feverish credit markets of past societies. Historians and archaeologists have provided a rich pool of wisdom that many contemporary commentators neglect. We can extract from this rich history examples of civilizations, and where possible, stories of individuals, for lessons that are instructive.[2]

The societies of our world have developed a relatively few num-

ber of policies for dealing with the social and economic consequences of high-cost debt. While it is beyond the scope of this
chapter to explore every method societies have employed to battle the sometimes pernicious effects of high-cost credit, a small
number of policy strategies emerge as the most significant and
widely used in our far and recent pasts. To extend the metaphor of
high-cost lending as a constant but selective low-grade fever, we
might think of these strategies as widely accepted medical treatment regimes. The policies of each civilization have retained
unique characteristics, and often strategies are combined and per-
muted. Nevertheless, we can condense these strategies into seven
historical "treatments" which retain contemporary significance.[3]
Six of these historical strategies predate the United States and are
presented here. The seventh, a relatively recent strategy which
shall be a particular focus in this book, is saved for later. Unlike
most chronological histories, our purposes are better suited by
grouping different historical examples based primarily on policymaking tactics rather than upon dates. In this way, we may reduce
lessons of a long history into a much shorter story.

While the treatments of the past, and even recent history, have
attempted to temper the fervor of high-cost credit, a different approach is necessary to cure the current high-cost credit epidemic.
We will explain this promising and historically different approach
later.

POOR, NASTY, BRUTISH, AND SHORT: THE
INCEPTION OF HIGH-COST CREDIT REGULATION

The earliest form of credit was probably reciprocal gift-giving—
a variation on "you scratch my back and I'll scratch yours." Here,
as one historian puts it, the creditor is "in effect a gift-giver who
merely expects a 'delayed' reciprocal gift from the recipient."[4] Or
perhaps the recipient of the first gift will merely owe a debt of loy-

alty to the creditor. Historians and archaeologists speculate that interest itself probably originated some time between 8000 and 5000 B.C.E., during the late Paleolithic or early Mesolithic ages. By then agriculture was common. With the advent of farming, the accumulation of capital such as livestock, tools, and seed took on an importance likely unfamiliar to the nomadic hunter-gatherers of earlier eras. This desire to collect capital probably gave impetus to define more clearly the terms of previously ambiguous credit agreements. Loans were usually payable in either grain, animals, or metal. The earliest historic mainstream interest rates range from 20 to 50 percent per annum, later stabilizing at 33⅓ percent for loans on grain, and 20 to 25 percent for loans of silver.[5] Loans were made both for the purposes of investing in future production as well as for nonproductive purposes, the latter being accurately characterized as consumer credit. There is, of course, no reason to suspect that greed, or more charitably, the desire to compete successfully in a world of scarce resources, was any less a motive at the dawn of civilization than today. Because creditors often lent to those in desperate need of food or shelter, the relative bargaining position of debtors often placed them at a significant disadvantage. For these debtors, short-term loans with great risk and extremely high costs were common. Also, in the absence of standard currencies, ambiguity over what constituted acceptable payment of a debt left wide latitude for abuse. Thus, "[h]uman nature being what it is, trouble must have developed quickly. The rich exacted hard bargains and grew richer; and the poor fell into perpetual debt and forfeited their meager possessions."[6]

Although the earliest recorded prevailing interest rates are similar to the rates many regularly pay today, the penalties for default tended to be more severe in ancient times. In Mesopotamia, free males were entitled to send their wives, servants, or children into forced servitude to pay off debts. If a man could not produce a working dependent, his enslavement or imprisonment was common. Creditors who seized the human assets of a debtor were essentially free to do with the slave whatever the creditor chose. The treatment of debt slaves was harsh indeed, often including gouging out the slave's eyes to prevent escape, and only providing enough food to sustain life. With the stakes so high, we can expect the powerful and greedy took great advantage of the poor and vulnerable. While consumer credit was an important tool for managing poverty it also quickly became one of our earliest tools of forced poverty, social oppression, and enslavement.[7]

Treatment One
The Deceptively Simple Solution: Debtor Amnesty

Despite its drawbacks, the practice of borrowing has persisted because of its fundamentally useful nature. The task of consumer credit policy then, as it still is today, became separating the harmful obligations society is not prepared to embrace from the useful purposes of credit. In this regard, the Sumerians, generally considered the world's first civilization, took the lead as they did in many other areas of human concern. Occupying the southernmost segment of Mesopotamia between the Tigris and Euphrates Rivers, stretching roughly from modern Baghdad to the Persian Gulf, the Sumerians were eventually supplanted by the Babylonians. However, Sumerian civilization is nonetheless credited with developing the world's first wheeled vehicles, the first ox-drawn plows, the first system of writing, and the first city-states.[8] Alongside other trades, including pottery, weaving, metalwork, and masonry, the Sumerians traded in credit. Many documents dealing with credit have survived showing a system which carefully recorded and commonly extended loans. But like other early societies, the penalties of default were severe and violent. As credit grew in popularity, a significant portion of the Sumerian population—

mostly subsistence farmers—was sold into debt slavery to live alongside prisoners of war.[9]

The treatment of debt slaves, at times apparently offending even the ancient sense of social decency, led many Sumerian and later Babylonian kings to "make justice."[10] Kings often recorded their deeds for posterity, not only professing their power in war, but also claiming the adoration of their people. Included in these aristocratic boasts were references to royal decrees which canceled certain debts, especially those which forced free people to sell themselves or their families into slavery. For example, one of the earliest recorded legal codes, dating from about 2350 B.C.E., provided relief for debt slaves. Urukagina, the Sumerian king who promulgated the rules, gave amnesty to all persons imprisoned for failure to repay their debts. Similarly, Ammisaduqa (1646–1626 B.C.E.), a later Babylonian king, also canceled the debts of enslaved former citizens.[11]

Although the details of these royal decrees of amnesty are sparse, they begin to sketch the outlines of problems that have plagued similar strategies ever since. Initially, forgiving some debts did not solve the real problem, only treating its symptoms after the fact. Debtors would still borrow, creditors would still lend, and in the absence of state intervention, default and its attendant problems still developed. Moreover, each decree was a limited one-time treatment rather than a permanent systemic reform. These executive pardons did nothing for those not lucky enough to fall under their limited jurisdictions. The conundrum of whether a creditor or debtor should bear the losses associated with default still existed. All these amnesty decrees could do was temporarily reverse fortunes of those who managed to capture the attention of fickle authority.

As a social strategy, granting debtors amnesty from their debts persisted. In sixteenth-century Spanish Holland, the penalties for debt default were reminiscent of their distant Sumerian forbears.

In 1540, Charles V passed an edict, later described as the first bankruptcy statute in the Netherlands. In its preamble, the law justified itself as attempting to remedy the expense connected with creditor law suits against debtors and to provide for a pure administration of justice which would deal equally with the rich and poor. Hoping to deter debtor default, the law provided among other things that "all persons who absented themselves from their ordinary residences with the object of defrauding their creditors were to be regarded as common thieves, and if caught might be summarily dealt with and publicly hanged."[12] Ironically, the Spanish crown consistently defaulted on its own debts, finding itself bankrupt on *six* subsequent occasions during the sixteenth century alone.

Like Sumerian and Babylonian kings, Europe's princes also issued decrees canceling debts. The crucial difference, however, was that European princes usually canceled only their own loans or the loans of their closest allies and associates. For example,

> Philip the Fair (IV) of France, 1285–1314, borrowed heavily at unstated rates, but instead of repaying his bankers he banished them, canceled his own debts and decreed that the principal of all other debts must be paid to the Crown. His principal creditor, the Order of Knights Templar, which had become largely a banking organization, was utterly destroyed. Edward III of England, 1312–1377, likewise repudiated his debts . . . and ruined his Florentine bankers.[13]

Nobles would also at times orchestrate cancellation of their debts by availing themselves of lingering church doctrines prohibiting interest—especially against foreigners. While consumer and commercial debtors alike faced severe punishments, such as summary public hangings, even the deliberate and fraudulent default of royalty "could be punished only by the sanction of a future denial of credit."[14] This aristocratic abuse of power demonstrates central limitations with forgiving debt as a policy strategy: it is difficult to devise fair and efficient rules determining who deserves amnesty. Too often, those who receive discharge of their debts are those who least merit it. As we shall see, it is precisely this difficulty which more than any other afflicts the contemporary United States bankruptcy system.

Treatment Two
Separating "Good" Credit from "Bad" Credit: Interest-Rate Caps and Other Loan Format Restrictions

Mesopotamian societies were not content with market anarchy and the occasional capricious amnesty of their kings. The next great innovation in consumer credit policy is best exemplified in the famous Code of Hammurabi, written in 1750 B.C.E. Legend tells us the Babylonian King Hammurabi ascended a mountain where Shamash, the God of Justice, gave him a divinely inspired code of law. History tells us under the rule of Hammurabi, Babylon developed from an insignificant city to the national capital of probably the most complex society of its time. Following Hammurabi, Babylon remained the capital of the entire region for about fifteen hundred years. The code set out over two hundred laws addressing social problems ranging from divorce to theft. Audaciously, it attempted to create a comprehensive and timeless set of laws to govern Babylonian society. Hammurabi's laws included several distinct controls on the lending market designed to protect debtors. Foremost was the world's first recorded maximum allowable interest-rate cap, which limited rates to about 20 percent per annum for loans on silver and 33 percent on loans of grain. The text of the code bears a remarkable similarity to interest-rate caps adopted thousands of years later and which in many areas are still in force. It translates, "If a merchant has given corn on loan, he may take 100 sila of corn as interest on one gur; if he has given silver on loan, he may take 1/6 shekel 6 grains interest on 1 shekel of silver."[15]

A central insight behind interest-rate caps is the recognition that while some loans are useful social agreements, others cause more harm than good. For early Babylonians, the central difference between acceptable and unacceptable loans was price. Thus, loans at interest rates in excess of the statutory caps were banned. However, the code also prohibited dangerous loan characteristics not directly related to price. For instance, recognizing loans may have dangerous consequences not only for individuals but for whole families, the code required both a husband and a wife to sign loan contracts encumbering joint property. Other rules included a maximum allowable three years that a wife, servant, or child of a debtor could spend in slavery to pay off a man's debt. Creditors could not take payments by force without the consent of the debtor. Debts of either a woman or a man incurred before marriage were not binding on the other spouse after marriage. Moreover, to prevent violations, Hammurabi's Code required creditors and debtors make their loan contracts in the presence of an official and witnesses.[16]

Hammurabi's interest-rate cap, along with its other lending format restrictions, proved remarkably durable. The rate cap remained intact as law for twelve hundred years—well over an entire millennium. In two thousand years the only significant change was to equalize the maximum allowable rate of grain to match that of silver. It is nonetheless unlikely the interest-rate cap and other provisions were consistently enforced. Records still exist documenting loans at 400 percent per annum during the period. Still, the enduring legacy of the social approach testifies to the success of the law as compared to what must have come before.[17] Nevertheless, for a closer look at potential cracks in the construction of this impressive regulatory feat, we must turn to later civilizations with a more complete historical record.

Ancient Rome also set maximum allowable interest-rate caps. High-cost debt played a crucial and volatile role in Roman politics from the earliest stages. In the fifth century B.C.E., Romans were only one of several ethnic groups present in Italy, and were still far away from domination of the Mediterranean. Already, class struggle, which would reemerge in centuries to come, was dramatically manifesting itself. In 494 B.C.E., a violent civil revolt took place. A large number of poor plebeians withdrew from the city and gathered on a hill overlooking the Tiber River. There they proceeded to elect their own shadow legislature, officials, and tribunes, essentially seceding from the Roman Republic. The outcome of this revolt, known as the First Secession, and many others like it during the period is historically unclear. However, its cause is not. "By all accounts" one historian writes, "the principal cause of the first secession was a debt crisis."[18]

The situation facing poor Romans of the period should by now come as no surprise to readers. Many historians, both modern and ancient, have focused on one uncannily familiar story which may have lit the fire. Apparently, a war veteran's farm was destroyed during a battle with a rival tribe. This, combined with government tax demands, forced him to borrow money at dangerously high rates. When he was unable to pay, his creditor imprisoned and tortured him. Eventually, he appeared in the Forum, where those who heard his story were so enraged they took to the streets and rioted.[19]

About fifty years later, the first major codification of Roman law, the Twelve Tables, appeared. For reasons undoubtably similar to those of the Babylonians, the Tables included an interest-rate cap with some basic provisions for enforcement. Under the Twelve Tables, the legal maximum interest rate was set by weight at one ounce per pound per year, which amounts to 8⅓ percent per annum. Creditors found contracting for greater rates were liable in

Roman courts to fourfold damages. This basic legislative approach remained intact for the duration of the Roman Republic and the Empire, although the legal maximum varied with political tides. During the third century B.C.E. the maximum legal rate was lowered for a short time to about 4 percent. In 88 B.C.E., Sulla raised the interest-rate cap to 12 percent per annum. This rate remained the legal limit for centuries with the later Empire, as well as the Byzantine Empire, adopting it.[20]

Although these interest-rate caps provided some protection for Romans, they were poorly enforced throughout Roman history. Pawnshops and other lenders that catered to the more risky poor consistently charged three to ten times the legal maximum. The rate caps also proved too inflexible for the volatile Roman economy. In particular, the availability of gold and silver from mining and foreign conquest dramatically affected market prices for the use of money. Moreover, both the Empire and the Republic faced the persistent problem of currency hoarders, who would hide away vast fortunes in coins, thus decreasing the available supply of cash and raising prices for use of money.[21] During times when the supply of money was low, interest-rate caps were probably all but ignored, thus affording almost no protection to debtors.

Nor were these problems with interest-rate caps limited to Rome. Around two thousand years later, on the other side of the globe, fundamentally analogous problems plagued late Ming Dynasty China. Following a hundred years of foreign domination by Mongolians with the clan of Ghengis Kahn at their head, the Chinese leader Chu Yuan-chang (later referred to as the Hung-wu emperor) solidified control over many competing factions and succeeded in driving the Mongolians out of northern China. Chu Yuan-chang went on to found the Ming Dynasty in 1368, which would last through the reigns of sixteen succeeding emperors until its overthrow in 1644. By the late sixteenth century China suffered from the inept governance of rural agrarian masses by a literary bureaucracy. Chinese law at the time fixed a maximum allowable interest rate for loans at 36 percent per annum. The statutes also forbade collecting more interest than the original principle. Hoarders of coin wealth, supply limitations, and failed attempts to introduce paper currency made cash a rare and expensive commodity. Nevertheless, lending for consumption purposes appears to have been widespread. In 1587, over 20,000 pawn shops operated in China. Once again the interest-rate cap was poorly enforced. Wealthy families commonly lent money to poor farmers at illegal interest rates, employing local roughnecks to collect. Foreclosures on the homes of poor farmers undercut, on an enormous scale, the ability of the poverty-stricken to survive. One historian explains the failure of the Ming Dynasty's interest-rate caps as a social policy-making tool thus:

> Agrarian exploitation of the poor . . . was far from limited to . . . isolated incidents. It affected all walks of life and was carried out on a large and small scale without surcease generation after generation. Essentially, such exploitation was the economic basis of the bureaucracy as an institution. Official families, who collected rents from landholdings and interest from the moneylending business, were an integral part of the rural economy.[22]

The story of one eccentric civil servant explicitly shows the entrenched and economically fundamental role of high-cost lending at this time in China. Hai Jui was a civil servant who worked his way up the Chinese bureaucracy with a maverick attitude extremely rare in the orderly Confucian civil service. Hai Jui achieved notoriety with the Chinese masses early in his career by remonstrating against the son of a powerful dignitary for financially abusing his position. Having attained fame for his unostentatious lifestyle, Hai Jui did the unthinkable and openly criticized the emperor Chia-ching. Hai Jui wrote the emperor a letter describing him as "vain, cruel, selfish, suspicious, and foolish." Reportedly, Hai Jui purchased a coffin and said goodbye to his family before he sent the letter. Chia-ching apparently was deeply disturbed by the reproach, hesitating to punish Hai Jui, but eventually sentencing him to death for insolence anyway. Before the sentence was carried out Chia-ching passed away, with Lung-ch'ing ascending the throne in 1567. Lung-ch'ing commuted the sentence, and Hai Jui emerged from prison with more prestige than ever. Eventually, Hai Jui attained the rank of governor over the richest and most developed prefecture in the entire empire.

But, for Hai Jui, challenging high-cost lending proved more politically dangerous than even challenging an emperor. As governor, Hai Jui attempted to enforce previously ignored credit laws and stretched procedural rules in order to prevent poor farmers from losing their homes. In doing so he confronted the richest landowners in the province, who profited from moneylending, creating enemies who would eventually erode his power. When the poor learned that the governor had personally heard the complaints of dispossessed landowners, his offices were flooded with as many as three to four thousand petitions a day. Other civil servants, possibly linked to lending interests, accused Hai Jui of "encouraging hoards of riffraff to make false charges against men of substance." These accusations, fueled by otherwise impotent claims of personal impropriety, cost Hai Jui his post, forcing him into early retirement, from which he never politically recovered. All this transpired in spite of Hai Jui's formidable contribution in organizing the dredging of two commercially important rivers.[23]

Perhaps Ming society would have done well to incorporate the lending reforms Hai Jui attempted to establish. Within fifty years Ming society entered a period of peasant rebellions, hastening the overthrow of the dynasty by Manchurian invaders from the North. Hai Jui probably would not be surprised by the story which one

Chinese source attributes as the event which incited the first re-bellions.

The incident involved four soldiers and an oppressive mon-eylender, appropriately named Ch'ien (money). The money-lender bribed the commander of the garrison to join him in a plot to force the soldiers to repay much more money than they had actually borrowed. This piece of chicanery prompted the soldiers to mutiny and organize local famine victims to ally with them in rebellion.[24]

Neither should this story surprise us, given its remarkable similar-ity to the story of the war veteran thought to have provoked the first secession in Rome.

There can be little doubt that interest-rate caps were a signifi-cant improvement over the violent and chaotic markets of our earliest civilizations. As a social policy-making strategy, interest-rate caps combined with other lending format restrictions have endured at least since the Code of Hammurabi and are still in ef-fect throughout much of the United States and the modern world. Nevertheless, the experiences of Rome and China begin to show the limitations of the policy that dog the social strategy even today. Interest-rate caps and other lending format restrictions pre-sume to prevent mutually agreeable contracts. Effectively policing these rules requires more resources than most societies are willing to expend. Although extremely different societies have chosen the "oldest continuous form of commercial regulation," interest-rate caps and similar format restrictions have traditionally garnered limited success in curbing the harmful consequences of high-cost lending.[25] The policy has also tended to cultivate black-market cultures which have come to threaten the very foundations of oth-erwise successful governments.

Treatment Three
Separating "Us" from "Them:" Selective Protection Strategies

While some societies have attempted to separate harmful loans from beneficial credit, others have attempted to separate individuals "deserving" of protection from those who are not. This strategy of selective protection is nearly as old as, and possibly older than, interest-rate caps. The best example of its evolution is found not far from Babylon in ancient Israel. But, unlike Babylon to the east, which had a long tradition of monarchy, the Hebrew culture was tribally organized prior to roughly the first millennium B.C.E. The Hebrew people lived seminomadically in small ranges near towns. They relied on herding domesticated animals and occasional farming. They lived both in tents and in houses. Having settled on the land bridge between Africa and Asia, the Hebrews were subject to invasion from many directions and by many peoples. From early on, Hebrew culture developed a strong sense of tribal unity and cooperation in order to compete with outside threats.

The early Hebrew laws concerning high-cost lending reflect this sense of tribal unity, by extending legal protection only to other Hebrews. Deuteronomy, which describes Yahweh's laws as delivered by Moses (probably around the thirteenth century B.C.E.), states:

> You shall not charge interest on anything you lend to a fellow-country-man [*l'ahika*], money or food or anything else on which interest can be charged. You may charge interest on a loan to a foreigner [*nokri*] but not on a loan to a fellow-country-man, for then the Lord your God will bless you in all you undertake in the land which you are entering to occupy.[26]

Thus the Hebrews simultaneously took action both attempting to prevent corrosion of community bonds, yet still providing at least some outlet for the wealthy to lend excess capital. That protection against the dangers of agreeing to interest was not extended to rival outsiders was probably an added benefit in the competitive intertribal anarchy which characterized the ancient eastern Mediterranean coast. Moreover, by simply banning interest within the Hebrew community, the rule probably had lower administrative costs than legal systems forced to distinguish between legal and illegal loans by interest-rate caps. Recently two economists described the likely role of the Hebrew rules as attempting "to make sure that individuals did not reduce themselves to a level of poverty, where they would be burdens on the community."[27]

Not surprisingly, the Hebrew injunction against charging any interest to other Hebrews was also followed infrequently. The story of Nehemiah is enlightening. By the fifth century B.C.E. the Persian empire dominated Israel. During the reign of Artaxerxes I (464-424 B.C.E.), a Jewish cupbearer to the king, named Nehemiah, was appointed governor of Jerusalem. Nehemiah tells his own story in a rare firstperson-dictated book in the Old Testament. Apparently arriving in 445 B.C.E. from the Persian capital of Susa, Nehemiah organized the rebuilding of the walls around Jerusalem.[28] After this he instituted a number of reforms directed at high-cost lending. What has come down to us of his own words tells the story best.

There came a time when the common people, both men and women, raised a great outcry against their fellow-Jews. Some complained that they were giving their sons and daughters as pledges for food to keep themselves alive; others that they were mortgaging their fields, vineyards, and houses to buy corn in famine; others again that they were borrowing money on their fields and vineyards to pay the king's tax. "But," they said, "our bodily needs are the same as other people's, our children are as good as theirs; yet here we are, forcing our

sons and daughters to become slaves." ... I was very angry
when I heard their outcry and the story they told. I mastered
my feelings and reasoned with the nobles and the magistrates. I said to them, "You are holding your fellow-Jews as
pledges for debt." I rebuked them severely and said, "As far as
we have been able, we have brought back our fellow-Jews
who had been sold to other nations; but you are now selling
your own fellow-countrymen, and they will have to be
bought back by us!" ... "What you are doing is wrong ... Let
us give up this taking of persons as pledges for debt. Give
back today to your debtors their fields and vineyards, their
olive-groves and houses, as well as the income in money, and
in corn, new wine and oil." "We will give them back," they
promised, "and exact nothing more. We will do what you
say." So, summoning the priests, I put the offenders on oath
to do as they promised. ... And they did. ...[29]

There is no independently corroborating evidence of Nehemiah's actions. One historian interprets Nehemiah's credit reforms as similar to earlier acts of Sumerian and Babylonian Kings
who granted amnesty to those sold into slavery for debt. Although Nehemiah's reforms did not fundamentally change the
Hebrew rule in Deuteronomy, they do shed light on its social operation. It would seem that without strong leadership early Hebrews lent and borrowed from one another with serious social
consequences in spite of the injunction in Deuteronomy. From a
contemporary American perspective, the racially oriented character of Nehemiah's rhetoric also casts a disagreeable pall over
whatever success he might have achieved. It is unclear whether
moneylenders' new found filial charity—derived from Nehemiah's exhortations—had any enduring effect, but at least one
noted historian asserts that the situation facing Hebrew debtors
probably did not change for at least another three hundred years.

Their lot probably only improved when the Hebrew Hasmonean state expanded, making poor foreigners a suitable substitute for religiously protected Hebrews.[30]

Many other cultures have used formal and informal mechanisms to protect favored groups from the consequences of high-cost debt. For instance, the Indian *Dharmasastras* provides for different interest rates varying with the caste of the debtor. Under the rule, lenders provided much lower rates to Brahmins than other caste members without regard to the personal credit history of the individual.[31] While selective protection strategies may have some success for protected group members, they also probably have the side effect of encouraging class division and racism. Despite egalitarian pretensions of the United States, as we shall see, this strategy too was later imported to the New World.

BEYOND REGULATION: HARNESSING THE MARKET FOR PROTECTION

While the earliest high-cost credit policy strategies attempted to prevent or remedy undesirable credit outcomes with government or religious rules, later strategies began in one way or another to harness market forces. While microeconomic theory as we currently recognize it did not begin to develop until the eighteenth century, social and governmental strategies for mitigating the problems associated with high-cost debt began tentatively to rely on the benefits of using market forces much earlier. Reforms adopted in the surprisingly liberal society of ancient Athens are illustrative.

Treatment Four
Everyone for Themselves: Self-Help Free Markets

At the zenith of its power and cultural sophistication, ancient Athens had no law restricting interest rates. Foreshadowing the economic arguments of thinkers such as Adam Smith, Jeremy Bentham, and David Ricardo, Athenian culture focused on individuality, personal responsibility, and balance in determining economic outcomes. The story of how Athenians arrived at this approach probably starts around the beginning of the sixth century B.C.E. At this time, Athenian society was intensely polarized. Recent advances in trading throughout the Mediterranean, the growing use of coined money, and competition from free slave labor had put pressure on subsistence farmers around Athens. Credit was already common and took on many different forms. Some credit was secured by land, but often it was secured by the freedom of the debtor, where, as in other early civilizations, default meant slavery. The gap between rich and poor became so wide that revolution threatened. Although this situation, like every other, was complex, early writers universally agreed that the primary cause of the crisis was high-cost debt.[32] Relying on Livy, one historian summarizes the situation thus:

> Solon tells us plainly of the overt abuses in his own day. A large part of the soil of Attica had come into the possession or at least under the control of the rich; many Athenians were suffering under a load of debt; some of these debtors, helpless to relieve themselves, had been forced into exile and had been living so long abroad that they had forgotten the good Attic speech; others, free-born though they were, had become slaves; and of these many had been sold into slavery abroad and so were in the worst case of all. Broadly speaking, the land and the greatest part of its products belonged to the rich; and the poor were constrained to toil for them as their

slaves without mercy or redress. Here were causes enough for bitterness and discontent. While the rich enjoyed their ease and all the luxuries and comforts that the times afforded, the poor were condemned to a life of hopeless drudgery at home or the worst of evils in the ancient world, exile in a foreign land.[33]

To stave off collapse of the city-state, the community appointed the poet and orator Solon, later called the father of Athenian law, to rehabilitate its government unilaterally. The gravity of the situation must have been deep, judging by the radical character of Solon's reforms and their acceptance. Solon took several onetime measures to stabilize the situation, including canceling or reducing many debts, freeing all enslaved for debt, and repurchasing those sold abroad for debt at state expense. Solon also permanently outlawed enslaving defaulting debtors. But this relief came at a price. For this law is attributed to Solon: "Money is to be placed out at whatever rate the lender may want."[34]

Solon's deregulation encouraged individual Athenians to rely on their own judgement.[35] Unregulated interest rates reflected Athens' commercially oriented values. Historians speculate it was this deregulation which helped creditors accept Solon's reforms. In any case, the changes appear to have had a lasting and generally positive effect on the Athenian society. Unregulated credit prices proved effective in encouraging the financing of maritime trade. Lenders could invest in shipping loans at whatever price the risks of the voyage demanded. Merchants engaging in risky long distance trade could shop for high-priced loans from respectable law-abiding creditors, rather than black market moneylenders. The fact that Athens gained great benefits from its open credit market is beyond doubt. "Bottomry loans," where a creditor advanced maritime traders the value of the ship's cargo before a voyage and assumed the risk of shipwreck, played a vital role in Athenian trade.[36] One scholar emphasizes that in Athens credit was more often used to the mutual benefit of people in similar economic situations, as opposed to the lending by the rich to the poor which was common in most of the ancient world.[37] Athens developed a banking system which "changed money, received deposits, made loans to individuals and states, made foreign remittances, collected revenues, issued letters of credit and money orders, honored checks, and kept complete books."[38] Although lending did not attain modern standards of complexity, it was nevertheless sophisticated in a way which was fundamental to sustaining the ancient Athenian lifestyle.[39]

But, for the poor and unwary, the historical record tells a different story indeed. Unregulated credit prices allowed unscrupulous lenders to charge the highest rates to those in extreme need. In this period we find some of the most expensive loans in recorded history—as high as 9000 percent per annum. Borrowers probably intended these loans, like most high-cost loans, to be short term, but they were nevertheless often compounded over long periods of time. Not unlike those who owe payday loans in contemporary America, Athenian debtors of this period came to dread "the end of the moon."[40] Moreover, creditors were free to calculate interest in whatever way they chose, probably charging interest compounded at frequent intervals. Because high-cost lending was so profitable, a class of creditors catering to the vulnerable poor and ignorant grew and thrived. High-cost lenders became prevalent enough to create a deep and lasting influence on Greek drama and literature. An ancient version of the modern loan shark was a staple character in Athenian plays. Perhaps it was the dramatic social pain associated with expensive debt which induced the contempt for lending of two of the world's greatest philosophers. We should not underestimate the fact that both Plato and Aristotle, observing the effect of unregulated interest rates on their society, concluded that all interest should be banned.[41] Plato, for example, condemns lenders for "planting their own stings into any fresh victim who offers them an opening to inject the poison of their money; and while they multiply their capital by usury, they are also multiplying . . . the paupers."[42]

The Athenian credit market exemplifies the free market strategy for controlling the harmful consequences associated with high-cost lending. Moreover, it mirrors much of the debate concerning credit regulation today. Athens demonstrates that unregulated interest rates (with basic limitations such as the elimination of debt slavery) can be socially and economically productive. Yet modern advocates of free-market lending should also stand warned that unrestricted interest rates left sophisticated lenders free to exact ruinous contracts on those in vulnerable bargaining positions.

Treatment Five
Give Them What They Want: Charitable Lending

Even societies deeply committed to controlling credit markets have come to realize the benefits of harnessing market forces in designing social policy. A fifth strategy, still often used in contemporary America, looks to undercut high-cost lenders by offering cheaper, less dangerous loans subsidized by the charitable impulses of powerful social or governmental institutions. An early example of this strategy for controlling the harmful consequences of high-cost debt evolved in late fifteenth-century Italy. Influenced by Aristotelian contempt for credit as well as the ancient Hebrew impulse to protect vulnerable group members, medieval Roman Catholic religious doctrine strongly condemned taking any interest. Most historians agree the prejudice fundamentally retarded commerce. Merchants had difficulty devising strategies to finance business ventures. Throughout the Middle Ages the poor were afflicted in the extreme, due in no small part to the lack of strong international and domestic trade.

But toward the end of the late fifteenth century, things began to change. The threat from the Black Death diminished considerably. Increased international and domestic trade invigorated the economy. The printing press was invented. And the ideological grip of medieval scholasticism finally began to loosen. Questioning the wisdom of their outright interest ban, Italian religious and secular authorities began to search for new ways to alleviate suffering of the poor. Black market moneylenders and pawnshops catering to the desperate poor had long existed in spite of religious condemnation. In this period many Italian leaders came to agree small loans to the poor were inevitable and even necessary to save those in extreme need.[43]

As a result, religious leaders established charitable pawnshops which intended to charge only enough to cover costs of operation. Called *mons pietatis*, such pawnshops were controversial, but nevertheless found papal approval at the Fifth Lateran Council in 1515. The term translates literally as "mountain of piety." Appropriately, the Latin word for mountain often carries a loose proverbial reference to making large promises followed by small performances. Papal authorities reasoned that where the *montes* charged more than the original principal they were not receiving usury, but contributions to defray operation costs.[44]

The *montes* offered key theoretical advantages which may explain their acceptance in the face of strong opposition from many Catholic thinkers. Unlike simply prohibiting certain types of loans, the *montes* required no one to do anything against his will. Thus there was no risk of motivating a black market. By offering cheaper credit to the poor, the *montes* would harness the market force of demand to put private lenders out of business. Debtors would have no reason to pay the high prices of traditional pawnshops, since they could obtain money from a more trustworthy source at a lower price. It is probably exactly these reasons which have fed charitable attempts to undercut private lending throughout history.

The *montes pietatum* did find some success. By 1509, eighty-seven of these pawnshops had been set up in the Italian peninsula. Over the next two centuries the idea spread throughout the continent under sponsorship of the church, municipalities, and independent charities. As the Catholic Church lost influence, many of the *montes* failed, but others were taken over by municipal governments. A few of the largest and strongest still exist today.[45]

Unfortunately, the *montes pietatum* and similar strategies have faced several drawbacks in spite of their visionary appeal. First, charitable attempts to undercut private lenders such as the *montes pietatum* are subject to the tides of ideological fashion, whereas private lending is supported by the inexorable and constant desire for profit. For instance, the most vocal advocates of the *montes* at their outset were the Franciscan Observant Order of Friars. Their charitable motives were at least supplemented and possibly dominated by their demagogic anti-Semitism. "Paced by Bernadino da Feltre (d. 1494)," writes one historian, "the Observantine preachers regurgitated the oft-discredited charges of ritual murder, incited mobs to attacks on Jewish life and property, and harangued the people and their magistrates to destroy the Jews. . . ."[46] The noble intentions of early administrators of the *montes* were polluted by the desire to drive Jewish pawnbrokers from business and from Italy itself. Whether the *montes* would ever have grown from infancy without the fuel of racial hatred is unclear.

Charity on a much smaller scale is also easily corrupted, often with the same ill consequences. English attempts to institute charitable pawnshops in the early 1700s are illustrative. The first major charitable pawnshop, called the Charitable Corporation, to appear in England was founded in 1699, and chartered in 1707. It operated without incident for about thirty years until, as one historian explains, "rumors that huge amounts of money were being embezzled on the basis of fictitious pledges began to gain credence." After Charitable Corporation officials fled the country, an enormous scandal ensued creating a longstanding public mistrust against charitable alternatives to pawnbrokering in England.[47] Lamentably, in consumer credit as elsewhere, the motivation of charity is rarely more contagious than that of hate or greed.

A separate drawback to charitable attempts to displace private lenders derives from private lenders' desires not to be displaced. Obviously pawnbrokers resent attempts by government or charitable institutions to drive them out of business. This resentment may be more acute where the social reformers engage private lenders in subsidized competition, rather than merely instituting uniform command-and-control style rules such as interest-rate caps. The former attack private lending at the root of its business—the demand for credit—whereas the latter merely regulates the way business may be conducted. Such private opposition to charitable lending often stifles charitable lending institutions in their infancy. A hundred years after the Charitable Corporation debacle, British reformers again tried to organize a charitable pawnshop which again met with failure. This time private lenders organized a strong resistance at government, investment, and customer levels. The opposition proved so effective as to convince one disgruntled ex-pawnbroker to state:

> A little more reflection convinced us that a few individuals with a limited fund could not hope to withstand for more than a very short period the opposition of a body so powerful in number, riches, and their union as the pawnbrokers of the Metropolis, and that if a successful competition should ever be established against them, it must be by a body as numerous, as rich, and as united as themselves.[48]

Neither need this opposition be merely at the level of mobilizing support and resources for charitable lending projects. It is easy to imagine private pawnbrokers strategically engaging in marketing and price campaigns to drive vulnerable charitable lenders, who still require customers to pay overhead, out of business. But even where private lenders do not intentionally besiege charity credit, benevolent lenders usually advocate thrift and are unwilling to encourage indebtedness, thus carrying a much lower profile and therefore a smaller base of customers. Charitable lending strategies have historically lacked the profit-driven zeal to compete successfully with private lenders.

However, the most formidable obstacle faced by charitable lending regimes is mobilization of sufficient capital resources. This problem is also doubtlessly engendered by the opposition of private lenders, but is still a menacing limitation to the strategy in its own right. Even the earliest of the *montes pietatum*, founded at the headwaters of the social current creating the most successful of Europe's charitable pawnshops, often found accumulation of capital reserves for their nonprofit venture prohibitive. Wealthy Christians, despite the considerable religious pressure towards charity exerted by the fourteenth-century Italian Catholic Church, were simply unlikely to invest in the *montes*. Although some of the *montes* survived past infancy, quite simply, "many suffered or failed from undercapitalization."[49] Without profit there is little or no incentive to supply the necessary assets to conduct charitable lending on any meaningful scale.

Often advocates of this strategy will turn to governments to help mobilize the capital when they realize the support of private beneficiaries is inadequate. A noted British scholar has concluded, based on failed British attempts to establish charitable lending, that governmental support is a virtual prerequisite to any meaningful success.[50] But successful governmental rent-seeking behavior is costly, inconsistent, and unpredictable, especially when opposed by powerful and organized private lobbies. While the supply of expensive capital for consumer lending has continued unabated for millennia, the supply of governmental subsidies for low-cost loans to the poor has been meager and sporadic. Governments, almost always controlled by the society's elite, face the same absence of incentive to provide charitable lending to the poor as private citizens. And additionally, government strategies are burdened in stimulating low-cost loans by the costs of immobile bureaucracy and tax collection.

The limitations of charitable attempts to undersell private lenders aside, the strategy nevertheless has retained advocates and limited successes for centuries—and for good reason. The strategy harnesses the demand for lower priced loans to extend protection to vulnerable debtors. Unfortunately, as the *montes pietatum* begin to show, these successes are limited by serious structural problems, particularly supply problems, which have come to afflict similar American strategies in the twentieth century.

Treatment Six
Strength in Numbers: Cooperative Lending

For thousands of years, families have extended low-cost and noninterest bearing loans to family members to insulate the family from the dangers of high-cost debt. This informal cooperation can be an effective method of pooling a small and trusted group's resources to overcome short-term deprivation and income shocks. However, the potency of this familial cooperation is limited by the size of the family's resource pool, as well as by the strength of the familial bonds tying the group together. In eighteenth- and nineteenth-century Europe, some groups began to expand and organize this cooperative lending strategy. The earliest formally organized cooperative lending groups were probably the British building societies. In the late eighteenth and early nineteenth century, Great Britain, in the early stages of industrialization, was also undergoing a revolution in financial markets. A new class of urban salaried industrial workers was emerging. Demographic shifts from rural agricultural work to urban industrial work contributed to widespread housing shortages. The Enlightenment fostered a new focus on self-help and entrepreneurialism.

Seeking to cope with the Industrial Revolution, a small group in Birmingham found a new way to pool resources to purchase homes. In 1775, a small club, called Ketley's Building Society, formed with that purpose. None of the members alone could gather enough cash to cover the cost of building a new house. But in the new club, members would contribute a specified amount each week into a common building fund. As soon as enough resources were gathered, the club would purchase land and build a home for one of the members as determined by lot. Members who had received homes were obligated to continue making their weekly contributions. When the club had purchased a home for every member, the society was terminated. Although the first Birmingham building society and the others which soon followed were limited to providing purchase money for home building, they nevertheless furnished their members with the permanent ability to acquire relatively inexpensive credit. After a group member acquired a home, the member would have significant real property upon which to secure relatively low-cost loans to overcome short-term needs or income shocks. By establishing a building society, a group could insulate member families, and in turn entire neighborhoods, against financial predators.[51]

As Germany began to experience the same structural precedents which spurred British building societies, it too developed organized cooperative lending institutions. Unlike British building societies, German institutions did not limit themselves to financing homes. Modern credit unions trace their genealogy to two upper-middle-class German financial innovators. Herman

Schulze, mayor of the town of Delitzsch, sought to create an institution which could lend capital to mechanics, tradesmen, and other local merchants. After unsuccessfully pursuing charitable investments from wealthy benefactors, Schulze turned in 1850 to organizing cooperative societies which would pool resources. These early Schulze-Delitzsch credit cooperatives sold shares and then lent the proceeds to members who could demonstrate efficient operation and a likelihood of profit for their small businesses. Members bought their shares in the union on an installment plan, similar to British building societies' weekly investment requirement. Because every member of the union shared equally in the risk that a borrowing member might default, Schulze-Delitzsch organizations excluded all but relatively stable small merchants from membership. Frederick William Raiffeisen, mayor of the village of Flammersfeld, organized similar cooperatives hoping to focus not on merchants, but on impoverished families. After many failed ventures, Raiffeisen forswore all charitable efforts and instead focused on self-sufficiency and mutual benefit. Thereafter, he limited membership to individuals with unimpeachable character, widely vouched-for moral responsibility, and steady incomes with successful results. Typical members were urban industrial workers and shopkeepers. With careful management, both men organized credit unions which successfully loaned money not based on collateral, but upon the character of the borrower as judged by all other members of the union. With widespread and growing demand for these basic financial services, these early German credit unions grew quickly. By 1882, Germany boasted over 3,000 Schulze-Delitszch credit cooperatives. By 1888, there were 425 Raiffeisen credit unions. Taking cue from British and German predecessors, cooperative credit organizations spread to Italy, Austria, France, Belgium, and then throughout Europe. Organized cooperative lending spread across the Atlantic first into Quebec and then into the United States. In the latter half of the nineteenth century and throughout the twentieth century, cooperative lending institutions grew rapidly both in variety and in numbers throughout the western world.[52]

Nevertheless, when viewed as a strategy for providing protection against the dangers of high-cost debt, cooperative credit organizations have, like other social strategies, encountered significant structural limitations. For instance, vulnerability to fraud and incompetence tends to make cooperative lending institutions unstable. Cooperative credit organizations have a strong incentive to add more members, and thus pool more resources. More members mean each member suffers less loss upon loan default. But as the union's membership grows, losses may become more likely, since members are less capable of judging the credit-worthiness of individual members applying for loans. Moreover, the larger the group, the more conflicting perspectives to accommodate.

Thus, as cooperative lending groups became larger, they were forced to adopt democratic ideals and management checks and balances in order to safeguard the common pool of funds. For instance, the New World's first credit union, the *Caisse Populaire* in Quebec, organized trustees into different committees to oversee the operation of the credit union. Some members were assigned to a *conseil d'administration* which watched over the day-to-day affairs of the union, while the *commission de surveillance* was responsible for guaranteeing the books were properly kept. The spirit of cooperation was essential because those with oversight responsibilities were ineligible to receive loans in order to avoid conflicts of interest. And, unlike commercial banks, trustees received no compensation.[53] While these policies and their natural outgrowths, such as salaried professional management, have made large-scale cooperative lending possible, they have not succeeded in removing its risks. As the savings and loan scandal of the 1980s makes clear, cooperative lending may be as vulnerable to fraud and mismanagement today as it was two centuries ago.

But perhaps more importantly, cooperative lending by its nature tends to exclude those who are in most desperate need of it. From the beginning, organized cooperative lenders have rigorously limited their membership to those with common bonds and relatively stable financial backgrounds. The first British building societies confined membership to groups of no more than twenty close neighbors and friends. Many German cooperatives required costly entrance fees which functionally excluded undesirable members. Early Quebec credit unions excluded all but respected French-speaking Catholics and garnered community support with anti-Semitic hate speech.[54] Moreover, many potential members who met the racial, religious, and character prerequisites of cooperative credit did not meet formal and informal financial requirements. It took little time for cooperative lenders to recognize impoverished applicants had nothing to offer other members in the way of mutual benefit. These applicants sought not cooperation but charity, and were therefore excluded.

This sampling of historical examples helps to illustrate six of the seven most important policy strategies attempting to treat debt fever. However, too often these "treatment regimes" have been too little, too late. Time and again, the ravages of high-cost debt have led to revolution or radical last-minute reform. The first secession in Rome, the Solonic crisis in Athens, the reforms of Nehemiah in Israel, and the peasant rebellions in the late Ming dynasty all offer dramatic lessons about the role high-cost debt has played in many diverse societies and could perhaps one day play in our own. This is not to suggest American society is on the verge of similar crisis, but only that, without care, it could be. For today, we should feel certain the high-cost lending problems we face are immensely common and old. The unending demand by the impoverished for consumer credit in small amounts should remind us of the beneficial and necessary role it can play in poverty management. But most importantly, we should understand that the simple solutions to such a difficult problem, often still defended have never, and in all likelihood, will never, succeed in eliminating the debt problems faced by the vulnerable working poor.

CHAPTER 3

A Survey of America's Struggle to Control High-Cost Lending: Echoes of the Past and Confusion in the Present

The borrower is a slave to the lender.
　　　　　　　　　　　　　　　　　　　—Benjamin Franklin

Don't leave home without it.
　　　　　　　　　　—Corporate slogan of American Express

E ACH OF THE MAJOR HIGH-COST consumer credit policy strategies so far discussed exist in the United States in various permutations. Debtor amnesty, interest rate-caps and other format restrictions, selective protection, deregulated free markets, charitable lending, and organized cooperative lending have all become among the market medications found within the satchels of American policymakers for at least a century. However, American high-cost consumer credit policy has followed no logical pattern, instead tracking the twists and turns of history and cultural change. We will now look briefly at this evolution, focusing on the recurrent strategic limitations which have plagued our imported high-cost credit policy strategies, while also introducing the radical cultural revolution in middle-class American values with respect to consumer credit. There is, however, one important, distinctly American, and relatively recent policy strategy which will be discussed separately.

AMERICAN HIGH-COST CONSUMER CREDIT POLICY PRIOR TO 1900

The original laws of the European colonies in North America dealing with high-cost credit followed the English pattern of the time. The basis for most modern state usury laws comes from imported English interest-rate-cap statutes. In particular, the colonies used the model of the Statute of Anne, which set a maximum allowable interest rate of 5 percent per annum. Passed in 1713, this statute was deeply influenced by receding but still influential medieval predispositions against the taking of interest. "The statute," according to commentator Lawrence Katz, "bear[s] witness to the Church's continued prejudice against the practice of usury in any form." Specifically, the statute forbade charging interest "above the value of five pounds for the forbearance of one hundred pounds for a year."[1] The statute attempted to send a strong message of deterrence by including a damages provision establishing a fine, triple the amount lent, for charging above the 5 percent cap.[2]

Early American caps were set at different levels, ranging between 4 and 10 percent. After independence, most states set their maximum interest rates at 6 percent. Many of these interest-rate caps, now called "general usury laws," have survived in one form or another until today. The colonies also created debt enforcement laws following the English pattern of strongly favoring creditors. States at times would raise or lower their ceilings. In 1867, Massachusetts followed the lead of England and other European countries in abolishing its interest-rate cap. A few states in turn followed Massachusetts. Nevertheless, the legislative approach of low interest-rate caps was relatively stable, normally involving only mild tampering.[3] "With very few exceptions," writes Kathleen Keest in *The Cost of Credit*, "these general usury laws were the only statutes regulating credit costs in the United States prior to the twentieth century."[4] The simplicity and durability of the early state interest-rate caps echoes many historical precedents. Thus, note Sydney Homer and Richard Sylla, the American "combination of rigorous enforcement of debt and legal maximum rates of interest comes down from Hammurabi through Rome, through seventeenth-century England, to the modern United States."[5]

The American Thrift Ethic

Early America viewed debt supporting commerce as necessary and enterprising, but conversely stigmatized borrowing for personal consumption purposes.[6] In 1838, one author explained the widespread American comfort with commercial lending in terms of personal trust:

> As the credit system is the offspring of confidence, and as no man reposes confidence where he deems it likely to be abused, this extensive and universal system of credit may be taken as evidence of *a general belief* among those who have commodities for sale, that those who desire to obtain them, have the disposition, and will have the means of paying for them, in such a manner and at such times as may be agreed upon.[7]

This focus on confidence is enlightening in regard to the reluctance of mainstream lenders to also extend credit for consumption. Quite simply, unlike commercial debtors, consumption borrowers were not trusted. A comment from the papers of Benjamin Franklin reveals the popular attitude toward consumer credit:

Think what you do when you run in Debt; *you give to another Power over your Liberty.* If you cannot pay at the Time, you will be ashamed to see your Creditor; you will be in Fear when you speak to him; you will make poor pitiful sneaking Excuses, and by Degrees come to lose your Veracity, and sink into base downright lying; for, as Poor Richard says, *The second Vice is Lying, the first is running in Debt.* . . .[8]

Nevertheless, despite strong social messages condemning personal debt, historians agree personal borrowing existed, often at high prices. Shame drove negotiations for personal loans behind closed doors. Colonial custom ensured few families would openly acknowledge or discuss their debts.[9] The low general usury law interest-rate caps were a reflection of this cultural norm. It was not possible for lenders to profit from short-term loans for small amounts without charging rates in excess of the legal limits. Accordingly, normal citizens generally could not purchase the use of money from legal lenders. In this way, the law acted as an agent of socialization against all borrowing for consumptive purposes.[10]

The American thrift ethic stifled development of debtor amnesty policies. Defaulting debtors, particularly consumer debtors, found little public sympathy. In addition to interest-rate caps, colonists also imported another English institution, the debtor prison. Imprisonment for debt was surprisingly common in the eighteenth and early nineteenth centuries.

[I]n 1830, there were in Massachusetts, Maryland, New York, and Pennsylvania three to five times as many persons imprisoned for debt as for crime. The Suffolk County Jail in Boston alone for the decade 1820–1830 contained 11,818 imprisoned debtors from a total populating ranging from 43,000 to 63,000.[11]

Although some states pushed for reform in the 1830s, debt peon-age was not federally outlawed until after the Civil War. Northern states only felt compelled to outlaw debtor prisons when Southern whites began circumventing emancipation with debt peonage.

Gradually, the bankruptcy system evolved to become the primary mechanism of providing American debtor amnesty. Throughout Europe, the earliest bankruptcy rules were exclusively creditor-collection remedies which provided virtually no protection for debtors. It was not until 1706 that a short-lived English bankruptcy law included discharge for a limited number of debts for a limited number of debtors. Nearly a century later, in 1800, the United States adopted its first bankruptcy law. Like early American interest-rate caps, the debtor amnesty provisions included in early American bankruptcy laws bear a surprising resemblance to their ancient Mesopotamian predecessors. Like the occasional Sumerian and Babylonian royal decrees forgiving debts for favored subjects, nineteenth-century American amnesty rules for bankrupt debtors responded to financial crises, were short-lived, and were capriciously limited in scope. For example, a financial panic spurred the 1800 Bankruptcy Act, which was repealed only three years later. While the act included narrow provisions providing for discharge of some debts, only merchants were eligible. And, while the law allowed release from debtor prisons for those obtaining discharge, there is some evidence that only the relatively influential consistently acquired this amnesty. For instance, Robert Morris, a member of the Constitutional Convention and a prominent financier, managed to liberate himself from a Pennsylvania debtor prison. The less prominent were not so lucky.

Our second and third bankruptcy rules were similarly inconsistent in providing amnesty for imprisoned and defaulting debtors. The Bankruptcy Act of 1841 was repealed in 1843 after becoming effective only in 1842. Perhaps contributing to its short life was the controversial innovation of extending limited debt-discharge

rights to non-merchant debtors. The post-Civil War economic crisis spawned the relatively enduring Bankruptcy Act of 1867. It
also provided limited debt-discharge rights, but survived for less
than a decade.[12]

The Origin of American Selective Protection: Our Tradition of Credit Discrimination

The American credit culture prior to the twentieth century can
only be understood against a backdrop of formal and informal discrimination against non-Europeans and women. Despite interest-
rate caps forbidding all forms of high-cost lending, ethnic
minorities and women often suffered terrible consequences resulting from their credit bargains. It is easy to overlook this fact in
light of the stark absence of treatment of race and gender in most
financial and credit histories.

For example, at the end of the Civil War, high-cost credit
played an important role in perpetuating the power of the white
elite over recently emancipated African Americans. Over 90
percent of blacks lived in the South and former slaves usually
had no resources aside from their own labor. With a white elite
determined to preserve as many of the economic aspects of slavery as possible, sharecropping developed as a contract-based
substitute. The cycle of poverty and debt engendered by sharecropping enforced the subordination of black workers. Sharecroppers received no pay for their work until the sale of the crop
at harvest time. With no available cash source, black agricultural
workers were forced to turn to high-cost credit to survive. Interest rates on supplies and money loaned to Southern blacks were
high, often exceeding fifty percent. When the farming season
ended and black workers sold their share of the crop, there were
rarely enough proceeds to cover debts from the previous season.
Thus, sharecroppers borrowed year after year, each time hoping

the next crop would provide enough to pay off their debt. Moreover, white landowners and creditors often cheated black workers. In Texas, for example, the courts sanctioned the widespread practice of shutting out black workers without compensation immediately before harvest, after they had farmed the entire agricultural season. Although a very few African Americans were resourceful enough to gather enough cash and credit to purchase their own farms, almost all black agricultural workers lived in the grips of poverty exacerbated by and entrenched in high-cost lending.[13]

Similarly, it is somewhat futile to speak of access to inexpensive credit when women had little or no property rights, nor even the right to vote. For women, access to credit has often been a function of their relationships to men. The ability to borrow requires a creditor's trust that the debtor will be able to raise and turn over the amount loaned plus interest. Because women were excluded from the basic mechanisms of the market economy, they could not consistently guarantee repayment without enlisting in some way the cooperation of a male. Where women did try to borrow, their exclusion from lower-priced lenders forced them to turn to pawnbrokers or other high-cost lenders, often with what one historian described as "devastating effects on a family's real income."[14] The story of one single mother in New York is illustrative:

> Mrs. Zulinsky . . . one day found her entire life's savings of six hundred dollars had been stolen from her mattress. Charity could not support three children, so Mrs. Zulinsky was forced to become, in the slang of the day, "a furniture dealer." Her table, her two beds, all her chairs, and "even the marble clock surmounted by a bronze horseman armed with a spear" were hauled down to the pawnshop and "put up the spout." When night fell, Mrs. Zulinsky's family was "sitting on boxes

and sleeping on the floor," but the immediate emergency had been bridged.[15]

Throughout the nineteenth century, approximately three quarters of pawnshop customers were women, usually borrowing at rates around 300 percent per annum.[16]

The Rise of Salary Lending

Nevertheless, high-cost consumer debt has by no means been limited to ethnic minorities and women. In particular, the latter half of the nineteenth century saw an upsurge in lenders catering to a clientele of married working-class white men with steady jobs. These creditors, known as salary lenders, were the precursor to today's payday lenders. Two historians explain salary loan borrowers as "frequently regular employees of large organizations: government civil servants, railroad workers, streetcar motormen, and clerks in firms such as insurance companies."[17] Such workers, often recent immigrants or former agricultural laborers, formed the foundation of the emerging lower-middle class of urban American society. For the lender, they represented good credit risks. These men usually borrowed to meet unexpected costs such as family illness or moving expenses. Nevertheless, they held steady jobs and had family obligations which prevented them from skipping town. High-cost lenders targeted such workers because their steady supply of disposable income made them likely to repay. Moreover, frequent minor income shocks made the workers likely to borrow.[18]

It was these high-cost lenders who the working class in eastern U.S. cities first came to describe as "loansharks." Although the term was new, the tactics of the lenders were not. Initially, these loansharks charged very high interest rates. In fact, rates in excess of 1000 percent annually were common. Like high-cost loans in ancient Athens, principals were generally small, and due in a short period of time. But very often the loans would end up compounding over longer periods of time. The records of one salary lender in New York City showed that out of approximately 400 debtors, 163 had been making payments on the loans for over two years. Nor was the length of these loans merely a result of the debtor's unwillingness or inability to pay. The most essential characteristic of these early salary lenders was the tendency to manipulate loans into "chain debt." This was accomplished by a broad variety of means. Perhaps the most important were late fees, which were often assessed even if the creditor was only minutes or hours late. Mark Haller and John Alviti found creditors often "deliberately maneuvered a borrower into a late payment, by falsely suggesting that a late payment would be overlooked or by claiming that a payment sent by mail arrived after the deadline." Sometimes, individual late fees were nearly as much as the principal itself. For salary lenders the key was to collect the most money while reducing the amount owed as little as possible.[19]

In a typical transaction a debtor might borrow five dollars on Monday, and repay six on Friday. This 20-percent-per-week loan translates into a 1040-percent-per-annum rate. African Americans borrowing in the South were often charged rates twice as high in the same type of transaction, where a loan of five dollars was repaid with seven at the end of the week.[20] The charge of one or two dollars itself seems fairly innocuous for any one given week. But, where a debtor lost a job, was not paid for his work, became ill, had a family member become ill, or was prevented from paying by some other emergency, the simple transaction rapidly swelled into an enormous drain on an already strained budget.

Profits from extended-term salary lending fueled the late-nineteenth-century upsurge in high-cost lending.[21] As the industry grew, so too did horror stories, which were often the only circulated evidence of what was becoming a crisis. Moreover, the surge in high-cost lending would significantly contribute to a transformation in American culture.

There was, for example, the employee of a New York publishing house who supported a large family on a salary of $22.50 per week and had been paying $5 per week to a salary lender for several years, until he had paid more than ten times the original loan. Or the case of a Chicagoan who borrowed $15, paid back $1.50 per month for three years before fleeing the city to escape the debt. Or the case of a streetcar motorman who in 1912, had seventeen Chicago loan companies attempting to collect $307 on an original loan of $50 after he had already paid $360. Or the claim of another Chicago borrower that he had borrowed $15, ten years later he had repaid $2,153 and still owed the original $15.[22]

In this period, pawnbrokers also grew quickly alongside salary lenders. In 1812, New York City had ten licensed pawnbrokers, but by 1897 the number had grown more than ten times to 134 licensed pawnbrokers. Similarly, by 1897, San Francisco, where there were no state usury laws, was home to 237 pawnshops.[23] Although the individuals indebted to salary lenders and pawnbrokers could not have known it, their stories bore remarkable similarity to those told for thousands of years.

Unfortunately, as in Babylon, Rome, and Ming China, government interest-rate caps provided little or no protection for those in the grips of such high-cost lending. First, many lenders evaded usury caps by phrasing the contract as a purchase or assignment of future wages, rather than a loan.[24] Second, lenders could easily take advantage of the common law time-price doctrine to avoid interest-rate caps. A physical good was purchased over time on installments, which was not considered a loan for purposes of a statutory interest-rate cap. This led some lenders to avoid interest-rate caps by, for example, requiring the debtor to "purchase" a worthless painting at the time the loan contract was signed. The debtor still owed the same amount of money, and could immediately throw the painting away, but the transaction was still at least superficially legal.[25] Third, statutes indicating the interest-rate cap often did not clearly describe how interest was to be calculated under the cap, leaving wide ambiguity over the actual amount it was legal to charge. Some lenders engaged in "note shaving," where a loan would be offered at a legal rate, but additional mandatory fees created a true price well above that contemplated by legislators. Other lenders charged interest on money already repaid by the debtor, thus dramatically increasing the overall amount the debtor had to repay.[26] Fourth, some lenders also required debtors to sign forms granting the creditor power of attorney. When and if the debtor tried to challenge the contract, he might find out he had already waived his right to do so. Whether or not this was in fact legal, power of attorney forms no doubt deterred many debtors from trying to contest the contract. Even if the debtor was not dissuaded, the creditor could, without the debtor's knowledge, appear in court and confess judgment on an unpaid debt, thus enlisting the power of the state to help in collection. Fifth, some state court systems were structured so that lower justices' of the peace and magistrates' incomes were provided for through court fees. Thus, "[j]ustices who found for salary lenders could often attract a good deal of business and thus earn tidy sums, so that it was in the economic interest of justices to look with favor upon suits by lenders."[27] Sixth, loans made above interest-rate caps prior to the turn of the century must have made their way to the courts for adjudication only relatively infrequently. This is not to say that there were no cases of courts finding loans above the statutory limit. But, compared to the number of illegal loans which were made, we can expect only very few ever made it to court. After all, anyone who had the money to hire an attorney needed to sort through salary lenders' complex legal contracts would use that money to pay off the debt. Finally, public prosecutors very rarely took the initiative to seek out those lending in excess of legal limits. Outside of New York, there was not one state officer specifically charged with enforcement of usury laws.[28] This left the complex and time-consuming business of enforcing interest-rate caps easy for officials to ignore. In this way, generations of lenders offered and collected on loans which violated certainly the spirit, if not the letter, of general usury laws. High-cost lenders' legal ingenuity helped them to maintain a thin veil of legality throughout much of the nineteenth century.

Even without resorting to the judicial system, creditors could place enormous pressure on debtors. A nineteenth-century creditor was free to confront the friends and family of a debtor who already paid the principal of a loan thrice over, subjecting the borrower to terrible social embarrassment. A common tactic was

to employ a "bawler-out"—usually a woman with a stentorian voice and a rich vocabulary. The bawler-out went to the borrower's place of work or neighborhood and, in a loud voice, denounced him for his dishonesty in refusing to repay the loan. To avoid further embarrassment or the possibility of being fired, the borrower might well seek a settlement.[29]

The lender could also threaten to try to garnish the wages of the debtor, which in the social climate of the time was tantamount to threatening many debtors with unemployment.[30] Lingering Victorian condemnation of personal debt created a culture of silence which masked the increasingly pervasive indebtedness of the working and lower-middle class. With debtor prisons only recently outlawed, debtors kept their obligations private. Although there are many surviving records of commercial lending at legal or nearly legal rates, there is very little surviving documentation of higher-priced illegal loans.[31] In the late 1880s, Congress became concerned enough to direct the census of 1890 to estimate the total amount of private debt.

Robert Porter, the census superintendent, "feared that the people regarded their debt . . . as a part of their private affairs, and that they would resent any inquiries in regard to it." The image was not a pleasant one: unarmed census workers thrown out of the homes of angry debtors resentful of governmental prying into their personal affairs. Porter concluded that any attempt to ask the people about their debts would cause collateral damage to the rest of the survey, enough to wreck the entire 1890 census.[32]

Realizing the citizenry would never reveal the extent of their personal debts, census officials relented and instead tried to estimate private debts on the basis of public records.

Policy Responses to the Late-Nineteenth-Century High-Cost Credit Boom

The social havoc associated with late-nineteenth-century salary lenders and pawnbrokers forced American credit policy into a period of dramatic evolution. Elites, as well as the working and still vulnerable middle class, united to adopt a variety of policies new to America, but not to world history. For instance, many Americans searched for redress in philanthropy by the rich. Social elites founded several charitably motivated lending institutions in the late 1800s. Following the lead of the European *mons pietatis* and, later, municipal pawnshops, in 1859, a group of wealthy Boston citizens organized a philanthropic pawnshop called the Collateral Loan Company. Like its European predecessors, the Collateral Loan Company aimed to provide relatively inexpensive pawn loans to a poor clientele in need of emergency credit. One of its primary goals was to encourage thrift and responsibility. If loans were not repaid, the pawned security would be sold at public auction. A board of directors chosen by shareholders who had invested capital in the company, as well as the mayor of Boston and the governor of Massachusetts, led the company. Shareholders received limited dividends on their capital investments, but the real appeal of the business was almost certainly charitable.[33]

Other institutions, both in Boston and elsewhere, emulated the Collateral Loan Society. In 1888, Massachusetts expanded charitable lending beyond philanthropic pawn loans by incorporating the Workingmen's Loan Association in Boston. The Massachusetts state legislature acted to create a business "for the purpose of loaning money upon pledge or mortgage of goods or chattels or of safe securities of every kind or upon mortgage of real estate."[34] A similar company was allowed to form in Worcester, Massachusetts, a short time later. Other examples from 1895 include an Ohio act inviting the public to create a charitable lending company patterned off the Massachusetts model and the Workingmen's Loan Association in Providence, Rhode Island. However, the most prominent example of a charitable lending company in the United States is the Provident Loan Society of New York, which was founded in 1894. Key charitable investors included J. Pierpont Morgan, Percy Rockefeller, and Cornelius Vanderbilt. The company charter stated "[n]o member or trustee of the society shall receive any compensation for his services, or any profit other than lawful interest on money loaned to it."[35] The founders of the society feared that personal financial problems exacerbated by high unemployment rates following the recession of the early 1890s were jeopardizing the social conditions of the working class.[36]

Widespread high-cost lending also spurred the middle class to organize more aggressively cooperative lending associations in order to insulate themselves from the risks of high-cost debt.

While the first American building society, modeled after its earlier British counterparts, formed in 1831, the late nineteenth century saw the entrenchment of savings and loan associations. By 1893, thirteen states including California, Illinois, Indiana, Iowa, Kansas, Maryland, Massachusetts, Missouri, New Jersey, New York, Ohio, Pennsylvania, and Tennessee boasted more than 100 savings and loan associations. While the first credit unions modeled on German and then Canadian institutions did not appear in the United States until 1909, they thereafter quickly followed on the heels of British-styled societies.[37]

Finally, the rise of the loansharks combined with the financial panic of 1893 to create momentum for a new attempt at a federal bankruptcy law. Opposition to a federal bankruptcy law by western and southern representatives who feared northern bias stalled the law until 1898, when numerous amendments favorable to debtors secured its passage. Growing middle-class access to credit, as well as increasing sympathy for the plight of non-commercial debtors preyed upon by unscrupulous lenders, wrought a fundamental change in the purpose of American bankruptcy law. While previous laws were primarily creditor collection devices, with parsimonious discharge provisions meant only to ease temporary financial crises, the 1898 act aimed to give bankrupts a fresh start. Although the inordinate focus of Congressional debates was still upon commercial transactions, under the new law, consumers and merchants alike were free to enter bankruptcy voluntarily. Discharge was no longer contingent upon creditor consent. The list of restrictions on the right of discharge was significantly narrowed. In fact, only a few debts were excepted from discharge. And, perhaps to limit the use of bankruptcy as a salary loan collection device, creditors could no longer force wage-earners into involuntary bankruptcy proceedings. Thus, the 1898 law not only secured an equitable division of property among creditors, it also dealt out discharge of debts to deserving debtors.[38]

But with more generous discharge provisions came increasingly complex and costly procedural rules for administering bankrupt estates. Lawrence King states that "[a]t least 70 percent of the [1898] Bankruptcy Act, if not more, was procedural."[39] The process rapidly became so complex, a specialized subdiscipline of law emerged. Creditors now elected a trustee. Creditors also organized into a creditors' committee. And although federal district courts were the venue, it was necessary to appoint "referees in bankruptcy." Federal judges delegated almost all of the judicial and administrative duties to referees, who eventually evolved into today's bankruptcy judges. The subject of bankruptcy policy debate switched from whether to grant discharge to the best way to grant it, thus charging the courts with a whole new system of commercial administration. After 1898, bankruptcy debates became contests between efficient formalistic rules versus justice-oriented discretionary standards. Despite these complexities, the law became America's first nontransitory bankruptcy law, and although it was often amended, it remained in force for eighty years.[40]

HIGH-COST CREDIT POLICY FROM 1900 TO WORLD WAR II

Nevertheless, the progressive new bankruptcy law, combined with interest-rate caps and fledgling charitable and cooperative lending efforts, proved incapable of stemming the growing and dangerous tide of late-nineteenth-century high-cost credit. As the twentieth century began, the numbers of high-cost creditors and debtors continued to grow. By 1907, 90 *percent* of the employees of New York's largest transportation company made weekly payments to salary lenders. An influential study estimated one in five American workers owed money to a salary lender. Others have argued, based on analysis of data from Pittsburgh, that this ratio actually underestimated the number of debtors obligated to turn-of-the-century loansharks. Moreover, the rates paid by working-class debtors to salary lenders were over a hundred times the rates paid by more affluent borrowers. Debtors who could offer some security or borrowed greater amounts over larger periods of time could usually find rates that were lower, but still nowhere near those offered to the wealthy. While rates from 20 to 300 percent were normal, rates well in excess of 1000 percent were also still common. The situation of many of the nation's poor was becoming so acute, socially sensitive elites could no longer ignore it. Newspapers around the country ran exposes and aggressive editorial campaigns on the evils of loansharks, with headlines indistinguishable from those of today.[41] Even the slow-to-change judiciary began to respond with a smattering of harshly worded opinions. One federal judge characterized a high-cost lender as having "brought on conditions which were yearly reducing hundreds of laborers and other small wage-earners to a condition of serfdom in all but name."[42]

For the first time in American history, significant numbers of wage-earning consumer debtors began to seek amnesty from their creditors by declaring bankruptcy under the 1898 law. But salary lending and other forms of high-cost credit persisted. Prior to becoming solicitor general in the Hoover administration, Thomas D. Thatcher noted many consumer debtors only declared bankruptcy after a struggle to pay off their debts, which often included turning to salary lenders as a last resort. Borrowers often attempted to negotiate a repayment plan to satisfy their obligations. But, using aggressive collection tactics, salary lenders undermined the effectiveness of these informal agreements by crowding out other creditors. Salary lenders often served as the final weight breaking a wage-earner's back and forcing him into bankruptcy.[43]

Charitable and cooperative lending societies grew in response to wider awareness of high-cost lending problems. In 1909, fifteen philanthropic lending societies existed throughout the United

States. By 1915, this number more than doubled to thirty-eight. Moreover, cooperative lending institutions also grew quickly between the turn of the century and the stock market crash of 1928. But, while these charitable and cooperative endeavors helped many people, there were not nearly enough of them to deal with the problems associated with high-cost lending. Much like their European predecessors, inadequate capital and staying power bedeviled United States charitable lenders. Of the early charitable lending societies, almost all failed due to years of operating losses, either falling by the wayside or reverting to regular commercial pawnshop operations.[44] Early twentieth-century scholars explained:

> Important as the service has been which these remedial loan societies have rendered, their facilities are not adequate to the need and cannot be used by the poorer type of borrower. It must be remembered that these societies were organized as, and for the most part remain, semi-philanthropic in purpose. Though their capital has grown, it has not kept pace with the needs of the borrowers.[45]

The notable exception was the Provident Loan Society of New York. It survived by commanding greater charitable capital from its fabulously wealthy benefactors, deriving a unique advantage from New York City's unusual population density, more than doubling its original interest rate of 12 percent, and by highly underestimating the value of security in comparison to normal pawnbrokers. But even this rarest of charitable organizations failed to displace traditional commercial pawnbrokers in New York City.[46] Ultimately, charitable lenders suffering from haphazard management and undercapitalization were, as Lendol Calder explained, "no more effective in solving the problems of illegal lend-

ing than the publicity campaigns run by the newspapers. . . . their
loans amounted to a drop in the bucket."[47]

Although cooperative lenders were becoming more important
for the upper middle class, the vulnerable working and lower middle class were still excluded. Almost a full century after the first
American building societies appeared, a scholar complained:

> Not even the savings institutions, which are commonly
> thought of as workingmen's banks, have served the masses
> with credit. While the average savings banks have accepted
> deposits from people of small means, they have not, except in
> the rarest instances, been willing to make them loans. Unlike
> the commercial banks, they have offered only a small part of
> the traditional banking services to their customers.[48]

Like their British counterparts, cooperative lenders could only
function by limiting cooperation to relatively small, homogeneous, and stable groups. Those who most needed the benefits of
cooperation were precisely those who were excluded.

The Small Loan Laws

The failure of non-governmental responses to problems associated with high-cost loans contributed to a growing dissatisfaction
with general usury laws at the state level, largely unchanged since
the founding of most states. Before the Great Depression, Americans, distrustful of the government, were not ready to ask it to help
provide credit for the disadvantaged. Instead, reformers hoped to
raise interest-rate caps in order to attract legal private capital to
markets for consumer loans. The intellectual roots of the position
were not new. Classical economists, following Jeremy Bentham,
had consistently argued that legislating interest rates only forced
the high-risk loan market underground, thus requiring the bor-

rower to pay a premium to the lender to cover the risk of being caught. By making a special exception to general usury laws and allowing higher rates for small loans, reformers hoped to make consumer lending profitable to banks and other commercial creditors. Honest, respectable private lenders would flow into the market for costly consumer loans, creating healthy competition and driving the dishonest loansharks out of business. Thus was born the first of what are now commonly called "special usury statutes." Special usury laws provided certain specified lenders licenses to lend at rates in excess of a state's general interest-rate cap. At the time, these special usury laws were commonly called small loan laws. The new statutes allowed lenders, who would agree to licensing, bookkeeping, security interest, and collection practice rules, to lend less than $300 at between 36 and 42 percent per year. Statutes also typically assessed a flat tax on small loan lenders which gathered revenue to cover administrative costs.[49]

The primary advocates of the small loan laws were scholars and businesspeople associated with the Russell Sage Foundation, a charity fund established by the wife of a railroad tycoon. The foundation sponsored several groundbreaking studies and organized lobbying efforts to raise interest rates for small personal loans. Most importantly, the foundation made several drafts of uniform small loan laws, which many states adopted or relied upon in passing their own legislation. With the backing of the powerful nonprofit foundation, small loan lenders began to regard themselves as performing a social service by lending at reasonable terms to disadvantaged people in need.[50]

The passage of the small loan laws was a watershed event in both the law and culture of American high-cost credit. Legally, the small loan laws opened the door for states to amend the hitherto untouched general usury laws descended from the Statute of Anne. Once the dam broke, a wide variety of different creditor organizations began lobbying for their own exceptions to state general usury laws. One state legislature and one interest group at a time, a simple and common body of law was transformed into an obscure and arcane patchwork of legal exceptions, restrictions, fees, limitations, and definitions. State legislatures passed a hodge-podge of industrial loan laws, installment loan laws, retail install-ment sales acts, insurance premium finance regulations, and home equity loan laws, all at different times, with different terminology, and with substantively different provisions. After the small loan laws each state cultivated its own unique regulatory environ-ment.[51]

Culturally, governmental approval of licensed high-cost lenders dramatically changed the social symbols and discourse Americans had used to refer to high-cost lenders for over two centuries. After passage of the small loan laws, consumer creditors began a steady march toward legitimization. Small loan legislation, along with the Bankruptcy Act of 1898, began a process of erasing the government-sponsored stigma which had separated commercial and consumer lending in Western culture for centuries. These were the first steps in what has since been described as a "credit revolution."[52]

The Credit Revolution: Financing the Middle Class

From the 1920s through the Great Depression, the business of lending under the small loan laws boomed. The ranks of lenders seeking to earn a profit lending at rates below the special usury interest-rate caps of between 36 and 42 percent swelled. These lenders aggressively worked to distance themselves from the salary lending loansharks who dominated turn-of-the-century consumer financing. Many small loan lenders called themselves "personal fi-nance" companies, hoping to call up images of respected commer-cial banks rather than neighborhood pawnshops. Reflecting the optimistic expansion of the industry, one personal finance executive went so far as to say, "I think I can confidently predict that within a very brief period of time we will no longer be thought of as 'moneylenders' but as financial physicians to the American family."[53] Nevertheless, an increasingly overshadowed class of illegal or marginally legal lenders persisted in lending to and collecting from the most desperate debtors. While the numbers of debtors increased during the Great Depression, probably due to cautious lending based on fear of default, indebtedness was less severe than one might expect.[54]

Of more lasting influence was the new era of accepted middle-class durable consumer goods financing. Many commentators have pointed to this era as a turning point when the culture of thrift and rugged individualism of early America gave way to one of consumerism and personal debt.[55] Beginning roughly in the 1920s, businesses began to realize the advantages of not merely advertising products, but also promoting new ideas and ways of life. As David Tucker wrote in his book, *The Decline of Thrift in America*, "Through newspapers, magazines, billboards, radios, and motion pictures, advertising invaded the countryside as well as the city—pushing new ideas, habits and tastes."[56] Led by automobile dealers looking to expand their markets, installment lenders charged rates in excess of the old general usury laws, but still far below what turn-of-the-century salary lenders expected. This new class of creditor used installment loans to finance home furnishings, sewing machines, pianos, washing machines, vacuum cleaners, phonographs, and jewelry. Not shady, backdoor, fly-by-night loansharks, these lenders included many of the nation's most respected businesses. Although the older, more dangerous high-cost lenders were still around, they were more than happy to let the new, brash, and well-capitalized middle-class corporate financiers take the spotlight. High-cost lenders had always preferred relative anonymity. It was in this era that names like General Motors,

Sears, Singer, Montgomery Ward, and Steinway and Sons changed forever the way middle-class America viewed debt.[57]

HIGH-COST CREDIT POLICY AFTER WORLD WAR II

By the time of the American economic boom following the Second World War, consumer credit had already become a culturally and morally accepted part of life. However, the depth of the "credit revolution" had only just begun. A leading cultural historian on the subject of consumer credit summarized the entire postwar period with one word: "more,"[58]: more installment lending, more lending from cooperative lenders such as credit unions and mutual savings banks, more lending from retailers, and even more lending from the biggest and last player to embrace consumer credit—large banks. The movement toward the suburbs created demand for housing, automobiles, and household furnishings. The cultural trend away from early American thrift became even more pronounced as themes like "be the first on your block to own . . ." were pushed by advertisers and accepted by millions. But most of all, the tremendous prosperity following the war led to a surplus of disposable income, readily consumed by the durable goods efficiently churned out by the converted war industrial base. Middle-class Americans took on previously unheard of levels of debt and gradually paid it back without unmanageable difficulties.[59]

The social acceptance of consumer debt in America became complete with the coming of the credit card. As early as 1914, retailers had issued charge cards specific to their stores to encourage loyalty in their most wealthy customers. Gasoline suppliers and airlines made similar efforts beginning in the 1930s. The first "third-party universal" card, which has become the contemporary norm, was issued by Diner's Club in 1949. The credit issuer acted as broker between customers and firms (usually restaurants). Customers enjoyed the convenience of not carrying cash, and the ability to borrow money over a short term. Sellers gained access to market share by catering to a card-carrying clientele. In spite of early growing pains, credit cards steadily gained in popularity, gelling into the currently recognizable industry by the late 1960s. Eventually backed by the capital of the nation's largest banks, the credit card industry solicited business through advertisements in every media. In 1971, half of all American families used at least one credit card. In subsequent years, by sending out billions upon billions of mailed solicitations, credit card companies succeeded in making third-party consumer credit almost a medium of currency unto itself. By 1995, credit cards had "outstripped coins and folding money as the payment of choice for consumer transactions."[60]

Echoes: Modern Credit Policy and Mistakes of the Past

American credit policymakers have scrambled to keep up with sweeping cultural change. Turn-of-the-millennium consumer credit policy has become an astonishingly complex patchwork of federal, state, and local laws. But, while policies directed at controlling the excesses of the credit market have evolved to accommodate millions of new middle-class borrowers, its underlying nature echoes the strategies of the past.

Debtor amnesty rules, best exemplified by debt discharge in bankruptcy, have continued to provide an important safety valve, but have been unable to prevent the latest upsurge in high-cost lending. While bankruptcy laws retained the underlying structure of the 1893 Act until 1978, the protection afforded to consumer debtors lurched back and forth, often depending on little more than the mood of Congress, the influence of creditor lobbyists, and the economic circumstances of the day. For instance, Depression-era legislation focused on debtor rehabilitation and placed significant restraints on the ability of creditors to seize collateral. The Chandler Act in 1938 presumed to make the administration of bankruptcies fairer and more efficient. It included the introduction of Chapter 13, which allowed consumer debtors to discharge unpayable debts and adopt amortization plans under the oversight of the bankruptcy system. In 1946, Congress changed the compensation of bankruptcy referees from hourly fees to a full-time salary. In 1960, Congress created a committee on bankruptcy rules to explore ways to smooth out the grinding complexity and inefficiency of sorting through bankrupt estates which still plagued the system. And bankruptcy reform efforts during the pro-consumer Johnson era culminated in amendments which made discharge self-executing rather than an affirmative defense. In 1973, bankruptcy referees were renamed bankruptcy judges. After a decade of study and debate, Congress adopted a new bankruptcy code in 1978 which substantially expanded the jurisdiction of bankruptcy judges. The 1978 act also created a pilot program, later adopted throughout the country, dividing labor between bankruptcy judges and newly created bankruptcy trustees. Trustees handled administrative work, allowing judges to focus on adjudication. Soon after the new code took effect, at the instigation of creditors, Congress passed a series of laws making many different types of debt unsusceptible to discharge. In 1984, the United States Supreme Court forced Congress to clarify the constitutional status of bankruptcy judges, which created an opportunity for the credit industry once again to narrow significantly available consumer credit protections.[61]

These changes, and many others, occurred against the backdrop of growing personal bankruptcy filings. Diagnosing the cause of increased filings has been a subject of much dispute. The credit industry and its patrons have consistently complained of the decreasing stigma associated with personal bankruptcy. For nearly a hundred years, they have attributed growth in bankruptcy rates to this "loss of shame."[62] Others argue bankruptcy filings have simply tracked the rapid increases in consumer borrowing. By all accounts, mainstream credit card debt has become the type of credit most likely to send consumers into bankruptcy. But, in the last two decades, the growth of high-cost second-tier fringe debt has played a more important role, concurrent with a sharp decline in the median income of bankrupt families. Because bankruptcy only provides an after-the-fact safety valve, it has not, and cannot, prevent problematic high-cost debt situations before they arise. Obviously, an amnesty law so widespread as to cure the debt ills of all troubled debtors would ruin the credit industry, to everyone's detriment. The discharge provisions of our costly and complex bankruptcy system have doubtlessly improved on the capriciousness of Mesopotamian royal decrees of amnesty. But like their ancient Mesopotamian forebears, bankruptcy discharge only provides a lucky and sometimes undeserving few relief at the expense of their creditors—and, by driving up interest rates—at the expense of fellow debtors. In at least one respect, Mesopotamian amnesty decrees may have been better than our current system. The Sumerians and Babylonians did not sponsor bankruptcy professionals and services with costly taxpayer investments.

In the Postwar era, Americans also experimented with laws and programs that explicitly selected Americans of European ancestry for protection unavailable to other ethnic groups. An important example of such a selective protection strategy had its roots in Roosevelt's New Deal. In 1933, Congress created the Home Owners Loan Corporation ("HOLC"), a federal agency which sought to stimulate economic growth through homebuilding and to provide financial assistance for those who might not otherwise be able to purchase a house. The agency innovated long-term, self-amortizing mortgage loans with uniform payments over the duration of the loan. However, the agency also took the lead in developing racially discriminatory appraisal practices. Kenneth Jackson explains that for the agency, "[r]acial homogeneity was explicitly identified as a criterion for evaluating properties; but it was clear that not all homogeneous neighborhoods were equally valued." For example, the agency appraised a St. Louis County neighborhood as having "little or no value today, having suffered a tremendous decline in values due to the colored element now controlling the district."[63]

Perhaps more importantly, in 1934, Roosevelt and Congress created the Federal Housing Administration (FHA), which facilitated inexpensive home purchase financing by offering federal insurance for mortgage loans. By insuring lenders against the risk of default, creditors could offer more and lower-priced home loans. Unfortunately, this valuable federal program was reserved almost exclusively for the use of whites. The FHA's underwriting manual stated:

> Areas surrounding a location are to be investigated to determine whether incompatible racial and social groups are present, for the purpose of making a prediction regarding the probability of the location being invaded by such groups. If a neighborhood is to retain stability, it is necessary that properties shall continue to be occupied by the same social and racial classes. A change in social or racial occupancy generally contributes to instability and a decline in values.[64]

These policies created a legacy of discriminatory home financing which extended well past the Second World War and, many argue, continues today. For example, although from 1934 to 1959 the FHA financed 60 percent of home purchases in the United States, between the mid-forties and the mid-fifties, less than 2 percent of the FHA's loans went to African Americans. For middle-class Americans in the twentieth century, family homes have been the most important source of security for purchasing inexpensive credit. The difficulty black families had in finding cheap financing for home purchases was an important factor preventing their migration to the suburbs along with white America. Relegated to the decaying inner cities, black families rented their homes instead of buying them in disproportionate numbers. Because home equity is the most important security by which middle- and lower-income families can obtain long-term inexpensive credit, discriminatory mortgage insurance policies in the mid-twentieth century may well have significantly contributed to a greater African American vulnerability to high-cost lenders in latter twentieth century. By selectively protecting only European Americans, early federal home financing policies helped create a tradition of excluding racial minorities from access to the means to procure cheap credit.[65]

Charitable lending efforts also have continued to suffer from their historic limitations despite later-twentieth-century attempts to reinvent them. For instance, in 1977 Congress tried to recreate charitable lending as community reinvestment. The Community Reinvestment Act (CRA) is based on the premise that financial institutions have a duty to provide for the credit needs of their local communities. The law requires banks to identify their service areas and indicate how they are meeting the credit needs of low- and moderate-income groups within that area. If a lender does not adequately extend credit to its low- and moderate-income customers, then federal regulatory agencies are authorized to deny the lender's applications for deposit insurance, charters, establishment of branch offices, or other similar transactions.

Although the law has helped some low income communities, especially where activist and community watchdog groups have vocally sought enforcement of the law, in general the CRA's impact has been limited. Unfortunately, "federal regulatory agencies have rarely initiated any action on the basis of a CRA evaluation."[66] While some fair lending advocates insist the approach holds promise, community reinvestment suffers from the same problems as earlier charitable lending efforts. The motivation for creditors to lend in low income neighborhoods is based on the fear of enforcement efforts of federal regulators. The federal regulators are motivated based on the charitable ambitions of Congress. Despite Congressional good will, lenders have little incentive to lend and regulators have little incentive to find violations.[67] In 1989, one befuddled senator questioned the lack of regulatory enforcement:

> I think it somewhat incredible that the substance of the testimony is mostly that you haven't found any violations when the evidence is pretty clear out there that a lot of violations have been taking place. . . . We have incredible testimony. . . . I'm not trying to pick on anybody, but I want to suggest that I find it pretty close to remarkable that we never find any violations.[68]

Another congressman went even further saying "[t]he Community Reinvestment Act . . . has become a monument to regulatory inaction."[69]

The incentive structure behind community reinvestment does not harness the profit motives of lenders. The result is chronic undercapitalization. Moreover, where community reinvestment lending does occur, it tends to devolve into simple profit-seeking behavior. For instance, in recent years consumer watchdog groups have complained that banks have turned to purchasing dangerous subprime mortgage loans from shady brokers in order to satisfy their reinvestment requirements. Recalling the supply problems of the *mons pietatis* as well as late-nineteenth-century American provident loan societies, the recent comments of a community reinvestment advocate would have been as applicable centuries ago as they are today: "[t]he present state of access to capital in low-income communities is improving but nevertheless very inadequate. Although there have been major improvements with new institutions and instruments, there are still huge gaps."[70] Community reinvestment has not provided enough low-cost funds to displace aggressive, profit-seeking high-cost lenders in significant numbers. Although today the federal government has filled in where the captains of industry left off, whether community reinvestment will succeed in the future depends on the ability of regulators and advocates to overcome competitive market forces in a way charitable lenders of previous centuries could not.

In the Postwar era, credit unions became the prototypical American cooperative lending institutions. Drawing on war- and Depression-hardened leaders, as well as responsible yet credit-hungry consumers, in the two decades after 1945 the number of credit unions grew 155.2 percent and the number of credit union members grew 489.4 percent. Government and employer sponsorship facilitated the gains. Credit unions retained the significant advantage of freedom from taxation. And the groups which provided the common bond for credit union membership also tended to provide free or subsidized management assistance, overhead, and a ready pool of potential members. In 1970, Congress created the Federal Credit Union Administration and insured credit union deposits with federal funds, further stabilizing the industry. In terms of credit sales, credit unions have generally used their production cost advantages to offer below-market interest rates for similar credit products. During the Postwar era, the staple loan for most credit unions became automobile financing. In the late 1970s and early 1980s, almost half of all credit union loans financed car purchases, and these loans in turn constituted a little less than 20 percent of all car loans nationwide. For millions of Americans, there can be no doubt credit union membership has provided an invaluable and socially constructive source of financial services and inexpensive credit.[71]

However, as in past ages, credit unions and other cooperative lenders have not significantly altered the financial destinies of the

most vulnerable debtors. Despite the originating spirit of cooperative idealism, two noted credit union scholars concede:

> credit union leaders had to confront the fact that the nature
> of the movement had changed greatly and that they were
> serving members with different patterns of employment and
> needs. Adequate savings could not be derived from the lower
> income groups and the very poor were not good credit risks.
> The ultimate effect was that the credit union movement de-
> veloped more of a middle income orientation than one de-
> voted to lower-income groups. Thus, . . . the main thrust of
> management became one of establishing sound management
> practices designed to stabilize the individual units while per-
> mitting steady growth.[72]

Although the common bond requirements for credit union membership loosened around the country, management practices and
economies of scale pushed the credit union industry toward a
smaller number of larger credit unions. Beginning in the 1970s,
large credit unions focusing on economies of scale came to over-
shadow smaller unions that focused on responding to the needs of
a core common bond group. Many credit unions merged. In 1965,
credit unions with over five billion dollars in assets held only 27.5
percent of total industry assets. By 1980, credit unions with over
five billion in assets accounted for 77.2 percent of all industry assets. When the boom in second-tier lending hit during the early
1980s, credit unions were focused on providing costly services
such as automatic teller machines, credit cards, trust services, and
automated telephone services to middle- and upper-income
members, rather than moderately priced credit to high-risk borrowers.[73]

Deregulation and the Illusion of Interest-Rate Caps

In the 1970s, government expenditures on the Vietnam War overheated the economy, leading to inflationary pressures which made it harder for banks to gather funds to lend. By the late 1970s, growing unemployment exacerbated the impact of still rampant inflation. Federal monetary policy sought to slow the rapidly diminishing value of currency by allowing high interest rates. As a result, short-term commercial market interest rates rose to above 20 percent. Although constant creditor lobbying had reduced many state interest-rate caps to a confusing patchwork, most states still had some upper interest-rate limit. But as rising market equilibrium rates forced depository institutions' cost of funds higher, it became difficult for banks and others to lend profitably within these legal usury limits. "There was a fear," explains Kathleen Keest, "that creditors would be understandably reluctant to lend money at rates below their cost of funds and that mortgage loans and other kinds of consumer credit would dry up."[74] State legislatures responded with a variety of actions, but almost all significantly decreased regulation of chargeable rates. Keest further elaborates:

> Many states repealed general usury ceilings completely, allowing parties who were not regulated by special usury statutes to contract for the payment of any agreed rate. Other states modified their general usury laws so that the ceilings would fluctuate with some published market interest rate. For example, several states set their ceilings to five or six percentage points above the federal discount rate. Most states simply raised their interest ceilings to a point not binding on traditional lenders.[75]

Congress also joined in. Among other interest rate deregulatory actions, Congress banned any state interest-rate caps on home or mobile home first mortgages.[76]

These temporary economic pressures have proven less enduring than the United States Supreme Court's effort at deregulation in the landmark decision of *Marquette National Bank v. First Omaha Service Corporation*.[77] Interpreting Section 85 of the National Bank Act of 1863, the Court held the Civil War-era Congress had intended to preempt state interest rates to the extent that they conflicted with the rates charged by out-of-state lenders. The *Marquette* Court held the interest-rate caps of a card issuer's home state trumped the interest-rate caps of the cardholder's home state. This set off two races: first for credit-card lenders to move their operations to states with no interest-rate caps, and second for state legislatures to remove their usury laws in order to attract or hold onto rapidly expanding credit card companies. By the early 1980s, several states, including Delaware, South Carolina, South Dakota, and Utah, had abolished all interest-rate controls. Although even bastions of interest-rate regulation like Minnesota soon followed by raising interest-rate caps, the damage was already done. In theory, if every state legislature but one passed low interest-rate caps, then lenders could simply set up operations (either in fact or on paper) within that one state. Lenders could export that state's unregulated interest rates to every other state, regardless of objections of the other forty-nine democratically-elected state legislatures. In practice, nine Supreme Court justices eliminated two hundred years of democratic state interest-rate regulation of bank loans.[78]

Although the *Marquette* case involved credit cards, the doctrine has subsequently spread to other types of lending. By the 1990s, the best example had become payday lending. Because payday lenders typically charge between 391 and 550 percent, their services do not fit under any of the state usury laws which survived the 1980s. But many of the states which retained interest-rate caps, including Indiana, North Carolina, and Virginia, have had markets of impoverished potential debtors too tempting for payday lenders to resist. In order to circumvent these caps, payday lenders teamed up with FDIC-insured banks. By exploiting the Supreme Court's constitutionalization of perceived Civil War-era Congressional intentions, payday lenders have managed to capture the legal authority of the United States Constitution to justify loans with interest rates more than twice as high as those typically offered by mafia loansharks.[79] A University of Michigan law professor explained, these developments have "been hidden from the public and state legislators by the camouflage of usury laws on the books of almost all states that appear to cover loans to that state's debtors. Day by day these local laws have become a more exaggerated illusion; under the *Marquette* doctrine, the sternest state laws are the first to be undermined and the quickest to fall."[80]

For thousands of years social and governmental leaders have socialized their people with strong messages condemning high-cost personal debt. American government, by gradually removing or at least muddling the old general usury interest-rate caps, has abdicated this leadership role. This resignation, combined with the sweeping cultural changes wrought by an explosion in mainstream moderately-priced consumer credit, has eroded a once unified moral stance towards high-cost debt. Today's high-cost debtors are in at least one sense worse off than those of a century ago. Then, almost all debtors would have had a lifetime of socialization regarding the "evil" of personal debt. Today's high-cost debtors, however, sign credit contracts with the same prices as a century ago, but do so with none of the same moral condemnation to warn them of the risks they take. In a very real sense, America's culture has become one of reckless borrowing. For many who can afford such carelessness, the consequences are not severe and are perhaps in some ways even beneficial: monthly payments, overtime, mild anxiety about bills, and perhaps less time with the kids, all offset by the fiscal disciplining of credit contracts and the genuine value of consumer products. But for those who cannot afford imprudent credit decisions, the consequences have become as grave as they were more than a century ago when the first loansharks appeared.

Although the history of consumer credit in America is unique, the policies relied upon to protect vulnerable debtors from the danger of high-cost credit are in most cases older than the country. Sadly, these strategies have not reliably cured the social ills associated with high-cost debt nor prevented our most recent surge in the high-cost credit market. Ironically, many advocates of these policies are quixotically unaware of the histories of failure plaguing each policy option, dating back hundreds or even thousands of years. Debtor amnesty, interest-rate caps and other format restrictions, selective protection schemes, charitable lending, cooperative lending, and the over-reliance on unregulated markets have all had histories indicating inherent limitation. As a result our efforts have tended to protect those who least need it—the relatively affluent.

Today America is in the throes of an identity crisis with respect to consumer credit. Social conservatives do not know how to resolve Biblical injunctions against abusive money lending and their tradition of stalwart thrift with their embrace of laissez-faire capitalism. Social liberals do not know how to resolve their empathy for the plight of working-poor and lower-middle-class debtors with their newfound commitment to market decision-making. Conservatives and liberals alike have embraced mainstream moderately-priced consumer credit. But as of yet both groups have lacked the cultural sophistication to distinguish morally the comparatively new mainstream moderately-priced credit with the millennia-old high-cost credit sold in the second-tier alternative finance market. It is precisely this collective moral disorientation which has allowed payday lenders, pawnbrokers, rent-to-own retailers, rapid tax-refund lenders, car title lenders, and predatory mortgage lenders to cloak themselves in mainstream legitimacy like never before. This moral disorientation has allowed these lenders to slip under the jurisdiction of laws designed to protect the relatively affluent upper and upper-middle classes. It is this disorientation which has allowed some banks to depart from the honorable traditions of American banking by stooping to triple-digit interest-rate payday lending.

CHAPTER 4

The Unique Promise of Disclosure Law and the Trouble with Shopping: Imperfect Information and Debt Fever

Let me emphasize: competition does not protect the consumer because businessmen are more softhearted than bureaucrats or because they are more altruistic or because they are more generous, but only because it is in the self-interest of the entrepreneur to protect the consumer.

—Milton Friedman

Publicity is justly commended as a remedy for social and industrial diseases. Sunlight is said to be the best of disinfectants; electric light the most efficient policeman.

—Justice Louis D. Brandeis

CONGRESS HAS BEEN WELL AWARE of the moral disorientation created by the "credit revolution." In fact, the most important federal consumer credit legislation, the Truth-in-Lending Act (TILA), was a response to precisely this problem. This chapter describes how and why Congress passed TILA. It will also explain the limitations of TILA today in correcting the harmful consequences of high-cost lending. But most importantly, this chapter attempts to point out one way in which the market for high-cost credit currently malfunctions.

THE RISE OF TRUTH IN LENDING

Throughout history there has been no common terminology used in credit contracts. After the explosion of mainstream, moderately-priced consumer credit use following World War II, the different meanings different lenders ascribed to certain terms became more noticeable than at any other time in human history. Even the most basic contractual terms, such as interest rates, had no commonly shared definition. The result was that consumers neither shopped for cheap credit nor even understood how much they were actually paying for the credit they agreed to. A 1964 study asked families to estimate the average interest rate on their consumer debt. The average response was 8 percent—a third of the true cost of 24 percent.[1] The complexity of quoted credit prices was multiplying the confusion. For example, there are a wide variety of methods for computing interest, which can produce a wide variety of actual costs. Lenders might calculate rates through the discount method, the discount-plus-fee method, the add-on method, the actuarial method, or any other method. Some lenders would quote yearly interest rates, while others might quote monthly or even weekly rates. Moreover, as former Senator Paul Douglas of Illinois once explained, on many monthly loans "the interest was computed not on the declining balance actually owed by the borrower, but instead on the original amount borrowed." Thus these creditors charged interest on money debtors had already repaid, which "meant that the real rate of interest was approximately double the one quoted."[2] Compounding the problem, state governments also used a large and incompatible variety of terms and classifications in statutes regulating consumer credit.

Although this may have been less of a problem for sophisticated commercial debtors, the new breed of consumer debtors lacked the expertise and patience necessary for distilling the true meaning of credit contracts. Finally, lenders often charged a variety of closing costs which were not reflected in the interest rate. The result was that consumer debtors rarely understood the true price of their credit contracts.[3]

Truth in lending sought to remedy this confusion. The basic idea was that government should require creditors to calculate and quote interest rates and other important contractual terms in a clear and uniform manner. Former Senator Douglas is commonly credited with creating some of the first modern credit price disclosure proposals. Years later Douglas recounted a story of the first time he suggested such a requirement. Working at Roosevelt's National Recovery Administration for the consumer finance industry, Douglas served on a committee responsible for drafting proposed credit code revisions.

> At the first meeting of the code authority in 1934, I brought up these facts and suggested that the members of the industry should quote their rates on an annual rather than a monthly basis and charge interest only on the unpaid balance. Never did the temperature of a meeting drop so sharply and so far. A chilling silence set in and the authority shortly adjourned. A few days later, I received a letter suggesting that I might want to resign.[4]

Douglas did not dare to revisit the proposal for twenty-five years and until he had a decade of experience in the United States Senate.

When Senator Douglas did finally introduce the first federal credit price disclosure bill in 1960, the idea was not received any better than in 1934. An awesome array of opponents including the nation's automobile dealers, finance companies, mail order houses, the National Association of Manufacturers, the U.S. Chamber of Commerce, the American Bankers Association, the American Bar Association, virtually all Congressional Republicans, and most of the Southern Democrats denounced the bill. One commentator colorfully summarizes what followed:

> Congress spent the eight years from 1960 to 1968 debating the Truth-in-Lending Act. According to the military metaphor that is almost obligatory in these cases, the process must be counted as an epic battle. Forces were rallied, maneuvers undertaken, salvoes exchanged, and casualties incurred. While the reality was political rather than military, it was no less intensely fought and, at some points, no less gruesome.[5]

The magnitude of "Congress'" debate is somewhat tarnished when one realizes the bill did not leave the Senate Banking Committee for debate by the whole Senate until 1967. In reality, much of the struggle occurred between just a few influential members of a Senate Subcommittee. As for casualties, it is worth noting that Senator Douglas' defeat in the 1966 election bears a striking resemblance to the political demise of Governor Hai Jui in the late Chinese Ming Dynasty. Both eroded their political capital by alienating powerful commercial interests while fighting for widespread credit reform of regulatory systems based on inadequate interest-rate caps. And both fell from power despite their informed and passionate commitment to populist government policy.

While early bills all faltered, they did provide Senator Douglas and, later, Wisconsin Senator William Proxmire the excuse to hold extensive hearings exploring the issue and hammering out the details. Particularly influential were a series of four 1963 hearings held outside of Washington, D.C. in New York City, Pittsburgh, Louisville, and Boston. Supporters of the legislation hoped that these hearings would raise public awareness and pressure Banking Committee members to allow the bill out onto the Senate floor. Although the hearings failed to produce the latter goal, they were successful in generating state and local interest in the issue.[6]

In particular, the Boston hearings may have helped spawn one of the first statutes which can fairly be characterized as modern credit disclosure law.[7] In 1966 both the Canadian province of Nova Scotia and the State of Massachusetts adopted local versions of the Truth in Lending Act. Portentously, the Massachusetts legislation included almost the same disclosure requirements as the federal bill.[8]

> How effectively . . . [the Massachusetts law] was working was an open question, but clearly it had not produced the commercial Armageddon which the opponents of Truth-in-Lending had predicted. Small businesses had not closed overnight, nor had the state economy collapsed, no sales clerks had suffered nervous breakdowns at the credit counter, and no bank officials had hanged themselves from their fluorescent lights. With life in Massachusetts going on pretty much as it had before, the opposition found itself somewhat embarrassed by the vigor of its prior rhetoric.[9]

This, combined with 1968 election results favoring supporters of the disclosure bill led the Senate Banking Committee to allow the bill onto the Senate floor, where it quickly passed.

In the House, Representative Leonore Sullivan (D-Missouri) led a faster and more dramatic charge than the plodding Senate, culminating in the ultimate passage of a more robust statute. The composition of the House of Representatives was decidedly more liberal than that of the Senate. This enabled Sullivan to introduce a much more liberal bill, which included many substantive provisions in addition to the disclosure bill passed by the Senate. She and her Democratic colleagues on the House Banking Committee's Subcommittee on Consumer Affairs inserted provisions requiring more comprehensive disclosure, including those regarding first and second mortgages and credit advertising. Additional substantive proposals included a national interest-rate cap of 18 percent, prohibition of all wage garnishments and confessions of judgment in consumer credit cases, the establishment of a national commission on consumer finance, and creation of a presidential power to control consumer credit rules during economic crises.[10]

House Republicans reacted by supporting the comparatively conservative Senate bill. Many of the substantive provisions, including the national usury limit, were bargaining chips which House Democrats intended to trade away in order to strengthen the Senate bill. On the House floor, Republicans, looking to salvage a "tough on crime" theme out of the impending consumer legislation, added provisions making extortionate credit collection a federal crime. When the legislation surfaced from a joint House and Senate Conference Committee it "retained the structure and discourse of the parent Senate bill," but included many of the added House provisions on first and second mortgages, credit life insurance, credit advertising, wage garnishment, administrative enforcement, loansharking, and the National Commission on Consumer Finance. Because the final bill went far beyond disclosure, it was renamed the Consumer Credit Protection Act. However, Congress retained the "Truth in Lending" label for the disclosure provisions, which still made up the most important and influential bulk of the act.[11]

The most important requirements of the Truth in Lending provisions centered around the disclosure of the cost of credit based on standard uniform requirements set out by the act and by the Federal Reserve Board. The two most important disclosures were the "finance charge" and the "annual percentage rate." The finance charge is "the sum of all charges, payable directly or indirectly by the creditor as an incident to the extension of credit."[12] It includes all interest and fees that a creditor requires the debtor to pay. The annual percentage rate (APR) is an interest rate based on the actuarial method and calculated in accordance with regulations set out by the Federal Reserve Board.[13] The act was enforced with tough civil penalties. It also gave debtors the right to sue their creditors for failure to correctly disclose prices and other contract provisions. Creditors found in violation were liable for actual damages the creditor caused the debtor, statutory damages, attorneys' fees, court costs, and in extreme cases even criminal prosecution.[14]

THE UNIQUE PROMISE OF DISCLOSURE

Although neither industry nor consumer advocates have ever been entirely satisfied with Truth in Lending, the disclosure approach has in general garnered wide acceptance. Not only has TILA remained the cornerstone of Federal consumer credit regulation, but many state governments have also come to rely heavily on disclosure provisions. Industry, rarely welcoming regulation, has nevertheless come to a grudging acceptance of TILA. And consumer advocates, albeit wishing for stronger rules, still usually see disclosure as indispensable.

Congress' adoption of Truth in Lending was only possible because the price disclosure approach has distinct political and theoretical advantages over other consumer credit policy options. In theory, disclosure simultaneously provides consumer protection and promotes market outcomes consistent with the conditions classical economics prescribes for efficient market economies. This characteristic makes the disclosure approach unusually attractive in the American political climate. Economic discourse in the United States has typically been characterized by two strains of thought: that—anchored by Adam Smith—advocating relatively less or no governmental control in the distribution of scarce resources, and that—anchored (albeit in the American case very distantly) by Marx—advocating more or complete governmental control. This dichotomous characterization of economic thinking has had profound influence on policymakers seeking to deal with problems arising in the respective rights of debtors and creditors. The disclosure strategy for controlling the harmful consequences of high-cost lending has the rare advantage of falling within an ideological overlap palatable to those holding both of these usually divisive perspectives.

Disclosure is acceptable in the classical economic perspective because it promotes informed decision-making. For classical economists the ideal method of constructing social policy was to leave nearly all policy decisions to individual economic behavior. Classical economists believed society could rely on its individual members to protect their own best interests, and in turn protect overall social wellbeing at the same time. Individuals neither intend nor generally recognize that their selfish actions promote societal welfare, but these actions nevertheless do so. When every member of society is making well-informed decisions in their own best interests, the collective result is better policy than any government planning board might make. Adam Smith describes this prediction as "an invisible hand" guiding social policy to the optimal outcome. In Smith's words:

> [O]f which the produce is likely to be the greatest value, every individual, it is evident, can, in his local situation, judge much better than any statesman or lawgiver can do for him. The statesman, who should attempt to direct private people in what manner they ought to employ their capitals, would not only load himself with a most unnecessary attention, but assume an authority which could safely be trusted,

not only to no single person, but to no council or senate whatever, and which would nowhere be so dangerous as in the hands of a man who had folly and presumption enough to fancy himself fit to exercise it.[15]

Thus, in this view there is a presumption against government interference in each individual's own purchasing decisions, with credit being no exception.

Nevertheless, most economists are willing to agree governmental action is sometimes necessary to protect the market conditions which facilitate competition. Where the private decision-making process in some way breaks down, the government must intervene either to reestablish private decision-making or correct for the failure. One introductory economics textbook plainly explains:

> Adam Smith extolled the virtues of private markets, arguing that consumers and producers "promote the public interest" more effectively than any government. If this were always true, then government intervention could only harm the public interest. Smith's argument holds, however, only when certain ideal conditions prevail. When these conditions are not satisfied, market outcomes are not optimal. In such cases government may serve the public interest. Among these reasons for market failure, and therefore government regulation, are natural monopoly, externalities and *imperfect information.*[16]

Information is important because it is a necessary prerequisite to efficient market decision-making. Efficient market outcomes can only come about as a result of individuals selecting those product options with the lowest opportunity costs. That is, the costs of forgone alternatives to any economic decision. "[G]iven limited or scarce resources and time," explain two economists, "the undertaking of any activity or the expenditure of any funds means that we must forgo some other activity or some other use of these funds."[17] The driving force behind market-based policymaking is harnessing the good sense and local perspective of each individual so that person can make the best decisions available to him. Without accurate information about the quality and especially the price of any good, no person can minimize opportunity costs, since they cannot compare the value of that product to the next best option. Thus, in a policymaking system of private decision-making, where individuals act without accurate cost information, there is no policymaking at all, but rather the random and often tragic outcomes of market anarchy.

Disclosure regulation fits within the traditional classical economic perspective because it is directed at fixing a breakdown in the private decisionmaking process which guides markets to optimal outcomes. Traditional governmental regulation controls the private decisions of debtors. For example, where there are interest-rate caps, debtors are not free to choose loans at prohibited prices. Classical economics recommends debtors have the freedom to make whatever bargains they choose, provided they understand the consequences of their actions. Or, as Jeremy Bentham explained, "no man of ripe years and sound mind, acting freely and *with his eyes open*, ought to be hindered . . . from making such bargain in the way of obtaining money, as he sees fit. . . ."[18] But to the extent that a debtor does not have his "eyes open," for classical economics, all bets are off. Unlike interest-rate caps and other control devices, disclosure regulation—at least in theory—*increases* the freedom of consumers by offering the opportunity to open their own eyes. With disclosure regulation, consumers compare different contracts and thus control their financial destinies. In theory, each debtor is empowered to protect her own interests, and in doing so will contribute to the overall welfare of society.

On the other hand, disclosure regulation is also acceptable to the control-oriented perspective in American economic discourse. This perspective is skeptical that private decision-making by individuals in unregulated markets can actually create the society we all hope to have. Proponents of this view believe well-planned government intervention into private purchasing decisions can improve the overall welfare of society. Often these thinkers point to actual stories of economic injustice as well as empirical data demonstrating economic inequality to show market outcomes are not what we want. Apologists for government control of markets often also point to the assumptions of classical economic models, arguing these assumptions are false, and therefore generate flawed predictions. Although as a nation we certainly identify more with Adam Smith than Karl Marx, policymakers and the American public have not followed blindly the recommendations of classical economics. Although exceptions for various lenders are both common and complex, all but six states retain some interest-rate cap language in their state statute books.[19] For those who take this control-oriented statutory language seriously, the emphasis of governmental action should not be solely on facilitating private policymaking, but also on protecting society's vulnerable members.

This emphasis on protection is why disclosure regulation also fits well within the perspective of those who advocate governmental control of markets. Disclosure regulations provide consumers with an important opportunity to protect themselves from credit bargains that are not truly in their own best interests. Although thinkers with this control-oriented perspective are likely to hope for additional regulations which more completely clamp down on high-cost lending (such as interest-rate caps with stiff enforcement and penalties), disclosure regulations are at least a palatably good start.

Historically the basic strategy of modern price disclosure represents a fundamentally new approach to solving the problems associated with consumer credit. Other American efforts have been variations on older strategies invented long ago on other continents. The interest-rate caps enacted throughout most of American history were little different than those of Ming China, Rome, and Babylon. American charitable lending strategies, including provident loan societies and community reinvestment efforts, suffer from the same problems of the first Italian *montes pietates*. American cooperative strategies including savings and loan societies and credit unions, albeit important contributions, have not been able to include those who need their services most. And sadly, racially discriminatory mortgage loan policies such as used by the Federal Housing Administration in the Thirties are prime examples of selective protection of a favored majority from the risks of high-cost borrowing. Truth in Lending does not properly fit into any of these classifications. Although the relative novelty of modern disclosure regulation does not by itself demonstrate greater potential than these older strategies, the fact that so many of us can agree about the basic theoretical advantages of disclosure may hold promise. Both classical market liberals and control-oriented supporters of regulation tend to agree on the formidable theoretical potential of price disclosure policies in regulating consumer credit. This agreement is notable not just because it is rare, and not just because it facilitates legislative compromise, but also because the agreement itself speaks well about the value of the approach. None of history's other strategies for controlling the harmful consequences of high-cost lending capture the ideological overlap between laissez-faire capitalists and protection-oriented government regulators as well as price disclosure.

THE LOST PROMISE OF DISCLOSURE: TRUTH IS NOT ENOUGH

Sadly, the thirty-five-year history of modern credit price disclosure regulation has demonstrated a wide gap between Truth in

Lending theory and market reality. Although the basic notion of preventing credit problems before they develop with a uniform price tag disclosure sounds simple, the practical implementation of TILA turns out to be extremely complicated. The statute charged the Federal Reserve Board with ironing out the details of the law in what was called Regulation Z. In addition to Regulation Z, between 1968 and 1980 the Federal Reserve Board issued approximately 1500 advisory opinions interpreting the rules. In order to help creditors digest this vast amount of technical information, the Federal Reserve Board also issued informal pamphlets. In some cases, creditors relied on these pamphlets in designing their disclosure forms, only to have the courts later rule the pamphlets themselves were incorrect.[20]

Following passage, however, consumer advocates did not hesitate to make use of the new laws. The National Consumer Law Center explains:

> Legal Services attorneys made extensive use of the TILA on behalf of low-income consumers. In addition the private bar developed a consumer segment which relied heavily on TILA. Creditors who did not comply with the Act found themselves defendants in thousands of lawsuits filed on the basis of TILA noncompliance, or found themselves losing what had previously been routine collection actions because of TILA counterclaims.[21]

Between 1969 and 1980 over 14,000 suits alleging TILA violations were filed in federal court. By 1979 Truth in Lending litigation constituted about 2 percent of the civil case load in federal courts. Congress, hoping to ensure enforcement of the intentions of the act, included language urging courts to broadly interpret TILA requirements and hold creditors to strict letter of the law.[22] This requirement forced courts to impose penalties on creditors who made only minor disclosure errors. Just as advocates of TILA had seized on the horror stories of cheated debtors, opponents of the legislation found new ammunition in the woes of creditor compliance troubles. Amplified by the finest lobbyists the consumer credit industry could buy, the stories of creditor compliance problems gradually forced Congress to reconsider the ardor with which they passed TILA.

Independent of creditor complaints about litigation and the difficulty of compliance, the credit industry as well as many neutral academics led a rhetorical challenge to TILA, asserting the information provided to debtors was not useful. A body of academic literature had developed discussing Truth in Lending even before Congress adopted the Act, but now it grew larger and decidedly more skeptical.[23] The early objection which resonated most was the claim that TILA caused information overload. The argument rested on studies showing that debtors did not understand most of the disclosed information. Because TILA required disclosure of too much information, disclosures resembled just another legal form, which debtors did not bother to read. In 1977 Senate hearings, the Federal Reserve Board itself marched before Congress a Yale professor they had hired to study disclosure problems. Professor Stephen Permut argued the basic philosophy of disclosing all important elements of a credit contract was flawed. Embracing this view, a governor of the Federal Reserve Board told senators:

[I]n our opinion, the total present disclosure requirements are simply too extensive to permit effective use by the vast majority of consumers. This view is based in part upon Professor Permut's advice that the mass of information now provided may produce a kind of "information overload" that overpowers many consumers and renders the entire disclosure statement a forbidding and incomprehensible document. Indeed, behavioral research suggests that when confronted with more than a few "bits" of information, consumers cease to read or retain *any* of the material offered.[24]

Opponents of reform countered that most of the complexity of disclosures was due to creditors' unnecessary and over-aggressive contractual efforts to protect themselves in every possible circumstance of default. Consumer advocates also argued that information overload could be solved by visually segregating the most important information from less important disclosures. Thus, consumers could have simplified disclosure, but still have the important yet more complex information available if they chose to explore it.[25] But after the Federal Reserve Board—the very administrative agency charged with implementing the Act—called for abandoning many TILA disclosures, fundamental change was inevitable.

The 1968 Act endured small amendments to correct technical problems in 1970, 1974, twice in 1976, and again in 1978.[26] But by 1980, Congress bowed to the inescapable industry pressure and the growing tide of deregulation around the country. The Truth in Lending Simplification and Reform Act cut out many of the provisions giving creditors compliance trouble. At the same time, Congress preempted state interest-rate caps on first mortgage home loans, effectively allowing mortgage lenders to charge whatever interest rates to which debtors might agree.[27] The changes to Truth in Lending were so thorough the Federal Reserve Board considered the law a "new" Truth in Lending Act, rather than an amended version of the old statute. The most important changes included limiting statutory penalties to only "significant" violations of the act, elimination of itemization of the finance charge, and in some instances elimination of itemization of the amount financed. Also, the Simplification Act eliminated or streamlined a variety of secondary, but potentially important, disclosures relating to the legal right to acceleration, security interests, late charges, and rebates. Finally, and perhaps in practical terms most importantly, the Simplification Act required the Federal Reserve Board to promulgate "safe haven" forms which further encouraged uniformity and gave an added assurance to lenders about liability risks.

Many changes, however, had nothing to do with making disclosure documents simpler, but rather focused on protecting major players in the lending markets. For instance, in the 1968 Act, assignees of the original creditor were sometimes held equally liable for any Truth in Lending violations. This encouraged the secondary lending market to police loan originators. But under the 1980 Act, assignees became liable only for violations apparent on the face of the contract. The 1980 Act also reduced the maximum recovery for multiple class actions, eroding the incentive of plaintiffs' lawyers to engage in major litigation battles with large lenders. One scholar recently explained, "it was undoubtedly the onslaught of TIL lawsuits, most of which were being won by consumers, more than the failure of the Act to assist consumers in comparison shopping that led Congress to enact a major overhaul of the Act, effective in 1980."[28] It is also worth noting the claim that Truth in Lending lawsuits in the pre-1980 era were largely based on technical problems with secondary disclosure requirements is something of a myth. On the contrary, more than half of TILA litigation in this period challenged the accuracy of finance charges, which as two influential consumer attorneys explain is, "not a 'technicality,' but one of the two most fundamental disclosures mandated by TIL."[29] Nevertheless, when the Supreme Court quickly resolved several of the most important controversies Congress left unaddressed, many of creditors' compliance concerns were essentially eliminated. The result was that soon after simplification, the levels of litigation over TILA subsided to "relatively sparse" levels.[30]

The Market for High-Cost Credit Information

While industry has come to a grudging acceptance of Truth in Lending as litigation and compliance problems have largely been solved, it is far less clear whether the Act has achieved the ultimate goal of protecting consumers by creating informed credit decisions. Unfortunately there are strong indications that, at least in the market for high-cost credit, Truth in Lending has failed almost entirely in promoting price-informed borrowing decisions among the most vulnerable debtors. In the high-cost credit market there is troubling evidence that structural and market forces act, not to promote price competition, but to promote confusion and strategic lending behavior. High-cost lenders have a greater incentive to erect barriers to price shopping than moderate- and low-priced lenders. The reason relatively inexpensive lenders sell their loan products at lower prices is because their clientele are responsive to those prices. The lender offering the cheapest loan has every incentive to advertise that price. But for lenders who have abandoned price competition for other means of acquiring customers, the wisest course is to hide those prices for as long as possible. The ideal high-cost debtor is one who continues paying without even realizing the true opportunity costs of her purchasing decision.

One way of discouraging comparison of loan products is by making those products complex. After-the-fact legal battles are at least partially to blame in encouraging high-cost credit contract complexity. Because in our legal system courts take the text of contractual provisions seriously—often regardless of whether the parties actually understood their own bargains—creditors have a great incentive to pack their documents to preempt every contingency they can imagine. Affirmative defenses in litigation as well as statutory penalties for flawed disclosure and other debtor consumer protection rules creates perverse incentives to craft complex contractual provisions which undermine the ability of consumers to make meaningful comparisons between competing products.[31]

Even where the added complexity of a contract does not provide legal protection for a lender in the long run, the *threat* of protection can be just as effective. High-cost debtors do not know what lending practices are and are not enforceable. This means complexity which looks defensible is often good enough, especially if it can scare off the few overworked lawyers who serve the nation's most vulnerable debtors.

Even absent litigation risks, in the high-cost credit market, many creditors inject complexity into their contracts and the negotiation process preceding them simply for the strategic value of the complexity itself. High-cost mortgage debtors often complain lenders present stacks of irrelevant brochures, letters, and advertisements in addition to already complex settlement forms in order to cloak their true prices. The story of John Evans, an 87-year-old retired laundry pressman from Columbia, South Carolina, is indicative. Evans and his wife bought their home in 1960. Since his retirement seven years ago he has worked part-time bagging groceries at a local Kroger supermarket. A telemarketer from Collateral One Mortgage Company called Evans and convinced him they could refinance his loan with lower monthly payments. Anxious to stretch his small paycheck and social security income farther, he expressed interest. Collateral One, a seven-year-old mortgage lender with operations in Tennessee, Kentucky, and North and South Carolina, immediately sent a salesman to Evans' home. Soon after, Collateral One signed Evans up for a $71,000 mortgage with higher monthly payments and a 10.792 percent interest rate. Included in the financing were more than $6,100 in fees, which cost around $26,000 over the life of the loan. And, after thirteen years of regular monthly payments, Evans, at 101 years of age, will be due to make a balloon payment of $58,622. The spokesman for Collateral One insisted Evans was fully informed about the terms of his completely fair loan. Collateral One provided Evans all the required paperwork detailing all loan terms and other information prior to closing. They emphasize that Evans never objected or indicated he could not understand the loan terms. For his part, Evans says, "he thought the contract was all right," but admits he cannot read, having left school after the first grade. What he does know for certain is that he was not told his monthly payments would be more than $100 larger than before. With his limited, fixed income Evans can barely make ends meet and is afraid he "can't hang on much longer." If he stops making payments, he will lose his home in foreclosure.[32]

An anonymous former branch manager for Associates Financial Service, a major national high-cost lender, paints a similar picture of typical high-cost mortgage loan closings. The former manager confided to a noted investigative journalist from Virginia:

> "The sales methods are so deceiving.". . . [W]ith all the numbers and documents involved, it's easy for a loan officer to throw out some figures and say, "I can save you $25,000, isn't that great?" The loan officer nods his head up and down and makes eye contact. The bewildered customers nod their heads yes too. "They'll be signing their lives away. . . ." It's not until too late that they suddenly realize, "I have an $800-a-month house payment."[33]

Contrasting the legal doctrine of "informed consent" which governs doctors, the former high-cost lending manger emphasized in his business, the norm is to sell credit products under "the doctrine of *assumed* consent."[34] Such lax communication with potential debtors combined with the increasing complexity of creditor contracts threatens to undermine our system of rational choice policy making. Credit contracts are often the most important contracts a consumer will sign in a lifetime. When courts enforce contracts, as though there were a real meeting of the minds as to all material terms, when in fact there was not, an enormous potential exists for lenders to include provisions which charge more than the customer actually agreed to.

Independent of information barriers erected by high-cost creditors, high-cost debtors often have limited resources and skills to invest in price shopping. The costs of acquiring information must be evaluated relative to the resources of credit shoppers. Because current price disclosures only provide information about one credit contract in a vacuum, in order to make an informed decision, debtors must still compare prices by travelling to other creditors, learning the prices they offer, and then choosing the best deal. Those, like Evans, who rely on creditors to come to them as telemarketers or door-to-door salespersons take extreme risks. Comparing product price and quality in some markets can be a relatively easy task. At a grocery store, a consumer might compare the prices of several different breakfast cereals, looking at the ingredients and the convenience of packaging, recalling advertising claims, and contrasting the quantities offered, all in a matter of minutes or even seconds. This is because in the market for breakfast cereals, shopping costs are low.

But in the market for credit, making a similar comparison may involve traveling between different locations, asking for the relevant documentation, conversing with clerks, potentially negotiating on the purchase price of a similar financed good, and probably undergoing multiple credit checks. Moreover, the most inexpensive lenders may have short operating hours, intimidating employees and environments, congested parking, might frown on bringing children along for the application process, and might unintentionally or even intentionally assemble other more subtle, but nevertheless socially profound, barriers as simple as offhand rude remarks or disapproving stares. A debtor must also have an arsenal of resources to keep these shopping costs from skyrocketing. If, for example, a debtor uses public transportation, taking the bus to visit different potential creditors could take hours. If the debtor is mobility-limited by a disability, old age, or illness, traveling to more than one or two creditor locations may be impossible. If the debtor has difficulty reading, the time which it would take to wade through many different disclosure statements alone would be prohibitive. At some point shopping costs will outweigh any uncertain benefits of reduced prices which might be gained from shopping, making it irrational for many, if not most or all, consumers to do pre-transactional shopping.

The problems of cost comprehension and price comparison are only magnified for the growing number of Americans who speak little or no English. Bringing a friend or family member along to translate roughly doubles the shopping costs. One study found that, in practice, "Spanish speaking consumers essentially rely on the verbal promises of a salesman to get through the process."[35] Unscrupulous high-cost lenders aggressively target Spanish speakers to generate heterogeneously inflated prices. A Port Lavanca, Texas, consumer poignantly complained to the Texas Attorney General about the credit practices of mobile home dealers. The Spanish letter translates, "[t]hey are soliciting business amongst the folks that have poor English skills in order to cheat . . . unsophisticated buyers."[36]

Some economists predict that consumers adopt shopping strategies which effectively cope with these types of information problems. For example, when consumers face a wide diversity of product choices finding the best deal becomes prohibitive. Because the costs of examining the benefits of each possible option outweigh the potential gains from finding the optimal choice, consumers have no incentive to find the best deal. But if consumers use a few important criteria to screen out options which are unlikely to be ideal, they can come up with an option which is the best choice given their circumstances. Then the consumer selects the best option from the limited set of choices. Although the selected option may not in fact be ideal, if the consumer uses sensible screening criteria, it will still be close enough to force price and quality competition in the market. In these cases, consumers are thought to "satisfice" rather than "optimize."[37]

But even if we assume prospective high-cost debtors do attempt to satisfice, it is still unlikely they could effectively force price competition. In the market for high-cost lending, search costs are so high consumers must typically screen out all but one or two product options from more detailed investigation. For instance, a recent Consumers Union study of the Texas manufactured home market indicates buyers seeking financing must pay expensive credit report and application fees as well as place deposits long before they ever see a contract or price disclosure statement. The price of a manufactured home loan is almost always much higher at closing than when first quoted. Moreover, sales staff often caution borrowers not to shop around, since the outdated credit reporting system used by many manufactured home lenders penalizes the credit ratings of borrowers for whom lenders submit multiple report requests in a short time.

The story of Porfirio P. from El Paso, Texas, is typical of the direct financial charges imposed on those who try to shop. In order to find the best deal, Porfirio left a $100 deposit with one El Paso mobile home lender and then a $300 deposit with a second lender buying from a third. When he asked for his initial two deposits back, both mobile home dealer/lenders refused. Consumers Union explained his "exercise in comparison shopping . . . left him $400 out of pocket until the [Texas] Attorney General intervened." Sometimes manufactured home buyers are asked to sign blank documents and dealers often refuse to give buyers copies of loan contracts. Moreover, the Federal Reserve Board and the Department of Housing and Urban Development confirm that the practice of charging application fees to potential borrowers *before* providing any closing cost or finance charge estimates is frequent and widespread all around the country.[38]

Even "fast loan" businesses have subtle but significant ways of raising shopping costs. For instance, payday and car title lenders often telephone first-time loan applicants' bosses or human resource managers to verify the applicants are employed. Employment verification almost always occurs before debtors see a contract or any Truth in Lending disclosures.[39] Telephone employment verification serves the lender's interests in several respects. Obviously, the practice helps evaluate loan risk. But it also dramatically increases search costs for first-time loan purchasers. Payday lenders themselves admit their customers almost always have unsteady employment.[40] Most borrowers are understandably nervous about exposing their financial circumstances to their uncommitted and sometimes capricious employers. After the first employment verification telephone call, many prospective debtors immediately end their searches because they (perhaps correctly) predict that embarrassment and the risk of jeopardizing their jobs from additional phone calls will outweigh any potential savings from searching for a cheaper loan. Moreover, the practice encourages a form of artificial brand loyalty. By only verifying employment over the telephone for the first loan, lenders create a subtle but stiff "penalty" for borrowers who choose to look elsewhere in the future.[41] Under this incentive structure the priority for lenders is to make themselves the first option potential borrowers will inspect. Telephone employment verification creates an incentive to compete with flashy signs, promises of quick cash, location, and name recognition, rather than price reduction. Search costs may be so high that borrowers satisfice after inspecting only one or perhaps two market options—an insufficient number to force price competition.

Also adding to shopping costs, payday lenders systematically delay revealing accurate comparative price information such as the annual percentage rates of their loans. A nationwide survey found only 37 percent of payday lenders contacted for price information would divulge even a nominally accurate annual percentage rate over the telephone. According to the study, other lenders "claimed they 'didn't know' or that the APR was equal to the fee for a two-week loan." A smaller study found that even when approached at store locations, over 65 percent of payday lenders would not disclose the rate of their loans in annual percentage rate format. These results indicate nearly two-thirds of the nation's payday lenders are in consistent violation of the Truth in Lending Act's most basic requirement: to respond to oral credit rate inquiries only in terms of the annual percentage rate.[42]

Moreover, in the high-cost credit market, many of the inexpensive and more informal shopping strategies used by upper-class borrowers are not available. Some economists predict markets self-correct despite information asymmetries because consumers use abstracted information sharing strategies, such as business reputation, to offset seller advantages. This is to say, consumers can effectively shop through more informal channels, such as gleaning a producer's reputation from friends, co-workers, and family. But in the market for high-cost credit, competition through creditor reputation is unlikely to succeed. Initially, because entry and exit costs are low for high-cost creditors, the market is inundated with fly-by-night businesses that make only minor investments in reputational capital and other sunk costs.[43] Because many high-cost lenders do not invest time and effort in building solid reputations, they have little to fear from word-of-mouth criticism. Moreover, high-cost debtors often are less embedded within their communities. Because high-cost debtors tend to have more fragile workplace, neighborhood, community, church, and family relationships, they may be less integrated into effective reputation-based shopping networks. For example, an inner-city single mother of four working nights as a nurse is likely to have less access to reliable information about the reputation of various payday lenders than two affluent married suburban CPAs would have about the reputation

of various banks. Also, high-cost debtors are unlikely to share reputation information because they often suffer from embarrassment
and shame over past credit failures. One study indicates less than
a quarter of borrowers behind on their home mortgages ever mention their trouble to family or friends. Sharing word of mouth criticism of high-cost lenders often means exposing embarrassing
financial problems.[44] Finally, all reliable shopping information
must at some point be obtained on a first-hand basis. If virtually
no one in a family or neighborhood has access to reliable and effective shopping information, then there is no basis for an effective informal word-of-mouth shopping process to begin. One
Latino social advocate explains, "[i]n many white families, there is
a long history of home ownership, so there is someone to help
walk them through the process. Many Latinos are first generation
home-owners. There is no one to say, 'Here's what you should do
and here's who you should talk to when getting a loan.'"[45] Because
many low-income and minority communities are conspicuously
devoid of branches of lower-cost credit providers, such as credit
unions and some banks, shopping may become extremely time
consuming for entire social groups. As a result these debtors are
likely to select credit on the basis of familiarity, the "convenience"
of low initial shopping cost investments, and other non-price related factors.[46]

The Limitations of Current Disclosure Rules

Sadly, our current disclosure laws do not meaningfully address
these information distortions, and sometimes encourage them.
Initially, current disclosures come too late. Truth in Lending as
well as the Real Estate Settlement Procedures Act (RESPA) allow
creditors to manipulate the timing of information exchange to increase inefficiently the transaction costs of acquiring price information. Truth in Lending disclosures

come at, or very shortly before, the consummation of a transaction to which the consumer is already verbally and psychologically committed. At this point, comparative shopping by the consumer is unlikely. Moreover, it is equally unlikely that at this point the consumer will opt to pay with cash. Thus, . . . [Truth in Lending] does not put useable credit information into the consumer's hands at a time when it will affect transaction behavior.[47]

One study of lenders in the New Orleans area found that, even when specifically asked for disclosure information prior to signing an agreement, every lender surveyed "refused to issue a credit disclosure statement at this point in the transaction." Instead, such statements were "issued *only* at the time the loan is consummated, never prior to that time."[48] But by then, consumers have already invested significant time and effort into obtaining the loan. Even short delays in receiving disclosure statements, when encountered with every lender, can erode borrowers' willingness to compare loans.

Furthermore, Truth in Lending regulations have departed so far from the original vision of a simple, all-cost-inclusive price tag, the key material disclosures themselves can often be a source of *disinformation*. The credit industry has for years seized on the complaint that credit disclosures are not useful because they are too hard to understand. But a significant amount of confusion is attributable to the industry's unnecessarily complex contracts, which make current disclosures awkward. The complexity of disclosure statutes, regulations, administrative interpretations, and case law as well as the disclosure statements they produce is a symptom of creditors' evasion. As consumer advocates, regulators, and policymakers have attempted to respond to the endless evolution of new contractual provisions and practices, they have lost sight of a simple truth: *credit contracts do not have to be complicated.*

Creditors can always protect their investments by raising interest rates. Contract, and in turn regulatory and disclosure complexity, only develops when lenders seek to protect their investments through uncomparable contract provisions such as junk closing fees, pre-payment penalties, credit insurance, and other hidden revenue producers, rather than interest rates. The principle advantage of these relatively complex and difficult to compare provisions is that they forestall and confuse debtor price resistance.[49]

The "Finance Charge" Debacle

Perhaps the most serious among Truth in Lending's drafting problems is the increasingly misleading calculation of the finance charge disclosure. Theoretically, the finance charge is the total dollar amount debtors must pay to borrow the principle, including interest as well as other non-interest charges. Ideally, the finance charge should be equal to the total amount financed minus the principle of the loan. Original proponents of Truth in Lending believed the finance charge would be an extremely powerful shopping device for consumers, since it would make comparing prices a simple matter of comparing a single dollar figure representing all the costs associated with borrowing a given amount. If a consumer wanted to borrower $20,000, all she would have to do is compare each lenders' finance charge, and she would immediately know which contract was the least expensive. The finance charge is also crucial because the annual percentage rate is simply a yearly percentage expression of the finance charge.[50]

But in the thirty-five-year history of Truth in Lending, high-cost mortgage lenders have learned to exploit regulatory exceptions to the calculation of the finance charge disclosure. When Congress passed Truth in Lending in 1968, most mainstream lenders described all non-interest charges as "points." These points would cover all the incidental costs of closing a loan including title searches, appraisals, and others. One point is usually equal to 1 percent of the total amount financed. But over the past twenty years lenders have increasingly "unbundled" the costs, which originally justified charging points into a variety of fees. A treatise on Truth in Lending law explains:

> Now, *in addition* to points (sometimes outrageously high), those costs that points were designed to cover (and more) are unbundled and separately passed on: underwriting fees, warehousing fees, interim funding fees, loan processing fees, document preparation fees, loan disbursement fees, lenders' closing attorney's fees, courier and expedited delivery fees to ferry the paper between the lender and closing agent. Of course more familiar closing costs are also passed on: title-related fees, credit insurance, property insurance, mortgage guarantee insurance, broker's fees. The list goes on.[51]

These fees create enormous difficulty for regulators as well as federal and state courts. Courts must grapple with the invention of each new fee to determine whether it is properly calculated as a finance charge and therefore included in the annual percentage rate. Different types of lenders have different fees, and even the same lender will have different fees for different types of loan products. The result is a body of law which is rarely penetrable by the attorneys and judges who work in the legal trenches where—in the best case scenarios—high-cost lending disputes are resolved. Because high-cost lending cases are notoriously labor intensive for plaintiffs' attorneys, in practice if not in law, it is often left to the discretion of lenders whether to include junk fees in the finance charge.[52]

The Truth in Lending statute itself, its regulations, rare court oversight, and inadequate debtor access to trained attorneys, allows lenders to wedge more and more of these fees in as exceptions to the finance charge. Because the annual percentage rate is derived from the finance charge, these seemingly innocuous exceptions can completely undermine the whole transaction-cost-reducing value of Truth in Lending. In order to know the total price of borrowing a certain amount of money, consumers must search through the documents, find every non-finance-charge-inclusive fee, and then add those fees to the finance charge themselves. This is impossible until all of the final documents are prepared. Then debtors must start all over again and go through the documents for *each loan* they want to consider. Moreover, most home mortgage lenders still quote the old pre-Truth in Lending "interest" charges in addition to (and sometimes instead of) quoting the more accurate annual percentage rate. But even when customers want to rely on the annual percentage rate, there is no guarantee it is accurate, since it is derived from an often horribly distorted finance charge. In reality, most high-cost debtors have trouble understanding the simple notion of a finance charge itself. Few can distinguish interest from an annual percentage rate, or understand why the latter is much more reliable. And virtually no debtors can distinguish those fees not included in the finance charge and then comprehend why that is crucial to knowing the true price of the loan.

The result is there is no single, easily comparable figure which describes the price a borrower will pay for financing—but to the casual observer *it looks like there is*. In the high-cost credit market, these junk fees are almost always financed as part of the loan principle. Since they do not come directly out of the consumer's pocket, an unsuspecting borrower cannot tell the difference. In the end borrowers are forced to pay costly fees, as well as interest on those fees, in monthly payments over the course of years—sometimes over a lifetime. And, if the borrower refuses to pay, the lender may use well-paid veteran lawyers to quickly take the borrower's home—possibly reaping an additional home equity windfall in the process. Thus, the Truth in Lending Act as it is currently written may not provide *any* pre-transactional shopping protection to debtors. Since prospective borrowers can never tell beforehand which lenders are packing the loan with non-finance-charge-inclusive fees, Truth in Lending only serves to create a veneer of legitimacy and safety where there is none. Credit industry lobbying to preserve the legality of these practices has so successfully battered Truth in Lending with manipulative complications, ever expanding exceptions, unnecessary delays, and outright deception, even U.S. Circuit Judge Richard Posner, quarterback for the neo-classic economic analysis of law team, recently quipped "[s]o much for the Truth in Lending Act as a protection for borrowers."[53]

The irony is this system may hurt forthright and efficient lenders as much as debtors. Lax finance-charge-disclosure calculations and other disclosure distortions create a disincentive for all lenders to comply with the spirit of Truth in Lending. Lenders who in good faith include all fees within the finance charge, offer disclosures promptly, and do not bury key pricetag information in a stack of misleading and irrelevant information are likely to hurt their own competitiveness. For example, many believe throughout the 1990s, prime and responsible subprime mortgage lenders lost market share to more aggressive unscrupulous high-cost mortgage lenders. The mainstream bankers' opposition to uniform bright-line no-exceptions pricetag disclosure may be borne out of an instinctive reaction against government regulation, rather than good business sense. Because all creditors operate under the same field of government regulation, lenders who intend to comply with the law have much more to fear from easily circumvented disclosure regulations than bright-line uniformly enforced regulations. Lenders who are not afraid of efficiency and price competition have nothing to fear from robust disclosure rules. It is only creditors who have something to hide—namely the prices of their loans—who should fear more thorough and consistently enforced disclosure.[54]

Technological Innovation in Disclosure Rule Evasion: The Example of Yield Spread Premiums

One of the central insights of Ronald Coase's Nobel prize-winning career in economic theory is that business firms exist in order to conserve the transaction costs of doing business. By organizing in firms, entrepreneurs can save money. For example, in previous centuries individual merchants typically dealt directly with individual buyers, negotiating and enforcing each contract separately. Law developed to recognize that contracts formed when both parties reached a mutual meeting of the minds on material contract terms. This process of negotiating each individual contract was, however, complicated and took a significant amount of both the merchant's and the consumer's time. If disputes developed, it was even more costly to sort them out. One of the reasons firms develop is to centralize and streamline this contract preparation and enforcement. The transaction costs of reaching an agreement were cheaper when a firm hired one individual to specialize in preparing and enforcing all of the firm's contracts. This streamlining is a form of organizational *technology* which increases productivity and economic efficiency.[55]

In the market for high-cost home mortgages, firms have developed a variety of organizational technologies which increase profits, not by decreasing transaction costs for the firm, but by surreptitiously increasing information acquisition costs for buyers. The widespread and controversial mortgage industry practice of providing mortgage brokers "yield spread premiums" (YSPs)—also sometimes referred to as servicing release premiums, overages, back-end compensation, or premium pricing—is an excellent example of this strategic behavior.[56] Today's market for home mortgages has become so complex, most borrowers have come to rely on mortgage brokers to help them find the best deal for which they qualify. Traditionally mortgage brokers received compensation directly from the borrower either as a flat fee or as a small percentage of the loan amount. Borrowers either paid the broker in cash out-of-pocket or obtained funds from the lender beyond the purchase price of the home and paid the broker out of these funds. In the latter case, the lender turned the loan proceeds over to the consumer, and then the consumer turned a small portion of the proceeds over to the broker. About fifteen years ago, lenders and brokers began arranging to have brokers' compensation paid directly by the lender to the broker, eliminating the middle step. This method of compensating mortgage brokers is called a *servicing release premium* or a *yield spread premium*. The practice was seemingly innocuous since the broker's compensation ended up in the same place regardless. For sophisticated home buyers who can carefully police brokers, the practice may still pose no serious problem. But in the market for high-cost loans, taking payment for broker services out of the borrower's hands was a recipe for disaster.[57]

In the 1990s the relationships between unscrupulous lenders and brokers evolved to conceal kickbacks to brokers for delivering above par loans inside of yield spread premiums. Lenders constantly kept brokers up to date on the rates and terms lenders are willing to offer. Many lenders provided this information to brokers on a daily basis, taking full advantage of new information technology such as e-mail and fax machines. Many high-cost lenders commonly pay brokers an inflated yield spread premium if the broker can convince the borrower to sign up for a higher-rate loan than the borrower qualifies for. Under these arrangements the broker receives a percentage of the extra profit made by the lender. One former broker explained, "I understand all too well how consumers are manipulated by mortgage lenders to maximize the YSP on any given deal. In fact, as a mortgage loan officer, I averaged over a full point on every deal in 'back end' YSPs."[58] The arrangement is risk-free, since even if borrowers are more likely to default under the higher rate, the lender (or more likely a secondary player who purchases the loan from the lender) can always foreclose on the family home. Since the borrower never knows about the yield spread premium, the broker can still collect up-front cash compensation from the borrower in addition to the yield spread premium, which is paid through the loan proceeds. Not only does the broker hide a large charge in the paperwork, but the borrower is also stuck with a higher interest rate.[59]

Take the story of Beatrice Hiers, a single African American mother from Fort Washington, Maryland. Hiers struggled financially for years, supporting her two children and her elderly parents as a typist. After scrupulously saving for a down payment and carefully shopping for the right home for close to year, Hiers signed a contract to buy a small house for $159,750. On her own, Hiers found a 7 percent fixed-rate FHA mortgage loan. Hoping to find a cheaper deal, she engaged a mortgage broker at Homebuyers Mortgage Company. Relying on her broker, she did not take the 7 percent fixed-rate FHA loan, even though her home closing was fast approaching. At the last minute, the broker came through with a 7 percent variable-rate mortgage. The broker promised Heirs this loan was the best rate with the most favorable terms she could qualify for. Up against the deadline for her closing and thinking she had no other options, Hiers agreed to the loan.

It was not until later that Hiers came to understand how badly Homebuyers took advantage of her trust. She explained:

Homebuyers charged me extraordinary fees and points. My HUD 1 settlement statement reveals that Homebuyers charged me the FHA maximum 1 percent origination point—$1,544—plus loan discount points of 3 percent—

$4,736. On top of these fees, Homebuyers also collected a Yield Spread Premium from [the lender] of nearly 3 percent—an astonishing $4,538.87. In other words, I paid three discount points to *reduce* my interest rate and the broker was paid 3 percent by [the lender] to *increase* my interest rate.[60]

Although Hiers paid over $10,000 in closing costs, she still did not receive the lowest priced loan for which she qualified. The lender's own rate sheet showed she qualified for the same loan at about a 5½ percent interest rate with no yield spread premium to the broker.[61]

Most of the mortgage lending industry maintains that this sort of fee arrangement is both fair and legal. Brokers argue these expensive yield spread premiums are offset by lower upfront cash payments. However, a recent study of over two thousand mortgage loans by two Harvard law professors indicates otherwise. Professors Howell Jackson and Jeremy Berry found that in cases involving yield spread premiums "mortgage brokers received substantially more compensation than they did in transactions without yield spread premiums."[62] On average, brokers using yield spread premiums received $1,046 more per loan than brokers who did not use the device. Of course, in many cases the difference was much greater. The trouble lies in distinguishing how much of the yield spread premium is fair compensation for the broker and how much is simply a kickback for delivering an above par loan. But the difficulty in drawing this distinction is precisely the genius and innovation of yield spread premiums: the payment device provides lenders and brokers the elasticity to abuse borrowers whenever they can under the cover of a legitimate compensation.

As for the legality of the yield spread premiums, the industry may be right. Although a court battle between class action plaintiffs' attorneys and the lending industry is currently raging over whether yield spread premiums are prohibited under RESPA, for now, the payment method remains practically legal. This is due in no small part to the Department of Housing and Urban Development's regulatory interpretation of RESPA which allows for any "reasonable" yield spread premium. Rather than banning the practice, HUD has primarily relied on disclosure to check abuses. Lenders are required to disclose any yield spread premium on the HUD 1 Settlement Form usually provided to borrowers at or around closing. HUD reasons yield spread premiums should be allowed because it may be beneficial and convenient for some borrowers to finance their broker's compensation by having the lender directly pay the broker. What is important is to let the borrower make an informed decision. From HUD's perspective, if lenders disclose the information, borrowers can simply refuse to choose a yield spread premium if it is not in their best interest.[63]

But, once again, while disclosure may be promising in theory, the reality has proven disappointing. HUD's regulations do not specify *how* to disclose the information. Many lenders, especially high-cost lenders, bury the disclosure on back pages, cloaked in other legal terminology and often printed in a smaller font. Even if the customer manages to find the disclosure, virtually no one can understand it. Yield spread premiums are almost always disclosed with only cryptic abbreviations, such as "P.O.C. by lender" or "YSP" to denote the charge.[64] And finally, even if the borrower finds the disclosure and understands she is paying an extra fee, the borrower will still never guess the *reason* for the charge. Who would expect to pay an extra charge for the privilege of paying a higher interest rate?

Most insidious of all, yield spread premiums also allow lenders and brokers to engage in heterogeneous pricing based on the consumer's sophistication. Traditional microeconomic models assume each market player has perfect information. Under this assumption every buyer knows the prices of every seller. Therefore, sellers would have no incentive to charge different prices for the same product to different buyers, thereby creating homogenous prices. But as a former high-cost mortgage broker explained, yield spread premiums allow pricing "not by the quantum of services provided, but by how aggressive the broker/lender may be and how little the consumer knows."[65] Other things being equal, the less sophisticated the borrower and the more unethical the broker, the higher the yield spread premium. This perverse incentive structure may help explain the findings of Jackson and Berry. They found ethnic minorities pay significantly higher yield spread premiums than whites. Recalling the selective protection policies of past eras, the best available data indicates mortgage brokers on average charge black borrowers $474 and Hispanic borrowers $580 more per loan more than white borrowers.[66]

One-Size-Fits-All Credit Regulation and the Promising Example of the Home Ownership and Equity Protection Act of 1994

Perhaps the most disheartening legacy of Truth in Lending's unfulfilled promise deals not with the disclosure provisions of the act itself, but with its political consequences. The disclosure approach to addressing credit problems has displaced and supplanted other forms of substantive regulation, especially interest-rate caps. When in the early 1980s many state legislatures were raising or even entirely removing their interest-rate ceilings, TILA and other disclosure rules allowed state and federal legislators to characterize interest-rate caps as superfluous. Legislators, industry lobbyists, and many academics emphasized that the "market perfecting" function of Truth in Lending made other substantive consumer protections obsolete. If Truth in Lending actually did perfect the market its undermining of substantive consumer protections would not be troubling. Most sophisticated upper- and middle-class borrowers have not missed our muddled interest-rate caps because, usually, they can effectively shop for reasonably priced credit. But in the high-cost credit market, borrowers have been forced to accept the worst of both strategies: they cannot effectively use Truth in Lending disclosures and they no longer enjoy the substantive protections of our effectively repealed interest-rate caps. This combined absence of effective government leadership in the high-cost credit market explains why it has been possible for high-cost lending to grow so dramatically over the past twenty years. Despite all the promise and theoretical charm of Truth in Lending, disclosure rules have not produced understanding and price competition among high-cost borrowers. For this reason, although Truth in Lending has well served the relatively affluent, by the early 1990s it became clear that high-cost debtors may have been better off had Congress never adopted the Truth in Lending Act at all.

Key leaders in Congress have recognized this fundamental class disparity in credit protection rules. The Truth in Lending Act was designed as a one size-fits-all social protection strategy. But it is clear the strategy has thus far been a poor fit for vulnerable borrowers. The Home Ownership and Equity Protection Act of 1994 (HOEPA) was a response to this problem.[67] HOEPA's most significant innovation was to create disclosure tiers where more risky forms of credit merited more careful disclosure. HOEPA requires lenders who sell certain forms of high-cost home mortgages to give prospective borrowers special disclosures in addition to those provided under normal Truth in Lending requirements. HOEPA-enhanced disclosures are required when a lender sells credit at prices above either a rate-based threshold trigger or (more likely) a combined points-and-fees threshold trigger. This tiered approach allowed Congress to craft one set of rules for the mainstream market and a different, more protective set of rules for the high-cost credit market. In fact, it was the passage of HOEPA, more than any other event, which has caused a transition away from discussion of "usurious" loans to "high-cost" loans.

Unfortunately, despite its significant innovations, the past eight years have proven HOEPA to be far too inadequate to address meaningfully the plight of working-poor and lower-middle-class debtors. Foremost among its many limitations is its inanely narrow scope. Many high-cost mortgage lenders' most abusive fees are legally or illegally excluded from calculation under HOEPA's trigger provisions. Mortgage lenders commonly exclude costly yield spread premiums from calculation of the HOEPA points and fees trigger. This allows lenders and brokers to charge thousands of dollars above HOEPA thresholds and still avoid any additional disclosure. Also, because HOEPA only applies to closed-end home-secured mortgages, some lenders structure high-cost loans as open-ended revolving home equity lines in order to evade not only HOEPA, but also some key RESPA disclosures. As a result, a startlingly small percentage of home mortgage loans are covered by the federal "high-cost" disclosure provisions. The Commissioner of the Illinois Office of Banks and Real Estate estimates HOEPA's enhanced disclosures are applicable in *less than 1 percent* of all home mortgages. But above all, HOEPA only provides for enhanced disclosure in certain home mortgage loans. This means payday lenders, pawnbrokers, car title lenders, and all other high-cost creditors still operate under the same disclosure rules as church-sponsored credit unions and smalltown family-owned banks. Reflecting the upper-middle-class bias of federal credit law, home ownership is a prerequisite to access to HOEPA's enhanced disclosures.[68]

Still, high-cost debtors excluded from HOEPA's limited scope are not missing much. Even when HOEPA's disclosure rules do apply, they provide only lukewarm and typically ignored additional information for debtors. The disclosures themselves are worded far too cautiously and in language and terms much to difficult for many unsophisticated borrowers to understand. After all, even if a government form clearly discloses a 21 percent APR home-secured mortgage, without assistance, many debtors, particularly those targeted by unscrupulous high-cost lenders, simply cannot understand the significance of that price. HOEPA also does not slow the pace of borrowing to allow debtors more time to consider their actions. In the words of a joint Federal Reserve Board and Department of Housing and Urban Development report "there is too much information for [HOEPA borrowers] to absorb, particularly in the 'hurry, hurry, sign here' environment of a typical home-secured loan closing."[69] The sad result is that the sole federal credit protection which goes beyond a one-size-fits-all approach is nevertheless irrelevant for the vast majority of high-cost debtors.

IT'S NOT JUST THE CREDIT INDUSTRY: FINANCIAL ILLITERACY AND UNDERSTANDING IN HIGH-COST BORROWING

If there is one thing consumer advocates, government regulators, and the credit industry can all agree upon, it is the widespread lack of financial literacy among Americans. The Securities Commissioner of Texas recently complained, "[t]he general public is financially illiterate. That may sound harsh, but unfortunately it is true." Empirical evidence consistently indicates many consumers lack the ability to compare information to make sound borrowing and investment decisions, even if that information were easily available.[70] A risk study prepared by Visa explains that many borrowers:

- Are ill informed as to basic money-management skills;
- Do not understand the basic principles of credit;
- Increasingly overspend their ability to repay debt;
- Do not know or understand their alternatives when they become overextended;

- Do not make informed choices regarding the obligations of repayment;
- Do not understand the implications of poor credit choices; and
- Once having chosen the option, are unable to execute a plan to restore themselves to financial health and well being because they lack the skills and understanding that are needed to manage credit.[71]

For instance, only 57 percent of American adults understand the concept of compound interest. Fewer than 50 percent of American families make a household budget and stick to it. Sixty-three percent of American adults cannot demonstrate an understanding of the basic concept of inflation. Many consumers cannot distinguish interest rates from annual percentage rates. And few borrowers bother to read credit contracts, because they doubt their ability to understand them, even if they tried. Once again, virtually all researchers agree financial illiteracy is particularly pronounced for the nation's most vulnerable working-poor borrowers—due in no small part to underlying reading and math problems stemming from inadequate primary education. As a result, vulnerable debtors lack the skills to use what information resources are available to protect themselves. Or, as Secretary of the Treasury Paul O'Neill explained, "[t]he poor, the elderly, and minority groups can be victims of fraud and deception, predatory lending, and other such abuses. . . . Understanding personal finance is a consumer's first line of defense against financial rip-offs and scams."[72]

This general lack of personal finance knowledge and the harmful consequences associated with it are compounded by a growing throng of false counselors who prey on desperate consumers as they attempt to educate themselves. Many high-cost debtors are acutely aware of their financial illiteracy and actively seek to learn the skills necessary to protect themselves. Sensing a market demand, a thriving private sector sub-industry of consumer credit counselors has developed. Consumer advocates estimate more than two million Americans sought debt counseling in 1998 alone.[73] Many of these counselors, particularly larger, reputable, licensed nonprofit counseling agencies, provide invaluable services to confused debtors who would otherwise have nowhere to turn. But, as should be expected, a comparably large industry of false counselors has developed which thrives on the naivete of high-cost borrowers. Sometimes less reputable counselors demand upfront fees for services of dubious value. Sometimes excessive counselor fees are surreptitiously taken out of payments which unsuspecting borrowers thought would pay down their debts. Sometimes counselors promise fraudulent or nonexistent "credit repair" products that will remove past credit history blemishes. Sometimes false counseling agencies are merely camouflaged subprime lenders seeking to refinance unsecured debt at high costs with the borrower's family home serving as collateral. Vulnerable borrowers hoping to find their way out of the American debt maze must not only possess the financial literacy to distinguish between responsible lenders and predatory lenders, but also between those who will genuinely assist them with this task and those who will yet again exploit their trust.[74]

Nevertheless, for many borrowers, the most significant form of financial illiteracy stems not from an inability to understand the available services and service providers, but from an inability to understand themselves. Debtors rarely understand how lenders will evaluate them as a credit risk—which cuts to the heart of credit pricing. While creditors have always tried to limit their exposure to high-risk borrowers, the available tools for accomplishing this have dramatically changed in the information age. Today's lenders rely on sophisticated statistical models to estimate credit-worthiness and instantaneous automated underwriting systems to generate prices. The foremost statistical credit-worthiness model distills a borrower's reported credit history into a single convenient score which predicts the likelihood of repayment. This credit rating, commonly called a FICO score, after Fair, Isaacson and Co., which designed the statistical model, rates consumers with scores between 300 and 900. A score of 620 or below is roughly considered a poor credit rating. FICO score models rely on nationally collected consumer information which is compiled and offered at a price to lenders by one of three major credit reporting agencies: Equifax, TransUnion, and Experian. Eager to provide reliable information at the lowest cost to creditors, these reporting agencies have made full use of the latest advances in information technology, allowing them to communicate more quickly with lenders about past and potential future borrowers. The symbiotic relationship of reporting agencies and creditors has provided the nation's lenders with a system which, although far from perfect, provides a consistent and generally reliable source of risk information on virtually all potential borrowers.[75]

For years creditors and credit reporting agencies fought to keep credit score information out of the hands of borrowers. While a variety of justifications exist for preserving this monopoly on risk information, few doubt it provided creditors with decisive leverage in the credit bargaining process. If a borrower does not have access to credit score information, a lender can simply justify an offered price (or rejection) based on the borrower's credit score. It has only been in recent years that sophisticated borrowers have started actively managing their credit scores and using these scores in shopping for the most inexpensive credit available to them. Last year Equifax led the way by offering a combined FICO score and credit report over the internet to consumers for a small fee. The company plans to market the product to consumers through banks. More recently, Fair, Issacson and Co., in collaboration with Informa Research, has begun releasing comparative credit price information which, although only sparsely noted by popular media, has enormous potential to improve consumer shopping efficiencies. At no cost, consumers can view average interest rates within any state for various types of loans *correlated with FICO credit score ratings*. In more simple terms, this means a borrower who purchases a copy of his credit report can know with a significant degree of reliability what interest rate he qualifies for before ever approaching a lender. Rather than relying on the dubious promises of brokers or their own haggling skills, borrowers equipped with this information can demand the best price they qualify for or quickly move on to a different lender. These relatively unheralded developments promise to remove a prodigious amount of the guesswork from borrowing for those debtors with the insight to pay the relatively insignificant up-front fee to purchase their credit scores and reports.[76]

Unfortunately, virtually all consumer advocates, legal services attorneys, and nonprofit credit counselors who work with high-cost debtors agree these developments are unlikely to provide victims of predatory lending with any significant relief. Guadalupe Aguilar, a consumer advocate with the nonprofit group Consumer Action, who deals with high-risk borrowers on a daily basis, explains the new FICO-correlated comparative interest rate table would "serve a good purpose for a limited audience, but it would not serve the people who we might want it to serve."[77] This is because high-cost borrowers tend not to have access to the internet, have difficulty reading even simple information, and are not likely ever to even learn about the existence of the comparative information without the direct assistance of an ethical credit counselor. Given the wide digital divide separating Americans, the most recent technological innovations in credit shopping are likely only to increase the gulf separating high-cost borrowers and relatively affluent upper-class Americans.

These recent developments only highlight the defects in our present credit disclosure regulatory system. What the basic approach of Truth in Lending fails to capture is that truth and understanding are not always (or perhaps are rarely) synonymous concepts. One cannot have understanding based on false information, therefore truth is a necessary element of understanding. But one can have true information, and not understand it. In the best of current circumstances, status quo federal law is only concerned with whether disclosures truthfully and completely describe the cost of a loan. The true descriptions provided by federal disclosure rules only provide an *opportunity* to understand credit prices. If the past thirty years of high-cost consumer credit experience teach one lesson, it is that *truth* is not enough—vulnerable high-cost debtors need *understanding*.

CHAPTER 5

Deciding to Borrow: Irrational Decisions in the High-Stakes Credit Gamble

There is no reason to suppose that most human beings are engaged in anything unless it be unhappiness, and even this with incomplete success.

—*Ronald Coase*

Outlays for the manufacturing of a product are not more important in the strategy of modern business enterprise than outlays for the manufacture of demand for the product.

—*John Kenneth Galbraith*

WHEN CONSIDERING THE HIGH-COST credit market, with its endemic problems and questionable business practices, many ask one essential question: why do they do it? Why do high-cost borrowers encumber their futures with such risky financial decisions? A variety of explanations have been given. Some commentators mention the need to bridge short-term income gaps. Some cite the transaction costs associated with a lack of available inexpensive lenders in low-income neighborhoods. Some commentators rely on the exclusionary effects of borrowers' poor credit histories. Some argue high-cost credit is more convenient. And finally, many argue that consumers turn to high-cost debt because their desperate financial straits make these contracts worthwhile despite the costs. For instance, in this view an under-employed, cash-strapped single mother of four might quite literally be *happy* to richly compensate a risk-averse lender in order to feed her children with the proceeds of a short-term loan. Underlying each of these explanations for high-cost borrowing is the classical economic description of preference ordering.

WHY DO THEY BORROW? THE CLASSICAL ECONOMIC ACCOUNT OF PREFERENCES

Preferences, or tastes, are the consumer desires that fuel economic demand. Understanding these preferences is fundamental to the whole project of making economic predictions. Classical economic models consider separately the preferences consumers have and how prices affect demand. Price changes create movement along demand schedules, while changes in preferences or tastes create shifts in the entire demand schedule. In other words, if the price of a good goes up, the quantity consumers demand of that product will be less, but the underlying social demand itself remains unchanged. Or, as Gary Becker has explained, preferences are generally thought to remain "stable."[1] Analyzing the consequences of price change is a matter of looking at the cause and effect relationships between how much of a good consumers will purchase at any given price level. However, change in the underlying demand itself is a result of change in consumers' essential preferences. Traditionally, economics has had little or nothing to say about how preferences for one type of good over another develop because it is difficult to make generalizations about preferences or tastes in the analytical context of microeconomic models.[2] Paul Samuelson and William Nordhaus explain:

Tastes represent a variety of cultural and historical influences. They may reflect genuine psychological needs (for liquids, love, excitement). And they may include artificially contrived cravings (for cigarettes, drugs, or fancy sports cars). They contain a large element of tradition or religion (eating beef is popular in America but taboo in India, while curried jellyfish is a delicacy in Japan).[3]

Unlike consumers' relatively predictable responses to price changes, preferences themselves are volatile and idiosyncratic. The difficulty in predicting preferences arises because they come from many complex sources, or, in Cass Sunstein's words, an *"unruly amalgam of things"* generally considered beyond the scope of economics, including "aspirations, tastes, physical states, responses to existing roles, and norms, values, judgments, emotions, drives, beliefs, [and] whims."[4]

The normal way to account for preferences in constructing economic models is to ascribe what are sometimes called "preference maps" to every hypothetical consumer included in the model. This is to say that if we take any random consumer with, for example, twenty dollars, theoretically we can plot out a "map" of every purchasing option available to the consumer, starting with the products the consumer wants the most and ending with those he wants the least. The product placed highest on the preference list is that one which has the lowest opportunity costs and is the one the model predicts the consumer, other things being equal, will purchase. Assigning each product or group of products which the consumer could purchase a variable, a preference order might look something like this:

<u>Most Desirable</u>   <u>Least Desirable</u>

Preference Map {A > B > C > D > E > ... Z}

For this particular consumer, each letter represents one item which costs exactly twenty dollars, or more realistically a "basket" of several goods purchasable with the money.

In the classical economic world view, each individual is presumed to order her preferences in the particular hierarchy most likely to promote her own best interests. This is to say, consumers are "welfare maximizers"—each individual structures purchase preferences to promote the greatest welfare for herself. Thus, in classical economic view, market outcomes have a presumptive utilitarian moral ratification. Or, as a one Cambridge economics professor stated, in classical economic models "it is a basic article of faith" that "preference maps are identical with welfare maps."[5] Thus:

Preference Map $\{A > B > C > D > E > ... Z\}$ =
Welfare Map $\{A > B > C > D > E > ... Z\}$

While contemporary neoclassical economists often take a more sober view,[6] American culture has nevertheless deeply assimilated this notion that each individual may be relied upon to have sound purchasing preferences. Tocqueville perceived that in the United States, "everyone is the best and sole judge of his own private interest, and . . . society has no right to control a man's actions unless they are prejudicial to the common weal." This belief has served a primary role in our democratic government and market economic orientation.[7] Taking as a starting point respect for the preferences of other fellow citizens enables a community to avoid many dangers inherent in paternalistic government. It grants each individual the dignity and respect due to a person who cares for themselves in a market characterized by self-interested behavior and scarce resources. Moreover, the assumption that gives voice to this cultural belief, namely that preference order tracks welfare order, is usually uncontroversial. In the markets for most products, there is no reason to suspect that economic agents will not have preferences consistent with their own well-being. For instance, when a competent working adult goes to the supermarket to purchase ordinary household consumption goods such as bread or laundry detergent, there is no reason to suppose that the products the person prefers are not the same products that the individual will be best off purchasing. In the more theoretically safe world of a grocery store, there is little reason not to ignore the few anomalous cases where a grocery shopper might prefer a product which is not in his best interests.

In this view, any given debtor borrows at high costs because her preference order, constructed in light of all available purchasing options, suggest the loan is in the debtor's own best interest. For the classical economist, it is axiomatic that the underemployed single mother borrows at high cost because the cost of the loan is the best possible use of her limited means. The loan she chooses is the product highest in her hierarchical preference order and accordingly in her welfare order. To suggest her choice was in error flies in the face of the American ideological commitment to individual freedom and economic action. This belief that each individual, acting on her preferences, purchases what is in her own best interests, lies at the heart of efforts to justify government inaction in various markets, including the market for high-cost loans. In a word, classical economics explains high-cost debtors borrow because the decision to purchase a high-cost loan is *rational*.

Wanting What You Shouldn't: The Limits of Rational Preference Ordering as a Substitute for Government Policy

Even the most useful and productive assumptions can be stretched too far. Some individuals in the markets for some products may not choose what is in their own best interests. One economist explains classical normative economic thinking "requires that any individual's welfare be identical with his preference ordering. In other words, children, dope addicts, fiends, criminals, and lunatics, as well as all other people, always prefer that which is best for them."[8] The highly regulated markets for prostitution, illicit drugs, gambling, pornography, guns, alcohol, tobacco, prescription medications, and even fireworks all reflect widespread beliefs that, at least sometimes, socially harmful preferences drive demand in these markets. Similarly, government policy often attempts to shape preference orders in favor of behavior seen as socially beneficial. Tax breaks for individual retirement accounts, as well as the social security system, are government actions intended to correct consumer preference orders which value present consumption over saving for retirement. In each of these markets, characteristics of either consumers or products create consumption decisions which are less than perfectly rational in the classical economic sense. Every time legislators, judges, academics, and citizens advocate control over free-market outcomes in the markets for each of these products, they express their doubt that preference orders are always identical to welfare orders.

Perhaps the best example of an exception to the American faith in self-ordered preferences is the market for illicit drugs. For instance, many, if not most or all, heroin addicts have preference orders which place purchasing more heroin above virtually any other good. Many heroin addicts strongly prefer heroin over other products usually thought to have the highest opportunity costs, including food, shelter, and transportation. To suggest heroin addicts do not place the drug higher on their preference maps than other products is simply to misunderstand what economic demand is. Yet almost everyone, often including heroin purchasers themselves, is willing to concede these preferences for heroin are not in the best interests of the addict. Heroin devastates the physical, emotional, and spiritual health of people who use it. When addicts begin to value heroin more than essentials such as food and shelter, they often end up homeless and desperate. Because heroin is so dangerous and because its highly addictive nature makes stopping once one starts so difficult, almost everyone agrees something is unacceptably amiss with the way the addict makes his consumption decisions. Our usual faith in Benthamite utilitarian preference theory notwithstanding, there is a broad American consensus heroin addicts do not order their preference maps identically with their welfare maps. A more intuitive characterization of heroin purchaser welfare orders in this exceptional market is:

Preferences {A (Heroin) > B > C > ... Z} ≠
Welfare { B > C > ... Z > A (Heroin)}

Paradoxically, for the members of this consensus, it would be safer to reject the traditional assumptions of preference and welfare order equation, and characterize heroin consumers' highest preference as the one which in all likelihood generates the least welfare.[9]

American law reflects our intuitive rejection of classical economic prescriptions with respect to heroin by similarly rejecting market-based policymaking in this arena. Even the states that most fervently support non-interventionist economic policy in other markets are willing to take ultimate control over market decision-making with respect to heroin demand. All fifty state legislatures have made heroin illegal. Outlawing a product for which there is enormous economic demand is the paramount demonstration of faithlessness in market decision-making. As a society we realize that because heroin addicts recklessly order their purchasing preferences in a manner inconsistent with their own best welfare, the state must intervene by making a centrally planned economic decision to curtail heroin consumption and supply. So vehemently do we spit out our classical economic assumption of perfect preference ordering that we place in cages those consumers and dealers found transacting upon heroin preference. Ironically, our most laissez-faire legislatures have chosen a policymaking strategy of total government control over a free and competitive market. And, although we might quibble about the details of punishment with respect to our control-oriented strategy, few indeed hold true to their convictions of preference and welfare order consistency so tightly as to advocate a completely free market for legalized heroin.[10]

As the market for illicit drugs demonstrates, the mental process which humans use to order their preferences in the real world is not the same as it is in the classical economic model. In order for a consumer to have preferences that will generate outcomes with the greatest welfare for that person, the consumer must know what he is feeling, why he feels the way he does, and how to make himself feel better. But this kind of self knowledge can be extremely difficult to acquire. As one Yale political scientist explains:

> If people do not know either that or why they are happy or unhappy, the premises of prevailing analyses of markets and democracies have failed. . . . The fallacy is this: The belief that people know precisely what they are feeling, can explain why they are feeling that way, and on the basis of this knowledge, can, within their means, maximize their own utilities. Most people at one time or another are victims to these fallacious beliefs, fallacious because they require qualities that people rarely have. These qualities are capacities for introspection revealing to people the workings of their limbic systems; for authentic, ego-synoptic self perceptions; for achieving unity of thought and feeling; and for avoiding compensatory pursuits that do not fulfill their promise. Lacking these capacities, people cannot maximize their well-being.[11]

Unlike life, in economic models preference ordering is instantaneous. There are no costs associated with delay. There is no ambiguity and no moral conundrums. There are no cognitive biases. There is no addiction. There is no desperation. But, in the real world, deciding what one wants is a process very much intertwined with the fundamental difficulties of human existence.

Responsible national, community, and family leaders realize that in the real world, the process by which humans order their preferences is delicate, vulnerable to manipulation, susceptible to self-hatred, and in the most robust sense of the word, controversial.[12] The framers themselves appear to have realized this in creating constitutional rules which may be seen as an effort to prevent the private preferences of majorities from overwhelming the choices of vulnerable minorities.[13] In reality, according to Tversky, Sattath, and Slovic, "observed preferences are not simply read off some master list."[14] Rather, Sunstein explains that "preferences can be products of procedure, description, and context at the time of choice."[15] At best, humans *usually* make classically rational decisions, but not always. Although our comfort with classical economic ideology has led us into a peculiar and chancy habit of at times acting as though we believe otherwise, we all understand that it is not easy to know what is best for oneself. Making the choices that are in one's own best interest is not just difficult for children and drug addicts, it is difficult for everyone.[16] Each of us at one time or another can remember making an impulsive purchase which upon further reflection was not the best choice. In free markets where consumers are reckless—that is, where consumers do not carefully conform their preference maps to their welfare maps—ideal social outcomes will never materialize. Moreover, in free markets where producers have no shame— that is, where firms do not temper their profit acquisition with norms of ethical behavior—neither governments nor consumers themselves will be able to prevent abuse of the vulnerable. This is why sound moral leadership of government, business, community, and family leaders is so important. True leaders actively manage the social norms which underlie market preference orders. Sometimes the most efficient government policies do not control market behavior itself, but aim to shape the norms and values of the citizenry, in order to facilitate the citizenry's policing of itself.[17] Market decision-making only works where individuals are empowered with responsible values and the preference orders they generate protect them. It should come as no surprise that in a market where choices are hard, options are limited, sellers are sketchy, and buyers are desperate, many consumers will lose their way. In such markets, where consumers have dangerous purchasing preferences, society must respond or face the harmful consequences of relying on a free market that does not protect the welfare of either individual consumers or society itself.

THE "UNRULY AMALGAM": PREFERENCE ORDERING IN THE HIGH-COST CREDIT MARKET

Many debtors in the high-cost credit market have lost their way. These debtors order their purchasing preferences in hierarchies which do not maximize their own expected utility. Although behavioral research on the purchasing decisions of high-cost debtors is disappointingly absent, empirical research has identified several cognitive biases which may help explain why debtors borrow at high cost. For a variety of reasons, normal people in normal situations make decisions which are not in their best interests. High-cost debtors are susceptible to these same preference ordering mistakes—but often with devastating consequences.

"It Won't Happen to Me:" High-Cost Debtor Unrealistic Optimism and Fundamental Attribution Error

Consumers from all walks of life systematically underestimate their exposure to human problems and overestimate their ability to judge risk. For instance, studies show the vast majority of people, including senior citizens, overestimate their ability to avoid car accidents, bicycle accidents, and even accidents with power lawnmowers. People from every background tend to underestimate their chances of developing asthma, suffering a heart attack, and acquiring a variety of other diseases and health problems. Sexually active gay men underestimate their risk of contracting AIDS. Cigarette smokers are overly optimistic about the health dangers their activity entails. Workers overestimate their legal protections against employers' arbitrary firings. Similarly, consumers chronically underestimate their chances of losing property in floods and earthquakes as compared to objective probabilities. In the flood and earthquake insurance market, instead of relying on objectively verifiable risk, empirical data indicates consumers rely almost exclusively upon past experience with floods or earthquakes (either personally or through acquaintances). Moreover, even when consumers actually overestimate the probability of a catastrophe, they typically "think that they personally are peculiarly less susceptible to such events."[18]

We should not be surprised to find high-cost borrowers systematically overestimate their ability to repay debt. Like everyone else, high-cost debtors have difficulty correctly estimating their risks of car trouble, health problems, and unemployment. For high-cost debtors this cognitive error may be more serious since they tend to have less access to reliable transportation, less access to health insurance and quality health care, and tend to be underpaid and/or underemployed. Car repairs, sickness, and job loss are precisely the personal events which consistently force consumers into high-cost borrowing and debt default. In fact, the best available data indicate family illness and work-related problems are among the most significant instigators of bankruptcy. Approximately one in four bankrupt families cite an injury or illness as a cause of their bankruptcy. Just as upper-middle class consumers underestimate the chances they will lose their homes in floods or earthquakes, high-cost debtors chronically underestimate the chances they will lose their homes in foreclosures. In reality, unpredictable systemic forces such as regional economic downturns may be more important in determining high-cost debtors' ability to repay than their own capabilities. The tendency to ignore factors beyond their control leads high-cost debtors to accept unrealistic and dangerous credit obligations, to default on them, and then to suffer the consequences.[19]

It is also doubtful that mere statistical price information (which is all Truth in Lending disclosures provide under even the best of circumstances) is likely to consistently counteract overestimation bias.[20] Certainly not all borrowers overestimate their own abilities. For instance, empirical data indicates borrowers who self-report very great or very little knowledge about credit contracts are less likely to experience financial problems when they borrow. The former know enough to stay out of trouble by accurately estimating their true risks, and the latter understand so little, they tend to recognize the need to be careful. On the other hand, researchers argue "[m]ost problems occur among borrowers with a moderate knowledge. They overestimate their knowledge, therefore do not ask for more information and as a result make the wrong decisions." Significantly, borrowers who overestimate their own abilities are "mainly, if not exclusively, interested simply in obtaining credit and get[ting] it fast." These borrowers do not seek information about "the really important credit characteristics such as the term, the interest rate, and the form of credit."[21] Moreover, because consumers disregard future repayment problems, they do not consider the costs associated with refinancing a bad loan—often the only way to stop foreclosure. High-cost lenders know this and hide high revenue-generating prepayment penalties from consumers with this blind spot. In the prime mortgage market only 2 percent of mortgage contracts include prepayment penalties. In

contrast, 70 *percent* of subprime home mortgage loan contracts include prepayment penalties.[22] While Truth in Lending disclosures
may refer to the creditor's security interest in a family home, prepayment penalties, late fees, and other contingent charges, it does
not follow that mere awareness of these contractual provisions
consistently translates into wise credit decisions. Without at least
a thoughtful evaluation of a debtor's actual repayment abilities
and the predictable income shocks from forces beyond the debtor's
control, debtors are still unlikely to grasp the true personal risks associated with high-cost borrowing.

Similarly, unrealistic optimism with regard to moderately-
priced credit can force unsuspecting mainstream borrowers into
the high-cost credit market. For instance, many commentators
have lamented the submersion of the "MTV generation" in excessive debt. When college students irresponsibly run up tens of thousands of dollars in credit card debt, they are often forced into
bankruptcy and a life outside the financial mainstream. Callie
Rogers of Imperial Beach, California was eighteen when she
maxed out her first credit card. It took only a few months. Over
the next several years she ran up a $16,000 debt, financing
clothes, food, entertainment, and a new car. "I was a kid who just
didn't realize I'd have to pay all this back," she explained, "I
though it was free money."[23]

For young borrowers like Rogers, a combination of credit cards
and an all too common case of the "it won't happen to me" cognitive error can be a bridge into financial exile. As the pressure to
make minimum monthly payments mounts, many debtors become
vulnerable to credit repair scams and high-cost debt restructuring.
When the borrower begins missing monthly payments, available
bank credit dries up. And, with no savings, these borrowers turn
to pawnshops, payday loans, and car title lenders to bridge the inevitable income shocks and emergency expenses. Unfortunately,
this overconfidence is not limited to young Americans. Looking at

data for the past thirty years in all demographic groups, Federal Reserve Board researchers have expounded that credit cardholders' opinions "about their own experiences are almost the reverse of their views about consumers' experiences in general, suggesting considerable concern over the behavior of others and a belief that *'I can handle credit cards, but other people cannot.'*"[24] Their erroneous overconfidence can start mainstream borrowers of all types down the road to high-cost indebtedness. But for the most vulnerable, the risks are even greater. The overconfidence associated with a 91 percent increase between 1983 and 1986 in the portion of families with annual incomes below $10,000 holding a credit card may be a significant causal explanation for the explosion in high-cost lending starting in the early- to mid-1980s.[25]

Living in the Now: High-Cost Debtor Intemporal Bias

Consumers also tend to focus on the present benefits of their actions, while underestimating or ignoring long-term disadvantages. Or, as a famous Cambridge economist noted, we "see future pleasures . . . on a diminished scale."[26] Virtually everyone has difficulty curtailing present consumption in order to save for retirement. Patients often have trouble following their doctors' treatment plans, even though they recognize the long-term health benefits. Studies consistently indicate consumers tend to buy cheaper, energy-inefficient home appliances even though higher operating costs over the long term more than offset the lower initial purchase price. And those hoping to lose weight *still* eat ice cream. Hersh Shefrin and Richard Thaler explain "[t]he very term 'self control' implies that the trade-offs between immediate gratification and long-run benefits entail a conflict that is not present in a choice between a white shirt and a blue one."[27] Moreover, people as well as governments adopt a variety of strategies for dealing with this problem, such as pension plans and "Christmas Club" saving arrangements, which only allow withdrawal of funds around the holidays. Government tax incentives for individual retirement accounts as well as the collection of a significant portion of the Gross Domestic Product to fund the social security system are both recognitions that sometimes people need help conforming purchasing preferences to their welfare maps.[28]

In the case of overinvestment in energy-guzzling home appliances or neglect of a planned diet, the consequences of intemporal bias may not be severe, or even worthy of inclusion in economic models. However, intemporal bias can be extremely serious for some people in some situations. For instance, many are initially attracted to purchasing and using illicit drugs because the thrill of the moment disrupts their ability to weigh the long-term consequences of their actions. One book on drug control programs explains:

> Because of their rapid action on the brain, psychoactive drugs attract those who seek or need instant reward and gratification; a 'short circuiting of the pleasure pain principle.' In Freudian terms this 'deficient ego functioning' permits the user to revert to a state of instant infantile gratification and delay or avoid the challenges of a mature adult role.[29]

Early-stage drug users themselves cite short-term gratification as a primary reason for their consumption. In a study compiling nine national surveys of high school seniors' self-reported reasons for consuming drugs, short-term gratification stood as the most important indicator. Early-stage high school drug users wanted "'to have a good time with [their] friends'" (65 percent), 'to experiment or see what it's like' (54 percent), 'to feel good or get high' (49 percent), and 'to relax or relieve tension' (41 percent)."[30]

High-cost debtors make borrowing decisions amidst the same psychological forces which compel intemporal biases. But while we give the relatively wealthy valuable tax incentives to invest in individual retirement accounts, vulnerable high-cost debtors have few government-sponsored incentives to avoid high-cost debt. The result is a government-sponsored incentive structure to invest in the growing wealth gap. One columnist explains it is "this need for instant gratification" which has "fueled the proliferation of payday loan stores, rent-a-centers, check-cashing stores and other alternative financial services."[31] Just as appliance purchasers focus on purchase price rather than operating cost, and just as early-stage illicit drug users focus on instant gratification, high-cost borrowers are typically "cash dazzled." As a Wharton School of Business professor explained, "the prospect of pocketing a significant sum of money causes a complete lapse of judgement. They ignore where the money is coming from and what it is costing them." Rather than considering the serious long-term consequences of their borrowing, high-cost debtors are often irrationally "payment-myopic," focusing on whether they can make monthly payments instead of whether the contract as a whole is a wise decision.[32] High-cost mortgage lenders have a unique opportunity to capture intemporal bias by transferring the borrower's home equity into cash. By giving a cash-dazzled, payment-myopic borrower a few hundred dollars out of the loan principle, a high-cost lender can capture a windfall of tens of thousands of dollars in home equity accessed through various points and fees. Clever high-cost creditors know the right times and have polished the right deliveries to tap as much out of debtors' intemporal biases as possible. For instance, "seasonal pitches are common, offering a few hundred additional dollars for Christmas money or a summer vacation," to induce a home or car loan refinancing.[33]

High-cost loans, like all credit, are time-intrinsic products where the qualitative characteristics of the product must be evaluated over the duration of repayment. High-cost debtors suffering from intemporal bias have preference orders which fail to account realistically for surprising long-term hardships, and therefore do not reliably track welfare. All humans have difficulty measuring the value of a product that is purchased over time, but because high-cost debtors are economically vulnerable, the preference-ordering process is much more difficult for them. They face situations which are psychologically easier to ignore and unstable futures which are inherently more difficult to predict. When facing the immediate short-term gratification of "easy money," "hassle free," "no credit check," "quick cash," it should come as no surprise that many high-cost debtors form preference orders which do not match their own best welfare. This is to say that for them, as for illicit drug users, the "pleasure-pain principle" has short-circuited. It is perhaps ironic that it was none other than Jeremy Bentham, the first and perhaps most persuasive opponent of interest-rate caps, who invented the pleasure-pain principle.[34]

"I Just Couldn't Help Myself:" High-Cost Debtor Compulsivity, Habit, and Addiction

The classical caricature of consumption decisions describes each individual as acting autonomously to make the best possible self-interested decisions. However, sometimes even relatively benign intemporal biases focusing on instant gratification can degenerate into more serious behavior which even more distantly approximates the classical notion of freely-formed, perfectly ordered preferences. For example, we commonly describe some human behavior as the product of *habit*, rather than autonomous decision-making. Those with habits "continue in a form of behavior not because of the high physical or emotional costs of desisting," asserts Sunstein, "but simply because they have become comfortable with the behavior." As a result we commonly try to shape our behavior in beneficial ways through forming "good" habits and breaking the "bad" ones. Parents try to instill in their children a toothbrushing habit. Some people exercise as a matter of habit. Some people do not. Doctors exhort their heart patients to break the habit of salting their food heavily. And governments try to break the bad habit of failing to wear seat belts with the threat of a small fine.[35]

Some bad habits have a way of developing into compulsive addictions. Smoking cigarettes may start as myopia and then develop into a habit, but as those who try to quit years later can attest, it most certainly ends up as an addiction. With addiction, preferences are determined, not by a well-considered process of self-interested autonomous preference ordering, but by the past act of consumption itself. And, although sometimes addiction is physical, it can also be mental or emotional. When heroin addicts stop consuming heroin they experience a variety of serious physical symptoms such as runny noses, chills, fever, inability to sleep, diarrhea, and hypersensitivity to pain. Barbiturate addicts experience anxiety, inability to sleep, and sometimes lethal convulsions in withdrawal. Chronic alcoholics face tremors, nausea, weakness, tachycardia, delirium, seizures, and hallucinations. However, other drugs, such as cocaine, which are nevertheless highly addictive, do not cause physical withdrawal symptoms. Moreover, in many cases even after physical withdrawal symptoms have ceased, addicts still relapse. For example, one study showed between 56 and 77 percent of heroin addicts who had already outlasted physical withdrawal symptoms nevertheless relapsed into addiction. In this sense addiction is often a psychological dependency, where a simple craving for pleasure motivates the consumption behavior, rather than a physical need. This form of learned behavior can create compelling self-pressure to repeat consumption decisions even though the addict might sincerely want to quit. In the case of addiction, an outdated and ill-advised preference order becomes locked into place, preventing a consumer from revising her purchasing decisions.[36]

Just as many drivers have the bad habit of failing to wear a seat belt, many high-cost debtors may simply be in the bad habit of borrowing too much and shopping for the best deal too rarely. Some borrowers can correct their risky borrowing behavior with a self-enforced rule of willpower. For instance, there are those who do not allow themselves to borrow to finance current consumption. While even a relatively minor habit of risky borrowing may cause significant financial problems over the course of a lifetime, for other debtors, risky borrowing behavior is much more than a bad habit. The behavior of some borrowers is a pathological habit that is fairly characterized as an addiction.[37]

While students of the physiological processes of chemical dependency might be skeptical of the claim that some high-cost debtors are addicted to credit, thousands upon thousands of devoted members of the support group Debtors Anonymous are not. This group models its twelve-step plan for dealing with irrational borrowing decisions upon the successful strategies of Alcoholics Anonymous and Narcotics Anonymous. A central tenet of the organization is the recognition that borrowers can become compulsively addicted to borrowing. "Compulsive debting is a disease," explains the Debtors Anonymous organization, "it is a disease that never gets better, only worse, as time goes on. It is a disease, progressive in nature, which can never be cured but can be arrested." The comments of one member who found the rapidly growing network of support groups are illustrative of the earnestness of Debtors Anonymous members: "This disease will kill you. It will send you to prison, or bring you to commit suicide. I knew I was dying. I saw for the first time that my life was slowly wasting away."[38] Debtors Anonymous is not alone. Many web sites and message boards have developed which aim to bring compulsive borrowers together in an anonymous and supportive network.[39] Also demonstrative of debtor self-compulsion is the market demand which has funded dozens and dozens of "how-to" and self-help books targeted at helping out of control debtors rein in their borrowing.[40] Commentators seeking to counsel compulsive debtors and urge social reform often resort to the rhetorical devices and therapeutic techniques usually targeted at the drug dependant. One columnist urges compulsive borrowers to avoid debt by "just saying no."[41] A noted business professor explains, "[a]lcoholics who are on the wagon have trusted advisors to call when they feel their control weakening. Impulsive borrowers can do the same."[42] A consumer activist recently remarked while protesting outside a payday lending outlet, "I could put up a sign that says heroin is $8 and cocaine is $15, and there would be a line formed around the block. But that doesn't make it right or responsible."[43] At least some psychologists and psychiatrists agree. Compulsive borrowing is "a lifelong disorder," explains one University of Iowa psychiatry professor. "[T]he relapse rate is very high and . . . people have to maintain a great deal of vigilance over the problem." Some doctors even prescribe anti-depressant drugs as a form of therapy for compulsive borrowing.[44]

Holding on Too Tightly: High-Cost Debtor Loss Aversion

The classical economic account of rational decision-making suggests individuals should value their out-of-pocket costs the same way they value forgone opportunities: people should not be more displeased with losses than they are pleased with equivalent gains. However, an impressive body of empirical research indicates most people are averse to losses. Some data indicates consumers are actually roughly twice as displeased with losses as they are pleased with equivalent gains. A related tendency makes consumers willing to assume an objectively inordinate amount of risk when facing the loss of something they already possess. For example, people who have owned antique furniture or vintage wine for a significant period of time commonly refuse to sell their possessions for prices far greater than market value—even though they could buy a replacement and pocket the difference. Some economists explain this is because the owners have "endowed" their possessions with personal value. Similarly, many firms sell products with "a thirty-day trial offer" and a "no questions asked, money back guarantee," where the consumer does not have to pay until after the temporary period expires. The seller realizes the buyer will pay a higher price after endowing the product with personal value, or stated differently, the buyer will pay more to avoid losing something they already have. By holding on too tightly to the things they possess, many consumers exhibit a classically irrational bias for preserving the status quo.[45]

In the high-cost credit market, lenders have learned to exploit loss aversion. For example, car title lenders often extract more payment from consumers who do not want to lose their cars than the cars themselves are worth. From a classically rational perspective, the borrower would be better off allowing the lender to repossess the car and then spend her resources purchasing a different automobile of comparable or even greater value. But if consumers exhibit significant loss aversion for antiques, wine, and cars, we can expect far greater aversion to losing a family home. One branch manager of a large finance company testifying anonymously before Congress, confided how home mortgage lenders tap the loss aversion of home owners who fall behind in their payments:

> Delinquent customers made good flipping candidates because we could put additional pressure on them. We were instructed to tell those customers that they could either bring their account balance current or refinance the loan. We knew that these customers would almost always agree to refinance because they didn't have the money to pay on their current loan and did not want the finance company to institute foreclosure or collection proceedings.[46]

This behavioral phenomenon may help explain the extreme refinancing abuses consumers will undergo in order to prevent foreclosure. Borrowers late on their home mortgage payments are extremely vulnerable to manipulation. In each refinancing the creditor lends thousands of dollars to cover the points and fees for the new loan. Thus, by running a few weeks late on a mortgage payment, a debtor can be maneuvered into giving up thousands of dollars in home equity in order to hold onto the home itself.

Misplaced Trust: Displacing Debtor Preferences

Sometimes people make a rational decision to delegate their preference ordering which leads to ostensibly irrational results. People hire stockbrokers to help them decide which companies to invest in. People hire interior decorators to help them decide which paintings, drapes, and furniture to buy. Firms hire consultants to help them decide which employees to retain. In these instances the purchaser only orders her preferences with respect to hiring the broker or consultant. Afterwards, purchasing decisions actually made by the agent are often merely ratified by the principal. In most markets, this delegation of decision-making retains competitive or nearly competitive equilibria because agents fear the loss of business through erosion of good will and trust. Principals can generally be relied upon to carefully select only trustworthy agents. Nevertheless, in cases where an agent is willing to abuse a principal's trust, there is significant opportunity for less than optimal outcomes. Where the potential rewards from abusing the principal's trust are greater than the potential ramifications, a utility maximizing agent will make purchasing decisions in the agent's interest rather than the principal's. If legal, social, and economic conditions existed where such representation arrangements could persist consistently we should expect a systematic pattern of

Pareto dominated outcomes. Such a market would never reach an ideal equilibrium because purchasing decisions would not be made in the best interests of each economic actor.[47]

It is impossible to know the extent to which high-cost debtors unwisely trust the purchasing decisions of those who do not act in debtors' best interests. But the finance company branch manager spelled out to Congress that "victims of predatory lenders are generally passive, allowing themselves to be solicited by those who prey on others."[48] What one debtor calls a "terminal vagueness" with respect to borrowing allows unscrupulous lenders and brokers to organize purchases in a manner which is consistent with the lenders' or brokers' preferences rather than the borrowers'.[49] Consumers who borrow impulsively may be especially willing to rely on the judgment of others because, as a *Los Angeles Times* journalist explained, most impulse borrowers are unclear on "their account balances, monthly expenses, loan interest rates, fines, or contractual obligations."[50] A great variety of sales techniques allow unscrupulous lenders to take advantage of the naive debtors' trust. For instance, most consumers are averse to extremes. Sunstein points out that "[w]hen . . . people are choosing between some small radio A and a mid-sized radio B, most may well choose A; but the introduction of a third, large radio C is likely to lead many consumers to choose B instead."[51] Similarly, door-to-door credit salesmen, mortgage brokers, and high-cost lenders in general can seal high-cost loans with trusting borrowers by couching those loans within the context of *very* high-cost loans. Empirical research has also found that simply changing the way product information is presented— such as referring to identical investment risks as insurance instead of a gamble—can systematically alter consumer's demand for the product for both naive and sophisticated consumers alike.[52]

Once an initial decision to trust a lender or broker is made, many high-cost debtors become extremely vulnerable. Take the story of Rita Herrod. Herrod, a sixty-two-year-old grandmother, purchased a Clarksburg, West Virginia, home in 1994 for only $22,000. She financed the purchase with an initial 7.8 percent APR variable rate bank loan. She explained, "[i]n early 2000 my troubles started when we encountered a mortgage broker we thought we could trust." The broker, Earl Young, worked with Herrod's daughter and seemed both ethical and responsible. Young promised Herrod he could find her a loan with a lower interest rate, that he would find the best deal he could, and even said he would cut his own fee to give her a good deal. Instead, he charged a commission of $4000, a broker's fee of $2600, and took an additional yield spread premium of $3304 for delivering a higher interest rate loan to the creditor than Herrod qualified for under the lender's own underwriting guidelines. Recognizing her misplaced trust, Herrod lamented, "I am stuck with this loan, which requires that I make over $275,000 in payments at an APR of almost 10%."[53]

Because abusing the trust of naive borrowers often runs afoul of fraud rules as well as disclosure rules, many high-cost lending organizations are intentionally structured to insulate their deep pockets from legal challenges. For instance, many companies have made a profitable business financing door-to-door sales of satellite TV systems, water purification systems, and home improvements in low-income and ethnic minority neighborhoods. Door-to-door sales staff often act as independent contractors, making it difficult to challenge credit contracts based on misrepresentations made to the consumer. These roving salespersons may have no offices, simply working out of the back of a car or truck, which makes them difficult or impossible to sue. Lenders who provide the financing can often deny any knowledge of wrongdoing or inadequate disclosure and avoid liability. While federal and state regulators have had some success in holding assignees liable for fraud and inadequate disclosure in solicitation, the wide loopholes for holders in due course, as well as the need for assignee liability rules to begin with, demonstrate debtors' misplaced trust is a significant limitation on classically rational high-cost credit decision-making.[54]

Before It's Too Late: Debtor Anchoring in Preference Formation

Psychologists and behavioral economists have found people often rely too heavily on first impressions when making judgments of risk and value. People tend to "anchor" on information presented early on. When additional information comes to light, most people do not adequately revise their initial judgments. This anchoring bias can lead to serious miscalculations, particularly where bargaining or risk evaluation is an ongoing process. For example, anchoring tends to obstruct the resolution of lawsuits in settlement conferences because both sides hold firm to their initial estimates of liability. Thus, even sophisticated professionals often miscalculate because of anchored initial estimates.[55]

This heuristic bias can have devastating consequences for high-cost borrowers. The initial financing price estimates of an unscrupulous mortgage broker or used car dealer can lead a borrower into a dangerous sense of security. Even if the borrower receives more accurate disclosures when signing the contract, they may come too late. At that point an informal agreement has already been reached. It is extremely difficult and rare for debtors to reconsider such informal agreements and do additional shopping by the time accurate disclosures have been provided. Consumers have an emotional investment in believing their informal agreement was in fact the best decision. In order to reconsider an informal decision when disclosures are provided, consumers must overcome the cognitive dissonance created by rejecting their own prior emotional commitment. Creditors can place subtle pressure on debtors not to back out, appealing to a debtor's sense of fairness.[56] Because the borrower has already "anchored" his estimation of the price to earlier informal estimates, it is very unlikely he will adjust his price estimates sufficiently to account for the true risks.

Similarly, current disclosures typically come after the lender has decided the borrower is creditworthy. This creates the tendency for debtors to rely on the lender's decision to accept the debtor—not whether the debtor accepts the creditor. Because it is psychologically easier to ratify the affirmative decision of another person than it is to refuse to go forward with the transaction, this significant delay in disclosure again undercuts classically rational preference ordering and stymies pre-transaction shopping. The risk is especially acute in the high-cost credit market where debtors often have difficult credit histories. High-cost debtors tend to be afraid they will find no one else willing to lend to them. They typically await a lender's approval, fearing possible public humiliation at having their applications rejected. Making a similar point, Professors Landers and Rohner write "[t]he consumer's shopping energies may dissipate upon a favorable determination of credit worthiness; moreover, the creditor's continuing ability to revoke a favorable credit determination will likely act as a constraint upon overly aggressive bargaining by the purchaser."[57] High-cost lenders systematically use fear as a wedge to force poorly considered decisions. It should come as no surprise one study found 65 percent of randomly selected payday lenders refused to let potential customers look at a contract or any federally mandated disclosures until *after* approving the loan application.[58] Disclosure rules which permit disclosure late in the bargaining process facilitate this behavior.

One of our most important disclosure rules goes even farther by *encouraging* lenders to anchor debtors with inaccurately low early price estimates. Under the federal Real Estate Settlement and Procedures Act, mortgage lenders are required to make a "good faith estimate" of mortgage loan closing costs within three days after a debtor applies for a home mortgage. Regulations require the good faith estimate bear a "reasonable" relation to charges actually accessed. However, there is no definition of what constitutes an unreasonable deviation. And, federal law "does not impose liability on a creditor for an inaccurate or incomplete estimate . . . or for failing to provide one."[59] Accordingly, lenders have no incentive to incur extra costs guaranteeing accuracy. On the other hand, if behavioral accounts of consumer anchoring are correct, lenders have a great deal of incentive to provide unrealistically low price estimates. Compelling behavioral evidence suggests that once the borrowers see low good-faith estimates they are likely to anchor their judgments, insulating lenders from price resistance down the road. Lenders have an incentive to give inaccurately low estimates because it makes debtors less suspicious and more compliant at closing. Even the term "good faith" itself is likely to put pressure on borrowers to reciprocate similar good faith by not backing out once they learn the true price.

Cultivating Irrational Credit Decisions: The Example of Credit Insurance

Perhaps no product or business practice better encapsulate the preference ordering problems found in the high-cost credit market than does credit insurance. Credit insurance, which is offered in mainstream credit contracts as well as with high-cost loans, makes payments to the lender for the consumer when covered events occur. For example, credit life insurance typically pays off the debtor's remaining balance on a loan, home equity line, or credit card account if the borrower dies during the term of coverage. Involuntary unemployment credit insurance usually makes a limited number of monthly payments if the borrower loses her job. Credit accident and health insurance (sometimes called credit disability insurance) makes payments if the debtor becomes disabled. Credit property insurance pays to replace or repair property purchased with the loan proceeds. Each type of credit insurance is sold with various types of loans, including both prime and sub-prime home mortgages, car loans, home equity lines, retail installment loans, and credit cards. Sometimes several types of credit insurance are bundled into one insurance package; other times they are sold as individual plans. Credit insurance companies are often third parties with no relationship to the lender, but they can also be a wholly owned subsidiary of the lender. In the latter case, "insurance" is something of a misnomer, since when paying out on a credit insurance claim the lending corporation only loses a legal entitlement to a debt payment it probably would not have collected anyway. Where the insurer is a third party, the lender receives a commission for selling the insurance plan typically worth between 33 and 50 percent of the amount of collected premiums.[60]

In the traditional insurance market, the most reliable measurement of the value of an insurance plan is its loss ratio. Loss ratios describe the ratio of claims paid out by an insurer to customer premiums. If an insurer paid out ninety cents in benefits for every dollar customers pay in premiums, then the plan would have a loss ratio of 90 percent. Generally speaking, the more competitive the insurance market, the higher the loss ratio. This is because savvy consumers push insurers to offer the most generous benefits package for the lowest price. Actual historical loss ratios for traditional group life insurance plans are between 85 and 90 percent—and sometimes even higher. Typical health insurance loss ratios are around 75 percent. Car insurance loss ratios usually are between 65 and 70 percent. Life insurance tends to have higher loss ratios than car insurance because there are fewer claims with lower administrative costs, allowing insurers to offer more generous benefits packages for each dollar in customer premiums. People only die once, but have lots of fender benders, car break-ins, as well as more serious traffic accidents. While the traditional insurance market is not perfect, most providers in most states tend to offer plans producing loss ratios within these general ranges. The National Association of Insurance Commissioners' model regulations set an absolute minimum floor below which benefit payouts should never reasonably drop at a 60 percent loss ratio.[61]

Compared to traditional insurance, credit insurance is almost always a terrible investment. Loss ratios for credit insurance are stunningly low. And, as table 5.1 demonstrates, while the high-cost credit boom continued in the late 1990s, credit insurance loss ratios have steadily decreased. In 1995 the average national credit insurance loss ratio was a paltry 42.5 percent. But by the year 2000 the average national loss ratio for credit insurance dropped to 34.2 percent—roughly *half* the standard loss ratios found even in the labor intensive auto insurance industry. Some types of credit insurance are worse than others. Across the nation, the average year 2000 payout in benefits for every consumer dollar spent on credit unemployment insurance was a nearly worthless 5.8 cents. Credit unemployment insurers and lenders kept 94.2 percent of customer premiums to cover costs and line their pockets.[62]

TABLE 5.1

National average credit insurance loss ratios by credit insurance product, 1995–2000

Coverage Type	1995	1996	1997	1998	1999	2000
Credit Life	42.4%	42.3%	41.6%	41.2%	41.4%	40.7%
Credit Disability	50.6%	49.4%	48.6%	46.7%	44.2%	46.1%
Credit Unemployment	18.2%	14.6%	12.6%	10.3%	7.6%	5.8%
Credit Property	32.4%	32.0%	23.3%	20.3%	22.5%	14.7%
Total	42.5%	40.9%	38.7%	36.0%	34.9%	34.2%

Source: CFA and CEJA analysis of National Association of Insurance Commissioners Data[63]

In the information age, one would expect a standard national equilibrium price for a financial product, such as credit insurance, which should lend itself to digital commerce. A credit insurance provider does not need boats to ship products to Hawaii, warehouses to serve the rural south, or reliable trucks to cross long distances in the mountainous west. Yet, unlike more competitive financial service markets, credit insurance prices and loss ratios are inexplicably diverse across geographic locations. In reality, credit insurance prices are set based on political considerations rather than through market forces. Because states still have control over insurance regulation, credit insurers price their products based on this criterion: how far can we go before the local authorities intervene to protect consumers?[64] In tightly regulated New York, year 2000 credit life insurance loss ratios were a nearly reasonable 59.6 percent. But the North Dakota credit life insurance market generated an average loss ratio of only 24.4 percent. Credit life and disability premium charges in Mississippi and Louisiana are almost four times greater than in Maine. But even relatively progressive Maine logged a stunning 3.4 percent loss ratio for credit unemployment insurance.[65]

Credit insurance is generally a bad bargain even in the mainstream credit market. But in the high-cost credit market, unscrupulous lenders have found new and aggressive ways to "pack" their loans with highly profitable—but nearly worthless—credit insurance. Consumer advocates complain that insurance packing in the high-cost credit market is an abusive way to quietly tap the home and automobile equity of unsuspecting and naive borrowers. Many in the credit industry agree that this assessment is not far from the truth. Gene Marsh noted, "[t]o see an illiterate borrower who has had a loan 'renewed' five, six, or even eight times in two years, and who is sometimes sold as many as three or four credit insurance products (credit life, credit property, credit disability, 'involuntary unemployment insurance,' and nonfiling insurance, may appear individually or all together in one loan), is enough to make most traditional lenders shake their heads."[66] Even some credit insurance providers concede the "people who tend to use it [credit insurance] are people who earn a lower income and don't have other insurance. It tends to be more attractive to minorities and the less educated."[67]

Few can doubt the market for credit insurance suffers from serious informational imperfections. It is difficult, if not impossible, for borrowers to calculate the true value of credit insurance products. But credit insurance also reinforces and cultivates cognitive errors and biases in preference ordering. Often borrowers simply do not recognize the decision to purchase insurance as significant or as a distinct decision, separate from purchasing the loan itself. Lenders facilitate this behavior with an "if they don't ask, don't tell" policy for explaining credit insurance options and charges. The training manual of at least one lender explains, "don't shoot yourself in the foot by addressing objections concerns or questions you 'think' the customer 'might' have."[68] But when borrowers do ask questions about the credit insurance which lenders *sua sponte* include in contracts, credit sales staff describe insurance in terms of a protection for the borrower. Credit insurance helps create an illusion of creditor benevolence which engenders trust and complacency. By framing a costly ancillary fee as "insurance," creditors can gain debtors' trust, cultivate unrealistic optimism, and encourage compulsive borrowing. With credit insurance debtors can rationalize that, "I don't need to worry, because if anything happens, I'm covered." Credit insurance facilitates poor shopping habits and compulsive borrowing by helping debtors persist in the false belief that their borrowing is under control.

Gael M. Carter was fifty-five-years-old, and retired, a widow with blurred vision, high blood pressure, liver trouble, and asthma. She lived in the house where, since 1963, she and her deceased husband had raised seven children. Carter had a ninth grade education and had last worked as a cleaning lady in a movie theater. She maintained a reasonably comfortable lifestyle on her fixed social security income. Her troubles began when she borrowed a thousand dollars to buy Christmas gifts for her grandchildren. She explains, "over the next year, they [the lender] kept giving me advice on my finances and getting me to take out loans with them. Every time, they told me they were going to put my finances in order and consolidate all my bills. . . . They kept calling me and telling me they could consolidate my bills and save me quite a bit of money per month."[69] Soon a sales representative of the lender filled out a home mortgage loan, application over the telephone, and then came to Carter's home for her signature. When, at the closing, the representative mentioned insurance for the first time, Carter asked what it was for. The representative only explained that the policy would pay off the loan, protecting Carter's daughter if she died. The representative did not explain that the $100,000 policy would not cover the total outstanding debt and had a term of only ten years—this, even though Carter was required to pay interest on the loan for all of its fifteen-year duration. But it was not until too late that Carter wised up. Later she explained:

> You see, I now know that the way this company gets you to take out all these loans and buy all the insurance and extras is that they tell you some lies and they just don't tell you anything at all about a lot of things. When it comes time to sign the loan papers, they just sail right through them. When you arrive at the closing, they've already prepared all the papers, with the life insurance and the points and extras added on. At the closing, they point at this and that in the papers but they don't explain really what any of it means. There's a whole lot of fine print in the papers that even now I just don't know what it means. At the loan closing they don't give you any chance to figure it out. They don't want you to understand what's going on. And since they always act so nice and friendly, you come to trust them and rely on them to tell you all the important information about the loan.[70]

Not surprisingly, within a year of the first small loan, Carter's life-time home equity savings of $150,000 were gone.

Carter's comments would be less troubling if they were not closely echoed by industry insiders. A former branch manager with experience working for three different leading finance companies recently described common credit insurance sales practices:

> The "don't ask, don't tell" policy was successful because customers were not aware, until closing (if at all), that the loan included insurance. Once the customer indicated that we could schedule a closing regarding the loan proposed in the telephone solicitation, we merely presented the loan documents with insurance included, even though insurance had not been discussed previously. Through their training and experience, finance company employees know that customers are often desperate for the money, and usually will not object to the insurance once the loan reaches closing. If customers objected to the insurance at closing, we would add more pressure by telling them that if they wanted the loan without insurance it would be necessary to re-do their loan documents and the closing would need to be rescheduled for a later date. That was a half truth. We could re-do the loan documents in a few minutes. It wasn't really necessary to reschedule the closing for a later date, but we knew that customers would be more likely to cave in and accept the insurance if they couldn't get the money that day. In my experience, this was usually enough to persuade the customers to go through with the closing and take the insurance.[71]

High-cost lenders are conscious of typical cognitive errors and biases and design their sales practices to extract profit from the borrowers' mistakes.

Credit insurance is particularly profitable for lenders in the subprime home mortgage market because higher risk borrowers tend to refinance consistently and often. At each refinancing, the lender can issue a new batch of insurance plans. If any premium refunds are given back to the borrower at refinancing, the lender usually uses creative accounting techniques to minimize the refund.[72] Because high-cost lenders usually finance insurance policies in a single lump sum premium paid out of the proceeds of the loan, borrowers must pay interest on the policy for the duration of the loan. This tends to be poor value, since as the loan is gradually paid off, the insurance coverage is worth less and less. Moreover, since at the beginning of the term almost all of the borrower's payments go toward interest and fees rather than the principle, up-front single premiums forestall the borrower's chance to make headway on the loan. If the lender can convince the borrower to refinance every few years, the borrower will never accumulate any equity in the home, even after making tens or even hundreds of thousands of dollars in payments. Although a few lenders have stopped selling single premium insurance, usually under threat of lawsuits, the practice continues to be legal in all but a few states.[73]

Unfortunately, our current credit rules do far too little to discourage credit insurance packing in the high-cost credit market and provide little or no effective information to help consumers carefully order their preferences. State insurance regulators are notoriously indifferent and lax concerning credit insurance loss ratios and premiums. And the credit industry can always defend credit insurance by pointing to the exceptional cases where insurance products benefit consumers. But perhaps most fundamentally, Truth in Lending disclosures do not provide any useful information or warnings about credit insurance to help debtors avoid trouble in the first place. In general lenders are required to include credit insurance in calculating the finance charge disclosure. Theoretically, borrowers should be able to compare the end result price, if not the specific insurance plans, and in this way protect themselves. However, the credit industry successfully lobbied for an exception, which allows lenders to exclude credit insurance from the finance charge whenever the insurance is "optional." If the lender does not require the borrower to purchase the insurance as a condition of approving the loan, then lenders need not include the insurance cost in calculating the finance charge.[74] Everyone recognizes insurance premiums can dramatically affect the true annual percentage rate—whether they are "optional" or not. At a meeting of the American Financial Services Association in a seminar on "Credit Insurance: Current and Future Investment Opportunities" a representative of a major credit insurance provider explained, "start with a 12 percent loan; a credit life premium bumps it up to a 12.5 percent APR, and the 'full package' moves it up to an 18 percent loan."[75] However, because virtually all lenders now sell "optional" credit insurance, these premiums are not included in the finance charge, and therefore are not reflected in the disclosed annual percentage rate. As a result borrowers believe their annual percentage rate is only 12 percent—and, technically speaking, they are correct. But because the true costs of insurance-packed loans are much higher, vulnerable and naive borrowers pay more over a longer period of time to purchase essentially the same credit and never know the difference. Sadly, even if Truth in Lending finance charge regulations were changed to include optional as well as mandatory credit insurance in calculation of the finance charge and APR, there is no guarantee this would be enough to protect vulnerable debtors. Disclosures are usually not presented until closing, and it is typically too late to overcome debtors' anchoring on earlier estimates, the immediate lure of cash, and their misplaced trust in lenders.

Collectively, biases and cognitive errors, including those related to credit insurance as well as others, create a formidable constraint on the ability of markets to promote ideal social and economic outcomes in American high-cost credit transactions. Even in relatively well-functioning markets, cognitive biases can cause serious problems. But in the high-cost credit market, where poor decision-making, dishonesty, and desperation are endemic, these cognitive preference ordering errors can only be worse. With the equity-stripping character of some high-cost mortgage borrowing, a single poor decision can destroy a lifetime investment. With the chain debt structure of payday and car title loans, one poor purchasing decision can *lock in* an inescapable preference order. A single misdirected decision can lead to a sequence of events which drain the financial resources of low-income families. For those vulnerable to high-cost credit predators, financial health requires hundreds of smart decisions over the course of a lifetime. But poor financial health only requires *one* mistake.

SOCIAL NORMS, CULTURAL HISTORY, AND THE MYTH OF THE CLASSICALLY RATIONAL HIGH-COST DEBTOR

While debtors' various biases and cognitive errors have a profound effect on the market for high-cost loans, a related and perhaps more important (as well as more manageable) source of dysfunctional preference ordering arises in the norms emanating from American culture. Economists have long recognized cultural and historic forces shape consumer preferences and in turn create economic demand. Informal social regularities which individuals feel obligated to follow, but which are nevertheless not set as rules of law by governments, exert a profound influence on social and economic life.[76] As Sunstein explains, social norms tell us "when to sit, when to show anger, when and how and with whom to express affection, when to talk, when to listen, and when to discuss personal matters."[77] Norms help us live together in a civil society. Because social norms shape who we are and what we want, they fundamentally shape which products we prefer. Norms generate demand for many socially useful products and services including soap, pre-printed thank-you notes, and marriage counselors. Sometimes norms create demand for products and services which would not have any value absent the norm itself. They can generate drastically different prices for otherwise identical houses in demographically similar neighborhoods. Norms suggesting men wear ties in courtrooms create economic demand for an otherwise worthless product. Social norms defining beauty create demand to surgically alter our bodies themselves. Moreover, social norms are not always easily reconciled and are not always benign. Superiors deserve respect, but not obsequiousness. While loyalty is a virtue, too much loyalty can hide terrible crimes. And affection for one's family and appreciation of its traditions can sometimes evolve into hatred and contempt of diversity.[78]

It should come as no surprise some norms generate self-destructive purchasing preferences. Once again, the market for illicit drugs is telling. In this market, rebellious counter-cultural norms, magnified by peer pressure and media glamorization, often dominate mainstream norms condemning illicit drug use. Similarly, some suggest illicit drug use is often an unhappy outgrowth of social norms underpinning the benefits of modern medical reliance on drug therapy. In this view, when TV adds push sleeping pills, they acculturate us to drug use, thereby eroding social norms condemning more dangerous addictive drugs.[79] Social norms condemning illicit drug use sometimes give way to competing social norms facilitating or even encouraging it. These dangerous norms warp the preference maps of susceptible individuals, creating a wide disjuncture in preferences and welfare. This breakdown in classically rational decision-making helps explain aggressive government intervention in illicit drug markets. Criminal laws, quasi-militaristic eradication efforts, and public awareness campaigns can all be seen, in part, as a response to the self-destructive preferences generated by harmful social norms.

Analogously, radical change in American social norms regarding consumer borrowing has profoundly affected preferences for high-cost credit. For millennia human civilizations have produced both social norms and laws construing high-cost consumer borrowing as morally degenerate. Nearly five thousand years ago, Hammurabi invoked the divine authority of Shamash, the Babylonian god of justice, in justifying his 33 percent interest-rate cap. Hammurabi's message, and the social norms which undoubtably accompanied it, was one of unquestionable moral condemnation of high-cost borrowing and lending. Ancient Israel, Solonic Greece, Republican Rome, and Ming China all employed similar censuring social norms in controlling the consequences of high-cost debt.

Early America inherited these social norms. Laws nurtured and expressed anti-consumption debt norms with general usury interest-rate caps at around 6 percent, debtors' prisons, and parsimonious discharge in bankruptcy. Leaders such as Benjamin Franklin espoused a strict thrift ethic which had no tolerance for consumption debt. Business leaders tended to fire employees found indebted. Respected commercial creditors excluded high-cost lenders from their social circles and professional organizations. American religious leaders uniformly condemned debt-oriented lifestyles. And family leaders who found themselves and their dependants in high-cost debt hid this fact to avoid shame and stigma. In the early American consciousness, consumer credit was inextricably associated with poverty, untrustworthiness, and the path to moral decay. This consciousness was reflective of a simple and universally publicized norm that consumer borrowing was *wrong*. Placing our more modern sentiments aside, this norm carried at least one undeniable advantage: all high-cost debtors walked into credit negotiations with the warning that their choices entailed risks.

However, over the course of the twentieth century a new breed of consumer credit developed. This new type of credit, extended primarily to the middle class, evolved for a variety of complex economic and demographic reasons. The growth of the American economy, the rising income of the middle class, expansion of consumer aspirations, a shift from an entrepreneurial middle class esteeming real property to a middle class of salaried wage earners esteeming consumer goods, and the bureaucratization of the work force with income-shock-limiting regular pay checks: are all factors cited as creating what would eventually become an explosion in lending to average relatively affluent middle-class citizens.[80] This new credit was different than the older more silent credit that often shady lenders had extended to the desperate poor for millennia. Although not as cheap as commercial credit, the new credit was relatively inexpensive compared to the contracts offered to the poor and was extended by businesses which included the nation's elite corporations.

As the market for this new, moderately-priced consumer credit rapidly developed, the old moralizing social norms condemning all consumption debt were no longer coherent with the sentiments of the increasingly credit-oriented middle class. Sparking a norm cascade, all major social leaders simultaneously began accommodating this change by reversing the ancient message that consumer debt was wrong. Leading the way were "norm entrepreneurs," businesses which, acting on their profit motive, aggressively sought to change our credit norms.[81] In his landmark work, *The Affluent Society*, the noted economist John Galbraith explains:

People have changed their view of debt. Thus, there has been an inexplicable but very real retreat from the Puritan canon that required an individual to save first and enjoy life later. In fact, as always, the pieces of economic life are part of the whole. It would be surprising indeed if a society that is prepared to spend thousands of millions to persuade people of their wants were to fail to take the further step of financing those wants, and were it not then to go on to persuade people of the ease and desirability of incurring debt to make those wants effective. This has happened. The process of persuading people to incur debt, and the arrangements for them to do so, are as much a part of modern production as the making of the goods and the nurturing of wants. The Puritan ethos was not abandoned. It was merely overwhelmed by the massive power of modern merchandising.[82]

Middle-class consumer debt became morally acceptable and financially preferable through advertising that advocated new ways of life in the many media of communication which, for the first time in American history, reached into virtually every home. Long before billions upon billions of credit card solicitations reached our doors, TV, radio, newspapers, magazines, billboards, and movies had already changed the values that had been developed by virtually all civilizations to protect the poor over thousands of years. The ancient thrift ethic which constructed a social norm condemning all consumer debt has been almost completely eclipsed by the mass marketing of debt extended to the middle class.

American government followed, facilitated, and encouraged this trend. Around the turn of the last century, states began passing small loan laws permitting small personal loans at interest rates between 36 and 42 percent. These watershed rules qualified the old stark message of moral condemnation sent by the uniform general usury laws traditionally set at 6 percent. Although the architects of the small loan laws were social progressives who hoped to help the poor, the lasting cultural legacy of small loan legislation was the way it sparked later special usury statutes that allowed all types of middle-class oriented creditors to lobby for more and more exceptions to general interest-rate caps. Congress also passed, and the legal profession embraced, a national bankruptcy code which, in historical terms, provided generous and organized amnesty to consumer debtors. This sent the revolutionary message that even bankrupt consumer borrowers should sometimes be forgiven.

When the federal government eventually passed the Truth in Lending Act in 1968, this law only further erased the moral distinction between the old high-cost credit extended primarily to the poor, and the new moderately-priced consumer credit offered to the middle class. Truth in Lending's uniform disclosures make all loans look the same on facial inspection. After Truth in Lending, every consumer loan referred to the same terms and used the same terminology. Content aside, disclosure forms for the most expensive credit look virtually identical to the disclosure forms for the cheapest. For the illiterate and the financially illiterate, high-cost credit disclosures and mainstream credit disclosures are indistinguishable. The message, intended or not, is that all credit documents are on equal moral and legal footing; the only difference is price. At its most basic level, Truth in Lending seeks to create movement along an existing demand curve through price shopping, not to affect change in the preferences which shift demand schedules themselves. In this respect, Truth in Lending stands in stark contrast to the pre-twentieth-century governmental policies which sought to create and nurture social norms that would decrease demand for consumer credit by stressing its immorality.

When mainstream corporate lenders acting as norm entrepreneurs revised American taste for credit, their older and less savory high-cost cousins came along for a free ride. The dramatic cultural changes of the consumer credit revolution had the side effect of propping up social norms that facilitate dangerous, high-cost indebtedness as well as mainstream, moderately-priced installment buying. For affluent Americans, moderately-priced loans have become just another product or service to be evaluated in terms of price and opportunity cost. Credit cards, price-competitive car financing, and prime mortgages are not only respectable, they are encouraged by social norms and even, at times, government subsidies. Moreover, these norms have served the middle class well, having helped millions of families acquire the products that create comfortable and prosperous lifestyles. However, the tragedy and market failure for our nation's economically vulnerable is this: the credit they purchase today is still the same old silent, shady, high-cost debt that has been around for millennia, but the social norms which once protected them have been forgotten. High-cost debtors too, have adopted the same cavalier attitudes toward credit, along with their relatively affluent upper-middle-class counterparts. With the previous condemnation of personal consumption debt muddled, high-cost debtors walk into the arms of modern loansharks with the same moral predispositions and lazy shopping habits that one might expect at a corner grocery store. The chain debt lamented since the inception of civilization has taken on the moral character of laundry detergent. In the market for high-cost loans, where the personal risks are great, this otherwise acceptable attitude can only be described as reckless.

Because the fragile and norm-dependent human process of preference ordering has broken down, today's high-cost debtors do not have preference orders identical to their welfare. In this market, the classical economic presumptive utilitarian ratification of rational free market outcomes is little more than a hollow myth.[83] Indifferent and even reckless preference ordering is fine when one is buying the everyday household products and services which make up the vast bulk of the American economy. Such preference ordering may even be acceptable for relatively affluent upper-middle-class families purchasing moderately-priced loans. But indifferent and reckless preferences cause crushing breakdown in the efficacy of market decision-making when the precariously impoverished gamble their futures away on high-cost chain debt. We cannot expect that the free market alone will correct this cultural taste for what responsible social leaders characterize as reckless borrowing, since after all, it was the free-market-induced media blitz soliciting mainstream borrowers which, as much as anything else, created the problem in the first place.

CHAPTER 6

Families and Communities: Production Externalities and the Spillover Effect in High-Cost Debt Transactions

Those who lend small sums of money at high rates of interest . . . take more than they ought and from the wrong sources.

—Aristotle

O my unhappy friends, you must be mad indeed. . . . Do you think that a Greek could offer a gift without treachery in it? Do you know Ulysses no better than that? Either some of their men have been shut inside this timber-work and are now hiding in it, or the horse itself is a machine for overcoming our walls, . . . or it hides some other confusion for us.

—Laocöon, warning the Trojans

M ANY DISMISS HIGH-COST CREDIT market failure by thinking of the problem as one caused and solved only by individuals. The American ideology of individualism charges each citizen with caring for his or her own economic needs. Barring extenuating circumstances, such as fraud or disability, we expect all consumers to make wise decisions or live with the consequences. Thus far, we have treated high-cost credit market failure as a problem faced by individuals, dislocated from the people and institutions around

199

them. After all, there is a grain of truth underlying the comment often heard in discussions of high-cost credit: "Well, it was her own fault for agreeing to such foolish a loan." Nevertheless, in the market for high-cost credit, the consequences of ill-advised borrowing are not borne by individual debtors alone. High-cost debtors do not live in a vacuum. To expect that our most valued social institutions would be insulated from the reckless credit decisions of our most vulnerable is folly. We will now explore the effects of high-cost borrowing and lending for third parties, including debtors' families, neighborhoods, and communities, as well as our nation itself.

THE LIMITS OF INDIVIDUALISM AND THE PROBLEM OF EXTERNALITY

We tend to think about market transactions in isolation. Firms gather raw materials, overhead, and labor with a view toward creating a final product. When the product is complete, they offer to sell it at prices which will allow them to recover their production costs and provide a profit, which makes the time and effort of manufacture worthwhile. The price the firm charges for the widget must be at least as much as the sum of the cost of every input. Otherwise the firm would lose money in the transaction. A consumer, in deciding whether to purchase, must weigh the utility gained from purchasing the product against the utility lost by foregoing the next best option. If the price is right, the consumer will buy. In such a case the manufacturer receives the value tendered, while the consumer enjoys the utility garnered from the purchase. The manufacture of the product benefits both consumer and producer. Importantly, one need look no further than the two parties who negotiated the contract. In the typical transaction, the purchased product confers a personal and private benefit upon only the buyer. Economists usually label these products *private goods* because in Paul Samuelson and William Nordhaus's definition they "can be divided up and provided separately to different individuals with no external benefits or costs to others."[1] In a perfect market this is the end of the matter.

However, in the real world prices do not always reflect the true costs associated with a product. In such cases what economists have termed as *externalities* may develop. Again we turn to Samuelson and Nordhaus: "An externality occurs when production or consumption inflicts involuntary costs or benefits on others. More precisely, an externality is an effect of one economic agent's behavior on another's well-being where that effect is not reflected in dollar or market transactions."[2] The phenomenon of price externalization was first explored in 1920 by a Cambridge economist named A. C. Pigou. Pigou explained that there are many goods which the public enjoys, but for which there is no effective way to make all who enjoy the good help to pay for its production. For instance, "it may easily happen that the benefits of a well-placed lighthouse must be largely enjoyed by ships on which no toll could be conveniently levied." Conversely, there are goods which many suffer from, but are not compensated for their suffering. With these goods the marginal private net product is greater than the marginal social net product. For example, in Pigou's time, all of London suffered from the contamination of the air with "smoke from factory chimneys: for this smoke . . . inflicts a heavy uncharged loss on the community, in injury to the buildings and vegetables, expenses for washing clothes and cleaning rooms, expenses for the provision of extra artificial light, and in many other ways." Both the navigational guidance of lighthouses and the products manufactured at smoke-belching factories are public goods. This is because the benefits and losses associated with these two products are not limited to the parties involved in the buying and selling of the two, but spill over to third parties. All of the consequences of the buying and selling of products which affect the well-being of otherwise uninterested parties are consequences external to the market transaction itself.[3]

The market externalities which have a beneficial effect on those not part of a contract are called *external economies*. This is the case of the lighthouse. Sailors who had nothing to do with the building or maintenance of the lighthouse receive a beneficial external economy from the market transactions which caused the light-house to function. The owners of the ships that the noncontributing sailors navigate, and the buyers of the products that the ships carry, also receive external economies from the lighthouse. Today, most use the term *externality* in reference to external diseconomies, which produce a harmful effect on those non-contracting parties. The smoke-emitting factories create such an external diseconomy in the production of their goods.

Sometimes externalities inhibit the efficient functioning of otherwise competitive markets. In competitive markets we expect buyers to purchase the more inexpensive of two identical goods, since the opportunity costs of the cheaper product are lower. In order to attract buyers, firms must keep prices low, which in turn creates an imperative to keep production costs as low as possible. A firm can satisfy this imperative better than its competitors if it succeeds in creating an otherwise equivalent product manufactured with costs external to the price the firm will charge. If the firm can organize its production so third parties pay the firm's production costs, then the firm will have more inexpensive inputs and can attract more customers with lower prices. The buyer of the product also has virtually no incentive to prevent the cost externalization, since the buyer receives a benefit from the producer in the form of a lower price. Production externalities generate Pareto inefficient outcomes. A Pareto efficient outcome is a situation where no individual may become better off without making some other individual or group worse off. In a Pareto optimal market there are no trades or government policies which might increase production without decreasing someone's share of produced economic value. Production externalities are Pareto dominated because the product price, which is determined by a firm's private production costs (usually including payments for labor, materials, overhead, etc.), does not include the external social costs inadvertently imposed on third parties. In the traditional account of externality, a market is Pareto inefficient unless external costs are zero. Externalized production costs of this sort create a pocket of misallocation which swamps social resources. Society in effect *subsidizes* the overproduction of the product by absorbing the manufacturer's foisted production costs. Moreover, the subsidy is involuntarily granted because the contracts between the manufacturer and its buyers are sealed without the adversely affected non-parties ever having a say in the outcome.

Returning to Pigou's example of London factories, smoke and the suffering it caused were external to the market transactions between the manufacturer and its buyers. When a transaction between a buyer and the manufacturer took place, there was no (or at least very little) financial incentive to consider the consequences of the smoke released into the city air. While there are small private costs for the buyer and the factory, since they too must breathe the dirty air, these private costs are insufficient to change production behavior. This is because the marginal private benefit the parties would gain from displacing production costs would dwarf the private cost of their incremental suffering from the smoke produced as a result of their transaction. The incentive to keep private costs, and, in turn, prices, low, would almost always eclipse any incentive to avoid the externality. Thus, all of the London residents downwind from the factory would indefinitely suffer from the consequences of the market transaction, but nowhere would this suffering be reflected in contract prices. All these Londoners were involuntary victims of the mu-

tually beneficial exchange between the manufacturer and its
buyers. This outcome is inefficient since it may promote the best
welfare of the steel mill, but it does not promote the greatest welfare for society at large. What is more, all manufacturers had no
incentive to invest in cleaner production technology, since that
would only limit the manufacturers' ability to drop production
costs—at the expense of the general public.[4]

Many economists believe externalities provide one of the most
persuasive rationales for government regulation.[5] Externalities,
such as manufacturer pollution, are traditionally addressed by
charging a government regulator with setting a limit to pollution
discharge, which prevents excessive externalization. This response places the government in the position of policing an industry with the same financial incentive to pollute. Government
agencies use measurements and penalties to monitor and punish
noncompliance with the rules crafted to correct for the market
flaw. While the predisposition in market economies is against
government action, transaction-cost-insulated externalities have
long provided an important exception. Without government action, the market will fail in the goal of promoting society's best
interests. In some cases of externality, the price of government action will be cost-prohibitive because the social costs of regulation
will be greater than the marginal increase in efficiency generated
through deterring externalization. But even imperfect government action can significantly increase market efficiency where
the social costs of the externality are high. Particularly where the
government can prevent externalization beforehand by creating
an incentive to take precautionary measures, most agree government intervention in the form of liability or regulatory oversight
is advisable.[6]

DRAINING SOCIAL CAPITAL:
EXTERNALIZATION IN HIGH-COST LENDING

Although pollution provides one of the simplest and most common examples of externality, it is of course not the only one. Any economic behavior which has an effect on another's well-being, where the effect is not reflected in a market transaction, is an externality. Some externalities have far-reaching effects, while others are much smaller and less apparent. Samuelson and Nordhaus observe "[w]hen a carrier of bubonic plague entered a town during the Middle Ages, the entire population could be felled by the Black Death. On the other hand, when you chew an onion at a football stadium on a windy day, the external impacts are hardly noticeable."[7] Like pollution-intensive industries, the transactions of the high-cost lending industry have serious external effects for people not party to credit contracts.

Fresh Starts and False Starts: Bankruptcy, Foreclosure,
Families, and Externalities

An excellent first example of an externality associated with high-cost credit transactions is the social costs incurred in bankruptcy. Bankruptcy has proven to be an inevitable result of high-cost credit transactions. It is difficult to make accurate generalizations about the way high-cost creditors use bankruptcy courts to collect debts.[8] Sullivan, Warren, and Westerbrook explain, "[s]ome creditors suffer repeatedly in bankruptcy, whereas others dodge the bullet. Some are passive victims of unavoidable circumstance, whereas others are knowledgeable, repeat players in the credit game, including the end game of bankruptcy."[9] There is a tendency to presume that bankruptcy is an accidental and unpredictable side effect of a commercial society. Such an assumption portrays creditors as hapless victims of irresponsible debtors who make poor choices. Nevertheless, professional creditors in general, and high-cost creditors in particular, anticipate that a certain percentage of lent assets will not be repaid. High-cost creditors often lend out as much money as possible, relying on collection practices, rather than the ability to predict the likelihood of repayment, to turn a profit. Part of the collection process all too often involves bankruptcy. Creditors specializing in high risk loans, in particular, offer loans which are likely to end in bankruptcy.[10]

When debtors declare bankruptcy, creditors often sustain important financial losses. For creditors, bankruptcy losses are more accurately considered production costs. This is to say that creditors must expect an uncertain amount of bad debt as an input in order to conduct business. Creditors absorb this production cost by transferring it into credit prices. Because creditors anticipate that some of their assets will be written off when debtors declare bankruptcy, the creditors rationally choose to charge higher prices to reflect that anticipated business cost. But the financial losses suffered by creditors are not the only costs of bankruptcy. It takes a great deal of money to hire the judges, clerks, and administrative and organizational support staff to deal with the millions of American consumer bankruptcies. Each bankruptcy judge must have a courtroom and chambers in a federal courthouse. Each federal courthouse must have the security and custodial resources to run a professional building. Every federal judicial district in every state must have these facilities. And the more bankruptcy cases there are, the more these services cost in sum. Although bankruptcy courts do recover some of their costs in court fees, the best estimates suggest American taxpayers foot the bill for roughly half of the bankruptcy court budget.[11]

Unlike the bankruptcy costs borne by creditors, the costs of operating a bankruptcy system are an example of costs which are not reflected in the price of credit. A creditor does not anticipate that the government will have to spend money on providing a bankruptcy system, and therefore adjust prices upward, in order to help defray that social cost. Instead, taxpayers, and thus society in general, are left to deal with the financial burden of operating a bankruptcy system. Those creditors who tend to have a large portion of their obligations repaid when a debtor declares bankruptcy have a financial incentive to rely on the bankruptcy system as a collection device.[12] Creditors who do not fare well in bankruptcy have an incentive to structure risky debt to provide better shelter in the event of bankruptcy. Because the federal bankruptcy code strongly favors secured debts in determining which obligations may be discharged and ordering which obligations are to be repaid first, there is an incentive for the high-cost credit industry to filter its lent assets into secured transactions wherever possible, and then rely on the bankruptcy courts to create and enforce repayment plans.[13] Not every debt can be so restructured. This is only possible where the debtor has some valuable property, preferably a home, and where the debtor will agree to leverage themselves against that property. Nevertheless, creditors, particularly high-cost creditors, can run highly profitable businesses by using the federal bankruptcy system as a collection tool, which eliminates the need to use expensive default risk-evaluation tactics. Quite simply, for many creditors it is cheaper to lend to debtors who will declare bankruptcy than it is to figure out which debtors are likely to repay.

However, bankruptcy is not the only example of externalities associated with high-cost lending borne by society through tax revenue. Courts also bear the collection costs of creditors through judicial devices such as wage garnishment, writs of execution, replevin, attachment, and discovery of assets. Such devices can be a more effective means of collecting debts than actions which creditors might take alone. By enlisting the aid of the courts, creditors co-opt the moral authority and intimidation of a state's police powers. High-cost creditors employ these collection devices, garnishment in particular, with much greater frequency than other creditors. Moreover, courts garnish from minorities and economically disadvantaged people at relatively greater rates.[14] Like the bankruptcy system, these remedies for payment disputes so frequently employed by high-cost lenders are subsidized by the tax revenues which keep the courts open.

While the operation of the bankruptcy system entails externalization, the existence of the system itself is also evidence of a larger problem. In bankruptcy, the government intervenes at least in part to limit the consequences of an individual's financial collapse for others. When a consumer is saddled with inescapable high-cost debt, many individuals and groups suffer. If a borrower is paying a significant portion of her monthly income to a payday lender, her landlord may not receive the rent on time or at all. An ill-advised credit decision can prevent high-cost debtors from making utility payments, harming telephone companies, electricity providers, and natural gas companies. Servicing high-cost debt can also prevent consumers from making payments on medical bills. It is easier to ignore doctors' and hospitals' efforts to collect payment, than it is to ignore the aggressive and unregulated in-house bill collectors employed by high-cost lenders. Churches and charitable organizations also suffer. Few have the faith to pay tithes or the benefaction to donate to favored causes before paying loansharks. Jumping to the head of the line, high-cost lenders also draw payments away from mainstream lenders by collecting payments on more recent, yet higher-cost, obligations. As a last resort the bankruptcy system exists, in part, to organize the repayment of obligations equitably among a bankrupt borrower's many creditors, thus minimizing the spread of externalities throughout the community. Similarly, two noted economists speculate the ancient history of interest-rate restrictions discussed earlier evolved to check externalities associated with dangerous borrowing:

"[I]n biblical Israel (and even earlier in Babylonia), interest rate restrictions seemed to have been intended to limit the degree to which an individual could become indebted. If the community paid some of the price of bankruptcy (perhaps in having to care for the bankrupt), then the community sensibly wanted to restrict the individual's ability to overcommit himself to loans."[15]

We should not be surprised to find high-cost debtors turn in greater proportions to the state for financial assistance in the form of unemployment insurance, medicaid, food stamps, housing assistance, and welfare. High-cost debt often preempts and frustrates the tenuous social links between the debtor and other unsuspecting third parties.[16]

The external consequences for communities and neighborhoods can only be greater where a borrower's high-cost debt results in home foreclosure. The stability of neighborhoods is intertwined with the economic health of the collection of families which comprise it. And for the vast majority of American families, a house is the largest investment they will ever make. When entire neighborhoods have difficulty finding safer low-cost credit, they will eventually turn to higher-priced options, one family at a time. Low-income neighborhoods are often targeted by high-cost mortgage lenders hoping to extract the value of residents' home equity. Using aggressive marketing tactics, and unclear price disclosures, entire neighborhoods can eventually be signed up for extremely high-cost second or third mortgages. When this happens, entire blocks of families risk losing their homes. Each time a family loses its residence to foreclosure the fabric of the neighborhood as a whole is weakened. The social bonds that take time to form are eroded as one family after another is forced to relocate to an even less desirable location, or struggle on encumbered with their financial obligations.[17] One study noted this effect in Boston, where in certain targeted neighborhoods between 1985 and 1993 as many as *82 percent* of the families lost their homes in foreclosure to a relatively small number of high-cost mortgage firms.[18] One senator explained that high-cost loans are destroying

> the pillars of strength that are out there, either older people or other families that have had homes over the years and really provide the bedrock in a community. . . . They're [high-cost loans are] pervasive and they're going on every single day in this country, and they're grinding down our people, and everybody suffers. When this happens, the whole community is lesser for it. It's not right, it's not decent, it's not what the country should be about, and it's not what our laws should tolerate.[19]

Although each individual debtor decides to borrow, when many individuals make the same decision, greater collective consequences can result. The stability of an entire neighborhood can be undermined, one decision at a time. Because, as Ioannis Kallianiotis notes, "our wealth is a more social good than a personal good," even those who never borrow are affected by the high-cost credit contracts of their peers.[20] Everyone in a neighborhood, high-cost debtors and nondebtors alike, bear the consequences of lost stability. Neither is the evidence of the destructive power of misplaced high-cost credit production costs upon communities simply anecdotal. In the past twenty years, the national foreclosure rate has *quadrupled*, in step with the explosion of high-cost lenders.[21]

High-cost lending also erodes the stability of families. The person most likely to suffer immediately the external consequences of high-cost credit transactions is the debtor's spouse. Professors Sullivan, Warren, and Westerbrook's exhaustive study of American bankruptcy found bankrupts, both men and women, often argue "they were dragged into bankruptcy by the financial irresponsibility of spouses and cohabitees."[22] Another study of defaulting mortgage debtors found spouses often end up making payments on loans to which they never agreed. And the courts have developed a great deal of case law forcing one spouse to deal with debts errantly incurred by the other.[23]

History also provides precedents for state intervention to prevent the external effects of a high-cost debtor's borrowing from spilling over upon a spouse. Toward the end of America's last high-cost credit boom, legislatures attempted to prevent intrafamilial high-cost debt externalization by requiring the consent of husbands and wives prior to sealing small short-term loans. For example, in 1908 the Massachusetts state legislature passed a law requiring that married men seeking to borrow money against the security of future wages (an early form of payday lending) obtain the written consent of their wives. In a constitutional challenge, the United States Supreme Court found that Massachusetts had a reasonable interest in protecting wives from the foolish credit decisions of their husbands.[24] Other states passed similar provisions. Indiana, for example passed a law stating that:

> No assignment of his wages or salary by a married man, who shall be the head of a family residing in this State, shall be valid or enforceable without the consent of his wife, evidenced by her signature to said assignment executed and acknowledged before a notary public or other officer empowered to take acknowledgments of conveyances, and no wage broker or person connected with him directly or indirectly shall be authorized to take any such acknowledgments.[25]

The Supreme Court of Indiana similarly upheld the statute, arguing that it legitimately protected the wives and families of debtors from consequences of the debtor's own actions:

Improvident debts of the head of the family constitute an important factor not only in the destitution and illiteracy of the State's youth, but hinders the normal development of their physical, mental and moral powers. By restricting the power of the householder to pledge his future earnings and those which he has not yet received, the tendency to heedless extravagance is measurably curtailed, and we are of the opinion that the legislation here in controversy is well within the limits of the State's police power, and offends no provision of either State or Federal Constitution.[26]

These early statutes and their successful defenses in court are evidence of the fundamental and widespread risk externalities pose for healthy marriages and families in general.

Recent data corroborates this conclusion. Empirical research has consistently found financial hardship, such as that posed by ill-advised high-cost borrowing decisions, threatens marital quality and often leads to divorce. Most agree that the ever-increasing divorce rates of recent decades show changing gender roles and social expectations have left the institution of marriage fragile. The added stress of unmanageable debt burden can be more than enough to crush the already frail bonds that tie together many contemporary families. One survey found that 38 percent of respondents reported debt troubles had adversely affected their marriage. Sixty percent reported debt trouble had an adverse effect on the rest of their families.[27] Perhaps more surprising, financial hardship associated with high-cost debt may prevent families from forming by deterring marriage in the first place. External consequences can unfurl into the extended families of debtors as well. One study found that just under 25 percent of a sample of debtors in default on mortgage payments received help in making payments from their extended families. It is no doubt even more common for debtors to tap their familial resources in more informal ways, such as providing daycare, food, clothing, and transportation, when the debtor can no longer make these purchases. Even when such care is not extended, a debtor's family is likely to endure emotional pains of sympathy and regret when they learn of the debtor's financial troubles. Collectively, when one family member unwisely signs a high-cost credit contract, the rest of the family suffers.[28]

Furthermore, the severity of externalization in high-cost lending is compounded by what may be called a *saturation effect*. Returning to the example of pollution, saturation effects are often seen in droughts when rivers run unusually low. Firms continue to discharge pollutants into the water at the same rate as normal. But, because water levels are so low, the same volume of pollution can lead to a much higher pollution content. In such cases fish and other wildlife able to live in the presence of low or moderate concentrations of pollution are often poisoned to death *en masse*, even though the actual behavior of polluters has not changed. In droughts the pollution-assimilative capabilities of the environment may dramatically decrease.

Just as rivers may face droughts, so too can families, communities, and even whole cities. Neighborhoods and families regularly experience times when they are less able to absorb the financial hardship of debtors. When times are good, a family can help a member in debt trouble by making a payment, providing food, free childcare, or even just offering emotional support and love. But when times are rough, the ability of the family to absorb financial hardship of a debtor is substantially curtailed. Just as ordinary levels of pollution during a drought may destroy entire rivers or estuaries of fish, so too may ordinary levels of the financial discord associated with poorly considered credit contracts permanently damage entire groups. These social costs of high-cost credit transactions are not reflected in the price of credit contracts, and are therefore externalities, for which the market cannot successfully account. Because affected nondebtors never enter into a credit transaction at all, such nondebtors never have the chance to receive a mutual benefit from the transaction, or to negotiate for lower prices. The destiny of all members of a community or a family can be deeply affected by the decisions of a relatively small number of members. Just as the destiny of people downwind from a smoke-belching factory might suffer from the purchase of the factory's manufactured products, so too can the members of a family or community be affected by one person's decision to borrow.

HIGH-COST CREDIT EXTERNALITIES AND UNIQUELY VULNERABLE GROUPS

Not all groups suffer from the consequences of high-cost debt in the same way. It is worthwhile to explore separately groups who are targeted by high-cost debtors, as well as groups who disproportionately suffer external consequences of high-cost debt.

Exploiting the Elderly

Senior citizens are uniquely vulnerable to high-cost creditors, particularly high-cost home mortgage lenders. High-cost lenders target the elderly for a number of reasons, but most importantly because senior citizens are likely to have built up equity in a family home over a lifetime. Just under 80 percent of Americans over the age of fifty own their own homes, with the majority having free and clear possession. House-rich but cash-poor retirees are often bombarded with solicitations urging them to tap their home equity by borrowing. Moreover, many elderly individuals face visual and physical impairments resulting from the natural process of aging which limit their abilities to scrutinize closely credit contracts. U.S. Department of Education data indicate "a steep decline in all measures of literacy—prose, information processing, and quantitative—among age groups 55 to 64, and an even greater one among those 65 and over."[29] Senior citizens with regular social security checks or pension payments have steady and reliable income sources which makes them a relatively good credit risk, even if they had credit problems when they were younger. Finally, many senior citizens live in older homes needing repair. This creates a demand for home-improvement financing—a market notorious for high-cost lending abuses. Combined these factors make a target too tempting for many high-cost lenders to pass up.[30]

Horror stories of high-cost lending abuses of the nation's elderly are startlingly common and tragic and are repeated in variations on a common theme around the entire country. Johnnie Edge, a 76-year-old Atlanta retiree, borrowed $3,000 to sort out a short-term financial jam. Afterwards, his finance company convinced him to refinance the original loan into a $50,000 obligation secured by the home where he lived with his wife Flora. Next, the company refinanced the $50,000 debt twice again in the space of only three months. As a result, Edge was paying 16 percent interest and had borrowed over $12,000 to pay fees included in his contracts. When Flora died his monthly mortgage payment was *more* than his monthly social security income. And, after four years of payment, his principle had decreased only $1200, with the rest going to interest. Edge explained, "I thought they were trying to help me."[31]

Similarly, Mary Stuart, a 75-year-old widow from Roxbury, Massachusetts, had lived in her home for over thirty years when a man approached her and claimed she could be fined because her rundown front porch was not in compliance with the municipal code. He offered to fix it for only $10,000 and arrange for "market-rate financing." When Stuart expressed concern about the cost, the contractor told her he would give her a senior citizen discount price of $8,000. Several days after the contractor began work, he brought a loan contract from the "We Care Finance Company" for

$22,500 at a 16 percent interest rate. When Stuart objected, the contractor told her that since the work was already half done, he would abandon the project and put a mechanic's lien on the house if she refused to sign. She signed. But she also fell behind on the payments quickly. Each time she was delinquent, the lender would call and urge her to refinance. After relenting twice, her loan principle grew to $75,000, allowing We Care to capture almost all of Stuart's accumulated equity in her $105,000 home.[32]

Finally, 66-year-old Annie Johnson of Buffalo, New York, was tricked into a $20,400 home improvement loan. Her lender passed out fliers in her low-income neighborhood, which city officials described as a "shark pool." Johnson lived on a social security check of $472 a month, but the lender signed her up for a $424 monthly mortgage payment anyway. In short order, the lender initiated foreclosure proceedings, even though Johnson's serious health problems had recently led to the amputation of both her legs.[33]

There is no way to know to what extent these tragedies represent the high-cost credit market norm. But we can be certain that even in less dramatic cases, harmful consequences are not borne solely by the elderly victims. In many ways, the costs of these transactions are also borne by independent third parties who had no opportunity to prevent the transaction. For instance, because senior citizens live on fixed incomes, extended family members often take up the burden of paying high-cost loan payments in order to prevent foreclosure. When seniors do lose their home in foreclosure, decades of memories are lost—both their own, and their children's and grandchildren's. Senior citizens are also often pillars of local communities with decades of involvement in church groups, volunteer organizations, and more informal neighborhood bonds. The loss of elderly families through high-cost credit home foreclosure can be a crushing blow for the stability of an entire neighborhood. Like everyone else, seniors often rely on others of their own age group for friendship and support. When the financial lives of one or two seniors are ruined, many others are likely to suffer.

After foreclosure, seniors must often turn to family members to provide alternative living arrangements. This can be taxing not only for the senior citizen, but also for the family which may have a limited income as well. And if a senior does not have family to rely on, government services may be the only substitute. Senior citizens who are at the mercy of high-cost lenders are less able to pay their own medical bills without government assistance and are more likely to require housing assistance, often at costly long-term care facilities. When elderly low-income parents lose a family home in foreclosure, the next generation can miss an important opportunity to climb out of poverty. Even if the elderly parents do not end up losing the family home, an ill-advised high-cost loan can quickly deplete retirement accounts and life savings, which would otherwise have provided a source of financial stability for both the elderly parents as well as for an entire extended family. For instance, Professor Dalton Conley of Yale University has recently emphasized how many aging parents deflect poverty from their children by temporarily tapping their retirement nest eggs. A non-interest bearing intrafamily loan can help newlywed children or young parents come up with the down payment on a house, which secures safe, low-cost bank financing for the next thirty years.[34] High-cost loans deplete senior citizens' retirement accounts and thus transfer externalities to a second or even a third generation by eroding an extended family's ability to leverage themselves mutually for one another's collective benefit. Perhaps even more tragic are the senior citizens who pawn and then lose family heirlooms to make payments on high-cost home mortgages, thus destroying the continuity and intergenerational bonds which tie families together over time.[35]

Furthermore, the outlook for seniors and for the externalities associated with high-cost lending to seniors looks grim. As the

baby boom generation begins to retire, absent aggressive government intervention, high-cost creditor equity-stripping promises to
continue its rapid growth. Many are already concerned about the
ability of the shrinking American workforce to support our aging
population. But as market predators aggressively infiltrate the accumulated home equity savings of a generation, this problem may
become even more acute.

Race and High-Cost Credit Externalities

In recent years researchers have found overwhelming empirical
evidence suggesting race-related problems in the high-cost credit
market. African Americans, Latino Americans, and Native Americans all have less access to traditional lower-priced financial institutions. However, researchers have found indisputable evidence
suggesting minorities with comparable education and income are
nevertheless disproportionately served by subprime mortgage
lenders. Some commentators have argued informal discrimination, which is often imperceptible to lenders themselves, perpetu-
ates disparate access to low-priced financial services. For example,
ethnic minorities are often victims of what some call the "thicker
file" syndrome.[36] Here, a loan processor works harder to assemble
the file upon which a loan application will be granted or denied
for whites than for blacks or other ethnic minorities. This tendency was first identified in a landmark study by the Federal Reserve Bank of Boston in 1992. The study found that minorities in
the Boston area were 2.7 times more likely than whites to have
mortgage loan applications denied. Since then, further research
has, in the minds of most observers, confirmed suspicions of disparate access.[37]

Discrimination in the processing of applications for inexpensive
credit aside, geographic and historical barriers make simply *finding*
inexpensive loans to apply for more difficult for minorities. Many

commentators have pointed again and again to the absence of traditional banks in minority neighborhoods.[38] Simple distance can exert a great deal of influence over a community's ability to find cheap loans. Ethnic minority groups often face such obstacles as transportation problems, long work hours, and insufficient child care opportunities. Collectively, the formal and informal barriers to equal credit access have created what some describe as separate and unequal credit origination systems for whites and minorities. One civil rights attorney argued before Congress:

> Thirty years ago in the South, we had a system of dual waiting rooms, dual water fountains, and the like. Congress reacted. Today our nation is better. However, we still have a dual system of lending in this nation in which whites, in connection with home mortgage loans, more often than not receive the benefit of market rate loans from traditional sources of financing. A substantial number of African Americans only have one other source of lending on homes available; that is, loans at very high rates, very high pre-payment penalties, [and] very high points.[39]

While many disagree, few doubt there is truly equal access to low-cost financial services for some ethnic minority groups in America. In one recent national poll, 76 percent of Americans said that steering minorities to more costly loan products than they qualified for is a "somewhat serious" or "very serious" problem.[40] The Department of Housing and Urban Development appears to concur. It has concluded from its analysis of lender-reported data on nearly a million mortgage loans that "subprime loans are five times more likely in black neighborhoods than in white neighborhoods." And even more unnervingly, *high-income* homeowners in black neighborhoods are still twice as likely to have subprime loans as *low-income* homeowners in white neighborhoods.[41]

The consequences of exclusion from inexpensive mainstream credit create special problems when entire minority communities are systematically engulfed in expensive debt. It is one thing for a single family to be in debt trouble, but it is another for nearly every family in a neighborhood to be in debt trouble. Some have described the situation facing many of the nation's minority communities as "credit famines" that send millions of citizens into the arms of high-priced lenders. When these famines strike entire neighborhoods the results can be devastating. One community bank CEO described the high-cost debt problem facing Hispanic and black communities as the "rubber effect." When money comes into these communities in the form of wages, it is not spent on businesses within the community. Instead, it bounces back out in the form of loan payments to capital-rich outside lenders.[42]

Bishop C. Vernie Russell Jr., pastor of the predominantly African American Mount Carmel Baptist Church in inner-city Norfolk, Virginia, recognized high-cost debt was draining the life from his flock. He now holds "debt liquidation revivals" once a month where churchgoers gather together and raise money to pay off the debts of a lucky church member, selected by Bishop Russell at the door. Clapping and singing along with brass, keyboard, and drums, the group has to date raised $318,000 for various community members. At each revival, dancing and chants of "stomp, stomp, stomp on the devil" encourage the community members to help pay off the debts of the chosen family.[43] Regardless of whether debt revivals catch on elsewhere, Mount Carmel demonstrates the collective community consequences of individual high-cost debt costs, which are not reflected in the transaction prices paid by individual debtors. When a significant number of community members fall into high-cost debt, the entire community—even those who do not borrow—suffers.

The disparity of access to low-cost credit is nowhere greater than for many American Indian tribes. During the high-cost lending boom of the past twenty years, mainstream lenders had almost no success reaching out to Native American borrowers. Through 1994, not a single conventional mortgage had been closed within the Navajo Nation, an Indian reservation located in New Mexico, Arizona, and Utah, a land area larger than that of nine states.[44] In that same year, the Department of Justice brought a suit against the Blackpipe State Bank of South Dakota. The Department found that the bank had a long track record of discriminating against Native Americans by "refusing to make secured loans where the collateral was located on a reservation, . . . for placing credit requirements on Native Americans that it did not require of whites, . . . [and charging] greater interest rates and finance charges than those it charged to whites." This in spite of the fact that the bank was the major lender in the area, the local branch was located in a city bordered on three sides by reservation land, and Native Americans represented the majority of the local population. Bank policy refused to secure loans with collateral subject to tribal court jurisdiction, even though tribal courts had repossession and collection remedies available. Additionally, all of the bank's competitors operated under the same cross-jurisdictional transaction costs, insuring the bank would suffer no cost disadvantages relative to its local competitors. Because none of the Native Americans living on tribal lands could use their property to secure inexpensive credit, they simply had no access to lower cost financial products from the area's major bank.[45]

Perhaps even more effective at excluding Native Americans from inexpensive credit were subtle and informal methods of discrimination. The Justice Department also noted "an absence of Native American employees" at the bank.[46] Furthermore, small-scale capital is virtually nonexistent on reservation land. For most tribes, what little capital investment has occurred has been large-scale infusions of federal funding. As for the property of Native Americans themselves, it is often held in trust by the government, leaving tribal members without access to mortgages or home equity loans.[47] This leaves many Native Americans in a situation where, realistically, their only source of credit is payday lenders, car title lenders, pawn shops, or subprime mortgage lenders—particularly if they choose to stay on the reservation and live traditional lifestyles.

TABLE 6.1

Percent of conventional home purchase loans from subprime and
  manufactured home lenders, 2000

	White Borrowers	All Borrowers	Native American Borrowers
New Mexico	15.3%	28.1%	78.8%
South Dakota	17.4%	18.4%	35.1%
National	10.4%	13.2%	26.3%

Source: *Indian Country Today* Analysis of National Community Reinvestment
Coalition Data[48]

When Native Americans turn to these lenders for financing, the results are predictable. In 2000, Native Americans were nearly three times as likely to have a subprime or manufactured home loan when compared to white borrowers. In New Mexico, a shocking 78.8 percent of new mortgage loans to Native Americans were issued by subprime or manufactured home lenders. On reservations many of these loans can only be described as predatory.[49] The Associates was the nation's top lender to Native Americans, providing more than twice as many mortgages as the next largest competitor. The Associates, called a "poster child for abusive lending" by the *National Mortgage News*, has been dogged by allegations of unfair practices and predatory lending for years. Its record in Indian country is little better. One community activist explained, "[s]omebody in the hierarchy of Associates painted a bull's-eye on the back of American Indians."[50]

Like other communities, Native American tribes suffer collectively from the unwise financial decisions of individuals. One Native American man living on tribal land in Eastern Oklahoma with his disabled nephew, was only a few years away from paying off his home loan in full through a subsidized government program. Nevertheless, a high-cost lender persuaded the uncle to refinance his $50-a-month mortgage payment for a higher-rate loan with monthly payments of over $500. Almost immediately the uncle found himself unable to pay his monthly payments and in jeopardy of losing his home. When the uncle turned to the tribal council for help, the underfunded local government paid off the new mortgage, saving the home. But the council, which had thought of the deed as an isolated case, was stunned when within weeks several other families living around the reservation turned up with the same problem. Even if the uncle had initially turned the lender down and managed to pay off his home loan, he would not have been safe. Authorities from the Chickasaw tribe report that high-cost lenders scour court records on a regular basis looking for Native American families who have just acquired free and clear title to their homes. Upon finding a likely target, lenders bombard the unsuspecting family with flyers, mailed solicitations, telephone calls, and unannounced visits. Only the most skeptical and tight-fisted homeowners stand a chance. And when a foolish decision is eventually made, the community, with its already overextended resources, will almost certainly be unable to come to the borrower's aid. Even as many tribes are scrambling to create stopgap predatory lending education campaigns, it is clear Native American communities cannot absorb the external consequences of high-cost loans as quickly as lenders can issue them.[51]

The Perfect Target: Enlisted Military Personnel

High-cost lenders have targeted junior military personnel for thousands of years. The First Secession in Republican Rome and the northern Chinese peasant rebellions at the end of the Ming Dynasty were both sparked by public outrage over high-cost lending targeted at war veterans. America at the beginning of the twenty-first century has proven susceptible to the same problem. Historically, the military personnel of major international powers generally receive a steady but shallow stream of income. Today's junior military personnel are typically cash-strapped and often find themselves waiting eagerly for the next paycheck.[52]

Payday lenders, car title lenders, and other high-cost creditors have learned to target military personnel with telephone solicitations, mailings, and fliers. Payday loan outlet stores line the streets surrounding major military bases such as Louisiana's Polk Army Base, Utah's Hill Air Force Base, and Norfolk, Virginia's Naval Installation. When the Virginia legislature recently gave in to payday lenders by passing an industry-friendly bill, heavy brass from the Navy and Marine Corps turned out to protest. As more payday lenders flocked to Norfolk, Rear Admiral David Architzel, commander of the Navy's mid-Atlantic region, complained, "[w]e're going to see more of our young sailors in trouble. This isn't going to help them."[53] Similarly, Navy Captain Robert Anderson recently lamented his young cash-strapped sailors too often become trapped in a "financial death spiral" through payday loans. He elaborated, "I have one sailor who is writing $2,893 in checks to cover $2,550 in cash advances."[54]

The consequences of high-cost borrowing spread throughout the military community. Janice Barnes, head of the Air Force Aid Society at Robbins Air Force Base in Georgia, oversees the distribution of the Society's voluntary donations to airmen in financial crises. Air Force personnel commonly donate a few dollars a month to a fund aimed, among other projects, at preventing high-cost loans before they happen by offering small no-interest loans. Barnes explains, "[c]ar repair is probably the No. 1 [*sic*] loan we give." But bailing out enlisted borrowers after the fact is also common. Loans to pay off 600 percent car title debts are not unusual.[55] The Navy-Marines Corps Relief Society provides similar services. Debra Prall, manager of the Norfolk office, sees sailors and marines every week, desperate because they can no longer meet their family and community obligations due to payday loan debt. She reports some payday lenders "intimidate the borrower by threatening to take the matter to the service member's commanding officer." Faculty at the Judge Advocate General's School report that military legal-assistance attorneys now commonly deal with the aftermath of payday lending. Unfortunately, even with legal assistance, "rarely does the service member emerge from these situations in better financial condition and often only gets deeper in debt."[56] Recent military surveys revealed nearly a third of enlisted service members reported moderate to severe difficulty in paying bills. As a result, top brass have become so concerned with the effect of high-cost lending on the wellbeing of enlisted personnel and their families, as well as the nation's military readiness itself, new inductees are now required to receive mandatory financial education.[57] Whether the education will stem high-cost credit externalization throughout the military community remains to be seen.

Doing More than Their Fair Share: Women and the Consequences of High-Cost Debt

The experiences of women mirror those of racial minorities historically excluded from access to inexpensive credit. For centuries, in countries all around the world, predatory lenders have extracted hard bargains from poor women. As economies evolved from agrarian to industrial bases, the central importance of land in determining wealth gave way to the ability to command capital. No longer was the family farm central to the average household's economic welfare. Increasingly, household goods such as clothing, furnishings, and simple tools were purchased with cash, usually supplied from wages earned by fathers and husbands. This decreased the relative value and importance of the handmade goods traditionally fabricated by women, particularly beginning in the nineteenth century, when most production moved outside the home. The result was a lessened ability of women to contribute to the overall financial welfare of the family and the deepening of their subordinate relegation in the private sphere of domestic arrangements. A tradition of social engagement evolved which left women, in their role as homemakers, increasingly isolated from one another and from interaction in the evolving market economy.[58]

Because women have commonly lacked influence, power, and respect in the traditionally male public sphere of society, they too have been subject to discrimination in access to the forms of credit offered in that world. Accordingly, women have been forced in comparatively greater numbers to turn to whatever alternatives are available to them. Pawnbrokers in particular have historically been the creditor most willing to serve female customers. But even amongst pawnbrokers there is some evidence suggesting that women paid a higher price than male clients, owing in part to the lack of other credit options available to them. Until only recently, even affluent women with extensive security assets had difficulty acquiring low-cost credit without a husband or father serving as a cosigner. In English common law married women lacked the right to contract without the approval of their husbands or other male relatives. The credit options available to ethnic minority women must have been especially narrow.[59]

Many women still report sexist underwriting policies and sales practices. For instance, in 1994 the Federal Trade Commission (FTC) won a significant settlement against a manufactured home lender for refusing to aggregate the income of unmarried co-applicants. By only aggregating the income of married couples, the lender sent a message that female borrowers were only a reliable source of income when attached to a husband. Similarly, in 1999 both Ford Motor Credit Company and the Franklin Acceptance Corporation paid hefty sums to stop FTC lawsuits challenging policies which refused to consider the income of unmarried women in issuing credit. The FTC found Franklin had also discriminated against women whose income came from public assistance and child support payments. Many women report difficulty obtaining low-cost automobile financing. Many also report paying higher prices for car repairs. Because car repairs are a leading cause of high-cost borrowing, many women are forced relatively deeper into high-cost debt than their male counterparts in similar situations.[60]

Today women disproportionately bear the consequences of high-cost debt. Both industry and consumer advocate studies show the typical payday loan borrower is female. One industry-sponsored study found women constitute 62 percent of the payday lenders' clientele. Yet when women borrow from payday lenders, it is more difficult in aggregate terms for them to escape the weekly debt cycle associated with these loans. At the turn of the century, women still earn only about 77 cents for every dollar earned by men. Tracking the high-cost credit boom of the past twenty years, bankruptcy filings by women have grown nearly 800 percent. "Indeed," according to Harvard Law Professor Elizabeth Warren, "women are now the largest demographic group in bankruptcy, outnumbering men by about 150,000 per year." Warren projects over a million American women will declare bankruptcy in 2003—"more than will graduate from four-year colleges."[61]

Because high-cost debt continues to hurt women disproportionately, it is one factor among many preventing progressive and healthy reformation of damaging gender roles. A woman indebted to a payday lender or fighting off foreclosure proceedings on a predatory mortgage loan has no time to advance the cause of women in general through serving on community boards, volunteering, or campaigning for local political office. A woman who loses her car to a car title lender, and then loses her job when she misses the bus, also loses her chance to become a supervisor and hire more women. Historically, the disparities in credit prices offered to women have helped entrench gender roles associated with the public-sphere subordination of women. This continuing side-effect of the high-cost credit boom should be viewed as one more externality associated with the malfunctioning market.

Those without Protection: Children

The often stated and more often implicit "they deserve it" rationale for non-intervention in the high-cost credit market is weakest for those who are most vulnerable. The children of debtors suffer grave consequences from their parents' decisions to borrow at high cost. Children are the largest group of poverty-stricken Americans, comprising 40 percent of all people below that line. "[O]ne of four American children live in poverty, the highest rate across seventeen developed nations."[62] When high-cost debt service payments deplete low-income communities of already meager resources, children are unavoidably deprived of care and opportunities. Parents who devote greater and greater portions of their disposable income to debt service have less money available to provide for their children's food, housing, transportation, clothing, and educational needs. A parent deeply mired in high-cost debt might be more likely to take shelter in a cheaper apartment in a more dangerous neighborhood, where their children undergo greater exposure to violence, drugs, or other social problems. Another parent struggling with high-cost debt might be less likely to save to help the child attend college or purchase a family computer. Moreover, "[t]he struggle to make ends meet might also leave parents with little time to spend with their children or leave them feeling too drained to interact with their children when they are with them," explain three influential sociologists.[63] Studies show economic hardship consistently reduces parental responsiveness, warmth, and supervision while increasing erratic discipline practices and the use of unnecessarily harsh punishments.[64] And, even temporary poverty spells can seriously erode the cognitive capabilities and school-readiness of young children. As these children grow older, they tend to acquire less education, transmitting the consequences of high-cost debt to subsequent generations. Girls raised in poverty are more likely to become teenage mothers. There is nothing to suggest that a relationship between money spent servicing high-cost debt and money spent in a family's child-rearing are zero sum. But there is ample evidence to suggest that when parents face the most difficult problems of indebtedness, these problems inevitably transfer to their children.[65]

The high-cost debt externalities faced by children in single-parent families are particularly acute. Initially, high-cost debt often interferes with the child support payments by absent parents. Children in single-parent families are also less likely to have health insurance, less likely to have a primary earner in a stable job environment, and less likely to have reliable transportation. They are thus more vulnerable to income shocks and the resulting high-cost debt. To this effect, a recent study of bankrupt families found "[h]ouseholds without a male present were nearly twice as likely to file for bankruptcy giving a medical reason or identifying a substantial medical debt as households with a male present."[66] And when debt trouble does occur, single parents have less time and fewer resources to insulate their children from its consequences. For instance, a single mother who takes a second job to pay off a high-cost loan may be forced to leave her children unattended in the evenings. Her children receive less supervision in their television, radio, and internet choices; less help with homework; less access to transportation; and less guidance on interaction with peers. Empirical evidence consistently finds an association between single-parent families and a variety of social, health, and financial impairments. Children in single-parent families are more likely to suffer from high-cost debt and have less ability to overcome it in later years.[67]

The grave consequences of high-cost debt borne by children are in the most fundamental sense an externality. The lost opportunities of the children themselves, as well as our nation's foregone productivity, are not reflected in the prices charged by high-cost lenders and paid by high-cost debtors. Because the children of debtors are not parties to loan agreements, current consumer lending regulations, which focus on the disclosure of key loan costs, offer no protection beyond any warning a parent may or may not heed. The "he got what he deserved" justification for laissez-faire high-cost credit policy is irrelevant in the context of debtors' children. Children never "deserve" to suffer for the financial mistakes of their parents. They are defenseless.

AS IF IT WEREN'T BAD ENOUGH: REFUND ANTICIPATION LOANS, MANDATORY ARBITRATION, AND INVOLUNTARY HIGH-COST CREDIT SUBSIDIES

The normal governmental, legal, and market mechanisms for correcting negative externalities have not succeeded in the high-cost credit market. In part this is due to the defuse and complex nature of high-cost credit itself, but it is also due to the deliberate efforts of high-cost lenders to circumvent government mitigation efforts.

Tricking the Tax Man: Refund Anticipation Loans and the Earned Income Tax Credit

Tax refund anticipation loans and their effects on the earned income tax credit offer a provocative example of high-cost creditor subversion of the very government policies directed toward correcting the poverty often associated with high-cost debt. Tax refund anticipation loans allow consumers to skip the wait for their tax return checks by borrowing against their expected refunds. Tax refund anticipation loans are usually offered by tax document preparation services such as H&R Block and Jackson Hewitt, along with banks working in cooperation with the document preparers. Historically, consumers have been consistently misled into thinking of tax refund anticipation loans as quick refunds rather than loans. Consumers also do not realize that with current electronically-filed refunds available at tax preparation services, the normal wait is only about ten days. In a typical transaction, generalized from H&R Block records, a consumer would pay $121 finance charge for a loan on a $2,500 expected tax return. Scholars with the Brookings Institution estimate out of a $121 finance charge, H&R Block typically keeps about $43 and gives the remaining $78 to its partner, Household Bank. This taxpayer only saves between a week and ten days, since these preparation services all take advantage of the IRS' speedy new electronic filing program. The APR on this typical $2,500 tax return works out to about 250 percent.[68]

In order to lend at such high prices, refund anticipation lenders actively circumvent state interest-rate caps as well as Truth in Lending disclosure. Virtually all refund anticipation loans exceed virtually all state interest-rate caps. But, like payday lenders, H&R Block and other tax preparation services pair up with banks in order to take advantage of the Civil War-era National Bank Act provision, which has been interpreted to allow banks to lend under their home state's interest-rate rules. This allows a tax return preparer to ignore any state's interest-rate cap by paying a fee to a bank located in a state with lax regulations. Under this interpretation of the law, H&R Block is free to charge whatever interest rate it chooses anywhere in the United States, so long as it partners with a bank. Moreover, consumer advocates charge that under current Federal Reserve Board regulations, tax preparation services are allowed to calculate the annual percentage rates based on the almost always false assumption the loan will be repaid over the course of an entire year instead of in a week to ten days. Tax preparation services exploit the rule, often disclosing their loans as having APRs between 1.8 to 21 percent—even though true annual percentage rates are almost always between 67 and 774 percent. Neither are these charges justified by the risk of the loan, since lenders can arrange to have the government directly deposit the tax refund into a temporary bank account set up and controlled by the lender. The tax preparer's low-income, cash-dazzled consumers, who are self-selected by their inability or unwillingness to wade through complex financial documents, never know the difference.[69]

A significant portion of these misleading finance charges are actually *paid by the federal government*. The earned income tax credit program is currently our nation's largest anti-poverty program. Created in 1975, the policy delivers federal financial assistance to working families with children who have incomes below roughly 200 percent of the poverty level, or to individuals and childless couples earning less than about $10,000. The program is dubbed the "earned income tax credit" because eligibility is determined through income tax forms, and the assistance is distributed through families' tax return checks or direct deposits. Although recipients can have the assistance paid in installments, most recipients choose delivery in one lump sum. Widely heralded as an effective and efficient government assistance program, the earned income tax credit "lifts approximately 4.7 million people, over

half of them children, from poverty, more than any other federal program," according to a joint National Consumer Law Center and Consumer Federation of America report.[70]
Tax preparers who cater to less-educated and low-income consumers have flocked like vultures to the earned income tax credit. Recognizing the enormous potential to feed on the displaced generosity of American taxpayers, refund anticipation lenders have clustered in low-income communities during the past decade. A recent geographic study found zip codes home to a high percentage of families qualifying for the earned income tax credit have 50 *percent* more tax preparer outlets than zip codes with few working-poor families. Jackson Hewitt, which has based its recent rapid corporate growth on catering to such families, has an even more skewed concentrated of outlets. As a result, 68 percent of the families qualifying for an earned income tax benefit turn to preparation services to file their returns. Currently, refund anticipation lenders skim the top off of nearly half of all earned income tax refunds. Scholars estimate that in 1999, tax preparers and their bank partners diverted 1.75 billion dollars out of the U.S. Treasury and out of the pockets of the working poor.[71] While industry officials defend refund anticipation loans as a valuable convenience, there is a distinct irony in the arrangement. Intentionally or not, high-cost creditors have found a way to dilute directly the most important anti-poverty program that might otherwise buffer vulnerable debtors from the negative externalities more generally associated with high-cost debt.

Arbitration and the Circumvention of Pigouvian Externality Corrective Liability Rules

In recent years many law and economics scholars have come to view rules which assign liability to individuals and corporations as legal devices to correct for externalities. For instance, in a groundbreaking article, Federal Court of Appeals Judge Guido Calabresi explained that much of tort law is best understood as a relatively crude regime designed to internalize the externally located social costs of production.[72] A playground equipment manufacturer which sells dangerous products to public park agencies risks liability to the parents of children injured on the equipment. The injuries are an externality: the social cost of the accident is not reflected in the private costs of the manufacturer or the equipment purchaser. In this view, liability rules create a quasi-market which aims to raise the private costs of production to approximate the dislocated social costs foisted on third parities. Liability rules provide an incentive for firms to take precautions to protect the safety and health of those not privy to purchasing decisions made by the manufacturer and its customers. Debtor/creditor laws which hold creditors liable for unconscionable business practices and improper disclosure serve a similar externality-corrective role. Even debtor amnesty provisions which merely forgive debts, such as Truth in Lending's recision remedy for improperly disclosed home mortgages, as well as discharge in bankruptcy, are best seen as attempts to address externalities associated with ill-advised credit contracts.[73]

If lender liability for unfair business practices aims to correct the externalities associated with credit contracts, the growing predominance of mandatory binding arbitration clauses is an attempt to circumvent that market correction. Mandatory arbitration clauses are usually fine-print contractual provisions which stipulate the parties will resolve any disputes using a private arbitration company, rather than the courts. Arbitration agreements have been around since before the Federal Arbitration Act of 1925, which attempted to encourage the practice. Congress wanted to decrease the strain of litigation on courts and, more importantly, to provide a low-cost alternative to public litigation. Following the lead of the Supreme Court, courts generally enforce even one-sided arbitration agreements. The decision reached by an arbitrator is final and almost never disturbed by the courts on appeal.[74]

Originally, arbitration clauses were mutually agreed to by parties with equal bargaining power. In the archetypal case cited in favor of mandatory binding arbitration, two merchants agree to waive their respective rights to the court system in the hope of employing a cheaper and faster alternative with simpler discovery rules, greater flexibility, and a less adversarial atmosphere.[75] In recent years, mandatory binding arbitration clauses have become a standard method of shielding corporations from liability under consumer protection statutes. Unlike mutually agreeable decisions amongst merchants, today's mandatory binding arbitration clauses are often made between merchants and their customers. Even if a customer actually reads an arbitration clause, merchants' form contracts are not open to negotiation and are offered on a take-it-or-leave-it basis. By simply inserting an additional clause, many businesses drastically reduce their exposure to liability. Generally unconcerned with whether consumers actually notice the arbitration clause or even understand what it means, a University of Missouri-Columbia law professor notes that courts have upheld "clauses contained in small writing and inconspicuous location in form contracts, in fliers contained in mailings with bills and other statements, in packaging that arrives with a computer, and in medical consent or HMO forms or contracts."[76] As a result, according to University of Houston law professor Stephen Huber, "[a] decade ago consumer arbitration hardly existed. Today it is found everywhere."[77] But nowhere have mandatory binding arbitration clauses caught on more quickly and with such aggressive draftsmanship as in the high-cost credit market.

Consumer advocates and plaintiff attorneys complain high-cost credit arbitration has not proven itself a fair dispute-resolution mechanism since arbitrators have an overwhelming financial incentive to protect lenders. Arbitrators are almost always selected by the lender who drafted the loan contract. Because arbitration companies are financially dependant upon being selected by lenders, arbitrators have a long-term incentive to defer to the wishes of the industry. Those arbitrators who do not comply with industry wishes may have trouble competing with more deferential rivals.

Evidence of impropriety and unfairness in arbitration abounds. Because creditors draft the contracts, they usually contain questionable provisions, selecting inconvenient forums, often in far away cities or states, barring punitive damages, eliminating the right to appeal, and prohibiting class action suits or even joinder with other debtors. Consumer attorneys complain arbitrators make overt suggestions about favorable results in solicitations and advertisements. Creating at the least an appearance of impropriety, some arbitration companies, including the National Arbitration Forum, provides litigation assistance to companies seeking to enforce arbitration clauses in court. The National Arbitration Forum often files *amicus* briefs on behalf of lenders.[78]

The financial forces driving industry-friendly arbitration results are not without precedent. The current system of mandatory binding arbitration clauses bears an uncanny resemblance to late-nineteenth-century practices for compensating justices of the peace and magistrate judges. During America's last high-cost credit boom, the salaries of magistrate judges were paid by litigants' filing fees. Under these systems, salary lenders, the first loansharks and the antecedents to today's payday lenders, only filed their collection lawsuits with sympathetic judges. Judges who refused to participate in the fatuous legal fiction of treating salary loans as an "assignment of future wages" (rather than a loan subject to low state interest-rate caps) simply received no business. But judges who were willing to ignore externality corrective interest-rate caps were busy, respected by the superficial, and rich.[79]

One hundred years later, and under the guise of different names, mandatory arbitration creates similar pockets of suppressed market forces. The mandatory and unilaterally chosen character of arbitration "agreements" have eliminated most or all of the original benefits of alternative dispute resolution. The primary advantage of arbitration used to be the lower costs imposed on parties. Both parties would voluntarily agree to arbitrate because each recognized the benefit of foregoing the more expensive court system. But in today's mandatory arbitration market, businesses, in this case high-cost creditors, have no incentive to choose inexpensive arbitration services. On the contrary, the more costly the up-front arbitration fees, the less likely it is that a consumer will bring a complaint. Not only is there no market competition between rival arbitrators to offer low costs, there is a perverse incentive to incur the *highest* costs. This is because, until the government intervenes, the higher the arbitration costs charged to high-cost debtors, the more attractive the arbitrator is to various creditors. As a bonus, plaintiff attorneys' contingent fee arrangements are no longer an effective method of enforcing externality corrective liability rules since few attorneys are willing to advance to their clients the funds to litigate before an arbiter handpicked by and economically dependant on the lender. The result is a gulf between traditional court filing fees and up-front arbitration fees. According to Joan Claybrook of the nonprofit organization Public Citizen, "the fee to bring an $80,000 claim for an illegal home mortgage in federal court would be $150, as opposed to $11,625 at the National Arbitration Forum or $6,650 at the American Arbitration Association." At least in the high-cost credit market, the claim that arbitration is better and cheaper than civil courts has become little more than an "oft-repeated canard."[80]

High-cost credit arbitration clauses undermine the ability of the courts to apply externality corrective legislation. The rules which seek to protect not only consumers, but in turn society, from ill-advised high-cost credit arrangements are watered down and often ignored entirely through arbitration agreements. Lenders have a financial incentive to displace the costs associated with their products on third parties who were not considered in or protected by the lenders' credit-purchase contracts. Arbitration acts as a buffer against the liability rules which attempt to raise lenders' private costs of engaging in socially destructive lending practices. Once arbitration promised to make markets more efficient by decreasing the costs of dispute resolution. But in today's high-cost credit market, arbitration facilitates inefficient, unfair market outcomes by protecting lenders' ability to foist costs on families and communities.

Sponsoring Your Neighborhood Loanshark: How Debtors' Families and Communities Provide an Involuntary Market Subsidy to High-Cost Lenders

The primary social force for the correction of externalities is neither government benefit payments to affected third parities nor liability rules. In many markets third parities internalize dislocated social costs through private bargains with the externalizing party. As Ronald Coase explained, those who bear the public costs associated with a producer's nuisance externality can contact and negotiate a mutually agreeable solution with the producer.[81] If we assume there are no transaction costs inhibiting bargaining between the victim and the perpetrator, the victim may be willing to pay the perpetrator to have the nuisance removed. Coase uses the example of a neighboring cattle rancher and a farmer. Suppose that without protective measures, such as fencing, the rancher's cattle inevitably escape onto the farmer's land and damage his crops. Other things being equal, the rancher's price for her cattle will not reflect the crop damage costs imposed on the farmer. But if the farmer can, without cost, contact and negotiate with the rancher, he might be willing to pay the rancher to install better fencing or hire additional hands for herding. Presumably, the farmer would be willing to pay for these protective measures until the marginal value of more protection was less than the marginal cost reduction from prevented crop damage. If the amount the farmer were willing to pay to prevent intrusion from the cattle exceeded the rancher's cost in erecting fences and other protective measures, the two would enter into a bargain to do just that. On the other hand, if the farmer's reservation price were less than the rancher's, the cattle would continue to intrude, "but in either case the outcome would be efficient."[82] No externality is present, since the farmer and the rancher have incorporated the social costs into a private transaction. The opportunity to bargain *internalizes* the externality, allowing the market to function efficiently without any government intervention.[83]

In view of what has since been dubbed the Coase theorem, many economists have come to believe the problem of Pigouvian externalities can only develop where transaction costs, such as imperfect information or high administrative costs, prevent the victim of externalization from negotiating a mutually agreeable solution with the producer. While the Coase theorem is good news where externalities develop amongst a small number of sophisticated parties, such as merchants in a long-term commercial relationship, it is small consolation to large, diffuse groups. "In the standard case of a smoke nuisance," Coase writes, "which may affect a vast number of people engaged in a wide variety of activities," the prohibitive administrative and transactional costs make negotiating an efficient bargain "impossible."[84] Like communities downwind from smoke-belching factories, families and communities ravaged by high-cost debt problems cannot cost-effectively negotiate private bargains with high-cost lenders to prevent the harmful social consequences of ill-advised high-cost debt. Because there is no way for the many affected third parties to organize privately and negotiate a mutually agreeable solution with high-cost lenders, high-cost credit prices are involuntarily *subsidized* by those who do not borrow. Drawing on the words of Judge Calabresi, the market gap which prevents charging a high-cost lender with the dislocated social costs of its behavior "leads to an understatement of the true costs of producing its goods; the result is that people purchase more [high-cost credit] than they would want if the true costs were reflected in the price."[85]

Perhaps the reluctance of courts, administrators, and legislatures to protect aggressively families and communities from the high-cost debt spillover effect stems from a failure to recognize these social consequences as externalities. This may be due in part to the non-corporeal nature of credit transactions. Unlike externalities where a side effect of production is pollution, in credit transactions there is no substance to point to. When a steel mill releases smoke into the air, everyone sees and smells the smoke. Credit products have no smell, no physical appearance, and no weight. This is because credit is an idea—a purchased social obligation. Just as the externalities in the manufacture of corporeal steel are also corporeal, so too are the externalities of credit transactions often born of the social ties that create obligations. These ties include those between husband and wife, between parent and child, person and community, and citizen and government. Simply because one cannot see or hold these obligations, they are no less real or influential on market behavior. Where steel manufacturers without adequate pollution abatement technology release harmful chemical compounds into the air, high-cost lenders without adequate disclosure procedures release harmful social dependency, confusion, hopelessness, and financial desperation into the community. Because our species is social, social obligations often provide *the* most important controlling factor on human behavior. If a particular type of transaction impedes the healthy fulfillment of various social obligations, and does so for people not represented in that transaction, then the transaction creates an externality no less real or important than the physical smoke of which Pigou wrote eighty years ago. Just as polluting manufacturers often discharge dangerous carcinogens into the physical means of commerce, so too do high-cost lenders discharge financial discord into the social means of commerce.

CHAPTER 7

Information-Based Regulation of High-Cost Credit: Two Policy Case Studies on Learning How to Learn

I do not feel obliged to believe that the same God who has endowed us with sense, reason, and intellect has intended us to forego their use.

—Galileo

HIGH-COST CREDIT POLICY HAS fallen behind the times. All of the basic policy strategies used to correct high-cost credit problems have origins in past centuries and millennia. The one exception—disclosure rules such as the Truth in Lending Act—is an information-based strategy which predates the widespread use of computers. Truth in Lending's basic approach and technologies have not changed since its passage in 1968. Moreover, rather than protecting low-income borrowers, many credit policy strategies, such as our abandoned use of interest-rate caps and upscale cooperative lending institutions, are now geared toward facilitating the voracious consumer credit demand of the relatively affluent upper and upper-middle classes. Despite the revolution in information technology over the past twenty years, comparatively vulnerable high-cost debtors have not improved their ability to price-shop, organize preferences, or insulate families and communities from the inevitable spillover effects of ill-advised credit decisions. With stagnation or decline in real wages and net worth amongst the working and lower-middle classes, vulnerable borrowers have become less capable of repaying high-cost debts.

In contrast, the high-cost credit industry has been quick to embrace innovative contract and legal strategies, organizational tactics, and new information technology. In the years since Congress passed Truth in Lending, the high-cost credit industry has embraced mandatory arbitration clauses, rapid refinancing practices, prepayment penalties, non-amortizing loans, balloon payments, a host of junk closing costs, high late payment fees, penalty interest rates, and personal check security arrangements. Bank charter renting by payday and tax refund anticipation lenders, mortgage-broker kickbacks and yield spread premiums, as well as credit insurance abuses, have only become widespread in the past two decades. Sophisticated marketing databases, demographic modeling, openly traded telemarketing information, inter-office networking, and automated underwriting guidelines have all increased the productivity of those in the business of transferring wealth away from vulnerable families and communities. Creditors are correct in explaining how each of these contract strategies, organizational tactics, and technological innovations *can* help consumers by giving more options, flexibility, and protection. For instance, if lenders use greater productivity to generate lower operating costs and then pass those costs on in the form of lower prices, consumers *can* benefit. But in the high-cost credit market, where there is no true price-shopping and borrowers consistently make cognitive errors, lenders' greater productivity merely allows deeper penetration into high-risk markets by extracting debts more efficiently. Without meaningful price competition, technological innovation merely allows high-cost creditors to command more of the disposable income of more debtors. The shameless entrance of major corporations and banks into the high-cost credit market has given the ancient industry an infusion of talent and a youthful vigor not seen in at least a hundred years. High-cost debtors and creditors now sit on opposite sides of the digital divide. High-cost lenders are becoming smarter, but borrowers—as well as their advocates and the government agencies charged with protecting them—are not.

High-cost credit policymakers need to innovate. What follows are plausible suggestions to refine disclosure rules, drawing lessons from regulatory strategies that address social and economic problems analogous to those found in the high-cost credit market. Case studies of two promising policies are presented. First, the medical doctrine of informed consent may offer useful lessons in understanding and comparing credit prices. And second, the evolution of health hazard warnings on tobacco products and advertisements suggest an inexpensive method of encouraging rational preference ordering and recapturing social leadership.

FROM TRUTH TO UNDERSTANDING: A HIGH-COST CREDIT INFORMED CONSENT DOCTRINE

Many American legal strategies attempt to address social problems by helping an uninformed individual or group understand the costs of a choice or agreement. Food and Drug Administration nutrition labels aim to help consumers make healthy eating decisions. The Supreme Court has required police to apprise criminal suspects of their *Miranda* warnings prior to custodial interrogation. Similarly, judges must conduct a colloquy of questions and explanations with criminal defendants prior to accepting a guilty plea. Companies with publicly traded stock must disclose earnings information to the Securities Exchange Commission for the benefit of small investors. Political candidates must disclose the source and dollar amount of campaign contributions, in part to help voters evaluate those candidates. Each of these communication-based policies has different strengths and weaknesses and each is designed to fit within the context of the problem it addresses.

In searching for a cure for the feverish high-cost lending market, it is perhaps appropriate that we turn first to a medical doctrine for lessons which might help treat high-cost credit market imperfections. The doctrine of informed consent addresses problems structurally analogous to those addressed by high-cost credit price disclosure. Both attempt to compel an informed party to share information with an uninformed party. Both hope to empower an uninformed individual with the information needed to make a responsible choice. Both deal with uncertain consequences—in one case the risks of medical procedures, and in the other indeterminate future repayment. Both referee a relationship with an imbalance in bargaining power. Both anticipate the prevention of fraud and duress against an uninformed party. Both struggle with practical limitations to implementing theoretical goals. Both deal with an often reluctant informed party. Both deal with an often unsophisticated uninformed party. And both seek to balance the implementation costs of the rule with gains in individual autonomy. In much the same way that debtors have traditionally had difficulty understanding credit prices, so too have patients had difficulty understanding the risks associated with medical procedures. Surgeries may entail hidden future risks, physical therapy can include a long and painful commitment, and drug treatments can cause side effects worse than the disease. In order to protect patients' ability to choose well, medical practitioners are usually expected not simply to obtain the consent of a patient, but first to help the patient understand the possible consequences the treatment might entail. By requiring doctors to explain potential side effects and alternative treatment options, the medical doctrine of informed consent seeks to empower individual patients with autonomy, self-respect, and greater health.

The Evolution of Informed Consent: Medical Beneficence and the Rise of Autonomy

Doctors have an ancient tradition of ambivalence toward informing patients about their treatment and acting on the wishes of those patients. Professor Jay Katz, a leading medical historian, explains "[d]isclosure in medicine has served the function of getting patients to 'consent' to what physicians wanted them to agree to in the first place," not unlike disclosure in the high-cost credit market.[1] The earliest documents espousing medical philosophy show doctors are inclined to treat patients consistent with their judgments rather than with the values and choices of the patient. The Hippocratic Oath makes no mention of the need to explain the risks of a proposed treatment or to solicit agreement from a patient. Instead, the oath suggests "concealing most things from the patient, while attending to him . . . turning his attention away from what is being done to him; . . . [and] revealing nothing of the patient's future or present condition."[2] Because the primary task of the physician was to prevent harm to patients, doctors were instructed to foster the patient's confidence and trust—even through deception if necessary. What constituted harm or injustice was a matter for the doctor's, not the patient's, consideration. Where there was a disagreement about what was best for the patient, doctors were to follow their own opinions. This approach to making medical decisions, called "Hippocratic authoritarianism," is the archetype of the disposition in medical culture towards a beneficence model of decision-making.[3]

Hippocratic beneficence has exerted immense influence over medical ethics and clinical behavior in the Western tradition. By the Middle Ages, written medical philosophy generally espoused the view that doctors should engage in manipulation and deceit in pursuit of what the doctor viewed as the patient's best interests. For instance, the French surgeon Henri de Mondeville (ca. 1260–1325) instructed his pupils to "promise a cure to every patient, but . . . tell the parents or the friends if there is any danger."[4] Some Enlightenment medical theorists began to acknowledge that patients had a very narrow role in making decisions about their treatment. But, by and large, describes Katz, the "traditional view that physicians must assume sole responsibility for protecting the ignorant public from its folly" dominated the medical profession.[5]

Although early American culture followed the European tradition, our cultural and legal commitment to individualism, autonomy, and freedom began to chip away at medical paternalism early in the twentieth century.[6] For example, in 1914, Supreme Court Justice Benjamin Cardozo famously opined in the *Schloendorff v. Society of New York Hospital* case that "[e]very human being of adult years and sound mind has a right to determine what shall be done with his own body; and a surgeon who performs an operation without his patient's consent commits an assault, for which he is liable in damages."[7] This approach to preserving patient autonomy required doctors to obtain consent before touching the patient. However, a doctor obtained legal consent merely by informing the patient of the nature of the proposed touching. Failure to do so was legally a battery, just as any other unwanted touching might be, even if the patient was not injured. Moreover, physical injury was not necessary to show a doctor's liability. Nevertheless, this intentional tort approach to consent had a serious limitation. Doctors could obtain consent without allowing the patient any meaningful choice simply by withholding the true potential consequences of the procedure. For example, a physician could simply disclose he was about to preform a routine surgery, leaving out information on the risks of the procedure.[8]

Commentators generally agree informed consent as we now know it was born in the 1957 California Court of Appeals decision in *Salgo v. Leland Stanford Jr. University Board of Trustees*.[9] Martin Salgo was a 55-year-old man suffering from cramping pains in his leg. Under the advice of his doctor, Salgo underwent a diagnostic procedure involving the insertion of a needle through his back into his aorta to deploy a dye which would appear under x-rays. When Salgo awoke the next morning he was permanently paralyzed below the waist. He later argued that he was not informed of the risks of the diagnostic procedure. In considering whether the doctor had failed in his duty to explain the dangers of the test, the court stated "[a] physician violates his duty to his patient and subjects himself to liability if he withholds any facts which are necessary to form the basis of an intelligent consent by the patient to the proposed treatment." Relying on *Schloendorff*, the court ordered the jury be instructed that the physician was required to disclose medical risks "consistent, of course, with the full disclosure of facts necessary to an informed consent."[10]

Three years later the Kansas Supreme Court more firmly pioneered the doctrine of informed consent in *Natanson v. Kline*. Irma Natanson sued her radiologist after an experimental cobalt radiation treatment for breast cancer burnt beyond recognition her left chest and rib cage. Natanson acknowledged that she consented to the treatment but argued that "the nature and consequences of the risks of the treatment were not properly explained to her." Distinguishing the traditional battery approach, the *Natanson* court allowed recovery under a negligence theory of tort. The Kansas majority found that the radiologist failed to warn Natanson adequately of the inherent risks of cobalt radiation therapy, which was then a new, unstable, and poorly understood treatment. The court's landmark decision held the law:

> in effect compels disclosure by the physician in order to assure that an informed consent of the patient is obtained. The duty of the physician to disclose, however, is limited to those disclosures which a reasonable medical practitioner would make under the same or similar circumstances. How the physician may best discharge his obligation to the patient in

this difficult situation involves primarily a question of medical judgment. So long as the disclosure is sufficient to assure an informed consent, the physician's choice of plausible courses should not be called into question if it appears, all circumstances considered, that the physician was motivated only by the patients's best therapeutic interests and he proceeded as competent medical men would have done in a similar situation.[11]

This new negligence-based reasoning formed the basis for the current doctrine of informed consent in all but a few states. Under this rule, a doctor must explain the risks of treatment to help the patient understand the implications of the patient's treatment choice. If the doctor fails to make a reasonable effort to help her patient understand, she is exposed to potential liability. How much information a physician is required to give depends on an estimate of what a reasonable doctor in the situation would explain. After *Natanson v. Kline*, patients had the right to expect information with which to make their own choices about health care.[12]

The final case necessary for a basic understanding of informed consent came in 1972. In *Canterbury v. Spence*, the U.S. Court of Appeals for the District of Columbia developed a new standard for determining how far a doctor is required to go in helping a patient understand the risks of a proposed treatment. In that case, a 19-year-old man suffered paralysis and permanent incontinence after agreeing to undergo back surgery. Instead of basing disclosure on what a reasonable doctor might consider appropriate, the D.C. Circuit Court of Appeals required that doctors disclose so a reasonable patient might understand. The court argued customary medical practice should merely offer evidence on the adequacy of disclosure, rather than itself defining the standard. Instead "the patient's right of self determination shapes the boundaries of the duty to reveal."[13]

Following the *Canterbury* decision, many jurisdictions quickly adopted similar approaches to informed consent. Today a slight majority of states retain the reasonable practitioner standard advanced in *Natanson*, with most of the remainder adopting the *Canterbury* "reasonable patient" position. During the eighties and nineties some legislatures and commentators have questioned whether there has been an overemphasis on autonomy in medicine. Moreover, several important defenses have evolved. Nevertheless, informed consent has entrenched itself as an important aspect of American health law.[14] For every scholar willing to criticize the doctrine, another looks to expand its influence to other social issues, including engineering, workplace hazards, the nuclear power industry, and even geography.[15] Moreover, some scholars have argued for much greater protections of patient autonomy, including an actual patient standard of disclosure, where liability would turn on whether each individual patient understood a doctor's disclosures. Informed consent has similarly achieved wide acceptance in bioethics, leading one writer to assert, "there are relatively few bioethicists who argue that respect for autonomy is not the preeminent value governing the actions of health care providers."[16]

Understanding vs. Truth in Producing Informed Decisions: Lessons for High-Cost Credit Policy

There is little agreement about what constitutes informed consent. Bioethicists tend to describe informed consent in terms of whether or not a patient has had sufficient information to enable an autonomous decision. Thus, for bioethicists, informed consent is "an ethical doctrine, rooted in our society's cherished value of autonomy, that insures to patients their right of self-determination when medical decisions need to be made."[17] Others emphasize that informed consent is not one simple act, but is rather an exchange between a doctor and a patient:

> Consent is a process, not a form. . . . [C]onsent is the dialogue between the patient and the provider of services in which both parties exchange information and questions culminating in the patient's agreeing to a specific medical or surgical intervention. On the one hand, the patient needs certain basic details in order to decide whether to a accept the treatment. On the other, the physician also needs information from the patient in order to tailor the disclosure of risks and benefits to him. This process, if it is to be effective, requires active participation of both parties.
>
> A document called a consent form can never replace the exchange of information between a patient and a health care provider.[18]

Finally, legal doctrine recognizes a narrow definition of informed consent based on whether physicians make reasonable disclosures. As the D.C. Circuit Court of Appeals decision explained:

> While we recognize the general utility of shorthand phrases in literary expositions, we caution that uncritical use of the "informed consent" label can be misleading. . . . In duty to disclose cases, the focus of attention is more properly upon the nature and content of the physician's divulgence than the patient's understanding or consent. Adequate disclosure and informed consent are, of course, two sides of the same coin—the former a *sine qua non* of the latter. But the vital inquiry on duty to disclose relates to the physician's performance of an obligation, while one of the difficulties with analysis in terms of "informed consent" is its tendency to imply that what is decisive is the degree of the patient's com-

prehension. As we later emphasize, the physician discharges
the duty when he makes a reasonable effort to convey sufficient information although the patient, without fault of the
physician, may not fully grasp it.[19]

However, even in this narrow legal sense of the term, the underlying objective of the rule is to promote understanding on the
part of an otherwise uninformed person. In practice and in law, informed consent aims to promote *informed* decision-making by
helping the patient understand her choice. Distilling the principle
might yield:

*Lesson #1: Disclosure rules should attempt to promote understanding
rather than mere truth.*

Like informed consent, consumer credit disclosures aim to create informed choices. But, unlike informed consent practices and
rules, consumer credit disclosure legislation focuses not on promoting true *understanding*, but upon promoting *truth*. Case law interpreting consumer credit disclosure rules makes little or no
reference to whether a debtor actually understood the terms of a
loan. Instead, debate focuses on whether the loan contract included disclosure provisions satisfying federal code requirements.
And, in turn, the federal code is preoccupied with whether disclosures truthfully and completely describe the true cost of the loan.
If the value one hopes to promote is the informed use of credit, the
means to that end must not be merely true descriptions of loans,
but also *understood* descriptions of loans.[20]

In crafting rules, a focus on understanding helps to avoid the
problems of overly complex disclosures. There are often instances
where a true disclosure will not advance a patient's or a debtor's understanding of the choices at hand. Courts applying informed consent law focus on the promotion of understanding by requiring

doctors to disclose only those risks which are material to a patient's choice in undergoing a proposed treatment. "For example," notes Professor Fay Rozovsky, "patients who undergo hemodialysis three times a week do not need to be informed of the risks each and every time they report for treatment." Similarly, doctors are not usually required to disclose very remote risks.[21] Moreover, a focus on whether a party understood disclosures helps allow courts to look beyond boilerplate formalities such as consent forms. Professor Paul Applebaum has explained that in most states consent forms "actually provide very little legal protection."[22] Or, as the Maryland Court of Appeals wrote, a signed consent form is "simply one additional piece of evidence for the jury to consider. . . . [U]nless a person has been adequately apprised of the material risks and therapeutic alternatives incident to a proposed treatment, any consent given, be it oral or written, is necessarily ineffectual."[23] By comparison, Truth in Lending liability turns on the compliance of boilerplate forms with regulations, regardless of whether a debtor read or even had an opportunity to read the forms. In order for government regulation to promote meaningful price competition, consumer understanding will ultimately have to supplant accurate price description as the criterion of successful disclosure.[24]

A renewed focus on price understanding in the context of high-cost credit is not beyond our capabilities. Recent advances in industry-, community-, and government-sponsored home purchase and credit counseling hint at a future where disclosure regulations might focus on price comprehension, rather than mere contractual truth. For instance, the laws governing reverse mortgage disclosure have recognized the need for price understanding is especially acute when a family home is at stake. Reverse mortgages are designed to produce income for cash-poor/house-rich senior citizens by gradually selling the senior's home back to a bank. The house is usually turned over to the purchasing bank upon the senior's death. Federal law currently *requires* that individuals contemplating reverse mortgages undergo pre-transaction counseling through the Department of Housing and Urban Development's Home Equity Conversion Program. HUD has also taken a positive but incomplete step in the right direction by advocating that Congress should require creditors to recommend certified home counseling to high-cost home mortgage loan applicants. Similarly, Chicago's National Center on Poverty Law has brought together banks, regulators and other community groups in its "Financial Links for Low-Income People" initiative. This program offers low-income participants who complete financial literacy classes a no-fee, no-minimum balance savings account and Illinois Department of Human Services matched funds for savings of up to $1,000. Some progressive credit unions have also successfully expanded membership in lower-income households by relying on one-on-one counseling. While history suggests the charitable resources and cooperative spirit of these programs will inevitably fall short, it does demonstrates industry and consumer advocates can work together to promote government policies which in turn promote financial literacy.[25]

The nonprofit Homeowner Options for Massachusetts Elders, or H.O.M.E. program, goes further. In cooperation with federal and state regulators, this federally supported group has organized a collection of sixty-three Massachusetts lenders who, in exchange for participation in the program, agree to lend only to elders who have received counseling by an independent third party *before consummation* of any mortgage loan.[26] Price understanding in general, and pre-transaction counseling in particular, should not be an optional charitable programs, but should be incorporated into federal disclosure law as doctrinal requirements. In smaller high-cost credit contracts such as payday loans, pawnshop loans, and rent-to-own transactions, it would not be cost-effective to require pre-transaction counseling. But a renewed focus on understanding could still provide great benefits of consumers. Federal disclosure regulations should incorporate elements of Texas' new "plain English" rules which require creditors to leave out incomprehensible jargon and use only the most simple syntax in writing credit contracts. Credit disclosure regulations must be *scientifically tested* to ensure those with only the most rudimentary literacy skills can understand them. In the case of more complex high-cost home mortgages, a focus on understanding argues for independent pre-transactional counseling prior to the consummation of every high-cost home mortgage.

Understanding as a Counterweight to Autonomy: Diagnosed Understanding in High-Risk Circumstances

In order for informed consent to occur, a patient must be able to understand the information provided to her. But some patients, such as those who arrive unconscious in hospital emergency rooms, are unable to understand anything at all. In these cases, doctors may temporarily dispense with informed consent in deciding the patient's course of treatment. More difficult cases are those where individuals are conscious, but still incapable of understanding the medical information needed to make an informed decision on a procedure. Such a patient might be incompetent to accept or reject a proposed treatment, and thus their choices may be put to one side.[27] Doctors determine the competence of patients to consent through assessing the psychological and intellectual capabilities of their patients. Often they will give competency assessment tests which aim to measure the abilities of disabled patients and help the clinician make an informed decision about the patient's capability. Among other things, these tests are intended to assess the patient's apprehension of his disorder, his understanding of the treatment's risks, and of the treatment itself. Although the test results are not intended to determine the physician's decision on whether a patient will be considered competent to make treatment decisions, it is a method which structures and guides assessment interviews, and a patient's performance can strongly influence doctors.[28]

In normal circumstances, competency to consent to treatment is not an issue, because as Becky White explains, "there is no reason to question the patient's competence. Just as the law assumes people are innocent until proven guilty, clinicians generally presume patients are competent until their incompetence is proven or until there are good reasons to suspect it." When patients behave erratically, or express interest in an extremely risky treatment option, standard medical practice is to question whether the patient truly understands the danger. "Competence does not vanish just because professional decisions are contested, nor does compliance guarantee its presence. The point is that refusing therapies that will most likely restore health or minimize disability triggers the suspicion that patient decision-making abilities are impaired." Although consent is commonly cloaked in language of "competency," what is at issue, speaking generally, is whether the patient understands the risks of a decision. When patients cannot understand the situation so as to make a decision about treatment, doctors will not allow the patient to proceed with his choices. The heightened risk in such circumstances necessitates that doctors suspend a patient's treatment choice until the doctor can diagnose the patient as capable of understanding the situation. Although distasteful in a society which values individual choices, "[a]ssessing competence is the necessary first step in the process of obtaining informed consent. If the patient is not competent, he is not the appropriate decision maker. . . . Unless determinations of patient competence are possible, the validity of consents cannot be assured."[29] The overall policy objective of informed consent is only served when individuals make decisions that take into account the potential consequences of those choices. By refusing to proceed where the ability of a patient to make an informed decision is in doubt, health care providers ensure that the autonomous decisions remain pure. This brings us to:

Lesson #2: In high-risk circumstances, do not proceed without diagnosed understanding.

In informed consent, where a decision threatens to undermine the integrity of the policy, the decision does not proceed. This protects the autonomy and well-being of all concerned by only allowing rationally informed medical decisions. In high-cost credit negotiations, there is no equivalent guarantee of an informed decision. Homeowners who repeatedly refinance their mortgages with virtually no benefit to themselves engage in behavior so risky impartial observers must suspect something is amiss in these borrowers' decision-making. High-cost debtors' willingness to agree to payday loans with annual percentage rates in excess of 1000 percent provides strong evidence that some procedure is needed to preserve informed decision-making. The great personal and financial risks associated with high-cost debt provide a forceful argument for considering an assessment procedure theoretically similar to competency assessments used in obtaining informed consent. Bioethicists recognize that even the highly esteemed value of autonomy must sometimes be set aside when it is exercised by a patient without informational capacity and will cause serious consequences for the patient and perhaps society. The harmful consequences of uninformed high-cost credit decisions are every bit as serious and much more common than many contemplated in medicine. Moreover, at least in medicine, the uninformed party is protected by the doctor. Thus, to the extent informed consent and Truth in Lending are disanalogous, these differences argue for greater protection of high-cost debtor understanding and autonomy. Healthcare practitioners have a shared professional interest with their patients in healthful outcomes. Physicians have a long cultural tradition of sincere caring. They are consistently members of widespread and influential societies dedicated to professionalism. And medical practitioners tend to have a robust fear of tort liability. High-cost lenders, however, have *no shared incentive with debtors, no culture of beneficence, only limited professional associations*, and a *long history of successfully evading liability*. If anything, the procedures designed to protect high-cost debtor autonomy should be *more* robust than patient protection procedures, rather than less. A policy where no course of action is undertaken until *after* an informed decision has been made is even more suited to the communication and decision-making realities of high-cost lending than it is to medical treatment decisions.

A high-cost credit price understanding assessment strategy could be structured as a pedagogical tool to help debtors understand the serious risks of their behavior. If high-cost debtors were required to demonstrate price understanding on loan application forms, they would be less likely to ratify a creditor's subsequent application approval. Debtors might also avoid the trap of failing to adjust their first impressions by requiring accurate price understanding early in the loan negotiation process. If all high-cost debtors had to demonstrate a basic understanding of a loan in order to have the loan application approved, it would be against creditors' interests to pressure debtors not to read the loan's basic contractual provisions. Debtors could no longer succumb to information overload. And, over the long term, such a policy would improve the overall familiarity and comfort with credit terms for the people who need such familiarity the most.

The obvious concern is that individuals should be free to make contracts without understanding them if they choose to do so.[30] Certainly this is true as a general rule. There are, however, many exceptions. People cannot make contracts to practice law without first passing a "competency assessment" known as the bar exam. The same is true in medicine, engineering, and real estate appraisal, to name only a few. Even the most basic freedom to move about is constrained by competency assessments. Individuals cannot drive cars without first proving a basic level of traffic rule comprehension. Moreover, those seeking to contract for the purchase of firearms are often required to pass hunters' safety courses. Finally, people cannot make contracts for the purchase of many of our most effective medicines without first demonstrating to a state-licensed medical practitioner an actual need and some form of competency to take the medicine in the way the doctor will prescribe. The freedom to contract, like all freedoms, is subject to limitations in a democratic society.

A rule requiring debtors to demonstrate credit price understanding prior to completing a transaction is not without precedent. Several states require notaries to assess the competence and willingness of home mortgage borrowers when notarizing deed transfers or liens. For instance, in Georgia notaries cannot be compelled to notarize a document where the notary "feels such act is ... for a person whose demeanor causes compelling doubts about whether the person knows the consequences of the transaction requiring the notarial act."[31] A persuasive case can be made for expanding this approach by requiring that notaries conduct simple mental competency exams on elderly mortgage borrowers. This would deter scam artists who prey on desperate and cognitively impaired elderly homeowners going through foreclosure proceedings.[32]

A more generally applicable model for demonstrated price understanding can be found in the laws governing federally subsidized student loan programs. Congress requires colleges and universities to provide loan counseling to students before any student can borrow federally subsidized student loans. Many universities have adapted to the requirement by designing student loan orientations on university computers and over the internet. Computer counseling programs include *detailed tests which students must pass prior to receiving student loan funds.* These tests examine students' understanding of basic credit concepts and personal financial planning, as well as some of the important laws which could effect their repayment plans in future years. In most programs, after passing the test, students receive a certificate indicating they have completed their pre-transaction counseling. Placing a hurdle in the path of students helps to foster basic financial literacy. But more importantly, they all but guarantee that no American student can borrow federally subsidized loans without a tested demonstration of the borrowers' credit knowledge. Theoretically similar to medical competency tests, student loan orientation tests are a relatively cheap and effective procedural device for preventing uninformed and ill-advised credit decisions. It reflects badly on the equitable undercurrents of our credit disclosure rules that they provide a technologically advanced understanding assessment device for relatively well off and educated college students, when working-poor high-cost debtors receive only cursory and boilerplate lender-drafted documents long after all the real decisions have already been made. Testing procedural devices for student loans are particularly generous when one realizes federally subsidized loans are among the safest and lowest cost credit options available to American consumers. If anything, working-poor debtors borrowing high-cost chain debt to finance daily consumption are more in need of procedural safeguards than are our future college graduates.[33]

The costs and implementation problems for a similar high-cost credit policy could be tempered by requiring that debtors demonstrate a basic understanding of the prices of their individual loans. Many critics of informed consent argue that most patients can never truly understand the risks of treatment options because they lack medical and scientific training. So too have critics of price disclosure argued that debtors can never truly understand credit bargains. For example, some have suggested that a genuinely informed and rational credit decision is beyond the capabilities of consumers, since it cannot be made without understanding judicial case law which controls who will pay how much in the event of default.[34] This overstates the problem and ignores important gradations of understanding. Just because most high-cost debtors will never understand pre-default contractual posturing, it does not follow that with understanding of basic prices, consumers, especially poor and undereducated consumers, will not be a great deal more capable to protect their own best interests.

For the nation's vulnerable borrowers, Truth in Lending and other state disclosure rules at best provide the *opportunity* to understand credit contracts. For a variety of reasons, virtually all high-cost debtors have not been able to capitalize on this opportunity. Like college students applying for student loans, high-cost debtors do not need opportunities, they need results. They need a law which is aimed at guaranteeing high-cost credit bargains are not sealed until the debtor does in fact understand at least the basic provisions of the bargain. Truth in Lending law should not allow creditors to lend money at high costs without first making sure both creditors and debtors have made a genuine effort at informed borrowing.

Price is Relative: The Disclosure of Alternatives in Overcoming Cost Barriers to Shopping

Informed consent doctrine requires disclosure of not only the risks of a proposed treatment, but also the risks of feasible alternatives to the treatment.[35] Moreover, for medical practitioners the risk of losing the revenue of a procedure to a competing hospital or doctor is not a reasonable justification for failing to disclose an alternative procedure. The Wisconsin Supreme Court recently went so far as to hold material a doctor's failure

(1) to divulge the extent of his experience in performing . . . [a particular] type of operation; (2) to compare the morbidity and mortality rates for this type of surgery among experienced surgeons and inexperienced surgeons like himself; and (3) to refer the plaintiff to a tertiary care center staffed by physicians more experienced in performing the same surgery.[36]

The court argued that because the doctrine of informed consent requires disclosure of all alternatives and risks which might be material to a patient's choices, an inexperienced doctor could not hide the fact that experience might have a substantial impact on the efficacy of the procedure.[37] Theorists defend this position on the grounds that informed consent is premised on the assumption that healthcare should be provided in line with the patient's values. Various treatment options for the same medical condition can reflect the values of different people. In order to truly empower patients with control over their medical destinies, they must have knowledge of medically acceptable options and the risks and benefits associated with each option.[38] This principle yields:

Lesson #3: Disclosure must include reasonable alternatives.

Like medical patients, high-cost creditors must be able to compare the reasonably available alternatives to a contemplated loan. Because shopping costs in the high-cost credit market prohibit effective comparison of credit prices, lenders have little or no incentive to price their products competitively. Even if prospective debtors have a great deal of information about any one given loan product, this information will not drive competition without comparison of loan prices offered by different lenders. This conundrum regarding high-cost debt can just as succinctly be expressed, as one commentator does, in terms of laundry detergent.

[T]he complaint that consumers do not have sufficient information available for intelligent decisions misses the point. . . . Even if all relevant information on, for example, laundry detergents, could be printed on packages, comparisons of price and quality would still be required. Search calls not only for collecting information on the individual brands and versions of the product in question but for comparing brands as well. What is needed, therefore, is not so much *more* information but rather more *efficient* information, that is, information not only "complete" but also provided in a form which permits comparisons with maximum efficiency. This would lead to a reduction in the incremental cost of search, and so the process would be pushed further than if these conditions were not met.[39]

In most markets we hardly notice the technology and organizational arrangements which permit cost-effective price comparison. Grocery stores shelve all of their laundry detergent products in one aisle so consumers can quickly compare prices. Different brands of laundry detergent are not located at opposite ends of the store. Similarly, medical patients could not assemble all the scientific evidence and medical training necessary to compare various treatment options without their medical practitioner's assistance. The disclosure of alternative treatments in informed consent is an effort to facilitate efficient comparison of potential choices.

Unlike grocery stores and medical practices, the high-cost lending market and the disclosure rules governing it do not facilitate efficient price comparison. High-cost debtors' relatively limited shopping capabilities, lenders' active construction of barriers to price comparison, and the complex nature of most credit documents all inhibit efficient shopping. In comparison, mainstream lending markets have developed extremely efficient methods of comparing price information. Investors considering lending money to publically traded corporations have access to daily stock price listings every day in every major newspaper across the country. Collected bond price listings are also easy to find.

Reform-minded consumer advocates and government leaders have for years crept toward the policies which attempt to make price comparison faster and easier for vulnerable borrowers. Some state small-loan laws have included an ineffective attempt to reduce shopping costs by requiring that lenders post interest rates on signs in their offices. Moreover, in the late 1970s the Senate contemplated directing the Federal Reserve Board to experiment with the preparation and dissemination of APR brochures for this purpose. Scholars have half-heartedly posited and then dismissed similar programs using newspaper listings. A small minority of court decisions also hint at the importance of efficient price comparison. But each of these policies and suggestions have eventually been dismissed as either too slow, too haphazard, or too expensive.[40]

New information technology may have made these strategies feasible for the first time in human history. Up-to-date comparative price lists for mainstream, moderately-priced consumer credit are now common on the internet. Private internet companies have begun to provide comparative price information on more moderately-priced standard-duration mortgage loans, credit cards, and auto loans. At least one organization provides a similar service in purchased newspaper advertising space. However, these new listing services are based on voluntary participation of lenders, and therefore have not attracted high-cost creditors, who rarely wish to advertise their prices. That market forces alone led to the development of alternative price listing services for mainstream credit further demonstrates breakdown in the high-cost loan market.[41]

Hoping to facilitate efficient price comparison amongst its citizens, the New York State Legislature requires the New York State Banking Department to publish price information on credit card lenders doing business within its borders. For every credit card issuer, a summary of available open-ended credit plans lists annual percentage rates for purchases and cash advances, grace periods, annual fees, late payment fees, and over-the-limit fees. The Department also lists annual percentage rates, fees, and conditions for auto loans. For home mortgages the website lists terms including annual percentage rates, interest rates, points, down payment requirements, and application fees. The website also compiles the average interest rate for different types of loans as well as the lowest and highest offered rates. Telephone numbers and addresses are listed for each lender, allowing consumers to inquire further if they have more detailed questions. Savvy mainstream credit shoppers can log on and find the best credit bargains in the state of New York in a matter of minutes.[42]

These valuable services are not provided to high-cost debtors, and the great majority of high-cost debtors would not know how to take advantage of them if they were available. No internet service lists the prices of payday, pawnshop, or rent-to-own loans. Price lists for automobile loans and home mortgages do not assume problem credit histories. Contrary to standard medical informed consent practices, where doctors provide the most careful disclosure of alternative procedures when the risks of treatment are highest, in our national credit market, cost-effective alternative price information is least available where it is most needed. If potential high-cost debtors were given access to information about the prices of similarly accessible credit each time they applied for a loan, debtors would have not just the tools to search out cost comparisons as provided by Truth in Lending, but actual cost comparisons at their fingertips. If society could feasibly implement such a strategy, high-cost debtors would at last have a "meaningful disclosure of credit terms" as originally contemplated by the Congressional statement of purpose under the Truth in Lending Act.[43] The legal doctrine of informed consent cannot be transplanted into high-cost credit law. But the theoretical principles which drive informed consent do point toward ways to improve credit disclosure law.

FROM UNDERSTANDING TO WISDOM: HIGH-COST CREDIT FINANCIAL HAZARD WARNINGS

Truth in Lending price disclosures bear many similarities to cigarette packaging and advertising health hazard warning labels. Both try to encourage consumers to make healthy and responsible decisions. Where cigarette warning labels seek to help consumers make physically healthy choices, TILA disclosures seek to help consumers make financially healthy choices. Where cigarettes create shackling addiction, high-cost credit creates coinciding cyclical use patterns. Conflicted cultural values have historically insulated both products from government regulation and social disapproval generally. Powerful and active industrial lobbies back both products and have actively concealed their harmful side effects. And most essentially, many high-cost debtors and many smokers base their demand on preferences for products they would be better off not purchasing. Accordingly, this section looks for lessons applicable to high-cost lending from our experiences with cigarette health hazard warnings.

Social Norms, the Intractability of Tobacco, and the Rise of Health Consciousness

Tobacco was widely consumed in North America prior to the arrival of European explorers and colonists. Like other New World agricultural products, such as potatoes and tomatoes, tobacco rapidly permeated European culture with "royalty, physicians, and philosophers" giving "glowing reports of its medicinal properties."[44] Nevertheless, some European and American leaders had misgivings about the wisdom and morality of tobacco use. John

Quincy Adams, for example, smoked and chewed tobacco as a young man, but later came to vigorously gainsay its use. Adams stopped using tobacco after a three-month struggle to quit. In a noted 1845 letter he wrote:

> I have often wished . . . that every individual . . . afflicted with this artificial passion could force it upon himself to try but for three months the experiment which I made, sure that it would turn every acre of tobacco land into a wheatfield, and add five years to the average human life.[45]

Still, the economy of much of the Southern colonies before and after the Revolutionary War focused on the production and export of tobacco as a cash crop to Europe. In the early United States, adult males were the principal consumers of tobacco products, with consumption growing at a gradual but steady pace.[46]

In the 1880s a cigarette rolling machine made the mass production of cigarettes economically feasible. Near the turn of the last century, growing quantities of easily consumed, inexpensive cigarettes fostered fear that tobacco on this scale would erode the moral fiber of society. Unlike chewing and pipe tobacco, cigarettes were relatively palatable to women and relatively accessible to children. By 1890, twenty-six states had passed legislation forbidding the sale of cigarettes to minors. But by 1909, these fears had developed into a full-fledged prohibition movement where the sale of cigarettes was banned altogether in seventeen states. Unlike contemporary anti-tobacco efforts, this movement focused on tobacco use as a moral issue rather than a health issue. Tobacco, and cigarettes in particular, were thought by many to be morally debilitating.[47]

However, the antismoking movement faltered after World War I.[48] In the 1920s, factors, including the association of cigarettes with (masculine) returning soldiers, effective marketing to women, and a growing connection between cigarettes and a new stylish urban lifestyle all contributed to a widespread acceptance of cigarettes. Later, the failure of alcohol prohibition, the Hollywood glamorization of smoking, and free distribution of cigarettes to soldiers in World War II solidified the tobacco industry's social, market, and legal gains. In the early 1920s all legislation banning the sale of cigarettes was repealed. By the 1930s and 1940s the ranks of smokers were rapidly expanding while the social acceptability of the practice became almost unquestioned.[49]

It was not until the mid-1950s, when scientists began to develop more sophisticated epidemiological studies, that questioning of cigarette smoking again resurfaced. The results showed dramatic statistical correlations between smoking, the incidence of certain diseases, and even death. Although the tobacco industry aggressively contradicted the scientific evidence, mounting data would soon render their protests hollow. By the early 1960s, scientific evidence had escalated to the point that influential leaders began to take notice. For example, Lee Fritschler recounts a story from 1962 when a reporter surprised President John F. Kennedy at a live televised news conference by asking the president what he intended to do about health concerns over smoking. After an embarrassing pause Kennedy admitted that he did not have enough information to comment and would respond next week. Fritschler writes, "[a]s a result of the press conference, . . . [Kennedy] was now publically committed to initiating some action within the bureaucracy." Soon after the conference, Kennedy initiated actions in the Public Health Service which led directly to a high-level advisory committee study ultimately culminating in the famous Surgeon General's report of 1964.[50] That report summarized previous scientific studies on the consequences of smoking concluding, for example, that "[i]n general, the greater the number of cigarettes smoked daily, the higher the death rate."[51] The nation's news media seized the report and treated its conclusions as "certain and authoritative." The ensuing shift in public perception of cigarettes set the stage for a governmental response.[52]

Despite fierce industry objections, the Federal Trade Commission issued regulations seeking a health warning on cigarette packages and in cigarette advertising less than a year after the Surgeon General's report. Congress, heading off the agency response, began hearings to issue legislation of its own, preempting the agency action. The next year, at least two important social trends converged to allow Congress to pass legislation requiring a health warning label on every cigarette package sold in the United States. The first was a shifted focus from the moral condemnation of tobacco use prevalent at the beginning of the twentieth century to objections based on scientifically demonstrated health risks. The prestige of government health institutions and the scientific elite gave health concerns a tacit objectivity which the earlier moralizing prohibitionists lacked. Second, the regulatory strategy which sought to empower consumers with the ability to protect themselves from marketplace hazards emerged. For instance, only a year after the House Committee on Interstate and Foreign Commerce held its cigarette package labeling hearings, it held even longer and more extensive hearings on fair labeling of food packaging. Also, and perhaps more relevant for our purposes, hearings on Truth in Lending, which sought to empower debtors to protect themselves from creditors, were simultaneously in progress in the Senate.[53] The two changes allowed Congress to compromise on a strategy which warned consumers of the health risks associated with smoking. In the words of Senator Maurine Neuberger the legislation was

> clearly a compromise. Cigarettes, after all, are habituating, stimulate disease, and finally are death dealing. I receive many communications each week asking for cigarette prohibition legislation. . . . I have rejected these counsels because I believe in the ability of the American people to make in-

telligent decisions when given all the facts. . . . Therefore, I have turned to the health hazard warning statement as the most satisfactory middle ground.[54]

Although public health activists criticized the Cigarette Labeling and Advertising Act of 1965 as a Congressional attempt to protect the tobacco industry from more extensive administrative regulations, the warning label strategy endured. The "rather bland" 1965 warning label read: "Caution: Cigarette Smoking May Be Hazardous to your Health."[55] However, cigarette warning labels were popular enough with the public, and sufficiently uncontroversial for Congress, that the warning label was strengthened in 1970. Congress required that a warning label appear in all print advertising for cigarettes in 1972. In the deregulatory climate of the early 1980s, the Truth in Lending Act was austerely narrowed, but cigarette warning labels were strengthened and expanded. After 1984 Congress mandated that cigarette packages carry four different warning labels, which would rotate in order to preserve their "freshness." These still-current labels read:

- SURGEON GENERAL'S WARNING: Smoking Causes Lung Cancer, Heart Disease, Emphysema, And May Complicate Pregnancy;
- SURGEON GENERAL'S WARNING: Quitting Smoking Now Greatly Reduces Serious Risks to your Health;
- SURGEON GENERAL'S WARNING: Smoking by Pregnant Women May Result in Fetal Injury, Premature Birth, And Low Birth Weight; and
- SURGEON GENERAL'S WARNING: Cigarette Smoke Contains Carbon Monoxide.[56]

The warning label strategy was not limited to the United States. By 1982, approximately thirty-seven countries had adopted some form of cigarette package warning labels. By 1991, seventy-seven countries all around the world required warning labels.[57] The success of cigarette warning labels has also provided the justification for similar labels on alcoholic beverages. Then-Senator Albert Gore Jr. (D-Tenn.) explained at a hearing debating requiring warning labels on alcoholic beverages:

> I have strongly supported product labels to identify both the contents of products, as well as particular hazards associated with their use. I was deeply involved in an effort with regard to the labeling of cigarettes. Labels are proven, effective means for consumers to become informed about a product and any unique characteristics associated with that product. Consumers can then make more intelligent decisions about whether to use or not use the product in question, or how to use it safely.[58]

Neither has support for cigarette warning labels been limited to Democrats. By the early 1980s Senator Orrin Hatch, an influential and conservative Republican, was on the record arguing tobacco warning labels are one of the most cost-effective public health programs possible.[59] Today policymakers have reached a virtual consensus which has rendered the existence of tobacco warning labels essentially uncontroversial.

Criticisms of the form, content, and strength of cigarette warning labels have persisted, as have claims that warning labels alone are not enough. Nevertheless, in comparison to many strategies, cigarette warning labels combined with other health education have proven surprisingly effective in changing consumer preference ordering, particularly where the labels are strongly worded. For instance, Dr. Edwin B. Fisher, Jr. representing the American Lung Association at the House of Representatives' 1983 Smoking Prevention Act Hearings, said:

In Sweden, when rotating warning labels were incorporated as part of a comprehensive, affirmative program of health education regarding the risk of smoking, there was a 9 percent decrease in the rate of smoking among adult males and females. . . . [A] 50 percent decrease was realized in the teenage population.[60]

During the same time period, similar programs achieved similar results in Norway and Finland as well. Furthermore,

A study from Turkey suggests that health warnings caused consumption there to fall by about 8 percent over six years. In South Africa, when serious warning labels were introduced in 1994, there was a significant fall in consumption. More than half (58 percent) of smokers questioned for that study said they were motivated by the warning labels to quit or reduce their smoking.[61]

Even in countries which have had relatively high exposure to cigarette health information over a long period, strong warning labels can produce impressive results.

In Poland in the late 1990s, new warning labels that occupy 30 percent of each of the two largest sides on the cigarette pack have been found to be strongly linked with smokers' decisions to quit or cut down their smoking. Among Polish male smokers, 3 percent said they had quit following the introduction of the labels; an additional 16 percent said they had tried quitting, and a further 14 percent said they understood the health effects of smoking better because of the warnings. Among women, the effects were similar.[62]

Recent data also shows promising results from cigarette warning labels in Canada and Australia.

In the U.S., the variety of health information sources make it difficult to separate behavioral change attributable to warning labels from change attributable to other sources. Nevertheless, one noted study estimated that by the mid- to late-1970s, per capita cigarette consumption in the U.S. dropped 20 to 30 percent due to the collective anti-smoking campaign.[63] Finally, the value of warning labels should not be judged only in terms of decreased consumption, since that is not their only goal. Helping people to think for themselves regardless of their choices about consumption, as well as providing social leadership, avoiding government hypocrisy, and correcting false or misleading advertising are all objectives which have been admirably served by cigarette warning labels.

Over thirty-five years after warning labels were first introduced in the United States, cigarettes provide one of the best twentieth-century examples of how consumers can change the way they order their purchasing preferences. In fact, a standard college economics textbook seeking to explain the very concept of change in demand schedules writes that "changes in preferences can and do manifest themselves in market behavior. As the medical consequences of smoking have become more and more clear, for example, more and more people have stopped smoking. As a result, the demand for cigarettes has dropped significantly."[64] Another economist more dramatically expressed the change caused by greater consistency in preference and welfare ordering in the market for cigarettes:

> Half of the men who ever smoked in this country have quit, and nearly half the women. In my generation three-quarters of young men smoked; the fraction is now less than one third and going down. Fifty million [American] people have quit

smoking, and a hundred million who would have become smokers since 1945 did not.[65]

Government leadership through cigarette package and advertising warning labels must be seen as an important step along the road to this cultural change. Cigarette warning labels helped spark a remarkably beneficial cascading change in the social norms which inform consumer preference ordering.

Moral Condemnation vs. Personal Health in Socializing Cautious Preference Ordering

The highly moralistic efforts condemning tobacco use at the beginning of the twentieth century were ultimately ineffective. The basic, underlying rationale for cigarette bans was that cigarette smoking was immoral. In comparison, "concerns for the harmful effects of cigarettes played a minor role." Mass-produced cigarettes allowed women to smoke, which challenged the traditional symbol of exclusively male tobacco use threatening the moral system associated with gender hierarchy. Moreover, as one sociologist explains, "[o]pponents associated cigarettes with depravity. The cigarette was described as an accompaniment to crime, lust, insobriety, and a general looseness of social obligations." Although this view had a simple, easily understood message, its usefulness was nevertheless relatively short-lived.[66]

However, the health focus of later twentieth-century antismoking messages stand in stark contrast to earlier moralizing. Cigarette warning labels did not seek to condemn smoking as immoral, but rather to accurately stigmatize it as unhealthy. This new approach had several advantages, which may help account for the success of cigarette warning labels. Unlike moral claims, health claims are empirically verifiable. Where moral objections based on religion, philosophy, and personal values, such as social etiquette, grounded efforts to ban cigarettes, scientific epidemiological studies grounded later health objections. This shift in the debate from claims such as "one ought not smoke," to claims such as "smoking is unhealthy," avoided an important measure of unresolvable controversy. Empirical claims about smoking proved less vulnerable to the changing tides of fashion and moral values. Empirical claims were also more resilient against subversion into other social agendas. For example, claims that cigarettes were immoral were manipulated to buttress gender hierarchy by equating social movements advocating women's suffrage with the moral stigma of cigarettes.[67] Moreover, a health-based rationale more successfully fostered consensus because supporters of intervention could cite compelling empirical evidence, rather than hoping moral arguments would persuade those who had an incentive not to listen. Additionally, because health claims were grounded in empirically verifiable facts, opponents could characterize the advertising claims of cigarette manufacturers as false or at least misleading. It was exactly this that gave the Federal Trade Commission, a body responsible for addressing false advertising, the jurisdictional hook to issue its first regulations on cigarettes. And although these regulations never went into force, they did compel a Congressional response which ultimately led to passage of the Cigarette Labeling and Advertising Act of 1965.[68]

But, perhaps most important for our purposes, a focus on health allowed a reconceptualization which was cognizant of the tragic breakdown in market forces associated with cigarettes. In the fight over warning labels, the cigarette industry most feared recognition of the addictive character of cigarettes. This is why they have argued "that smoking is a matter of 'personal choice,' and that tobacco companies should not, therefore, be held responsible for adverse health effects attributed to smoking. If the industry were to admit that nicotine is addictive, it would have a much harder time arguing that people can choose to quit smoking any time they want."[69] A focus on scientifically demonstrated personal health risks exposed the addictive characteristic of cigarettes, which not only makes them so dangerous, but also disrupts normal market decision-making. Cigarettes are unhealthy because smokers become addicted, locking hurtful preference orders into place. It is only through a focus on the unhealthy side-effects of tobacco that our current policy response acknowledged that once consumers are addicted to cigarettes, they will no longer have autonomous and rational preference ordering systems. Counter to the presumptions of classical economic ideology about product demand, preferences supporting cigarette consumption do not consistently track welfare. This market breakdown justifies market-corrective action: the government must try to help consumers become aware of the risk and thus protect themselves with more carefully ordered preferences. The first, most basic step in what has become a government campaign to produce awareness of unhealthy addiction—or counter presumptively inflexible market demand—for cigarettes was a health hazard warning label. Health-based objections to tobacco have led us to recognize that when it comes to addictive cigarettes, the invisible hand alone cannot be trusted.

The important lesson is that the strategy of cigarette warning labels transcended moral questions, instead providing market-corrective leadership based on the personal health risks each consumer would face. This gives us:

Lesson #4: Market-corrective efforts based on empirically demonstrated personal risk are superior to efforts focusing on moral condemnation.

Unlike the evolution of the debate over government policy towards cigarettes, the policy debate over consumer credit in general and high-cost lending in particular has not evolved beyond controversial moralistic arguments. As a noted historian explained, "the recipe for conventional analysis of rising consumer credit is the same today as it was in 1957 and in 1927." These arguments recount "that consumer credit has turned America into a nation of bankrupts . . . and pleasure-loving hedonists increasingly bereft of the capacity to discipline desire and postpone gratification. It is an old tired analysis. . . ."[70] Where the most fundamental policy tenet with regard to cigarette smoking has become the claim "smoking is dangerous," opposing sides in the debate over high-cost lending rely primarily on statements such as "debtors ought not [to] default so often," and "lenders ought not to lend at such high prices." Both creditors and debtors in the high-cost credit market rely on antiquated moral arguments.

Industry argues that contemporary consumers have lost the traditional American thrift ethic. In this view debtors borrow when they cannot afford to repay, and quit trying at the first sign of trouble. This view is firmly grounded in the American traditions of business, independence, and trustworthiness. Supporters of this position can call upon a formidable arsenal of scholarship bemoaning the erosion of stoicism in personal finance. Because debtors have lost the moral commitment to honor their contracts, bankruptcy has lost its stigma, in turn leading many debtors to abuse the system. Accordingly, this vision of the high-cost lending problem tends to lean in favor of tighter restrictions on consumer access to bankruptcy protections. Its advocates see themselves as seeking to revive a morality of commercial honesty.

On the other hand, debtors and consumer advocates accuse creditors with unethically abusing consumers. In this view, high-cost creditors viciously exploit desperately poor and unfortunately ignorant debtors. This view is grounded firmly in biblical injunctions against usury along with thousands of years of history condemning exploitation of the poor. Traditional American interest-rate caps brought over from England had their heritage in papal acceptance of lending at rates below 6 percent annually. Supporters of this position can call upon an equally formidable arsenal of scholarship ruing corporate creditor mistreatment of the poor and the working class, oblivious to our protective heritage. This vision of the high-cost lending problem tends to favor market-control strategies, such as interest-rate caps, which ban the most culpable credit products. Advocates of this view seek to revive a morality of commercial compassion.

However, the statement that "high-cost borrowing is financially dangerous" does not have the same polarizing effect as statements like "debtors ought not to default so often," and "lenders ought not to lend at such high prices." On the contrary, both industry and consumer advocates can agree that high-cost debt is a risky business for both parties. Debtors risk ensnarement in expensive loans they cannot easily pay back. Creditors risk writing off their investment. But perhaps more fundamentally, it is likely the social consequences of high-cost debt can be empirically demonstrated. Just as the physical health risks of smoking were demonstrated with epidemiological studies, so too might consumer advocates and social scientists show the financial health risks of high-cost borrowing. This is not to suggest the outcome of these studies is a foregone conclusion. The debate over whether smoking causes disease was robust, to say the least. But it was a debate where empirical facts governed and ultimately resolved the outcome. Similarly, a shift in focus onto personal financial risk-taking behavior itself, rather than continuing endless moral accusations, would be a useful development in the debate over high-cost lending. A rhetoric based on financial health risks might lead to practical, meaningful social leadership without moral condemnation of debtors or creditors.

This is not to suggest that all moral claims may be eliminated from the policy discourse surrounding high-cost credit. That would be neither desirable nor feasible. Both industry and consumer activists can simultaneously make the case for moral reform, and take steps to address the personal financial risks of high-cost credit. For example, it is obviously consistent to argue that high-cost lending is dangerous and that interest-rate caps ought to be adopted. The advantage of an approach focusing on the personal financial danger associated with high-cost credit is not that it removes *all* moral discourse, but that it has the potential to insert a nucleus of empirical fact into the debate which can ground and focus other moral arguments. All policies will ultimately turn on whether they *ought* to be implemented. But a focus on the empirical social consequences associated with high-cost credit use would give both sides a factual starting point. Just as a focus on health risks, rather than the morality of smoking, improved the tobacco debate, so too could a focus on the financial health risks, rather than the morality of high-cost lending, improve the usury and bankruptcy debates.

Hazard Warnings vs. Price Disclosures in Socializing Careful Preference Ordering

After the old moralizing anti-smoking movement collapsed, there was little or no social leadership actively encouraging American consumers to refrain from smoking. As cigarette smoking became accepted and normal behavior, consumers took the decision of whether to smoke or not lightly. After all, as Dr. Elizabeth Whelan, president of the American Council on Science and Health, put it "the cigarette . . . came to symbolize the all-American man and eventually the all-American woman. Controversy and rumblings of danger existed, but by the time the bad news [about health risks] became clear, cigarettes had become socially desirable."[71] From the 1930s through the mid-1960s, consumers had little or no socialized defense mechanisms to protect themselves from the addictive habit. After state governments abandoned their efforts to ban cigarette sales, they left a vacuum in anti-smoking social leadership. When the government began to shift its position to look for a method of helping consumers make careful decisions about whether or not to smoke, it made sense to try to communicate to the public the very same knowledge which had forced government leaders to change their own minds.

Unfortunately, the knowledge that forced change in government was complex and difficult to convey through ordinary discourse. Knowledge of the risks of smoking was derived from scientific studies of the effects of cigarette consumption on sample populations. This kind of evidence is expressed in terms of probability, percentage, researcher bias, and control groups. Just to comprehend the scientific significance of a single study would have been a demanding task for many citizens, regardless of their educational and cultural backgrounds. Knowledge about the health risks of smoking becomes even more complex after one begins the process of synthesizing the many different and sometimes conflicting studies. How does one compare the evidence produced by studies on different sample populations? How can one be certain that every study has effectively controlled for alternative causes of disease? How does one compare studies that have different mechanisms for controlling for alternative causes of disease? To what degree should a researcher's financial interest in a study's conclusions affect the credibility of that study's data? Understanding individual studies alone is difficult, but accurately synthesizing the evidence of many studies is even more difficult. Nevertheless, scientists can and do provide good answers to these difficult questions, coming up with passably accurate assessments of the health risks of smoking behavior. What the government needed was a way to summarize the results of multiple studies into a simple easily understood statement about risk. The government would only be able to recapture its role as a social leader, cautioning the public about the use of cigarettes, if it could intelligibly express those risks to the American public.

In the Cigarette Labeling and Advertising Act of 1965, the government turned to a simple health hazard warning to fill this need. It was clear from the beginning that reproducing the risk descriptions of scientists would not be an effective way to express the true risks to normal people. It would hardly have been feasible to reproduce epidemiological study results on the back of cigarette packs, on billboard and magazine advertisements, or within radio and television commercials. And even if it were, the vast majority of those who needed the risk information could not have understood the results anyway. Instead, warning labels gave consumers the bottom line: a simple message warning them that cigarette smoking was dangerous.

Health hazard warnings made a useful *inference* for consumers. Much different than accurately reproducing epidemiological risk evidence, cigarette warnings allowed the government to act on behalf of the people by reaching an official conclusion about the safety risks of the product. This simple regulatory tool was effective for a variety of reasons. Unlike other education strategies such as school curriculum, public service announcements, press releases, and government reports, package warning labels were provided directly to the consuming population. Similarly, advertisement warnings had a premade distribution system, piggybacking along cigarette advertisements. Very few government employees had to be hired, since tobacco manufacturers themselves provided the information whenever they advertised or sold a pack of cigarettes. Teachers did not have to modify their curricula, substituting cigarette education for reading or math. The strategy also did not have high compliance costs for industry. It does not cost more to print an ad or cigarette package label with a warning statement than it costs to print ads and labels without warnings. Even when rotating warning labels were adopted, industry compliance costs were insignificant. Warning labels made the false and misleading advertising images of health and pleasure that cigarette manufacturers hoped to link to their product implausible.

But perhaps the most important advantage of warning labels may have been the way they helped prevent consumers from deceiving themselves. For example, warning labels prevent smokers from making the rationalization that if smoking were truly dangerous, the government would do something about it. After all, the federal government had subsidized tobacco farmers for years, potentially ratifying cigarette manufacturers' deceptive advertising messages. Warning labels were a symbolically significant effort at correcting the hypocrisy (or, depending on your perspective, the appearance of hypocrisy) of cigarette regulation and tobacco subsidies. People often have trouble accepting what they do not want to be true. Smokers had a psychological tendency to avert their attention from less direct methods of consumer education. Cigarette warning labels helped force smokers to face up to the risks of their behavior.

Even though the scientific knowledge supporting conclusions such as "smoking causes lung cancer" were complex, communicating the essence of that risk was not. And, even though conducting the studies that established this as proven scientific knowledge was expensive, providing the most basic socialization about that knowledge was not. Although warning labels lacked the moral simplicity of earlier cigarette prohibition statutes, the warnings nevertheless provided an avenue of social leadership towards greater public health. The warnings on cigarette packages and in advertising provided a potent red flag, signalling to all Americans that the carefree method they had used to arrive at smoking consumption decisions needed reevaluation. With warning labels the government elegantly recaptured its role as an active agent of socialization on cigarettes. This suggests:

Lesson #5: Socializing caution, unlike communicating price information, is relatively cheap and simple.

During the first half of the twentieth century, American government abandoned its role as an agent of socialization regarding the risks of cigarettes. In much the same way it has now abandoned its role as an agent of socialization in the market for high-cost loans. Traditionally, state governments sent the simple and uncompromising moral message that lending and borrowing at prices above the old general usury law interest-rate caps was immoral. But as the revolution in credit products targeted at the upper-middle class complicated our collective cultural response to credit, the traditional moral message became outdated. Confusing exceptions to usury laws, such as multi-tiered interest-rate caps, the total elimination of all caps in some states, and federal policies allowing some lenders to export laissez-faire credit laws to other states, placed all consumer credit on the same moral footing. One unfortunate side effect of this cultural transformation left high-cost debtors without millennia-old traditions of lifelong socialization about the dangers of high-cost debt, making them vulnerable to sometimes deceptive and always risky contracts with high-cost debtors.

The socialization efforts of American government with respect to high-cost credit did not improve with the adoption of the Truth in Lending Act. Comparing the 1968 Truth in Lending Act with its cousin, the Cigarette Labeling and Advertising Act of 1965, exposes an essential weakness in TILA. Where cigarette legislation sought to make an inference from complex information for consumers, credit disclosure laws only provided the consumer with the complex information itself, no inferences attached. Cigarette warning labels distill complex information into a group of simple, rotating, cautionary messages, with one of the same four on every package. But TILA price disclosures are complicated, and different, for every loan. Each price disclosure requires the consumer to understand the terminology of lawyers and accountants. To make use of TILA disclosures, debtors must comprehend terms like "APR," "finance charge," "balance computation method," and "negative amortization." And, independent of problems with terminology, TILA disclosure statements are probably too long to warn consumers effectively of potential hazards.[72] The Truth in Lending Act attempts to reproduce complex, specialized, legal knowledge which, if carefully evaluated by a person with adequate legal and accounting skills, *may* yield information suggesting a possible hazard. If tobacco regulation had followed TILA's information description pattern, warning labels would have provided epidemiological study evidence, rather than a warning. The only people who would have understood the label would have been research scientists and medical doctors.

The differences in these approaches may make sense for moderately-priced consumer credit offered to the middle class. The authors of Truth in Lending did not intended to portray credit use as hazardous, but simply to facilitate price shopping. This is because unlike cigarettes, responsibly used, moderately-priced consumer credit is, by and large, not dangerous for consumers. The same cannot be said for high-cost loans. Virtually every government since ancient Babylon has recognized that high-cost consumer credit is fundamentally hazardous, not unlike cigarettes. That is why American states, along with so many other governments for thousands of years, banned high-cost credit with interest-rate caps. The Truth in Lending Act imprudently grouped the new, moderately-priced consumer credit extended to the middle class with ancient and dangerous high-cost credit extended to the desperate and ignorant working poor. The result was a myopic federal policy which further erased the traditional socialization of the immorality of high-cost lending and borrowing. Rather than providing a compensating message of caution, like that provided in cigarette warning labels, TILA may merely have helped facilitate self-deception on the part of desperate high-cost debtors who could not or would not try to understand complex price information. With TILA in place, it is easy for high-cost debtors to tell themselves that if this loan were so bad, the government would do something about it. Unfortunately, that is not true.

A simple hazard warning label for high-cost credit, such as those mandated by cigarette legislation, would allow American government to easily recapture its abandoned role as an agent of protective socialization regarding the dangerous risks of high-cost credit. Nothing in this argument should be construed to suggest credit price disclosures should be abandoned. Research on the willingness of consumers to read information about a product is directly related to the perceived hazardousness of the product. For decades scholars have complained that price disclosures are *least effective* for (often poor and relatively uneducated) consumers who are unfamiliar with credit. However, all of our past experience with hazard warning labels shows they are *most effective* for consumers who are unfamiliar with the products to which warnings are attached.[73] Unlike long, confusing, and technical price disclosures that most benefit consumers who are familiar with credit, a financial hazard warning on high-cost credit advertisements and contracts would most benefit those who most need help.

Obviously, a well prepared high-cost debt warning strategy will not be a silver bullet eradicating all the problems of high-cost debtors. Many high-cost debtors have already carefully ordered their preferences. Those debtors who borrow because they are desperate may do so regardless of warnings. A single mother might decide to borrow at high-cost to feed her children—even after carefully considering the potential harm, because the harm of her children's hunger is still greater. A factory worker with car trouble might borrow to fix his car—even after carefully considering the risks, because the risk of losing his job is still greater. Nevertheless, even these debtors would be well served with a warning reminding them to repay their high-cost debts carefully and quickly.

The advantages of a simple hazard warning label for high-cost credit are most persuasive when one considers their relative cost.

Unlike public education campaigns through schools and public service advertisements, which require government expenditures, requiring hazard warning labels costs the government little or nothing. And unlike relatively complicated price disclosures, which have compliance costs for industry, hazard warning labels are the same every time they are printed and are only attached to communication the creditor would purchase anyway. To the extent industry opposes costs associated with warning labels, it is likely the real concern is that consumers will purchase their products less often, if they think carefully about the risks. But sound free-market economic principals do not entitle industry to profits gleaned by selling hazardous products without fair warning.

Warning labels alone may not provide price information, but they may encourage consumers to *seek out* information by sparking more realistic preference and welfare ordering. Moreover, warning labels provide a hedge against government hypocrisy. Publicly taking a stance on the known consumer hazards of high-cost debt can catalyze other governmental efforts and spark further discussion. Still, a warning label strategy for high-cost loans should not be designed to decrease borrowing. Rather the goal should be to provide social leadership emphasizing careful decision-making in risky circumstances. Unlike Victorian anti-debt moralizing, an effective contemporary warning label strategy would not declare that high-cost debtors ought not borrow, but that *high-cost debtors should be careful.* The short-term gratification, combined with surprising long-term consequences, the cyclical nature of high-cost debt, and cultural changes leaving high-cost debtors without traditional moral defense mechanisms, have created a market breakdown where consumer preference orders do not track welfare orders. A government warning label strategy should focus on persuading at-risk consumers to consider carefully their credit-buying motives. Aggregate demand for high-cost credit will only change if debtors have been deceived either by their creditors or themselves into ignoring the risks of their behavior. Just as many right-thinking people still choose to smoke, so too will many high-cost debtors still choose to borrow.[74] The difference is that with the help of a warning label strategy they will do so more cautiously. One commentator remarked that even for ordinary products, such as household cleaners, over-the-counter medications, flammable liquids, and do-it-yourself power tools, "[t]he consensus of accident prevention professionals strongly recommends that warnings labels and cautionary instructions be provided on hazardous consumer and industrial products."[75] It is a testament to the pernicious silence and abject policy failure surrounding high-cost lending that such an equally hazardous product does not carry an equally conspicuous message of caution.

This discussion has drawn from two policy strategies in searching for lessons which might mature our high-cost credit price disclosure laws. As dramatic growth in the high-cost credit industry continues, a consensus on the necessity of meaningful reform is likely to emerge. Even the Mortgage Bankers Association of America (MBA) has come to agree that a technologically updated, comprehensive reform of disclosure rules is necessary to address the gap between understanding and truth faced by vulnerable debtors. John Courson, chairman of the MBA, recently testified before the Senate Banking Committee:

> [The] MBA believes . . . that ultimately, we can do much better. We can, and should, construct systems of consumer protection that go beyond mere disclosures. In the end, consumers run the risk of being tricked and deceived as long as consumers are subjected to the arcane and outdated disclosure system that is now mandated by federal law. As with predatory lending, we believe that it is absolutely essential to enact comprehensive reform of the current mortgage lending

laws. So long as the mortgage process remains confusing and perplexing, consumers will run the risk of being gouged and defrauded, whether through trickery involving yield spread premiums, or through other schemes that unscrupulous actors will continue to develop to exploit the unwary and unsophisticated.[76]

The medical doctrine of informed consent and cigarette health hazard warnings suggest promising guidance for "comprehensive reform" of high-cost credit disclosure laws.

CHAPTER 8

Towards a Cure: A High-Cost Credit Policy Agenda for the Twenty-First Century

Where the weak or oppressed assert the rights that have been so long denied them, those in power inevitably resist on the basis of the necessity for tranquility.

—Chief Justice Earl Warren

If you want to succeed you should strike out on new paths rather than travel the worn paths of accepted success.

—John D. Rockefeller

THIS BOOK HAS COMPARED THE American economy to a human body suffering from a persistent low-grade infection. Low interest rates have been an indicator of economic and social health for thousands of years. It is safe to say the United States could not have attained the social wellbeing, prosperity, and international power it has without a monetary policy effectively moderating the interest governments, banks, businesses, and ordinary citizens pay for the use of money. Unfortunately, the economic health of the nation has not been evenly spread. Persistent pockets of people in our society pay rates as high as the highest recorded rates in written history. For these debtors, high interest rates are an indicator of social and financial infirmity, just as high interest rates have been for other nations, communities, and individuals across time. The challenge of American consumer credit policy in the twenty-first century is to bring stability, understanding, and prosperity to these debtors without risking the financial health of the rest of the country. Unfortunately, thinking on the subject of high-cost credit has in many ways stagnated. The credit industry has come to control the attention of federal policymakers with self-interested, simplistic, and moralizing accounts of an old and complex problem. Consumer advocates have lost momentum in debates over credit policy because they offer no policies which simultaneously protect vulnerable consumers and do not burden the socially successful trade between creditors and debtors. The goal of this book has been to promote a more reasonable and productive understanding of high-cost credit and policy directed toward it.

In pursuing this goal, we have surveyed the problematic borrower and lender practices which create market imperfections and explored our knowledge of human interaction for regulatory methods which might enliven the policy debate over high-cost loans. Particularly, I have sought to explore the ideological overlap favoring consumer access to basic product information between free-market liberals and consumer-protection-oriented proponents of government regulation. The hope has been that we might find policies palatable to a broad political spectrum which might nevertheless substantially remedy the long-standing credit woes of America's impoverished and vulnerable working classes. Moreover, I have also sought to employ interdisciplinary methods in the hope of sparking new academic interest in an unjustifiably under-treated subject.[1] The high-cost lending problem in general, and credit information disclosure rules in particular, are strongly analogous to problems associated with obtaining informed consent from medical patients and problems attributable to broken preference ordering in the market for cigarettes. Now let us move beyond these interdisciplinary analogies to look at a tentative proposal for reform.

A twenty-first century agenda for reform must first and foremost come to terms with credit disclosure law. Credit disclosure is historically a unique and relatively new strategy. It contains enormous theoretical potential to bridge the ideological gulf in the high-cost credit debate that separates the political right and left. Credit disclosure may in fact show more promise as a treatment for the feverish high-cost credit market than any other policy device yet created. But credit disclosure as we know it today falls far short of this goal. Because disclosures are too inaccurate, come too late, do not require comprehension, do not provide comparative information, and do not make useful inferences for consumers about the contracts they disclose, they do little or nothing for vulnerable high-cost borrowers. America's short three-decade experiment with credit disclosure rules has degenerated into a tragic irony of Orwellian doublespeak. Our most recent medication for the ancient social disease of debt fever has been adulterated by an overreaching industry and its lobbyists, uncertain legislators, complacent regulators, indifferent jurists, and perhaps most important of all, consumers who do not shop around. Today, the most significant political, social, and economic function of credit disclosure rules is their ability to obscure market reality, deflect efforts to pass substantive consumer protection, and infuse faith in the myth of rational price-compared high-cost credit decisions. Truth in Lending inadvertently facilitated the high-cost credit boom of the past twenty years, destroying the financial lives of millions of Americans. The irony is this: "Truth" in Lending has become a collective lie.

While Truth in Lending has been ineffective in curing the high-cost credit fever, some progress has been made. First and foremost among promising developments in disclosure rules is the price-threshold trigger approach used in the Home Ownership and

Equity Protection Act ("HOEPA") amendments to the Truth in Lending Act, as well as recent predatory lending laws in North Carolina and New York. The idea here is that, if a lender offers credit above certain prices, or perhaps with particularly dangerous triggering contract provisions, the lender is governed by enhanced disclosure rules not applicable to more moderately-priced loans. For instance, under recent HOEPA regulatory amendments, lenders must make special disclosures if they offer a first lien loan with an annual percentage rate that exceeds by more than 8 percentage points the yield on comparable-duration treasury securities.[2] HOEPA protections are also triggered if the total points and fees are excessive, even if the annual percentage rate is not. In the future, credit contracts exceeding price-threshold triggers should only be formed after the completion of a heightened disclosure procedure aimed at helping consumers make informed and wise borrowing decisions.[3]

The notion of a price-threshold trigger can be used as the foundation for which a broader disclosure-reform agenda can be developed. Under this approach, 16 U.S.C. § 1602(aa) and 12 C.F.R. § 226.36 should be repealed and replaced with price-threshold triggers and heightened disclosure strategies for *all* high-cost loans. The current high-cost credit disclosure system, which protects only homeowners, is neither fair nor reasonable. Sweeping amendments should include—in addition to high-cost home mortgage loans—special price-triggered disclosure rules for payday loans, pawnshop loans, rent-to-own transactions, tax refund anticipation loans, high-cost automobile financing, and any other form of high-cost credit.

Price-threshold triggers should be set at different levels for different types of credit. A 30 percent annual percentage rate is a crushing and unconscionable rate for a secured home mortgage, but is a bargain for a payday loan. The levels at which price-threshold triggers should be set would be a matter of the utmost importance, since if thresholds were set too high, the new amendments would be irrelevant. Unreasonably low price-threshold triggers have rendered HOEPA largely irrelevant. In 2000, Federal Reserve Board Governor Edward M. Gramlich conceded that HOEPA only covered 1 percent of all subprime home mortgage loans. Moreover, HOEPA is currently hobbled by exceptions to the calculation of its triggers. Quite simply, if threshold triggers distinguishing high-cost credit from moderately-priced, mainstream consumer credit are not based on low bright-line annual percentage rate triggers, they will not work.[4] A fair system would set a bright-line APR trigger for all home-secured loans at 6 percentage points above the yield on comparable term Treasury securities.[5] A second APR trigger for automobile-secured credit should be set at around 12 percent. A third APR trigger covering all other open- and closed-end loans, including rent-to-own transactions, should be set at around 24 percent. Additional triggers based on abusive or dangerous credit terms should also be considered. For instance, Congress should include a separate monthly income-to-payment ratio trigger for home mortgages to insure heightened disclosure for lenders who target home equity irrespective of a borrower's ability to pay. Operating on the assumption of these triggers, the subsequent proposal sketches what a national *Understanding in High-Cost Credit Act* might look like.

A TWENTY-FIRST CENTURY HIGH-COST CREDIT DISCLOSURE STRATEGY: THE COMPONENTS OF A CURE

From Truth in Lending to Understanding in High-Cost Lending

Both the medical doctrine of informed consent and the Truth in Lending Act seek to require that an informed service provider gives information to an uninformed consumer. However, the objective of informed consent is to help the patient understand the risks and benefits of a potential treatment. The objective of the Truth in Lending Act is only to provide true information. Although one may not understand without truth, truth alone does not create understanding. For a variety of reasons, although high-cost debtors have had an opportunity to understand information about their loans, oftentimes they have not or could not take advantage of that opportunity. When these debtors borrow without understanding how much their credit costs, they undermine the very foundation of economic competition: shopping. A consumer cannot shop if she does not understand the price of any given product. This is why in the market for high-cost debt disclosure rules should attempt to promote understanding rather than mere truth. This suggests:

Recommendation #1: High-cost credit should be sold in packages where, prior to application, the debtor receives a uniform Plain English "price tag" prepared in advance by the Federal Reserve Board.

The basic approach of disclosure rules, at least for high-cost credit, should be to help the consumer understand the most important price and contractual information at the most important time—*before* contracting to a high-cost loan. Lenders who contemplate offering high-cost credit should be required to submit the terms of their contracts over the internet to the Federal Reserve, which would in turn prepare a uniform plain English contract. The Federal Reserve, either itself, or more preferably through a private contractor chosen in a competitive bidding process, should create software which designs uniform, consumer-friendly, credit disclosure documents. The internet-accessible software would work by prompting the creditor with a series of questions about the price of the credit. The software would be designed to incorporate all the contract terms which could materially affect the price of the credit into disclosure materials. It should also incorporate terms which materially limit the future legal rights of the debtor, such as arbitration clauses and prepayment penalties. The software would then organize all of the contractual terms into a disclosure document designed to disclose material price information to potential debtors contemplating applying for the loan. This form would then be e-mailed to the creditor, who could use the form to offer high-cost credit to potential debtors. Unlike current disclosures prepared by the creditor and presented after the debtor has applied and been approved for the loan, federal law would require high-cost lenders to present this document to borrowers before they apply for a loan.

Congress should require the Federal Reserve to conduct extensive scientific tests to determine what words, syntax, formatting, colors, and symbols generate the most easily understood documents for readers with only rudimentary literacy and financial literacy skills. The documents should be a radical departure from the current HOEPA high-cost mortgage command-and-control disclosure regulations. In the words of a respected legal treatise, HOEPA disclosures "need not be in any specific type size, or presented in any particular manner, or as part of any particular document."[6] Instead, the software should be designed to generate uniform disclosure documents that will grab consumers' attention, and highlight the most dangerous and costly loan provisions, rather than burying them in fine print, boilerplate legalese. Learning from more successful Food and Drug Administration nutrition labels, generated documents should integrate basic price disclosures and consumer rights information into one well-formatted document. Lenders would no longer have the option of hiding material credit terms until after the debtor has been approved for the loan. When problems were identified with disclosures, the agency could, on an annual or semiannual basis, alter e-mailed forms by changing the software used to issue disclosure documents. This would allow low-cost, gradual refinement towards disclosure forms that do more than present mere truth.[7]

Building on the past success of "safe harbor" credit disclosure forms, creditors would not have to submit every contract they make with every debtor for approval by the regulatory agency.[8] Rather, creditors would have a set of credit packages from which debtors could choose. Creditors would only have to obtain disclosure documents from the regulatory authority for each credit package. For example, a payday lender with hundreds of branches in many states might offer only a single type of payday loan. Even though the company might offer hundreds of thousands of individual loans per year, it would only need to obtain approval and disclosure documents once. Lenders who offer loans in amounts that vary with the purchase price of a product or who lend in variable amounts based on the value of security would have loan packages with set interest rates and terms on file with the central agency, allowing the lender to log on, enter the principal amount, and then print out a disclosure form designed by consumer-protection-oriented regulators, but nevertheless specific to the individual loan in every detail. Privately contracting internet service providers could be used to guarantee efficient and timely access to lenders' approved credit package files.

This approach would have several important advantages over the status quo. First, the wolves would no longer guard the chicken coop. Currently, lenders alone are entrusted with preparing the vital consumer-understanding documents that are the only basis upon which a successful market might function. Lenders, especially high-cost lenders, have no incentive to carefully explain the prices of their credit products. Today the process through which parties come to agreement on contracts is informal and vague. This ambiguous communication, although a seemingly natural way for humans to interact, leads to chronic consumer confusion and lender abuse. The same confusion and deception has been occurring due to the same vague pre-contract communication processes for thousands of years. High-cost lenders and borrowers need to communicate more precisely and in ways that prevent conflict and disappointments down the road. But to do so, they need the leadership of government to create a common language that both parties can understand. By having all high-cost lending documents drafted by a central regulatory authority computer program, a much more robust, uniform credit negotiation language would develop.

Second, pre-application price disclosure would more closely match the timing of price understanding in reality with the assumptions of microeconomic models. Currently, at-risk consumers hoping to shop for credit must complete the credit application process prior to receiving any meaningful price disclosure. Even for the most convenient "quick loans," this pre-disclosure process can be quite invasive and time consuming. Price comparison will never be feasible so long as payday lenders can call the applicant's boss or human resource supervisor to verify employment *before* accurately disclosing credit costs. In order to shop, the debtor must allow every potential lender to call his employer in order to get comparative price information. For an at-risk consumer this is an insurmountable burden to shopping, making any real price comparison infeasible. Simply stated, current Truth in Lending disclosures come too late. In the case of home mortgages, pre-approved package disclosure would do away with the Real Estate Settlement and Procedure Act's "good faith estimate," which probably detracts from efficient shopping more than it contributes. Also, Truth in Lending and RESPA disclosures should be combined and coordinated to replace the current disjointed mortgage loan disclosure process. Many progressive mainstream mortgage lenders have already advocated reforms which would include guaranteed closing-cost packages. Moreover, the Federal Reserve Board and

HUD have recommended Congress pass reforms which give all mortgage lenders the choice between selling closing costs in the form of price-guaranteed packages instead of imposed, prescribed price tolerances on closing-cost good-faith estimates.[9] Requiring high-cost lenders to sell credit in pre-approved packages would help force lenders to cover their risk through easily comparable terms such as the annual percentage rate, rather than covering costs in ad hoc fees assessed after consumers are already committed to the bargain. If lenders sold their credit in packages with disclosure forms pre-prepared by a regulatory agency, any prospective debtor would be free to shop *before applying for the loan*.

Third, agency-prepared pre-application disclosure would avoid many after-the-fact-disputes between creditors and debtors about whether disclosure was proper. The credit industry's most common and scathing complaint about the Truth in Lending Act is that drawing up compliant documents is difficult and time consuming. When even well-meaning lenders make mistakes, the door is opened for litigation. If the Federal Reserve Board or some other agency prepared disclosure documentation, lenders would be freed of this burden and subsequent litigation. Under such a system lenders would only be liable for improper disclosure if they failed to point out a blatant or obvious regulatory mistake or mischaracterized the terms of the contract in the disclosure document preparation process.

Fourth, using one central authority to prepare high-cost credit disclosure documents would make use of economies of scale. Under the current system, each lender is forced to understand the substantive intricacies of federal (and state) credit disclosure law. Also, each lender must invest time and money into making sure they keep abreast of changes in that law. If lenders could simply describe their loan contracts to a central document preparation service over the internet, and allow that central authority to prepare the disclosure documents for them, this slow and repetitive decentralized disclosure preparation could be avoided. The regulatory agency might achieve even greater speed in preparing the documents by using competitive bidding processes from computer companies seeking government contracts. Alternatively, multiple internet companies might be granted licenses from the regulatory authority to issue high-cost credit disclosure documents, allowing a market for disclosure document preparation to develop. This would allow lenders to specialize in lending, and document preparation services to handle price communication.

Finally, even if difficulties were encountered during transition to the new system, important long-term strategic gains would be made in consumer credit policymaking. Unlike most regulatory strategies, which attempt to curb the harmful consequences of high-cost lending, such as interest-rate caps, bankruptcy, and charitable subsidized lending, disclosure rules are a newcomer. When only the intelligentsia could read or write, disclosure was simply impractical. At the beginning of the twenty-first century, society's information-sharing technology and skills are undergoing one of the most remarkable transformations in human history. Yet our current information-sharing strategy for dealing with consumer credit problems relies on the information-sharing technology which existed in 1968 when the Truth in Lending Act first passed. An internet-based strategy of agency-prepared pre-application high-cost credit price disclosure would bring credit disclosure rules into the Information Age. Using internet technology for communication between credit regulators and lenders about how lenders should in turn communicate to debtors would help spread the benefits of information processing technology to those who have so far lacked access to that technology.[10] Moreover, it would radically expand the conceptual boundaries in policymaking, thereby opening doors to new techniques which might bring better credit protection to vulnerable high-cost borrowers.

*Mandatory Demonstrated Understanding: If You Don't
Understand, You Don't Borrow*

Doctors take special precautions when communicating risk information to patients in high-risk circumstances. For example,
when a patient agrees to an extremely risky medical procedure,
doctors will often not proceed with the medical treatment until
they have verified that the patient truly understands the danger.
One way physicians do this is through competency assessment
tests designed to verify that patients are in possession of their fac-
ulties and are capable of the understanding necessary to make an
informed decision. In informed consent doctrine, patients who do
not understand the risks of treatment options have no legal right
or ethical entitlement to make treatment decisions. This practice
teaches us in high-risk circumstances, do not proceed without diagnosed understanding. This lesson suggests:

> Recommendation #2: Consumers contemplating risky high-
> cost credit should not be allowed to borrow until they have
> demonstrated a reasonable understanding of the contract on
> a Federal Reserve Board high-cost credit application form.

The social and personal financial risks of high-cost debt are so
great, both to the debtor and to others, that to proceed without the
price understanding which microeconomics assumes all consumers
possess is unacceptably dangerous. Because families and communities suffer when borrowers make ill-advised high-cost credit decisions, consumers do not have the right to borrow without
demonstrating they at least understand the risks of their behavior.
Thus, high-cost credit applications should include a section entitled "credit terms" which provides an itemized list of simple questions reflecting the material provisions of the contract. Prospective
debtors should be required to complete these questions when they
fill out a high-cost loan application. While scientific study should

be done to identify the most effective pedagogical and measurement devices, examples of these questions might include: "The annual percentage rate of this loan is————;" "The finance charge is————;" and perhaps even, "*True* or *False*: I have agreed to binding arbitration, which means I do not have the right to appear before a judge or jury." This section of the application would be prepared by the regulatory authority over the internet and e-mailed to the lender along with any disclosure information through the same procedure previously described. Applicants for high-cost loans should have to demonstrate their understanding of the loan by correctly identifying a reasonable number of the material terms. Although the percentage of correct answers constituting a reasonable understanding could be set at different levels, a good benchmark might be 80 percent. Thus, applicants would have to correctly answer four of every five of the credit term questions on an application to be approved for the loan.

The austerity of this requirement would be tempered in several ways. Initially, all debtors should be allowed to apply for any given high-cost credit contract as many times as they choose. If the consumer has trouble demonstrating understanding of the contract the first time through, the second or third try might be much easier. Also, debtors should be allowed to bring friends or family to help them with the application. The creditors themselves should be encouraged to help customers (provided the lender does not simply fill in the form for the borrower) since this type of communication is exactly what Truth in Lending hoped to produce from the very beginning. And in the case of the disability or illiteracy, lenders should be required to provide additional help for debtors.

Moreover, because both the initial credit disclosure form and the credit application would be prepared by the regulatory authority over the internet, questions on the application would track the information presented on the disclosure form. Correctly filling out the application would only be a matter of reading the disclosure form and transferring the answers onto the application. The "test" would be designed to be easy to pass, since the point is not to make borrowing difficult but to provide debtors with a pedagogical device insuring a basic level of competence. In comparison to other government forms and tests, such as income tax forms or driver's license tests, these applications would be very simple indeed. Furthermore, borrowers *already* fill out long and complex loan applications. Even payday lenders require the borrower's address, phone numbers, employment history, and checking account information, as well as complete contact information on as many as five personal references. Many businesses have consumers fill out relatively long questionnaires simply for marketing purposes. The marginal increase in effort and time for the high-cost debtors beyond these application requirements would be relatively minor.

But the most assuaging recognition comes when one remembers that *credit contracts do not have to be complicated.* It is only when lenders try to preempt every possible contingency with boilerplate provisions that credit contracts become disorienting. If high-cost debtors were compelled to understand the contracts to which they bind themselves, creditors might begin to write less complex contracts. Some creditors would garner a competitive advantage by offering the simplest contracts possible, thus attracting consumers seeking easy, convenient applications. Currently, demand for fast credit drives lenders toward hiding abusive provisions in boilerplate forms, but under the proposed system the demand for fast credit would drive lenders toward offering easily understood, guileless contracts. In this way, the problem of uninformed credit use would be addressed from both ends: borrowers would become more sophisticated and loans would become simpler.

Finally, in the case of high-cost home and manufactured home mortgage loans, including refinancing where the stakes for individuals, families, and communities may be the highest, the Truth in Lending Act should be amended to require mandatory pre-transaction counseling from a Department of Housing and Urban Development-certified credit counselor. HUD has explained pre-transaction counseling would "provide counselors an opportunity to review the terms of applicants' potential loans, and advise borrowers whether they have the financial capability to enter into the loans (and whether the loans contain potentially abusive terms). Knowing that a borrower would seek counseling might deter less scrupulous lenders from attempting to entice the borrower into a loan that might not be to his/her benefit."[11] Under a system of pre-prepared regulatory price disclosures, counselors could help loan applicants decide between several mortgage applications and then help the borrower complete the application. Because mandatory pre-transaction counseling is already required for reverse mortgages, regulators would have a model to build upon in increasing the supply of certified private counselors to meet consumer demand.

Far from being paternalistic, requiring high-cost debtors to demonstrate price understanding prior to contracting would protect consumer choice and freedom. Under such a policy *any borrower can borrow any loan at any price*. Unlike fascist regimes which might restrict where their citizens can drive, all civilized countries have procedural safety rules which restrict *how* they can drive. Although there may be something invasive about speed limits, seatbelt laws, and drivers' licensing requirements, we all accept these minor inconveniences because the expected gains from safety are worth the trouble. To extend the metaphor: many high-cost debtors, with the encouragement of their lenders, are driving too fast with too little training and faulty brakes on the financial roadways of their lives. Requiring high-cost borrowers to demonstrate a basic understanding of their loans is merely a personal safety rule which has the valuable side effect of encouraging price competition. Furthermore, to the extent such a requirement is paternalistic, it is far less so than interest-rate caps which ban high-cost loans, or bankruptcy discharge provisions, which abate credit contracts altogether.

Comparative Understanding and the Cost of Shopping

Doctors seeking informed consent must not only explain the risks of a proposed medical procedure, but also the risks of alternative procedures. Only through comparative assessment of all the available options can a patient truly understand a treatment option within its context. If doctors did not provide this contextual information, patients would have to research all of the other potential treatments themselves in order to give truly informed consent. Informed consent doctrine requires disclosure of alternative medical procedures because it recognizes that patients do not have the capability of gathering information about treatment alternatives. For this reason, effective disclosure must include reasonable alternatives.

Recommendation #3: High-cost credit disclosure documents should include the average annual percentage rates on comparable credit within the borrower's geographic location correlated against the borrower's FICO credit score.

Information about high-cost loans is only useful if borrowers can use that information to shop for a lower price. For thousands of years, high-cost lenders have obstructed shopping. Today we have the informational technology to provide all borrowers with reliable comparative price information. Using this information, high-cost borrowers could force real price competition, driving down prices. To this effect, the Federal Reserve Board should expand and improve the New York Banking Department's current internet-based credit price-listing service. Because high-cost lenders would be submitting their contract information to the Federal Reserve Board in the disclosure document generation process, it would cost very little to record and compile that information into a database. At any given time, the Federal Reserve Board would have reliable data indicating the lowest, highest, and average interest rates offered on various types of high-cost credit in any given geographic area. This information should be updated regularly and posted on the internet, just as it currently is in New York for mainstream credit. To the extent that high-cost lenders have credit risk underwriting guidelines based on Fair, Isaac and Co. ("FICO") credit scores, this information should also be recorded and correlated against different FICO score ranges. An average price for comparable credit should be incorporated into the Federal Reserve Board disclosure document provided to consumers prior to application. The purpose of this disclosure would be to show the borrower instantaneously whether the contract under consideration was out of line with comparable contracts available to the borrower.

This technology is already available and comparative credit price information is now commonly used by savvy mainstream borrowers. Mainstream consumer credit price information sorted by geographic location and borrower credit history is now so cheaply produced companies literally give it away. Mainstream borrowers can obtain all of this information over the internet in a matter of minutes. But in the high-cost credit market, barriers to understanding and price comparison have prevented market forces from developing comparable technological resources. A program to incorporate this comparative price information into a Federal Reserve Board-prepared disclosure information system is both feasible and would help millions of vulnerable borrowers shop efficiently for the least expensive credit for which they qualify.

In the past, price listing services efficiently functioned for many products sold in smaller increments than high-cost credit, even with more expensive information-sharing technology. Newspaper classified listings in every city paper provide an aggregate price list for everything from used furniture to puppies. But unlike other consumer products, high-cost lenders have insulated themselves from shoppers by making the costs of comparing credit alternatives insurmountably high. The market for high-cost credit will never function efficiently until government leadership compels the innovation of a contextual price information-sharing strategy for high-cost debt. With the advent of the internet, credit-risk statistical models, and other information technologies, the twenty-first century offers a genuinely new opportunity to moderate the credit prices paid by the vulnerable.

From Moral Condemnation to Empirically Demonstrated Risk: Redefining High-Cost Credit Social Norms

In the earlier American debate over tobacco, ultimately unpersuasive moral arguments urging the prohibition of cigarettes hampered successful policymaking for generations. It was not until the late 1950s that discourse shifted to empirically verified public health arguments. This strategic shift subsequently produced many successful new policies, as well as a fundamental shift in the social norms restraining consumer preferences. Hundreds of thousands of lives have been saved as a result. In the case of tobacco market regulation, corrective efforts based on empirically demonstrated personal risk were superior to efforts focusing on moral condemnation. Accordingly:

> Recommendation #4: Government leaders, academics, creditors, and consumer advocates should place new emphasis on empirically demonstrated financial health risks of high-cost credit rather than the moral issues surrounding these loans.

The debate over high-cost credit has never yet evolved from unpersuasive moral arguments urging, on the one hand, prohibition in the form of interest-rate caps, and on the other, elimination of protections for remiss debtors.[12] Learning from the influential Surgeon General's reports in debate over cigarettes, government leaders at both the state and federal level should consider forming advisory committees to study the effects of high-cost lending on vulnerable families and then report their results. Although many regulatory institutions would suffice, employing state and federal attorneys general to conduct these studies might inject a new, relatively independent perspective into the high-cost credit arena. Legislators and the media should give the resulting reports careful attention and scrutiny. At the least, regulatory agencies gathering information on more mainstream financial institutions should expand their data collection to track trends in the high-cost lending industry more aggressively. Moreover, consumer advocates, economists, sociologists, family and consumer studies scholars, and law professors should refocus their attention on the neglected empirical risks to personal financial health associated with high-cost credit.

Toward Social Leadership on Public Safety: Warning in Addition to Informing

In the wake of the collapse of the cigarette prohibition movement during the early twentieth century, a vacuum of government leadership on tobacco facilitated the later unquestioning American acceptance of cigarettes. When government leaders came to realize the health risks of smoking they searched for a balanced policy which would allow them to recapture their role as social leaders. Cigarette advertising and package health hazard warnings admirably served this objective. Warning labels allowed government leaders to share their message of caution with little government or industry compliance costs. These labels, the debate leading up to them, and the mass media coverage of them helped

Americans revisit their personal assumptions and choices with respect to cigarettes. Warnings helped summarize a vast and complex body of scientific evidence about health risks, making a useful inference for consumers. In the case of tobacco regulation, socializing caution, unlike communicating risk information, was relatively cheap and simple. This implies:

Recommendation #5: High-cost credit advertisements, brochures, contracts, webpages, and other documents should carry strongly worded, scientifically designed financial hazard warnings.

Unlike cigarette warning labels, the Truth in Lending Act did not seek to help consumers make any important inferences. Rather it sought to provide the raw legal information which would give only the most attentive readers a rough guide to the price of credit. In addition to having much greater compliance costs than do warning labels, Truth in Lending provided no social leadership to help the most vulnerable debtors reflect on the way they value dangerous high-cost credit products. Moreover, as state interest-rate caps have been removed, camouflaged with exceptions, and watered down by federal law allowing lenders to export the lack of an interest-rate cap in one state to any other state, government has lost the protective social leadership role with respect to high-cost credit incumbent upon it for thousands of years.[13]

Taking a lesson from tobacco legislation, creditor's pamphlets, loan applications, contracts, and websites should all include warning labels. Advertisement warnings should be included in television, radio, and print advertising of high-cost credit. Warnings should use the simplest syntax and vocabulary, should include a pictorial symbol or government seal, and should use a strong signal word such as "DANGER." Such a government warning policy would supplement the Truth in Lending Act by providing a needed message of caution, in addition to mere price information. Unlike relatively costly price disclosures, which vary with each loan, financial hazard warnings could be cheaply added to documents and advertising that lenders would print and pay for anyway. Government would pay virtually nothing in passing the requirement, and the additional implementation costs for industry would be insignificant.

The objective of high-cost credit warnings should not be to reduce borrowing, but rather to help debtors carefully examine their own need and ability to repay. Government should not allow warning labels to be a throwback to Victorian anti-debt moralizing. The message of warnings should not be that high-cost credit is wrong, but rather that high-cost debtors should be cautious. Warnings should help debtors with the difficult human process of matching their purchasing preferences with their own best welfare. In one low-cost stroke, government leaders could recapture their time-honored and indispensable role as active agents of socialization on an important and neglected commercial issue.

LEARNING BY EXAMPLE: A HYPOTHETICAL TRANSACTION BETWEEN "KWIK-E-LOAN" AND "PENNY LESS"

A short hypothetical example will help illuminate how these proposals might improve the functioning of the market for high-cost credit. Let us suppose that a potential debtor named Penny Less is considering purchasing a "payday" check loan from a post-dated check lender called Kwik-E-Loan. If Kwik-E-Loan wants to offer credit at prices in excess of price-threshold triggers established by legislation or administrative rules, then it would only be able to offer credit packages for which a central regulatory agency had prepared disclosure documents over the internet. Suppose Kwik-E-Loan wishes to offer three different post-dated-check loans of $150, $300, and $500 respectively. When setting up its business, Kwik-E-Loan would have contacted a central regulatory authority over the internet. An online program would prompt Kwik-E-Loan with a series of questions describing in turn each of the three contracts the lender hopes to offer. The program would be designed to gather all contractual information potentially material to the price of each loan. Once this series of questions is completed, the regulatory authority computer program would design three documents for each loan: a loan disclosure "price tag" document, a credit application, and comparative price disclosure listing average payday loan prices in Kwik-E-Loan's geographic area. If Kwik-E-Loan has branch locations in different geographic areas, a different average rate sheet would be prepared for each area. These documents would then be e-mailed to Kwik-E-Loan. Regulators would require Kwik-E-Loan to review the e-mailed documents to check for any mistakes. Then Kwik-E-Loan would be free to print and photocopy the disclosure and application forms as many times as it chooses.

Now, suppose that our potential debtor, Penny Less, visits a Kwik-E-Loan outlet and asks to apply for the $300 post-dated-check loan package. Kwik-E-Loan would be required to provide Penny Less with two documents. The first would be the loan disclosure document and the second would be the most recently published comparative price listing for payday loans in Kwik-E-Loan's area. The loan disclosure document would begin with a financial hazard warning emphasizing the dangers associated with high-cost loans. The disclosure document would disclose in plain English all of the contract terms material to the loan's price. In addition to terms such as the annual percentage rate, the document would also disclose contractual provisions such as mandatory arbitration clauses, late fees, insufficient funds fees, and any security interests. Penny would also receive the separate comparative-price disclosure listing the average price offered by competing payday lenders in Kwik-E-Loan's area.

If Penny chooses to continue, Kwik-E-Loan would give her a copy of the Federal Reserve Board software-generated credit application. This application would begin with a second financial hazard warning label. Next would be a series of questions which Penny would be required to answer before Kwik-E-Loan could process the application. The application would explain that Penny must correctly answer at least 80 percent of the questions for her application to be approved. The Federal Reserve Board would have designed the questions to be as simple as possible. Moreover, the order of the questions would track the order and formatting of the credit disclosure document. Because the disclosure document provides all of the answers, Penny would be forced to read the disclosure document in order to apply for the loan. After these questions, a space would be provided for Kwik-E-Loan to ask personal information such as Penny's name, address, telephone number, references, and other applicable information. Kwik-E-Loan itself would be free to design this section of the application. Kwik-E-Loan would also be free to assist Penny in understanding the credit price disclosures. After Penny submits the application, a Kwik-E-Loan clerk would be required to review Penny's answers to the application questions. If Penny correctly identified 80 percent of the material price terms, Kwik-E-Loan would be free to approve the application and then give Penny a written contract. The written contract would be designed by the lender, except that Kwik-E-Loan would be required to include one final Attorney General's Warning Label next to the debtor's signature line. The promissory note would be consummated when Penny signs the contract.

Because in this simple example our imaginary lender offered a small number of identical loans, it would only have to contact the central regulator once in order to obtain the required documents. However, many high-cost lenders cannot offer identical loans, since the amounts of their loans vary with the purchase prices of products. For example, suppose a used car dealer provides relatively high-cost financing to many of its customers with problem credit histories. Because the amount of each loan will depend on the price of each car the dealer sells, dealers would need disclosure documents with many different principle amounts. However, most car dealers limit themselves to offering a small number of financing plans and fill in the details once the price for a car is reached. A similar system for preparing disclosure documents could be designed where these lenders initially set up each financing plan by visiting the regulatory website and answering a series of questions about every provision of each credit package, except the principle amount, the duration of repayment, and any other terms left unsettled until a car price is negotiated. This information would be saved in a password-protected file accessible only by the dealer. When the dealer later comes to an agreement with a customer about the price of a car, and this buyer wishes to obtain financing, the dealer would revisit the regulatory website. The dealer would open the file containing the credit package the buyer wishes to apply for and enter the principal amount of the loan. Then the Federal Reserve Board software would make any necessary last-minute calculations and allow the dealer to print a disclosure and application form.

The disclosure document preparation process would vary in its details with different types of credit. For example, special provisions would be made for new and unusual contractual provisions. More complex contracts, such as mortgage loans with graduated payments and variable interest rates, would require variations in the software and disclosure process. Special disclosure forms could be generated for open-ended credit solicitations. Provided that these processes were designed within the principles set out in this book and carefully tested prior to full-scale implementation, it is well within our technological capabilities to set up effective and provident disclosure systems for all forms of high-cost credit.

CONCLUSION

Prophesies of doom precede virtually all important social changes. In the 1960s opponents of the Truth in Lending Act predicted a "commercial Armageddon."[14] The National Small Business Association claimed in 1967 that the Truth in Lending Act would cause "racial strife and conflict," and that Truth in Lending was somehow "like a personal registration and identification act that forces citizens to carry an identification card or passport at all times."[15] The absurdity of these and similar predictions became clear after Massachusetts stepped forward and passed a state disclosure bill. As one professor explained:

> Small businesses had not closed overnight, nor had the state economy collapsed, no sales clerks had suffered nervous breakdowns at the credit counter, and no bank officials had hanged themselves from their fluorescent lights. With life in Massachusetts going on pretty much as it had before, the opposition found itself somewhat embarrassed by the vigor of its prior rhetoric.[16]

With the exception of paranoia, objections are the natural result of the healthy and progressive discourse that precedes all effective public policy. However, the one objection which, at the beginning of the twenty-first century, is inexcusable, is that we as a society can do no better than to repeat what has already been done. Today we possess new technologies, new legal strategies, and new minds. This book has presented a sketch of how one new and progressive disclosure-based approach to curing the harmful consequences of high-cost lending might look. I have argued that the formation of high-cost loan contracts requires a special enhanced disclosure process cognizant of the following suggestions:

- *High-cost credit should be sold in packages where, prior to application, the debtor receives a uniform, plain English "price tag," prepared in advance by the Federal Reserve Board.*
- *Consumers contemplating risky high-cost credit should not be allowed to borrow until they have demonstrated a reasonable understanding of the contract on a Federal Reserve Board high-cost credit application form.*
- *High-cost credit disclosure documents should include the average annual percentage rates on comparable credit within the borrower's geographic location, correlated against the borrower's FICO credit score.*
- *Government leaders, academics, creditors, and consumer advocates should place new emphasis on the empirically demonstrated financial health risks of high-cost credit rather than the moral issues surrounding these loans.*
- *High-cost credit advertisements, brochures, contracts, webpages, and other documents should carry strongly worded, scientifically designed financial hazard warnings.*

In addition to these specific proposals, this book has also touched on several other general themes. First is that both high-cost creditors and debtors alike must share in shouldering the long-neglected burden of better communication and more thoughtful self-reflection. High-cost creditors have a responsibility to help debtors understand their contracts. But so too do high-cost debtors have a responsibility to make carefully considered decisions. The American system of government and economic distribution presumes that the people will, in most circumstances, take care of themselves. Thus, our social and economic freedoms come with the price of responsibility. When sellers collude to de-

prive buyers of rational price comparisons, and when buyers neglect their responsibility to make those comparisons, all of society
suffers. Not only do debtors themselves suffer, but so too do their
families, their neighborhoods, and their communities.

Second, high-cost credit policy and credit policy directed toward the middle class must be treated separately. Throughout history, interest-rate caps provided important social leadership signals
to creditors and debtors on the danger of high-cost credit. But as
much of our society functionally abandoned interest-rate caps in
the late twentieth century, no rules offering a comparable social
message of restraint have taken their place. Twentieth-century
credit rules have neglected vulnerable debtors by focusing on
mainstream, moderately-priced consumer credit. The increasingly
prevalent view that all debts are morally equivalent has left many
mid-to low-income borrowers without a sense of caution appropriate to the risks of high-cost debt. Truth in Lending may have un-
wittingly facilitated this naïvety, by providing all lenders the same
veneer of legitimacy. Credit policy in the twenty-first century
must require heightened protections and new social leadership for
those who are most vulnerable.

Third, consumer credit disclosure is a relatively young strategy,
whose potential has not been fully explored. Bankruptcy rules,
interest-rate caps, selective protection rules, charitable lending
strategies, and cooperative lending strategies have all existed for
centuries or even millennia. While each of these strategies can
provide meaningful consumer protection for high-cost borrowers,
each also has fundamental limitations. Disclosure rules are com-
patible with each of these strategies and should not be seen as a
substitute for them. Disclosure has only been tried in earnest for
fewer than fifty years. Seen in this historical context, the limitations of current Truth in Lending rules may be the growing pains
of a policy strategy in its adolescence. The ideological overlap between free-market advocates and protection-oriented backers of

government regulation from which Truth in Lending sprang has not yet been fully tapped. Both sides can agree that for the market to function properly, high-cost debtors must make informed decisions based on comparative price information and carefully ordered preferences. Moreover, the revolution in information processing technology *must* be integrated into our consumer credit policies. Truth in Lending was designed to solve problems by sharing information. Naturally it relied on information-sharing technology designed in the mid-twentieth century when Truth in Lending was conceived. But, if we ever hope to achieve *understanding* in lending, our information-sharing policies must use our best information-sharing tools. Thus, there may yet be room for consensus-based consumer credit protections.

Fourth, the moralizing labels and superficial stereotypes of past centuries have become pointless and unproductive. Many still bemoan the loss of a Victorian thrift ethic. Many others curse the chicanery and plundering of high-cost lenders. In the future we should focus on high-cost lending as a public financial health issue. The very worst and most intolerable example of this mistake is the too frequent suggestion that victimized debtors deserve what they get. No one deserves a life of poverty. No one deserves to miss out on a fair share of the fruits of the coming century simply because he or she made imprudent financial decisions. And what is more, the children, spouses, extended families, and communities of debtors do not deserve privation. We must come to realize that the harmful consequences of high-cost debt are better conceived of as a social disease which affects not only debtors, but us all.

The final and most important message of this book is one of hope. We have failed before, but now we may succeed. The history of high-cost lending both in the United States and across the world has been one of failure: the failure of our moral institutions, the failure of our economic systems, the failure of governments, communities, families, and ultimately the failure of individuals.

High-cost debtors fail to make cautious, informed decisions in the face of danger. And high-cost creditors fail to play fairly by the presumptive rules of openly bargained for exchange. This long history of failure risks despair. Many casual observers of the problems associated with high-cost debt too easily shrug their shoulders as though there is nothing to be done. Perhaps academia has suffered from a similar malaise, explaining why, relatively, so little scholarship addresses this important topic. If nothing else, this book seeks to create hope. Times do change and many problems as old and daunting as this one have been solved. Diseases can be cured. Let us hope that in the twenty-first century, the long history of usury may become another.

NOTES

CHAPTER 1

1. Sidney Homer and Richard Sylla, *A History of Interest Rates*, 3rd ed. (New Brunswick, N.J.: Rutgers University Press, 1996), 2.
2. Adam Geller, "Payday Lenders Face Fiery Criticism: consumer advocates say federal law allows institutions to operate like loan sharks," *Salt Lake Tribune*, 28 January 2001, D6.
3. Lawrence Mishel, Jared Bernstein, and John Schmitt, *The State of Working America, 2000/2001* (Ithaca, N.Y.: Cornell University Press, 2001), 276.
4. Ibid.
5. Lendol Calder, *Financing the American Dream: A Cultural History of Consumer Credit* (Princeton, N.J.: Princeton University Press, 1999), 30–31.
6. Chuck Collins and Felice Yeskel, *Economic Apartheid in America: A Primer on Economic Inequality and Insecurity* (New York: New Press, 2000), 58–59.
7. Arthur B. Kennickell, Martha Starr-McCluer, and Brian J. Surette, "Recent Changes in U.S. Family Finances: Results from the 1998 Survey of Consumer Finances," *Federal Reserve Bulletin* (January 2000): 5, 11.
8. Mishel, Bernstein, and Schmitt, *State of Working America*, 278.
9. Alan Greenspan, "Economic challenges in the new century," *Remarks Before the Annual Conference of the National Community Reinvestment Coalition*, Washington, D.C., March 22, 2000, transcript available at http://www.federalreserve.gov.
10. Kennickell, Starr-McCluer, and Surette, "Recent Changes in

U.S. Family Finances," 3. See also Collins and Yeskel, *Economic Apartheid in America*, 39; James Medoff and Andrew Harless, *The Indebted Society: Anatomy of an Ongoing Disaster* (New York: Little, Brown and Co. 1996), 37–45.

11. Mishel, Bernstein, and Schmitt, *State of Working America*, 278.

12. Deanne Loonin and Elizabeth Renuart, "Less Than Six Degrees of Separation: Consumer Law Connections to Your Practice (Part I)," *Clearinghouse Review* (March–April 1998): 587.

13. Timothy H. Hannan, "Retail Fees of Depository Institutions, 1994–99," *Federal Reserve Bulletin* (January 2001): 1, 3–5.

14. Robert D. Manning, *Credit Card Nation* (New York: Basic Books, 2000): 199.

15. Kennickell, Starr-McCluer, and Surette, "Recent Changes in U.S. Family Finances," 9; Manning, *Credit Card Nation*, 199.

16. Michael Squires, "Short-term Loan Firms Prospering: Critics Say High Interest Rates, Easy Terms Have Led to Exploitation of Working Poor," *Las Vegas Review Journal*, 23 December 2001, 16; Dean Foust, "Easy Money: Subprime lenders make a killing catering to poorer Americans. Now Wall Street is getting in on the act," *Business Week*, 24 April 2000, 107; Geller, "Payday Lenders Face Fiery Criticism," D6; Editorial, "Time To Restore Loan-Sharking Laws," *Santa Fe New Mexican*, 9 April 2000, F-8; Editorial, "Borrowing Trouble: How Can Legislators Not Be Offended by Payday-Advance Businesses that Charge Outrageous Fees to Cash Strapped Consumers? Leaders, Step Forward," *Orlando Sentinel*, 17 April 2000, A10; John Roska, "How High Can the Finance Companies Go? With Interest Rates, the Sky Is the Limit," *St. Louis Post-Dispatch*, 16 July 1998; Jamal E. Watson, "Banking on a Costly Alternative: Low Earners Turn to Check Cashing Stores," *Boston Globe*, 28 February 2000, A1; Editorial, "Wolf At the Door: Vulnerable Need Protection Against Predatory Lenders," *Washington Post*, 10 March 2002, B10; Richard Newman, "Shark Attacks; An Encounter with Predatory

Lenders Can Leave You Without Your Money—Or Your Home,"
The Bergen County (N.J.) Record, 6 January 2002, B01; Molly
Ivins, "Feeding Off the Bottom," *Raleigh News and Observer*, 12
April 2000, A19; Jane Bryant Quinn, "Little Loans Come at
Staggering Cost," *Washington Post*, 13 June 1999, H02; Peter T.
Kilborn, "New Lenders With Huge Fees Thrive on Workers With
Debts," *New York Times*, 18 June 1999, A1; Editorial, "It Was Il-
legal When it was Loansharking," *Kansas City Star*, 2 March
2001, B6.

17. John P. Caskey, *Fringe Banking: Check-Cashing Outlets, Pawn-
shops, and the Poor* (New York: Russell Sage Foundation, 1994):
46 n.6, 62, 150; W. C. A. M. Dessart and A. A. A. Kuylen, "The
Nature, Extent, Causes, and Consequences of Problematic Debt
Situations," *Journal of Consumer Policy* 9 (1986): 311; Janet Ford,
The Indebted Society: Credit and Default in the 1980s (London:
Routledge, 1988), 126; T. C. Puckett, "Consumer Credit: A Ne-
glected Area in Social Work Education," *Contemporary Social
Work Education* 2 (1978): 121, 125; "Report of the Staff to Chair-
man Gramm, Committee on Banking, Housing and Urban Af-
fairs—Predatory Lending Practices: Staff Analysis of Regulators'
Responses," (23 August 2000), reprinted in *Consumer Finance
Law Quarterly Report* 54 (Summer 2000): 230–31.

18. Homer and Sylla, *History of Interest Rates*, 72.

19. For examples of courts and commentators using the term see:
Williams v. Gelt Financial Corp., 232 B.R. 629, 636 (Bankr. E.D.
Penn 1999); *DeBerry v. First Government Mortgage and Investors
Corp.*, 170 F.3d 1105, 1107 (D.C. Cir. 1999); *American Financial
Services Association v. Burke*, 169 F.Supp.2d 62, 68 (D. Conn.
2001); Deborah Goldstein, Note, "Protecting Consumers from
Predatory Lenders: Defining the Problem and Moving Toward a
Workable Solution," *Harvard Civil Rights-Civil Liberties Law Re-
view* 35 (Winter 2000): 232; Kathleen E. Keest, Jeffrey I. Langer,
and Michael F. Day, "Interest Rate Regulation Developments:

High Cost Mortgages, Rent-to-Own Transactions, and Unconscionability," *Business Lawyer* (May 1995): 1083–84.

20. Mark H. Haller and John V. Alviti, "Loansharking in American Cities: Historical Analysis of a Marginal Enterprise," *American Journal of Legal History* 21 (1977): 125, 127–28; Kathleen E. Keest, "Stone Soup: Exploring the Boundaries Between Subprime Lending and Predatory Lending," *Practicing Law Institute Corporate Law and Practice Course Handbook Series* (16 April 2001): 1111; Baxter Ware, "The Lure of the Loan Shark," *Harper's Weekly* 52 (11 July 1908): 32.

21. Jean Ann Fox, "What Does it Take To Be a Loanshark in 1998? A Report on the Payday Loan Industry," *Practicing Law Institute: Corporate Law and Practice Course Handbook Series*, 1047 (April–May 1998): 989–90; Deborah A. Schmedemann, "Time and Money: One State's Regulation of Check-Based Loans," *William Mitchell Law Review* 27 (2000): 974–76; Scott Andrew Schaaf, "From Checks to Cash: Regulation of the Payday Lending Industry," *North Carolina Banking Institute* 5 (April 2001): 341–42.

22. Comment, "Syndicate Loan-Shark Activities and New York's Usury Statute," *Columbia Law Review* 66 (1966): 167.

23. Indiana Department of Financial Institutions, "Summary of Payday Lender Examination: 7/1/99 Thru 9/30/99," (available at http://www.dfi.state.in.us), viewed 11 January 2002; Jean Ann Fox and Ed Mierzwinski, *Show Me the Money: A Survey of Payday Lenders and Review of Payday Lender Lobbying in State Legislatures* (Washington, D.C.: Consumer Federation of America & U.S. Public Interest Research Group, 2000): 7; Christopher Peterson, "Failed Markets, Failing Government, Or Both?: Learning from the Unintended Consequences of Utah Consumer Credit on Vulnerable Debtors," *Utah Law Review* (2001): 543, 564.

24. Contract on file with author.

25. Jean Ann Fox and Ed Mierzwinski, *Rent-A-Bank Payday Lending:*

How Banks Help Payday Lenders Evade State Consumer Protections (Washington, D.C.: Consumer Federation of America & U.S. Public Interest Research Group, 2001), 12–15; Al Guart, "'Loanshark' Banks Bite Apple," *New York Post*, 7 April 2002, 23; James J. White, "The Usury Trompe l'Oeil," *South Carolina Law Review* 51 (Spring 2000): 447–48.

26. Elizabeth McCaul, Superintendent of Banks, *Industry Letter on Payday Loans*, 13 June 2000, (available at http://www.banking.state.ny.us), viewed 11 January 2002.

27. Gregory Elliehausen and Edward C. Lawrence, *Payday Advance Credit in America: An Analysis of Demand* (Washington, D.C.: Georgetown University, McDonough School of Business Credit Research Center, 2001), 39; Indiana Department of Financial Institutions, *Summary of Payday Lender Examination*, 1–2; Fox and Mierzwinski, *Show Me the Money*, 8. Office of the North Carolina Commissioner of Banks, *Report to the General Assembly on Payday Lending*, available at http://www.banking.state.nc.us/, (July 3, 2001), 5–6; Sarah D. Vega, *Short Term Lending Final Report* (Springfield, IL: Illinois Department of Financial Institutions, 1999), 30.

28. Vega, *Short Term Lending Final Report*, 26 (emphasis added).

29. Danielle Herubin, "Some Check Cashers Charging Interest That Can Reach 520%," *Palm Beach Post*, (11 November 1998): 6B; Daniel A. Edelman, "Payday Loans: Big Interest Rates and Little Regulation," *Loyola Consumer Law Review* 11 (1999): 175.

30. Vega, *Short Term Lending Report*, 30.

31. Fox and Mierzwinski, *Show Me the Money*, 8.

32. Lisa Blaylock Moss, "Modern Day Loansharking: Deferred Presentment Transactions and the Need for Regulation," *Alabama Law Review* 51 (Summer 2000): 1725, 1729; John Hendren, "More states allow triple-digit loan rates," *Tuscaloosa News* 10, January 1999, 6B.

33. Peterson, "Failed Markets, Failing Government."

34. Keest, "Stone Soup," 1115.
35. Office of the Commissioner of Banks, *Report to the General Assembly*, 2.
36. Fox and Mierzwinski, *Show Me the Money*, 10.
37. See, e.g., John Conyn, Attorney General of Texas, "Be Wary of Payday Loans," *Ask the AG*, available at http://www.occc.state.tx.us, viewed 1 January 2002; Keest, "Stone Soup," 1115–16; Fox and Mierzwinski, *Show Me the Money*, 10; Moss, "Modern Day Loansharking," 1743–44; Deborah A. Schmedemann, "Time and Money," 977.
38. Fox and Mierzwinski, *Show Me the Money*, 19; Jean Ann Fox, "What Does It Take to be a Loan Shark?" 900; Office of the Commissioner of Banks, *Report to the General Assembly*, 5; Peterson, "Failed Markets, Failing Government," 561.
39. Mike Hudson, "Going for Broke: How the 'Fringe Banking' Boom Cashes in on the Poor," *Washington Post*, 10 January 1993, C01.
40. Fox and Mierzwinski, *Show Me the Money*, 8.
41. Hudson, "Going for Broke," C01.
42. Damian Paletta, "In Brief: Hawke Says Don't Overlook the 'Underbanked,'"*American Banker* 167(53) (19 March 2002): 4.
43. Comment, "Syndicate Loan-Shark Activities," 167; Fox and Mierzwinski, *Show Me the Money*, 8; X. M. Frascogna Jr., "Check Cashers: An Expanding Financial Service," *Mississippi College Law Review* 19 (Fall 1998): 231 n. 17; G. Edward Leary, "Report of the Commissioner of Financial Institutions," *State of Utah* 30 (June 2001), 158; Vega, *Short Term Lending Final Report*, 6–7.
44. Jaret C. Oeltjen, "Florida Pawnbrokering: An Industry in Transition," *Florida State University Law Review* 23 (Spring 1996): 995; Jaret C. Oeltjen, "Pawnbrokering on Parade," *Buffalo Law Review* 37 (1989): 757; Willis J. Wheat, "A Study on the Status of the Pawnbroker Industry in the State of Oklahoma," *Consumer Finance Law Quarterly Report* (Winter 1998): 87–90.

45. Kortney Stringer, "Best of Times is Worst of Times for Pawnshops," *Wall Street Journal*, 22 August 2000, B1.
46. Paul E. Kandarian, "Fortune's Fleeting, Pawnshops are Forever," *Boston Globe*, 20 February 2000, 1; Linda A. Moore, "Casinos, Economy, Attitudes Affect Both Sides of Pawnshop Business," *The Memphis Commercial Appeal*, 27 May 2001, C1.
47. Nicole Gull, "Pawn business not allowed to add check cashing," *Kansas City Star*, 30 January 2002, 14; Tom Sheehan, "Pawnshop to Trade in Name for Downtown Delaware Home," *Columbus (Ohio) Dispatch*, 23 October 1999, 7B; Beth Feinstein-Bartl, "Pines OKs New Ban on Flea Markets, City Ordinance Revision Also Bars Pawnshops," *Ft. Lauderdale Sun-Sentinel*, 9 January 2000, 15; Harry Hitzeman, "Village gives itself option to revoke pawnshop license," *Chicago Daily Herald*, 3 March 2001, 4; Janet McNichols, "Pawnshop plan in former hardware store meets opposition," *St. Louis Post-Dispatch*, 18 June 2001, 4; Tom Wilemon, "Pawnbrokers Question New Laws," *Biloxi (Miss.) Sun Herald*, 10 October 2001, A2.
48. John P. Caskey, *Lower Income Americans, Higher Cost Financial Services* (Madison, WI: Filene Research Institute, 1997), 27.
49. Moore, "Casinos, Economy, Attitudes," C1.
50. N. R. Kleinfield, "Running the Little Man's Bank," *New York Times*, 13 August 1989, 37. John P. Caskey, *Fringe Banking: Check-Cashing Outlets, Pawnshops, and the Poor* (New York: Russell Sage Foundation, 1994), 70–71; Bill Minutaglio, "Prince of Pawns: with a keen appreciation for the high-return, low-risk investment, Jack Daugherty is making hock shops a hot corporate property," in *Merchants of Misery: How Corporate America Profits from Poverty*, ed. Michael Hudson (Monroe, ME: Common Courage Press, 1996), 58–70.
51. Caskey, *Fringe Banking*, 12, 39–42; Kandarian, "Fortune's Fleeting, Pawnshops are Forever," C1; Hang Nguyen, "Pawnshops Hope New Loans Help Industry in Lean Times," *Dallas Morning*

News, 23 August 2000, 1A; Marla Dickerson and Stuart Silverstein, "In Tough Times, Pawnshops Are Thriving Lending," *Los Angeles Times*, 30 September 2001, C1.

52. Sara Nesbitt, "Borrowing a Better Image: Pawnshops Cater to a New Generation of Bargain Hunters," *The Colorado Springs Gazette*, 13 May 2001, 1.

53. Deb Gruver, "Pawnshop Owners in Wichita, Kan., Expect to Have Happy Holidays," *Knight Ridder Tribune Business News*, 11 October 2001.

54. Dickerson and Silverstein, "In Tough Times, Pawnshops Are Thriving Lending," C1; "Get Into the Pawnbrokers for Hard Times Ahead," *Sunday Business Post*, 17 June 2001.

55. Anderson, "Pawnshop Economics," F1; Debbie Blossom, "Pawnshops Fill a Niche," *Tulsa World*, 20 January 2002, 1; Elliot Brack, "Here's Why Pawnshops are Popping Up All Over," *Atlanta Journal and Constitution*, 10 July 2000, JJ4; Caskey, *Fringe Banking*, 139; John P. Caskey, "Explaining the Boom in Check-Cashing Outlets and Pawnshops," *Consumer Finance Law Quarterly Report* (Winter 1995): 6; Judy Waggoner, "Pawnshops in Appleton, Wisc. Area See Business Surge When Economy Slips," *Knight Ridder Tribune Business News*, 16 December 2001.

56. Caskey, *Higher Priced Financial Services*, 49–50; Alix M. Freedman, "Peddling Dreams: A Market Giant Uses Its Sales Prowess To Profit on Poverty," *Wall Street Journal*, 22 September 1993, reprinted in *Merchants of Misery: How Corporate America Profits From Poverty*, ed. Michael Hudson (Monroe, ME: Common Courage Press), 151, 158.

57. Federal Trade Commission, *Survey of Rent-to-Own Customers*, (Washington, D.C.), ES-4, 1, 55–57.

58. "Consumer Activists Opposing 'Rent-to-Own' Legislation," *Congress Daily*, 27 November 2001; Consumer Federation of America, et al., "Open Letter in Opposition to Industry-Supported Rent-to-Own Bill: HR 1701," 27 November 2001, available at

http://www.pirg.org, viewed 14 January 2002; Federal Trade Commission, *Survey of Rent-to-Own Customers*, 7–8; Jake Lewis, "Renting to Owe: Rent-to-Own Companies Prey on Low-Income Consumers," *Multinational Monitor*, 1 October 2001, 16.

59. Michael L. Walden, "The Economics of Rent-to-Own Contracts," *Journal of Consumer Affairs* (22 December 1990): 326; Lacy H. Thornburg, North Carolina Attorney General, "Statement on H 1108—Representative Hackney's Rent-to-Own Bill," 9 July 1987; Roger M. Swagler and Paula Wheeler, "Rental Purchase-Agreements: A Preliminary Investigation of Consumer Attitudes and Behaviors," *Journal of Consumer Affairs* (22 June 1989): 145; Susan Lorde Martin and Nancy White Huckins, "Consumer Advocates vs. The Rent-to-Own Industry: Reaching a Reasonable Accommodation," *American Business Law Journal* (Spring 1997): 40; Michael H. Anderson, "A Reconsideration of Rent-to-Own," *Journal of Consumer Affairs* 35(2) (1 January 2001). Robert Manning estimates the Rent-A-Center typically charges interest rates between 180 and 360 percent. Manning, *Credit Card Nation*, 210.

60. Freedman, "Peddling Dreams," 159 (alteration in original).

61. Ibid., 159–60.

62. Ibid., 157.

63. Margot Saunders, National Consumer Law Center, "Testimony before the Committee on Financial Services, Subcommittee on Financial Institutions & Consumer Credit regarding H.R. 1701," 12 July 2001, available at http://www.pirg.org, viewed 14 January 2002; *Kimble v. Universal TV Rental*, 65 Ohio Mic. 17, 417 N.E.2d 597 (1980); *Fassitt v. Rental, Inc.*, 297 So.2d 283 (La. Ct. App. 1974); Federal Trade Commission, *Survey of Rent-to-Own Customers*, 98–99 n.138; *State v. Stewart*, 288 N.W.2d 751 (Neb. 1980).

64. Freedman, "Peddling Dreams," 154, 164–65.

65. Lewis, "Renting to Owe," 16; Federal Trade Commission, *Rent-*

to-Own Customer Survey, 3; Manning, *Credit Card Nation*, 209; Michael Hudson, "Cashing in on Poverty: How Big Business Wins Every Time," *The Nation*, 20 May 1996; Loonin and Renuart, "Less Than Six Degrees," 587.

66. For example, the Illinois Department of Financial Institutions found an average APR of 290 percent on Illinois car title loans. Vega, *Short Term Lending*, 26. See also Lynn Drysdale and Kathleen Keest, "The Two-Tiered Consumer Financial Services Marketplace: The Fringe Banking System and its Challenge to Current Thinking About the Role of Usury Laws in Today's Society," *South Carolina Law Review* 51 (Spring 2000): 599; *Pendleton v. American Title Brokers*, 754 F.Supp. 860 (S.D. Ala. 1991).

67. Carol Marbin Miller, "'Car pawn' customers fight back," *St. Petersburg Times*, 16 July 1996, 1B.

68. Ibid.

69. Eric Stern, "Bill would limit 'payday' loans: Holden considers measure; Interest rates up to 400 pct. drew attention of legislators," *St. Louis Post-Dispatch*, 26 June 2001, B1.

70. Dalton Conley, *Being Black, Living in the Red: Race, Wealth, and Social Policy in America* (Berkeley: University of California Press, 1999), 38; Lisa A. Keister, *Wealth in America: Trends in Wealth Inequality* (Cambridge, UK: Cambridge University Press, 2000), 189–200.

71. Michael D. Larson, "It's buyer beware when you're shopping for a subprime loan," *Bankrate.com*, February 2, 2001, available at http://www.bankrate.com, viewed 31 May 2001. See also Glenn B. Canner, Wayne Passmore, and Elizabeth Landerman, "The Role of Specialized Lenders in Extending Mortgages to Lower-Income and Minority Homebuyers," *Federal Reserve Bulletin* (November 1999): 715–16; Neil J. Morse, "Coping with a wild market," *Mortgage Banking* 62(4) (1 January 2002): 107.

72. Edmund Sanders, "Ameriquest Defends Loan Practices: Sub-

Prime Lender Says it has Been Fair, But Activists See Examples of Predatory Lending," *Los Angeles Times,* 9 April 2000, C1.

73. Jennifer Larson and Frank Green, "Home Inequity Loans Hallmark of 'Predatory' Mortgage Lending Include Very High Interest Rates, Unneeded Credit Insurance and Balloon Payments. Such Practices Have Cost Consumers Billions," *San Diego Union-Tribune,* 21 August 2001, H1; Lew Sichelman, "Housing Scene: Subprime Lender Makes Effort to Address Consumer Concerns," *Origination News* 10(2) (24 August 2001): 8.

74. James MacPherson, "Carpenter Believes Would-be Financial Savior a Predatory Lender," *Alaska Journal of Commerce* 25(31) (5 August 2001): 8.

75. Russell Grantham, "Predatory Lenders Feel the Heat; Fed's Reforms Fall Short, Say Critics and Borrowers," *Atlanta Journal and Constitution,* 13 January 2002, C1.

76. Governor Edward M. Gramlich, "Remarks at the Federal Reserve Bank of Philadelphia Community and Consumer Affairs Department Conference on Predatory Lending," Philadelphia, Pa., 6 December 2000, available at http://www.federalreserve.gov viewed 10 December 2001; Patricia E. Obara, "Predatory Lending," *Banking Law Journal* (June 2001): 541 n.1.

77. Consumers Union Southwest Regional Office, *In Over Our Heads: Predatory Lending and Fraud in Manufactured Housing* (Austin, TX.: Consumers Union, February 2002): 4–6, available at http://www.consumersunion.org, viewed 23 February 2002; Consumers Union Southwest Regional Office and Austin Tenant's Council, *Access to the Dream: Subprime and Prime Mortgage Lending in Texas* (Austin, TX: Consumers Union, April 2000) available at http://www.consumersunion.org, viewed 23 February 2002; Gordon Oliver, "Manufactured Promises: Some Buyers of Manufactured Houses Find Themselves Trapped in Bad Deals," parts 1 and 2, *Portland Oregonian,* 20 and 21 August 2000, A01; Editorial, "Street of Broken Dreams," *Portland Oregonian,* 3 Sep-

tember 2000, F04; Heather Timmons, "Home Equity: Despite Potholes, Some See Gold in Prefab Lending," *American Banker* 163(148) (5 August 1998): 1.

78. Consumers Union, "In Over Our Heads," 2, 9–12, 14–15; R. A. Dyer, "Study cites complaints in mobile home sales," *Fort Worth Star-Telegram* 15 February 2002, 1; Robert Julavits, "Addition by Subtraction: GreenPoint Quits Prefab," *American Banker* 167(3) (4 January 2002): 1; Robert Julavits, "Economy's Streak Cited in Slump for Prefab Homes," *American Banker* 171(166) (7 September 2000): 9; "In Brief: FirstMerit to Close Prefab Lending Unit," *American Banker* 167(210) (1 November 2001): 6; Laura Pavlenko Lutton, "Small-Bank Lenders Feast on Surge in Prefabs," *American Banker* 164(77) (23 April 1999): 6; Canner, Passmore, and Landerman, "The Role of Specialized Lenders," 711.

79. Canner, Passmore, and Landerman, "The Role of Specialized Lenders," 719.

80. Teresa Sullivan, Elizabeth Warren, and Jay Lawrence Westbrook, *As We Forgive Our Debtors* (New Haven: Yale University Press, 1989), 303.

81. Lawrence M. Ausubel, "Credit Card Defaults, Credit Card Profits, and Bankruptcy," *American Bankruptcy Law Journal* 71 (Spring 1997): 256. Also, see George M. Salem and Aaron C. Clark, "Bank Credit Cards: Loan Loss Risks Are Growing," *GKM Banking Industry Report* (11 June 1996).

82. Karen Gross, *Failure and Forgiveness: Rebalancing the Bankruptcy System* (1997).

83. Elizabeth Warren, "The Bankruptcy Crisis," *Indiana Law Journal* 73 (1998): 1100–01.

84. U.S. House Committee on Government Operations, Manpower and Housing Subcommittee, *Mortgage Delinquencies and Defaults: Hearings Before the Manpower and Housing Subcommittee*, 97th Cong., 2d Sess. (1982), 1, statement of Representative Cardiss Collins.

85. Constance Perin, *Everything in Its Place: Social Order and Land Use in America* (Princeton, N.J.: Princeton University Press, 1977). See also, Sandra Fleishman, "Facing Foreclosure: It's an Owner's Nightmare, but Not All Houses Go to Auction," *Washington Post*, 2 February 2002, H01; Forrester, "Mortgaging the American Dream," 386; Mark Fried, "Grieving for a Lost Home," in *The Urban Condition*, ed. Leonard J. Duhl, (New York: Basic Books, 1963), 151; John Henretta, "Parental Status and Child's Homeownership," *American Sociological Review* 49 (1984): 131–40; John Henretta, "Race Differences in Middle Class Lifestyle: The Role of Home Ownership," *Social Science Research* 8 (1979): 63–78; John Henretta and Richard Campbell, "Net Worth as an Aspect of Status," *American Journal of Sociology* 83 (1978): 1024–1223; Keister, *Wealth in America*, 189.

86. David B. Lawrence, *Handbook of Consumer Lending* (1992), xiv; National Consumer Law Center, *Stop Predatory Lending: A Guide for Legal Advocates* (Boston: National Consumer Law Center, 2001), 13 n.34.

87. Ford, *The Indebted Society*, 120.

88. Debtors Anonymous, "History of Debtors Anonymous," available at http://www.debtorsanonymous.org/about/history.htm, reviewed March 28, 2003.

89. "Pressure As a Collection Tool: Turn Up the Heat to Get Paid," *Consumer Credit Collector* 5 (October 1997): 1.

90. "Set Deadlines to Create Urgency," *Consumer Credit Collector* 5 (October 1997): 3.

91. Dessart and Kuylen, "The Nature of Problematic Debt," Ford, *The Indebted Society*, 121–22; Martin Ryan, *The Last Resort, A Study of Consumer Bankrupts* (1995), 50, 114–17; D. Caplovitz, *Consumers in Trouble: A Study of Debtors in Default* (New York: Free Press, 1974): 298; T. C. Puckett, "Consumer Credit: A Neglected Area in Social Work Education," *Contemporary Social Work Education* 2 (1978): 121–23.

92. Anonymous autobiographical comment taken from Debtors Anonymous, *A Currency of Hope* (Needham, MA: Debtors Anonymous General Service Board, 1999): 131–32.
93. Puckett, *Consumer Credit*, 122; "Debts Drove Upholsterer to Kill Himself," *Northern Echo*, 30 March 2000; Christian Williams, "Combating the Problems of Human Rights Abuses and Inadequate Organ Supply Through Presumed Donative Consent," *Case Western Reserve Journal of International Law* 26 (Spring/Summer 1994): 322–23, n.36; Bruce Bongar, *The Suicidal Patient: Clinical and Legal Standards of Care* (Washington D.C.: American Psychological Association, 1991), 86–91; Frank Green and Mike Freeman, "The Debt Generation: Free Spending 20-Somethings Lured by Easy Credit," *San Diego Union Tribune*, 3 January 2002, A1 (discussing 22-year-old National Merit Scholar who committed suicide under pressure from $14,000 in unsecured debt).
94. "Title/pawn crackdown to be delayed," *Jacksonville Florida Times Union*, 21 March 1997, B1; Editorial, "What will they do? Predatory lenders are circling Florida's poor: It's up to state leaders to come to the rescue and fend off the sharks," *Orlando Sentinel*, 2 April 1999, A14.
95. Chris Johnson, Vice President Urgent Money Service, "Letter to the Editor," *Greensboro News and Record*, 7 January 2002, A6.

CHAPTER 2

1. Paul Einzig, *Primitive Money In Its Ethnological, Historical and Economic Aspects* (Oxford, New York: Pergamon Press, 1966), 363.
2. James M. Ackerman, "Interest Rates and the Law: A History of Usury," 1981 *Arizona State Law Journal* (1981): 61; Hugh Barty-King, *The Worst Poverty: A History of Debt and Debtors* (London: Sutton Publishing, 1997); Arthur Birnie, *The History and Ethics of Interest* (Glasgow: H. Hodge, 1952); Jeremiah W. Blydenburgh, *A Treatise on the Law of Usury* (New York: J. S. Voorhies, 1844);

Robert Buckley Comyn, *A Treatise on the Law of Usury* (London: T. Davison, 1817); Cheryl L. Danieri, *Credit Where Credit is Due: The Mont-de-Piete of Paris, 1777–1851* (New York: Garland Publishing, 1991); Raymond DeRoover, *Money, Banking and Credit in Mediaeval Bruges* (Cambridge: Mediaeval Academy of America, 1948); James G. Frierson, "Changing Concepts on Usury: Ancient Times Through the Time of John Calvin," *American Business Law Journal* 7 (1969): 115; Sidney Homer and Richard Sylla, *A History of Interest Rates*, 3d ed. (New Brunswick: Rutgers University Press, 1996); William Chester Jordan, *Women and Credit in Pre-Industrial and Developing Societies* (Philadelphia: University of Pennsylvania Press, 1993); Odd Langholm, *The Aristotelian Analysis of Usury* (New York: Columbia University Press, 1984); Paul Millett, *Lending and Borrowing in Ancient Athens* (New York: Cambridge University Press, 1991); J. B. C. Murray, *The History of Usury from the Earliest Period to the Present Time* (Philadelphia: J. B. Lippincott, 1866); Benjamin Nelson, *The Idea of Usury: From Tribal Brotherhood to Universal Otherhood*, 2d ed. (Princeton: Princeton University Press, 1949); John T. Noonan, *The Scholastic Analysis of Usury* (Cambridge: Harvard University Press, 1957); Mark Ord, *Essays on the Law of Usury*, 3d ed. (Hartford, Conn.: Printed for the editor, 1809); Franklin Winton Ryan, *Usury and Usury Laws* (Boston: Houghton Mifflin Company, 1942); Melanie Tebbutt, *Making Ends Meet: Pawnbroking and Working-Class Credit* (New York: St. Martin's Press, 1983).

3. This book omits strategies which have minimal relevance for contemporary policymakers. For example, the South Pacific Islander society on Rossel Island had a complex shell currency system, where certain types of shells were the only valid tender for certain types of transactions. Currency traders developed who borrowed from those who did not want a particular type of shell and lent to those who did. Interestingly, beliefs about magic of the currency traders, rather than laws, enforced the consumer

credit system. See Einzig, *Primitive Money*, 61–64. Far more influential, but still not particularly relevant to contemporary America, are the medieval Christian and Islamic doctrines forbidding taking any interest at all. Also beyond the scope of this book are totalitarian Marxist strategies such as those of the Soviet Union and the People's Republic of China.

4. Jordan, *Women and Credit*, 13.
5. Homer and Sylla, *History of Interest Rates*, 17–21; Jordan, *Women and Credit*, 13; Ackerman, "A History of Usury," 63.
6. Ackerman, "A History of Usury," 63; Homer and Sylla, *History of Interest Rates*, 18; Charles O. Hardy, et al., *Consumer Credit and its Uses* (New York: Prentice-Hall, 1938), 4–5; Alfred Marshall, *Principles of Economics*, 8th ed. (London: Macmillan and Company, 1970), 584.
7. Ackerman, "A History of Usury," 63–64; Samuel Noah Kramer, *The Sumerians: Their History, Culture, and Character* (Chicago: University of Chicago Press, 1963), 79–82; Hardy, et al., *Consumer Credit and its Uses*, 4–5; H. W. F. Saggs, *Babylonians* (Norman: University of Oklahoma Press, 1995), 97.
8. Kramer, *The Sumerians*, 79–82; Thomas H. Greer and Gavin Lewis, *A Brief History of the Western World*, 6th ed. (New York: Harcourt Brace Jovanovich College Publishers, 1992), 15–18; Homer and Sylla, *History of Interest Rates*, 26.
9. Greer and Lewis, *History of the Western World*, 15–18; Homer and Sylla, *History of Interest Rates*, 26.
10. Saggs, *Babylonians*, 97.
11. Kramer, *The Sumerians*, 79–82; Saggs, *Babylonians*, 97.
12. Louis Edward Levinthal, "The Early History of Bankruptcy Law," *University of Pennsylvania Law Review* 66 (1918): 223, 246.
13. Homer and Sylla, *History of Interest Rates*, 99.
14. Ibid., 94, 112.
15. G. R. Driver and John C. Miles, *The Babylonian Laws* (Oxford: Clarendon Press, 1955), 39. Homer and Sylla, *History of Interest*

Rates, 30; C. H. W. Johns, *The Oldest Code of Laws in the World: The Code of Laws Promulgated By Hammurabi, King of Babylon* (New York: Charles Scribner, 1903), 68.

16. Johns, *The Oldest Code*, 12–13, 20–22, 30.
17. M. I. Finley, *Economy and Society in Ancient Greece* (London: Chatto and Windus, 1981), 162; Homer and Sylla, *History of Interest Rates*, 27; Edward L. Glaeser and Jose Scheinkman, "Neither a Borrower nor a Lender Be: An Economic Analysis of Interest Restrictions and Usury Laws," *Journal of Law and Economics* 41 (1998): 1, 20 n.37, paraphrasing C. H. W. Johns, *Babylonian and Assyrian Laws, Contracts and Letters* (New York: C. Scribner's Sons, 1904).
18. T. J. Cornell, *The Beginnings of Rome: Italy and Rome from the Bronze Age to the Punic Wars (C. 1000–264 BC)* (New York: Routledge, 1995), 256–57, 266; Michael Crawford, *The Roman Republic*, 2d ed. (Cambridge: Harvard University Press, 1993), 31–42.
19. Cornell, *Beginnings of Rome*, 266.
20. Homer and Sylla, *History of Interest Rates*, 45, 52.
21. Ibid., 48–49, 59.
22. Ray Huang, *1587: A Year of No Significance: The Ming Dynasty in Decline* (New Haven: Yale University Press, 1981), 131, 138, 144–45, 149.
23. Ibid., 130–55.
24. James Bunyan Parsons, *The Peasant Rebellions of the Late Ming Dynasty* (Tucson: University of Arizona Press, 1970), 5.
25. Robin A. Morris, "Consumer Debt and Usury: A New Rationale For Usury," *Pepperdine Law Review* 15 (1988): 151.
26. Deut. 23:19–20 (Oxford Study Ed., 1976) (emphasis added). See also Nelson, *The Idea of Usury*, xix–xxii.
27. Glaeser and Scheinkman, "Neither a Borrower nor a Lender Be," 21.
28. H. Tadmor, "The Period of the First Temple, the Babylonian

Exile and the Restoration," in *A History of the Jewish People*, ed.
H. H. Ben-Sasson (Cambridge: Harvard University Press, 1976),
175–76.

29. Neh. 5:1–13 (Oxford Study Ed., 1976).

30. Finley, *Economy and Society*, 163; Kramer, *The Sumerians*, 82;
Saggs, *Babylonians*, n.14, 97; Tadmor, "The Period of the First
Temple," 175–76.

31. K.V. Rangaswami Aiyangar, *Aspects of Ancient Indian Economic
Thought* (Mylapore, Madras, India: The Madras Law Journal
Press, 1934), 108.

32. Ackerman, "Interest Rates and the Law," 68; Finley, *Economy and
Society*, 156; Fritz M. Heichelheim, *An Ancient Economic History:
From the Paleolithic Age to the Migrations of the Germanic, Slavic
and Arabic Nations*, trans. Joyce Stevens, 2d ed., vol. 1 (Leiden:
A.W. Sijthoff, 1958): 281–82 (giving a more thorough account of
the causes of the Solonic crisis); Ivan M. Linforth, "Solon the
Athenian," in *Classical Philology* (Berkeley: University of California Publications, 1919), 52; Millett, *Lending and Borrowing in Ancient Athens*, 181.

33. Linforth, "Solon the Athenian," 48–49 (citations omitted).

34. Millett, *Lending and Borrowing in Ancient Athens*, 50 (alterations
omitted). Finley, *Economy and Society*, 157; Homer and Sylla,
History of Interest Rates, 34–35.

35. Linforth,"Solon the Athenian," 67–68.

36. Homer and Sylla, *History of Interest Rates*, 35–36.

37. Millett, *Lending and Borrowing in Ancient Athens*, 219–20.

38. Homer and Sylla, *History of Interest Rates*, 38.

39. Millett, *Lending and Borrowing in Ancient Athens*, 220–21.

40. Homer and Sylla, *History of Interest Rates*, 35, 36, 40.

41. Ackerman, "Interest Rates and the Law," 69–70.

42. Ibid., quoting Plato, *The Republic*, trans. Francis Macdonald Conford (New York: Oxford University Press, 1945), 280.

43. Jordan, *Women and Credit*, 15.

44. The *montes pietatum* are also commonly referred to by their Italian name, *monti di pieta*. Ackerman, "Interest Rates and the Law," 76–77; John P. Caskey, *Fringe Banking: Check Cashing Outlets, Pawnshops and the Poor* (New York: Russell Sage Foundation, 1994), 13–14; Homer and Sylla, *History of Interest Rates*, 78–79; Jordan, *Women and Credit*, 37; M. R. Niefeld, *The Personal Finance Business* (New York: Harper and Brothers, 1933), 18–19; Nelson, *The Idea of Usury*, 19–23; Tebbut, *Making Ends Meet*, 108; Danieri, *Credit Where Credit is Due*; D.P. Simpson, *Cassell's Latin Dictionary* (New York: MacMillan Publishing, 1959), 379.

45. Caskey, *Fringe Banking*, 13, 14 n.3, 15; John Dornberg, "Vienna's Dorotheum: A Singular Auction House and Hockshop," *Smithsonian* 21 (Dec. 1990): 110–20; Nelson, *The Idea of Usury*, 19.

46. Nelson, *The Idea of Usury*, 19; Niefeld, *The Personal Finance Business*, 18.

47. Tebbutt, *Making Ends Meet*, 109.

48. Ibid., 110, quoting *A Report of the Proceedings in the Court of Common Council of the City of London, Relative to the Equitable Loan Bank Company*, 11 March 1825.

49. Jordan, *Women and Credit*, 37.

50. Tebbutt, *Making Ends Meet*, 111.

51. Barty-King, *The Worst Poverty*, 165–66; Mark Boleat, *The Building Society Industry* (London: George Allen and Unwin, 1982), 3; M. Manfred Fabritius and William Borges, *Saving the Savings and Loan: The U.S. Thrift Industry and the Texas Experience, 1950–1988* (New York: Praeger, 1989), 11–12.

52. Jack Dublin, *Credit Unions: Theory and Practice* (Detroit: Wayne State University Press, 1971), 142–46; Charles Ferguson and Donald McKillop, *The Strategic Development of Credit Unions* (New York: John Wiley and Sons, 1997), 15–17; Rolf Nugent, *Consumer Credit and Economic Stability* (New York: Russell Sage Foundation, 1939), 75–76; Olin S. Pugh and F. Jerry Ingram,

Credit Unions: A Movement Becomes an Industry (Reston, VA: Reston Publishing Co., 1984), 1–2.

53. Ronald Rudin, *In Whose Interest? Quebec's Caisses Populaires 1900–1945* (Montreal: McGill-Queens' University Press, 1990), 13–14.

54. Boleat, *The Building Society*, 3; Dublin, *Credit Unions*, 143–44; Rudin, *In Whose Interest*, 5, 11.

CHAPTER 3

1. Laurence M. Katz, Comment, "Usury Laws and the Corporate Exception," *Maryland Law Review* 23 (1962): 52.

2. Act to Reduce the Rate of Interest, 1713, 13 Anne, c. 15, reprinted in Katz, "Usury Laws and the Corporate Exception," 52; James M. Ackerman, "Interest Rates and the Law: A History of Usury," 1981 *Arizona State Law Journal* (1981): 85; Homer and Sylla, *History of Interest Rates*, 274; Kathleen E. Keest, *The Cost of Credit: Regulation and Legal Challenges* (Boston: National Consumer Law Center, 1995), 37; Tracy A. Westen, "Usury in the Conflict of Laws: The Doctrine of the Lex Debitoris," *California Law Review* 55 (1967): 123 n. 45, 131.

3. Ackerman, *History of Usury*, 86–87; Keest, *Cost of Credit*, 37; Westen, *Usury in the Conflict of Laws*, 133–34.

4. Keest, *Cost of Credit*, 37.

5. Homer and Sylla, *History of Interest Rates*, 274.

6. Lendol Calder, *Financing the American Dream: A Cultural History of Consumer Credit* (Princeton: Princeton University Press, 1999), 98; Homer and Sylla, *History of Interest Rates*, 274.

7. Henry C. Charles, *The Credit System in France, Great Britain, and the United States* (Philadelphia: Carey, Lee and Blanchard, 1838).

8. David M. Tucker, *The Decline of Thrift in America: Our Cultural Shift From Savings to Spending* (New York: Praeger, 1991), 9–10;

Leonard W. Labaree, *The Papers of Benjamin Franklin*, vol. 7 (New Haven: Yale University Press, 1963), 342–49.

9. Homer and Sylla, *History of Interest Rates*, 275.

10. Calder, *Financing the American Dream*, 112.

11. Vern Countryman, "Bankruptcy and the Individual Debtor—A Modest Proposal to Return to the Seventeenth Century," *Catholic University Law Review* 32 (1983): 814.

12. Countryman, "Bankruptcy and the Individual Debtor," 814–16; John C. McCoid, II, "Discharge: The Most Important Development in Bankruptcy History," *American Bankruptcy Law Journal* 70 (1996): 164–65, 181; Charles Jordan Tabb, "The History of the Bankruptcy Laws in the United States," *American Bankruptcy Institute Law Review* 3 (Spring1995): 11–22; Charles Warren, *Bankruptcy in United States History* (Cambridge, Mass.: Harvard University Press, 1935), 13–20.

13. Gerald D. Jaynes, *Branches Without Roots: Genesis of the Black Working Class in the American South, 1862–1882* (New York: Oxford University Press, 1985); Donald G. Nieman, ed., introduction to *From Slavery to Sharecropping: White Land and Black Labor in the Rural South, 1865–1900* (New York: Garland, 1994), *vii–viii*, x; Roger L. Ransom and Richard Sutch, *One Kind of Freedom: The Economic Consequences of Emancipation*, 2d ed. (Cambridge: Cambridge University Press, 1977); James Smallwood, "Perpetuation of Caste: Black Agricultural Workers in Reconstruction Texas," in *African American Life, 1861–1900: From Slavery to Sharecropping*, Donald G. Nieman, ed., (New York: Garland, 1994), 227, 229, 238–39.

14. Melanie Tebbutt, *Making Ends Meet: Pawnbroking and Working-Class Credit* (New York: St. Martin's Press, 1983), 1.

15. Calder, *Financing the American Dream*, 43, quoting Elizabeth Ewen, *Immigrant Women in the Land of Dollars* (New York: Monthly Review Press, 1985), 159.

16. Calder, *Financing the American Dream*, 47–48.

17. Mark H. Haller and John V. Alviti, "Loansharking in American Cities: Historical Analysis of a Marginal Enterprise," *American Journal of Legal History* 21 (1977): 128.

18. Ackerman, *History of Usury*, 89; Haller and Alviti, "Loansharking in American Cities," 128–29; Robert W. Kelso, "Social and Economic Background of the Small Loan Problem," *Law and Contemporary Problems* 8 (1941):15–20.

19. Haller and Alviti, "Loansharking in American Cities,"133.

20. Homer and Sylla, *History of Interest Rates*, 428.

21. John M. Glenn, et al., *Russell Sage Foundation 1907–1946*, vol. 1 (New York: Russell Sage Foundation, 1947), 65–66; Haller and Alviti, "Loansharking in American Cities," 125; Peter W. Herzog, *The Morris Plan of Industrial Banking* (Chicago: A.W. Shaw Company, 1928), 5–6; Keest, *Cost of Credit*, 38–39.

22. Calder, *Financing the American Dream*, 133–34.

23. Ibid., 46.

24. David J. Gallert et al., *Small Loan Legislation: A History of the Regulation of the Business of Lending Small Sums* (New York: Russell Sage Foundation, 1932), 17; Calder, *Financing the American Dream*, 50.

25. Calder, *Financing the American Dream*, 50; Keest, *Cost of Credit*, 37.

26. Evans Clark, *Financing the Consumer* (New York: Harper and Brothers, 1930), 69; Charles O. Hardy et al., *Consumer Credit and Its Uses* (New York: Prentice-Hall, 1938), 32; Keest, *Cost of Credit*, 39.

27. Haller and Alviti, "Loansharking in American Cities," 134.

28. Gallert et al., *Small Loan Legislation*, 53–54.

29. Haller and Alviti, "Loansharking in American Cities," 134.

30. *In re Home Discount Co.*, 147 Fed. 538, 546 (N. D. Ala. 1906).

31. Homer and Sylla, *History of Interest Rates*, 275.

32. Calder, *Financing the American Dream*, 39–40, quoting Robert

Porter, "Public and Private Debts," *North American Review* 153 (1891): 610–12.

33. Caskey, *Fringe Banking*, 23.

34. 1888 Mass. Acts ch. 100.

35. Gallert et al., *Small Loan Legislation*, 23, quoting the Charter of the Philanthropic Loan Society of New York.

36. Caskey, *Fringe Banking*, 24.

37. Jack Dublin, *Credit Unions: Theory and Practice* (Detroit: Wayne State University Press, 1971), 146; M. Manfred Fabritius and William Borges, *Saving the Savings and Loan: The U.S. Thrift Industry and the Texas Experience, 1950–1988* (New York: Praeger, 1989), 12–16; Charles Ferguson and Donald McKillop, *The Strategic Development of Credit Unions* (New York: John Wiley and Sons, 1997), 18–20; Rolf Nugent, *Consumer Credit and Economic Stability* (New York: Russell Sage Foundation, 1939), 76; Olin S. Pugh and F. Jerry Ingram, *Credit Unions: A Movement Becomes an Industry* (Reston, VA: Reston Publishing Co., 1984), 2.

38. *Bankruptcy Act of 1898*, ch. 541, §4, 30 Stat. 544–547; David A. Moss and Gibbs A. Johnson, "The Rise of Consumer Bankruptcy: Evolution, Revolution, or Both?" *American Bankruptcy Law Journal* 73 (Spring 1999): 312–14; Tabb, "History of Bankruptcy Laws," 23–26.

39. Lawrence P. King, "The History and Development of the Bankruptcy Rules," *American Bankruptcy Law Journal* 70 (1996): 218.

40. Moss and Johnson, "Rise of Consumer Bankruptcy," 312–14; Tabb, "History of Bankruptcy Laws," 23–26; Robert Weisberg, "Commercial Morality, the Merchant Character, and the History of Voidable Preference," *Stanford Law Review* 39 (November 1986): 5.

41. Calder, *Financing the American Dream*, 50, 52, 120; Clark, *Financing the Consumer*, 7–8; Gallert et al., *Small Loan Legislation*, 54; Homer and Sylla, *History of Interest Rates*, 428; Keest, *Cost of Credit*, 38–39.

42. *In re Home Discount Co.*, 546. See also *Wilson v. Fisher*, 75 Misc. (N.Y.) 383, 386 (1912); *State v. Hurlburt*, 72 A. 1079, 180 (Conn. 1909).

43. Moss and Johnson, "The Rise of Consumer Bankruptcy," 318–19.

44. Caskey, *Fringe Banking*, 24; Gallert et al., *Small Loan Legislation*, 54–55; Pugh and Ingram, *Credit Unions*, 2–3; Nugent, *Consumer Credit and Economic Stability*, 76.

45. Gallert et al., *Small Loan Legislation*, 13.

46. Caskey, *Fringe Banking*, 24–26.

47. Calder, *Financing the American Dream*, 121–22.

48. Clark, *Financing the Consumer*, 6.

49. Keest, *Cost of Credit*, 39, 48; Gallert et al., *Small Loan Legislation*, 89.

50. Calder, *Financing the American Dream*, 124, 150; Keest, *Cost of Credit*, 48.

51. Keest, *Cost of Credit*, 49–50.

52. Calder, *Financing the American Dream*, 156.

53. Ibid., quoting Burr Blackburn, "Financial Consultation Services," *Personal Finance News* 16 (1932): 22.

54. Calder, *Financing the American Dream*, 147; Clark, *Financing the Consumer*, 45.

55. Loren Baritz, *The Good Life: The Meaning of Success for the American Middle Class* (New York: Harper and Row, 1982), 64; Daniel Bell, *Cultural Contradictions of Capitalism* (New York: Basic Books, 1976), 21, 69–70; Thomas C. Cochran, *Challenges to American Values: Society, Business, and Religion* (New York: Oxford University Press, 1985), 86; John Kenneth Galbraith, *The Affluent Society*, 2d rev. ed. (Boston: Houghton Mifflin Co., 1969), 170–72; Christopher Lasch, *The Culture of Narcissism: American Life in an Age of Diminishing Expectations* (New York: Norton, 1978), 53; William E. Leuchtenburg, *The Perils of Prosperity, 1914–1932*, 2d ed. (Chicago: University of Chicago Press,

1993), 197; Tucker, *Decline of Thrift*, 114–15; Haller and Alviti, "Loansharking in American Cities," 140–42.

56. Tucker, *Decline of Thrift*, 115. See also Baritz, *The Good Life*, 64.

57. Baritz, *The Good Life*, 64, 80; Calder, *Financing the American Dream*, 164–65; Galbraith, *Affluent Society*, 171; Leuchtenburg, *The Perils of Prosperity*, 197.

58. Calder, *Financing the American Dream*, 291.

59. Paul R. Bears, *Consumer Lending*, 2d. ed. (Washington, D.C.: American Bankers Association, 1992), 11.

60. Teresa A. Sullivan, Elizabeth Warren, and Jay Lawrence Westerbrook, *The Fragile Middle Class: Americans in Debt* (New Haven: Yale University Press, 2000), 108. Lewis Mandell, *The Credit Card Industry: A History* (Boston: Twayne Publishers, 1990), xii–xiii, 2, 4, 22–23; Scott B. MacDonald and Albert L. Gastmann, *A History of Credit and Power in the Western World* (New Brunswick: Transaction Publishers, 2001), 227–230.

61. Tabb, "History of Bankruptcy Laws," 26–36, 38–39; King, "History and Development of Bankruptcy Rules," 218–19, 236; *Northern Pipeline Construction Co. v. Marathon Pipe Line*, 458 U.S. 50 (1982).

62. Moss and Johnson, "The Rise of Consumer Bankruptcy," 311–14.

63. Kenneth T. Jackson, *Crabgrass Frontier: The Suburbanization of the United States* (New York: Oxford University Press, 1985), 195, 200; Gregory D. Squires, "Community Reinvestment: An Emerging Social Movement," in *From Redlining to Reinvestment*, ed. Gregory D. Squires (Philadelphia, Pa.: Temple University Press, 1992), 1, 4–6.

64. Squires, "Community Reinvestment," 5, quoting U.S. *Federal Housing Administration, Underwriting Manual* 937 (1938).

65. Dalton Conley, *Being Black, Living in the Red: Race, Wealth, and Social Policy in America* (Berkeley: University of California Press, 1999), 42, 121, 150–52; R. Allen Hays, *The Federal Government and Urban Housing* (Albany: State University of New York Press,

1985), 79; Jackson, *Crabgrass Frontier*, 203; Squires, "Community Reinvestment," 6.

66. Squires, "Community Reinvestment," 11.

67. Allen J. Fishbein, "The Community Reinvestment Act after Fifteen Years: It Works, But Strengthened Federal Enforcement is Needed," *Fordham Urban Law Journal* 20 (1993): 296; Stephen A. Fuchs, "Discriminatory Lending Practices: Recent Developments, Causes and Solutions," *Annual Review of Banking Law* 10 (1991): 479–80; Richard D. Marisco, "Fighting Poverty Through Community Empowerment and Economic Development: The Role of the Community Reinvestment and Home Mortgage Disclosure Acts," *New York Law School Journal of Human Rights* 12 (Spring 1995): 282.

68. U.S. Senate Subcommittee on Consumer and Regulatory Affairs of the Committee on Banking, Housing, and Urban Affairs, *Discrimination in Home Mortgage Lending Hearing*, 118, 1990 (statement of Senator Alan J. Dixon).

69. House Committee on Banking, Finance, and Urban Affairs, *Discriminatory Mortgage Lending Patterns Field Hearing*, 101st Cong., 1st Sess., 1989, 2 (statement of Chairman Henry B. Gonzales).

70. Daniel M. Leibsohn, "Financial Services Innovation in Community Development," *Journal of Affordable Housing and Community Development Law* (Winter 1999): 128.

71. Dublin, *Credit Unions*, 166; Pugh and Ingram, *Credit Unions*, 12–13, 25, 34–35.

72. Pugh and Ingram, *Credit Unions*, 9.

73. MacDonald and Gastmann, *History of Credit and Power*, 231–32; Pugh and Ingram, *Credit Unions*, 10, 19, 26, 34–35; Ferguson and McKillop, *Development of Credit Unions*, 23–24; Melissa Allison, "Area Credit Unions Not Serving All, Study Says," *Chicago Tribune*, 15 February 2002.

74. Keest, *Cost of Credit*, 54.

75. Ibid., 55.

76. *Depository Institution Deregulation and Monetary Control Act of 1980* (DIDA), Public Law 96–221.

77. *Marquette National Bank v. First Omaha Service Corp.*, 439 U.S. 299 (1978).

78. William F. Baxter, "Section 85 of the National Bank Act and Consumer Welfare," *Utah Law Review* (1995): 1010–11, 1028; Richard P. Eckman, "The Delaware Consumer Credit Bank Act and 'Exporting' Interest Under Section 521 of the Depository Institutions Deregulation and Monetary Control Act of 1980," *Business Lawyer* 39 (1984): 1264–70; Donald C. Langevoort, "Statutory Obsolescence and the Judicial Process: The Revisionist Role of the Courts in Federal Banking Regulation," *Michigan Law Review* 85 (1987): 686; Moss and Johnson, "The Rise of Consumer Bankruptcy," 333; James J. White, "The Usury Trompe l'Oeil," *South Carolina Law Review* 51 (Spring 2000): 447–48.

79. Jean Ann Fox and Ed Mierzwinski, *Rent-A-Bank Payday Lending: How Banks Help Payday Lenders Evade State Consumer Protections* (Washington, D.C.: Consumer Federation of America & U.S. Public Interest Research Group: 2001), 12–16; Carol Hazard, "Payday Lending gets Warner OK," *Richmond Times-Dispatch*, 10 April 2002, B1; Ben Jackson, "Federal Courts at Odds Over Payday Lending Pact," *American Banker* 167 (108) (6 June 2002): 5; Amber Veverka, "Payday Lending Persists in NC: Some Lenders Keep up Practice After Linking to Out of State Banks," *Charlotte Observer*, 26 December 2001, 1A; *Marquette*, 439 U.S. 318–19 n.31; Comment, "Syndicate Loan-Shark Activities and New York's Usury Statute," *Columbia Law Review* 66 (1966):167 (reporting mafia loanshark interest rates averaging 250 percent annually).

80. White, "The Usury Trompe l'Oeil," 447–48.

CHAPTER 4

1. H.R. Rep. No. 1040, 90th Cong., 2d Sess., reprinted in *U.S. Congressional and Administrative News* (1968): 1962, 1970.
2. Paul H. Douglas, *In Our Time* (New York: Harcourt, Brace and World, 1968), 95.
3. John R. Fonseca, *Handling Consumer Credit Cases* 1, 3d ed. (Rochester, N.Y.: Lawyers Cooperative Pub. Co. 1986 and Supp. 1999), 301; Barry A. Abbott and John W. Campbell, "The Truth in Lending Act After 15 Years: Its Goals and Its Limitations," *Oklahoma City Law Review* 9 (1984): 1–2; *Ford Motor Credit v. Millhollin*, 444 U.S. 555, 559 (1980); *Mourning v. Family Publications Service, Inc.*, 411 U.S. 356, 363-69 (1973).
4. Douglas, *In Our Time*, 96.
5. Edward L. Rubin, "Legislative Methodology: Some Lessons From the Truth-in-Lending Act," *Georgetown Law Journal* 80 (1991): 242.
6. Ibid., 250–51.
7. Senator Douglas commonly called credit disclosure an old idea, citing the requirement that loan contracts be written down in Hammurabi's ancient Babylonian code. See Douglas, *In Our Time*, 100; Homer and Sylla, *History of Interest Rates*, 27. However, this may be rhetorical flourish since the Babylonian rule was probably directed not at debtor understanding so much as preventing false contracts and violations of other code provisions. The Babylonian rule is probably better characterized as an early version of the much more common statute of frauds.
8. Rubin, "Legislative Methodology," 252. One important difference between the Massachusetts rules and the federal bill was that Massachusetts did not include a private right of action for debtors to sue violating creditors. Instead, the state rule provided that "failure to comply barred recovery of finance charges and subjected the lender to a fine of up to $500 or imprisonment of

up to six months, or both." Ibid., n.116, citing 1966 Mass. Acts ch. 284 §§ 29-30; 1966 Mass. Acts ch. 587 §§ 10-11.

9. Ibid., 252–53 (footnotes omitted).

10. Kathleen E. Keest and Gary Klein, *Truth In Lending* (Boston: National Consumer Law Center, 1995), 31 n.4; Rubin, "Legislative Methodology," 256.

11. Rubin, "Legislative Methodology," 262.

12. 15 U.S.C. § 1605 (a); John R. Fonseca, *Consumer Credit Compliance Manual*, 2d ed. (Rochester, NY: Lawyers Cooperative Publishing Co., 1984 & Supp. 2000), §1:4; Dee Prigden, *Consumer Credit and the Law* (West Group: 2001), §§ 6:1, 6:2.

13. 15 U.S.C. § 1606 (a).

14. Keest and Klein, *Truth in Lending*, 34.

15. Adam Smith, *An Inquiry into the Nature and Causes of the Wealth of Nations*, Richard F. Teichgraeber, III, ed. (New York: Random House, 1985), 225–26.

16. James F. Ragan Jr. and Lloyd B. Thomas Jr., *Principles of Micro Economics* (Fort Worth: Harcourt Brace Jovanovich, 1993), 371 (emphasis added).

17. Robert B. Carson and Wade L. Thomas, *The American Economy: Contemporary Problems and Analysis* (New York: Macmillan, 1993), 508.

18. Homer and Sylla, *History of Interest Rates*, 81.

19. Jean Ann Fox and Ed Mierzwinski, *Rent-A-Bank Payday Lending: How Banks Help Payday Lenders Evade State Consumer Protections* (Washington, D.C.: Consumer Federation of America and U.S. Public Interest Research Group, 2001), 25.

20. Abbott and Campbell, "Truth in Lending After 15 Years," 3; Rubin, "Legislative Methodology," 279–80, 306; Elwin Griffith, "Truth in Lending—The Right of Recission Disclosure of the Finance Charge, and Itemization of the Amount Financed in Closed End Transactions," *George Mason Law Review* 6 (Winter, 1998): 192–94; Keest and Klein, *Truth in Lending*, 36; Ndiva

Kofele-Kale, "The Impact of Truth-in-Lending Disclosures on Consumer Market Behavior: A Critique of the Critics of Truth-in-Lending Law," *Oklahoma City University Law Review* 9 (Spring 1984): 126–29; Jonathan M. Landers and Ralph J. Rohner, "A Functional Analysis of Truth in Lending," *UCLA Law Review* 26 (1979): 713–25.

21. Keest and Klein, *Truth in Lending*, 34.

22. Federal Reserve Board, *Regulatory Analysis of Revised Regulation Z*, 46 Fed. Reg. 20,941, 20,942 (1979); Keest and Klein, *Truth in Lending*, 36; Willenzik and Leymaster, "Recent Trends in Truth-in-Lending Litigation," *Business Lawyer* 35 (1980): 1197 n.4; *Bizer v. Globe Financial Serivces*, 654 F.2d 1, 3 (1st cir. 1981); *Semar v. Platte Valley Federal Savings and Loan Association*, 791 F.2d 699, 704 (9th Cir. 1986).

23. An abbreviated sample of this literature includes: Abbott and Campbell, "The Truth In Lending Act After 15 Years;" Brandt and Day, "Information Disclosure and Consumer Behavior: An Empirical Evaluation of Truth in Lending," *University of Michigan Journal of Law Ref.* 7 (1974): 297; Jeffrey Davis, "Protecting Consumers from Overdisclosure and Gobbledygook: An Empirical Look at the Simplification of Consumer Credit Contracts," *Virginia Law Review* 63 (1977): 841; Jordan and Warren, "Disclosure of Finance Charges: A Rationale," *Michigan Law Review* 64 (1966): 1285; Homer Kripke, "Consumer Credit Regulation: A Creditor-Oriented Viewpoint," *Columbia Law Review* 68 (1968): 445; Kofele-Kale, "The Impact of Truth-In-Lending Disclosures," 117; Landers and Rohner, "Functional Analysis of Truth in Lending," 711; Rubin, "Legislative Methodology," 233.

24. U.S. Senate Subcommittee on Consumer Affairs of the Committee on Banking, Housing, and Urban Affairs, *Simplify and Reform the Truth in Lending Act Hearings*, 95th Cong., 1st sess., 16, July 11, 1977, statement of Philip C. Jackson Jr.

25. Keest and Klein, *Truth in Lending*, 36 n.37.

26. Ibid., 34 n.27.
27. Public Law 96-221 Title V, codified at 12 U.S.C. § 1735f-7a; 15 U.S.C. § 1604(b).
28. Prigden, *Consumer Credit*, § 4:2, 4:3.
29. Keest and Klein, *Truth in Lending*, 36.
30. Fonseca, *Consumer Credit Compliance*, §1:1; Keest and Klein, *Truth in Lending*, 35–6; Prigden, *Consumer Credit*, §4.3.
31. Michael I. Meyerson, "The Reunification of Contract Law: The Objective Theory of Consumer Form Contracts," *University of Miami Law Review* (1993): 1263, 1274–76; Kathleen E. Keest, "Whither Now? Truth in Lending in Transition—Again," *Consumer Finance Law Quarterly Report* 49 (Fall 1995): 361.
32. Rick Brundrett, "How Mounting Loans Devastated 87-Year-Old," *The State (Columbia, South Carolina)*, 24 February 2002; Editorial, "Predatory Lending A Shameful Practice That Must Be Ended," *The State (Columbia, South Carolina)*, 24 February 2002.
33. Michael Hudson, " 'Signing their Lives Away'—Ford Profits from Vulnerable Consumers," in *Merchants of Misery: How Corporate America Profits from Poverty* (Monroe, Maine: Common Courage Press, 1996), 47.
34. Ibid.
35. Reggie James, et al., "In Over Our Heads: Predatory Lending and Fraud in Manufactured Housing," *Consumers Union Southwest Regional Office Public Policy Series* 5(1) (February 2000): 16.
36. James et al., "In Over Our Heads," 16–17. Steven W. Bender, "Consumer Protection for Latinos: Overcoming Language Fraud and English-Only in the Marketplace," *American University Law Review* 45 (April 1996): 1027.
37. David M Grether, Alan Schwartz, and Louis L. Wilde, "The Irrelevance of Information Overload: An Analysis of Search and Disclosure," *Southern California Law Review* 59 (January 1986): 285–89; James G. March and Herbert A. Simon, *Organizations* (New York: Wiley, 1958), 140–41; Scott Plous, *The Psychology of*

Judgement and Decisionmaking (Philadelphia: Temple University Press, 1993): 94–95. Satisficing behavior c̣an be conceptualized as either a welfare maximizing response to imperfect information or as a problem of irrational behavior. See, for example, Avery Wiener Katz, *Foundations of the Economic Approach to Law* (New York: Oxford University Press, 1998), 268. I take satisficing behavior to be consistent with welfare maximization. Consumers rationally satisfice when the opportunity costs of pursuing larger product data sets outweigh the predictive potential gains to further shopping. Nevertheless, I do not mean to suggest high-cost debtors *always* behave rationally.

38. James et al., "In Over Our Heads," 4–6; Board of Governors of the Federal Reserve System and United States Department of Housing and Urban Development, *Joint Report to Congress Concerning Reform to the Truth in Lending Act and the Real Estate Settlement Procedures Act.* Washington, D.C., July 1998.

39. Christopher Peterson, "Only Until Payday: A Primer on Utah's Growing Deferred Deposit Loan Industry," *Utah Bar Journal* 15(2) (March 2002): 16.

40. One industry-purchased survey of payday loan debtors remarks, "[p]ayday advance customers are not deeply rooted in their employment. 50 percent of respondents have had their current job for three years or less, and 70 percent have had their current job for five years or less." Io Data Corporation, *Utah Consumer Lending Association: Utah Customer Study* (Salt Lake City: Io Data Corporation, 2001), 30.

41. Gillian K Hadfield, Robert Howse, and M. J. Trebilcock, "Information-Based Principles for Rethinking Consumer Protection Policy," *Journal of Consumer Policy* 21 (1998): 139.

42. Fox and Mierzwinski, *Show Me the Money!*, 6; Christopher Peterson "Failed Markets, Failing Government, Or Both?: Learning from the Unintended Consequences of Utah Consumer Credit

on Vulnerable Debtors," *Utah Law Review* (2001), 564–65; 15 U.S.C. § 1665(a).

43. Hadfield, Howse, and Trebilcock, "Information-Based Principles," 155.

44. Caskey, *Fringe Banking*, 70–71; W. C. A. M. Dessart and A. A. A. Kuylen, "The Nature, Extent, Causes, and Consequences of Problematic Debt Situations," *Journal of Consumer Policy* 9 (1986): 320, 328; Ford, *Indebted Society*, 126–30.

45. Ron Nixon, "Application Denied: Do Lending Institutions Overlook Hispanics?" *Hispanic* 11(11) (November 1998): 30, quoting Luis Artega, executive director of the Latino Issues Forum in San Francisco.

46. FED and HUD, *Joint Report*, 51; A. Charlene Sullivan, *Understanding the Consumer Credit Environment* (New York, NY: Executive Enterprises Publications Co.,1989), 35; Melissa Allison, "Poorer Areas of Chicago Also Remain Poor in Bank Branches," *Knight Ridder/Tribune Business News*, 26 November 2001.

47. Landers and Rohner, "Functional Analysis of Truth in Lending," 715–16.

48. Senate Subcommittee, *Simplify and Reform the Truth in Lending Act*, 333–34.

49. Keest, "Whither Now," 361.

50. Ralph J. Rohner, ed., *The Law of Truth in Lending* (Boston: Warren, Gorham and Lamont, 1984), ¶ 4.01[2][c][i].

51. Keest and Klein, *Truth in Lending*, 77.

52. Cynthia Vinarsky, "Youngstown, Ohio, Program Helps Homeowners Victimized by Predatory Lenders," *Knight Ridder/Tribune Business News*, 14 April 2002.

53. *Emery v. American General Finance, Inc.*, 71 F.3d 1343 (7th Cir. 1995); Keest, "Whither Now," 364.

54. Keest and Klein, *Truth in Lending*, 75.

55. Ronald H. Coase, *Essays on Economics and Economists* (Chicago: University of Chicago Press, 1994), 8; Ronald H. Coase, *The

Firm, the Market, and the Law (Chicago: University of Chicago Press, 1988), 5–7; Ronald H. Coase, "The Nature of the Firm," *Economica* 4 (1937): 390–97.

56. Keest and Klein, *Truth in Lending*, 87; Robert M. Jaworski, "RESPA Section 8: The YSP Waiting Game Continues," *Business Lawyer* (May 2001): 1207.

57. U.S. Senate Committee on Banking, Housing, and Urban Affairs, *Predatory Mortgage Lending Practices: Abusive Uses of Yield Spread Premiums Hearing*, 107th Cong., 8 January 2002, prepared statement of Ira Rhingold; Howell E. Jackson and Jeremy Berry, "Kickbacks or Compensation: The Case of Yield Spread Premiums," 8 January 2002, available at http://www.law.harvard.edu/faculty/hjackson/jacksonberry0108.pdf (viewed April 19, 2002), 24–25; Keest and Klein, *Truth in Lending*, 86–87.

58. Barren E. Ramos, "Materials on Residential Mortgage Litigation Preface," *Practicing Law Institute Corporate Law and Practice Course Handbook Series* 1242 (16 April 2001): 205.

59. Jackson and Berry, "Kickbacks or Compensation," 3–9; Keest and Klein, *Truth in Lending*, 87–88; Senate Committee, *Predatory Mortgage Lending Practices*, statements of Ira Rhingold, Howell E. Jackson, and David E Donaldson.

60. Senate Committee, *Predatory Mortgage Lending Practices*, statement of Beatrice Hiers.

61. Ibid.

62. Jackson and Berry, "Kickbacks or Compensation," 7.

63. *Culpepper v. Irwin Mortgage Corp.*, 253 F.3d 1324 (11th Cir. 2001); *Glover v. Standard Federal Bank*, 283 F.3d 953 (8th Cir. 2002); Robert M. Jaworski, "*Culpepper:* An Epic Battle Continues," *Consumer Finance Law Quarterly Report* (Winter 2001): 119; 24 CFR § 3500; Jackson and Berry, "Kickbacks or Compensation," 24; HUD Statement of Policy, 1999–2001, *Federal Register* 64 (1 March 1999): 10,080.

64. Senate Committee, *Predatory Mortgage Lending Practices*, n. 6, statement of Howell E. Jackson.

65. Ramos, *Materials on Residential Mortgage Litigation*, 206.

66. Jackson and Berry, "Kickbacks or Compensation," 9.

67. U.S. Senate Committee on Banking, Housing, and Urban Affairs, *Problems in Community Development Banking, Mortgage Lending Discrimination, Reverse Redlining, and Home Equity Lending Hearing*, 103rd Cong., 1st Sess., 24 February 1993, 3, 17.

68. National Consumer Law Center, "Why Yield Spread Premium Payments are 'Fees' For HOEPA purposes," in *Consumer Rights Litigation Conference Manual* (Boston: National Consumer Law Center, 2001), 571–73; Board of Governors of the Federal Reserve System, *Federal Reserve Board Public Hearing on Home Equity Lending*, Federal Reserve Bank of Chicago, 16 August 2000, 12, 26–27, statements of Michelle Weinberg and William Darr.

69. FED and HUD, *Joint Report*, 18 n.32. The Board's recent decision lowering the annual percentage rate trigger by two points for first lien mortgages and including optional credit insurance in calculation of the points-and-fees trigger is certainly a step in the right direction. However, it remains to be seen whether these changes will address the widespread problems faced by home mortgage borrowers. The changes certainly provide no additional protection for non-home mortgage borrowers. Board of Governors of the Federal Reserve System, *Amendments Designed to Curb Predatory Lending* (effective October, 1, 2002): *Final Rule*, 12 CFR part 226, Docket No. A-1090.

70. American Savings Education Council, "Youth and Money," 1999, available at http://www.asec.org/youthsurvey.pdf, viewed 22 May 2002; Americans for Consumer Education and Competition, "Key Findings from a National Survey of High School Seniors Regarding Personal Finance Issues," 16 February 2001, available at http://www.acecusa.org/reportcard/, viewed 22 May 2002; Consumer Federation of America, *College Student Con-*

sumer Knowledge: The Results of a Nationwide Test (Washington, D.C.: Consumer Federation of America, 1993); Consumer Federation of America, *High School Student Consumer Knowledge: A Nationwide Test* (Washington, D.C.: Consumer Federation of America, 1991); Consumer Federation of America, U.S. *Consumer Knowledge: The Results of a Nationwide Test* (Washington, D.C.: Consumer Federation of America, 1990); Employee Benefit Research Institute, "The Reality of Retirement Today: Lessons in Planning for Tomorrow," *EBRI Issue Brief*, no. 181 (January 1997); Jeanne M. Hogarth, "Financial Literacy and Consumer Sciences," *Journal of Family and Consumer Sciences* 94(1) (1 January 2002): 14.

71. Andrea Stowers and Mark Cole, "A Bankruptcy Wake-Up Call" *Mortgage Banking* 57 (5) (February, 1997): 13.

72. Ben Jackson, "Programs Tout Financial Literacy for All Ages," *American Banker* 167 (65) (5 April 2002): 5; Keest, "Whither Now," 366; U. S. Senate Committee on Banking, Housing, and Urban Affairs, *Hearing on the State of Financial Literacy and Education in America*, 107th Cong., 2d Sess., 5 and 6 February 2002, statements of Senator Paul Sarbanes, Secretary Paul O'Neill, Chairman Alan Greenspan, Esther Canja, and Securities Commissioner Dennis Voigt; Martha McNeil, "Ignorance Costs Plenty: Officials Promote Financial Literacy," *Washington Post*, 6 February 2002, E01; Sissy R. Osteen and Tricia Auberle, "Homebuyer Education: A Doorway to Financial Literacy," *Journal of Family and Consumer Sciences* 94(1) (1 January 2002): 29; Mary Radigan, "Predatory Lenders Bank on Ignorance: Extra Charges and Penalties Put Homes at Risk," *Grand Rapids Press*, 5 November 2001, A8; Mike Sorohan, "MBA Launches Consumer Fraud Web Site," *Real Estate Finance Today Electronic Ed.*, 11 March 2002, 4, available on Westlaw at 2002 WL 10349754.

73. Consumer Federation of America, "Large Banks Increase Charges to Americans in Credit Counseling: New Practices Will Hurt

Consumers on the Brink of Bankruptcy," *Press Release*, 28 July 1999, available at http://www.consumerfed.org/fairshare.pdf, viewed 22 May 2002.

74. Judy Artunian, "It Can Put You in a Real Fix: Credit Repair is Just a Scam, Experts Warn," *Chicago Tribune*, 21 May 2002, 5; Federal Trade Commission, "Credit Repair: Self Help may Be Best," available at http://www.ftc.gov/bcp/conline/pubs/credit/repair.htm, viewed 31 May 2001; Alan Joch, "Can You Deal Down Debt? Professional 'Negotiators' May Promise Quick Fixes, But the Best Counselors Aim at Roots of Debt," *Christian Science Monitor*, 10 December 2001; Lesley Mitchell, "Credit Counselors Warn Consumers to Be Wary of Scams," *Salt Lake Tribune*, 20 May 2002, D1; Prigden, *Consumer Credit and the Law*, §2:1.

75. Prigden, *Consumer Credit and the Law*, § 2:1; Liz Pulliam Weston, "Get Loan Rate Based on Your Credit Score," *Los Angeles Times*, 6 March 2002, C6; Ed Mierzwinski, *Mistakes Do Happen: Credit Report Errors Mean Consumers Lose*, (Washington, D.C.: U.S. Public Interest Research Group, 1998).

76. Elwin Griffith, "The Quest for Fair Credit Reporting and Equal Credit Opportunity in Consumer Transactions," *University of Memphis Law Review* 25 (Fall 1994): 37–43; Prigden, *Consumer Credit and the Law*, §2:1; Weston, "Get Loans," C6; W.A. Lee, "Fair, Isaac and Co. Taps Institutions For Credit Score Distribution," *American Banker* 167 (67) (9 April 2002): 1; "A Breakthrough for Borrowers," *Consumer Reports Online* (June 2001), available at http://www.consumerreports.org/main/deta . . . %3C%3Efolder_id=18151&bmUID=991247776473, viewed 19 June 2001; "Web Site Offers Credit Score Information," *Chicago Tribune*, 16 April 2002, 7.

77. Weston, "Get Loans," C6.

CHAPTER 5

1. Gary Becker, *The Economic Approach to Human Behavior* (Chicago: University of Chicago Press, 1976), 3–14.
2. Karl E. Case and Ray C. Fair, *Principles of Macroeconomics*, 4th ed. (Englewood Cliffs, N.J.: Prentice Hall, 1996), 81.
3. Paul A. Samuelson and William D. Nordhaus, *Economics*, 15th ed. (New York: McGraw-Hill, 1995), 40.
4. Cass R. Sunstein, "Social Norms and Social Roles," *Columbia Law Review* 96 (1996): 913.
5. J. De V. Graaff, *Theoretical Welfare Economics*, 1st paperback ed. (London: Cambridge University Press, 1967), 143.
6. For instance, James Coleman persuasively explains utilitarianism does not embrace all Pareto-optimal outcomes because not every Pareto-optimal distribution is the result of Pareto superior moves. Some Pareto-optimal outcomes are the result of uncompensated Caldor-Hicks moves, which have no utilitarian moral ratification. James Coleman, "Efficiency, Utility, and Wealth Maximization," in *Markets, Morals, and the Law* (Cambridge: Cambridge University Press, 1988), 95–132.
7. Alexis De Tocqueville, *Democracy in America*, ed. Phillips Bradley (New York: Vintage Books, 1945), 64. Robert A. Dahl, *A Preface to Economic Democracy* (Berkeley: University of California Press, 1985), 57; Robert E. Lane, *The Loss of Happiness in Market Democracies* (New Haven: Yale University Press, 2000), 283.
8. E. K. Hunt, *Property and Prophets: The Evolution of Economic Institutions and Ideologies*, 7th ed.(New York: Harper and Row, 1995), 192.
9. It is well taken that most contemporary economists no longer rely on preference and welfare order equation, focusing instead on "positive" or purely descriptive economics and eschewing any normative claims based solely on their models. In this vein, most contemporary economists take the word "utility" to mean noth-

ing more than the satisfaction of consumer preferences. This notion of utility does not implicate the normative utility of moral
philosophy. Daniel M. Hausman, *The Inexact and Separate Science
of Economics* (New York: Cambridge University Press, 1992),
18–19. Although this approach garners a firmer epistemic foundation, it also abandons the prescriptive persuasiveness of classical economics. Regardless, policymakers and the American
public have not been so quick to abandon the simple moral appeal of Benthamite arguments for non-intervention. They still
tend to conflate contemporary positive efficiency with classical
moral utility. So, to the extent that this chapter focuses on older
welfare economics rather than contemporary positive economics,
this focus may nevertheless be justified.

10. There are, of course, exceptions. Jefferson M. Fish, ed., *How to
Legalize Drugs* (Northvale, N.J.: Jason Aronson, 1998); Richard
Lawrence Miller, *The Case for Legalizing Drugs* (New York: Prea-
ger, 1991).

11. Lane, *Loss of Happiness*, 284.

12. Legal scholarship has begun to incorporate persuasively behav-
ioral challenges to the assumption of substantively rational util-
ity maximization. For an introduction, see Stephen M.
Bainbridge, "Mandatory Disclosure: A Behavioral Analysis,"
University of Cincinnati Law Review 68 (2000): 1023; Kenneth G.
Dau-Schmidt, "An Economic Analysis of the Criminal Law as a
Preference-Shaping Policy," *Duke Law Journal* (1990): 1; Melvin
A. Eisenberg, "The Limits of Cognition and the Limits of Contract," *Stanford Law Review* 47 (1995): 211; Larry T. Gavin, "Dis-
proportionality and the Law of Consequential Damages: Default
Theory and Cognitive Reality," *Ohio State Law Journal* 59 (1998):
339; Jon D. Hanson and Douglas A. Kysar, "Taking Behavioralism Seriously: The Problem of Market Manipulation," *New York
University Law Review* 74 (1999): 630; Jon D. Hanson and Douglas A. Kysar, "Taking Behavioralism Seriously: A Response to

Market Manipulation," *Roger Williams University Law Review* 6 (2000): 259; Jon D. Hanson and Douglas A. Kysar, "Taking Behavioralism Seriously: Some Evidence of Market Manipulation," *Harvard Law Review* 112 (1999): 1420; Samuel Issacharoff, "Can There Be a Behavioral Law and Economics?" *Vanderbilt Law Review* 51 (1998): 1729; Christine Jolls, "Behavioral Economics Analysis of Redistributive Legal Rules," *Vanderbilt Law Review* 51 (1998): 1653; Christine Jolls, Cass R. Sunstein, and Richard Thaler, "A Behavioral Approach to Law and Economics," *Stanford Law Review* 50 (1998): 1471; Owen D. Jones, "Time-Shifted Rationality and the Law of Law's Leverage: Behavioral Economics Meets Behavioral Biology," *Northwestern Law Review* 95 (2001): 1141; Russell Korobokin, "Inertia and Preference in Contract Negotiation: The Psychological Powers of Default Rules and Form Terms," *Vanderbilt Law Review* 51 (1998): 1583; Russell B. Korobokin and Thomas S. Ulen, "Law and Behavioral Science: Removing the Rationality Assumption from Law and Economics," *California Law Review* 88 (2000): 1051; Russell B. Korobokin, "The Status Quo Bias and Contract's Default Rules," *Cornell Law Review* 83 (1998): 608; Donald C. Langevoort, "Behavioral Theories of Judgment and Decision Making in Legal Scholarship: A Literature Review," *Vanderbilt Law Review* 51 (1998): 1499; Donald C. Langevoort, "Selling Hope, Selling Risk: Some Lessons for Law from Behavioral Economics About Stockbrokers and Sophisticated Consumers," *California Law Review* 84 (1996): 627; Richard A. Posner, "Rational Choice, Behavioral Economics, and the Law," *Stanford Law Review* 50 (1998): 1551; Matthew Rabin, "Psychology and Economics," *Journal of Economic Literature* 36 (1998): 11; Jeffrey J. Rachlinski, "A Positive Psychological Theory of Judging in Hindsight," *University of Chicago Law Review* 65 (1998): 571; Robert K. Rasmussen, "Behavioral Economics, the Economic Analysis of Bankruptcy Law and the Pricing of Credit," *Vanderbilt Law Re-*

view 51 (1998): 1679; Cass R. Sunstein, "Behavioral Analysis of Law and Economics: A Progress Report," *American Law and Economic Review* 1 (1999): 115; Cass R. Sunstein, "Behavioral Analysis of Law," *University of Chicago Law Review* 64 (1997): 1175; Cass R. Sunstein, "Legal Interference With Private Preferences," *University of Chicago Law Review* 53 (1986): 1129.

13. Sunstein, "Legal Interference with Private Preferences," 1141.

14. Amos Tversky, Shmauel Sattath, and Paul Slovic, "Contingent Weighting in Judgment and Choice," *Psychology Review* 95 (1988): 371.

15. Sunstein, "Behavioral Analysis of Law," 1176.

16. Lane, *Loss of Happiness*, 283–99.

17. Sunstein, "Social Norms and Social Roles," 913–14.

18. Sunstein, "Behavioral Analysis of Law," 1183; Laurie J. Bauman and Karolynn Siegel, "Misperceptions Among Gay Men of the Risk for AIDS Associated with Their Sexual Behavior," *Journal of Applied Social Psychology* 17 (1987): 329; Eisenberg, "Limits of Cognition," 216; Robin M. Hogarth and Howard Kunreuther, "Risk, Ambiguity, and Insurance," *Journal of Risk and Uncertainty* 2 (1989): 5; Pauline Kim, "Bargaining with Imperfect Information: A Study of Worker Perception of Legal Protection in an At-Will World," *Cornell Law Review* 83 (1997): 105; Howard Kunreuther et al., "Insurer Ambiguity and Market Failure," *Journal of Risk and Uncertainty* 7 (1993): 7; Langevoort, "Behavioral Theories of Judgment," 1504; Alan Schwartz and Louis Wilde, "Imperfection in Markets for Contract Terms," *Virginia Law Review* 69 (1983): 1387–1485; Susan Segerstrom et al., "Optimistic Bias Among Cigarette Smokers," *Journal of Applied Social Psychology* 23 (1993): 1615; Shelley E. Taylor, *Positive Illusions: Creative Self-Deception and the Healthy Mind* (New York: Basic Books, 1990), 10–11; Neil D. Weinstein, "Unrealistic Optimism about Future Life Events," *Journal of Personality and Social Psychology* (1980): 806–820; Neil D. Weinstein, "Optimistic Biases About

Personal Risks," *Science* 246 (1989): 1232; Neil D. Weinstein, "Unrealistic Optimism About Susceptibility to Health Problems: Conclusions From a Community-Wide Sample," *Journal of Behavioral Medicine* 10 (1987): 481; Neil D. Weinstein, "Why It Won't Happen To Me: Perceptions of Risk Factors and Susceptibility," *Journal of Personality and Social Psychology* 39 (1980): 431.

19. William N. Eskridge Jr., "One Hundred Years of Ineptitude: The Need for Mortgage Rules Consonant with the Economic and Psychological Dynamics of the Home Sale and Loan Transaction," *Virginia Law Review* 70 (1984): 1187; Julia Patterson Forrester, "Mortgaging the American Dream: A Critical Evaluation of the Federal Government's Promotion of Home Equity Financing," *Tulane Law Review* 69 (1994): 383–84; Rasmussen, "Analysis of Bankruptcy Law," 1694; Michael H. Schill, "An Economic Analysis of Mortgagor Protection Laws," *Virginia Law Review* (1991): 530; Teresa A. Sullivan, Elizabeth Warren, and Jay Lawrence Westerbrook, *The Fragile Middle Class: Americans in Debt* (New Haven: Yale University Press, 2000), 10, 239, 240–41; Visa Consumer Bankruptcy Reports, *Consumer Bankruptcy: Bankruptcy Debtor Survey* (Visa, U.S.A., Inc., July 1996), 438; Elizabeth Warren, "The Bankruptcy Crisis," *Indiana Law Journal* 73 (1998): 1100; Elizabeth Warren, Teresa Sullivan, and Melissa Jacoby, "Medical Problems and Bankruptcy Filings," *Harvard Law School Public Law and Legal Theory Working Paper Series*, Working Paper No. 008 (April 2000): 1.

20. Sunstein, "Behavioral Analysis of Law," 1184.

21. W. C. A. M. Dessart and A. A. A. Kuylen, "The Nature, Extent, Causes, and Consequences of Problematic Debt Situations," *Journal of Consumer Policy* 9 (1986): 332.

22. National Consumer Law Center, *Comments to the Federal Reserve Board's Proposed Revisions to Regulation Z Truth in Lending regarding Proposals to Address Predatory Mortgage Lending*, (9 March 2001), available at http://www.nclc.org/predatory_lending/com-

ments_frb.html, viewed 13 December 2001, n.36 and accompanying text.

23. Frank Green and Mike Freeman, "The Debt Generation: Free Spending 20-Somethings Lured By Easy Credit," *San Diego Union Tribune*, 3 January 2002, A1.

24. Thomas A. Durkin, "Credit Cards: Use and Consumer Attitudes, 1970–2000," *Federal Reserve Bulletin* (September 2000): 628 (emphasis added).

25. Lilian Y. Zhu and Carol B. Meeks, "Effects of Low Income Families Ability and Willingness to Use Consumer Credit on Subsequent Outstanding Credit Balances," *Journal of Consumer Affairs* 28(2) (22 December 1994): 403; Glenn B. Canner, "Changes in Consumer Holding and Use of Credit Cards, 1970–1986," *Journal of Retail Banking* 10 (1988): 13–24.

26. A.C. Pigou, *The Economics of Welfare*, 4th ed. (New York: St. Martin's Press, 1960), 25.

27. Hersh M. Shefrin and Richard H. Thaler, "The Behavioral Life-Cycle Hypothesis," in *Quasi Rational Economics*, ed. Richard H. Thaler (New York: Russell Sage, 1994), 93.

28. Kenneth Arrow, "Risk Perception in Psychology and Economics," *Economic Inquiry* 20 (January 1982): 8; Melvin A. Eisenberg, "The Limits of Cognition and the Limits of Contract," *Stanford Law Review* 47 (1995): 222; Jolls, Sunstein, and Thaler, "Behavioral Approaches," 1497; Sunstein, "Behavioral Analysis," 1193–94; Sunstein, "Legal Interference with Private Preferences," 163–64.

29. United Nations International Drug Control Programme, *World Drug Report* (Oxford: Oxford University Press, 1997), 47 (emphasis added).

30. Charles F. Levinthal, *Drugs, Behavior, and Modern Society* (Boston: Allyn and Bacon, 1996), 16; Lloyd Johnston and Patrick M. O'Malley, "Why Do the Nation's Students Use Drugs and Alcohol? Self-Reported Reasons From Nine National Surveys," *Journal of Drug Issues* 16 (1986): 29.

31. Tannette Johnson-Elie, "How to Avoid Debt: By Just Saying No," *Milwaukee Journal and Sentinel*, 4 September 2001, 01D.

32. Jack Guttentag, "Your Mortgage: Lenders Entice Passive Borrowers," *Los Angeles Times*, 30 September 2001, K4.

33. Gene Marsh, "The Hard Sell in Consumer Credit: How the Folks in Marketing Can Put You Into Court," *Consumer Finance Law Quarterly Report* 52 (Summer 1985): 297.

34. The first sentence of the first chapter of Bentham's landmark work reads, "Nature has placed mankind under the governance of two sovereign masters, *pain* and *pleasure*." Jeremy Bentham, *An Introduction to the Principles of Morals and Legislation*, J. H. Burns and H. L. A. Hart, eds. (New York: Oxford University Press, 1996), 11.

35. Sunstein, "Legal Interference with Private Preferences," 1161.

36. James G. Barber, *Social Work with Addictions* (New York: New York University Press, 1994), 20–25; Levinthal, *Drugs, Behavior, and Modern Society*, 38–39; D. Dwayne Simpson and Saul B. Sells, "Effectiveness of Treatment for Drug Abuse: An Overview of the DARP Research Program," *Advances in Alcohol and Substance Abuse* 2 (1982): 7; Jon Elster, *Strong Feelings: Emotions, Addiction, and Human Behavior* (Cambridge, MA: MIT Press, 2000), 190–91; Sunstein, "Interference with Private Preferences," 1158–60.

37. Shefrin and Thaler, "Behavioral Life Cycle Hypothesis," 96; Richard Elliot, "Addictive Consumption: Function and Fragmentation in Postmodernity," *Journal of Consumer Policy* 17 (1994): 159.

38. Debtors Anonymous, *A Currency of Hope* (Needham, Mass: Debtors Anonymous General Services Office, 1999), 17, 96.

39. Melissa Preddy, "Web Sites Help Make First Steps to Recovering from Debt," *Gannett News Service*, 9 March 2000.

40. A small fraction of debt self-help books include: Susan Abentrod, *The Ten Minute Guide to Beating Debt* (New York: John Wiley and

Sons, 1996); Jason Anthony and Karl Cluck, *Debt Free by 30: Practical Advice for Young, Broke, and Upwardly Mobile* (New York: Plume, 2001); Mark Bryan and Julia Cameron, *Money Drunk, Money Sober: 90 Days to Financial Freedom* (New York: Ballentine Books, 1999); Creflo A. Dollar Jr. *No More Debt! God's Strategy for Debt Cancellation* (College Park, GA: World Changers Ministries, 2001); Mary Hunt, *Debt Proof Your Holidays* (New York: St. Marin's Mass Market Paper, 1997); Stacy Johnson, *Life or Debt: A One Week Plan for a Lifetime of Financial Freedom* (New York: Ballentine Books, 2001); Steven D. Strauss and Azriela L. Jaffe, *The Complete Idiot's Guide to Beating Debt* (New York: Alpha Books, 1999).

41. Johnson-Elie, "How to Avoid Debt," 01D.

42. Guttentag, "Mortgage Lenders Entice Passive Borrowers," K4.

43. J. Andrew Curliss, "Loan Tactic Targeted," *Raleigh News and Observer*, 12 April 2002, B3.

44. Lauren Colemen-Lochner, "Disease of Affluence; Easy Credit, internet Malls, and the Thrill of the Hunt All Spell Trouble for Compulsive Shoppers," *The Bergen County (N.J.) Record*, 2 April 2000, B1, quoting Donald Black, Professor of Psychiatry at the University of Iowa; Jann Mitchell, "Kicking the Shopping Habit," *Sunday Oregonian*, 25 June 2000, L13.

45. Stephen M. Bainbridge, "Mandatory Disclosure," 1039–46; Colin Camerer, "Individual Decision Making," in *The Handbook of Experimental Economics*, John H. Kagel and Alvin E. Roth, eds. (Princeton, N.J.: Princeton University Press, 1995), 665–70; Daniel Kahneman and Amos Tversky, "Prospect Theory: An Analysis of Decision Under Risk," *Econometrica* 47 (March 1979): 263–291; Daniel Kahneman, Jack L. Knetsch, and Richard H. Thaler, "Experimental Tests of the Endowment Effect and the Coase Theorem," *Journal of Political Economy* 98 (1990): 1328; Richard H. Thaler, "The Psychology of Choice and the Assumption of Economics," in *Quasi Rational Economics*, ed.

Richard Thaler (New York: Russell Sage Foundation, 1994), 142–43; Amos Tversky and Daniel Kahneman, "Rational Choice and the Framing of Decisions," in *Rational Choice: The Contrast Between Economics and Psychology*, Robin M. Hogarth and Melvin W. Reder, eds. (Chicago: University of Chicago Press, 1987), 76–77.

46. U. S. Senate Special Committee on Aging, *Equity Predators: Stripping, Flipping, and Packaging their Way to Profits Hearing*, 105th Cong., 2d sess., 16 March 1998, testimony of "Jim Dough."

47. Professor Langevoort makes a similar argument with respect to securities brokers. Langevoort, "Selling Hope, Selling Risk," 676.

48. Jack Guttentag, "Your Mortgage: Confused Borrowers Can Make Easy Prey," *Los Angeles Times*, 23 September 2001, K5.

49. Debtors Anonymous, *Currency of Hope*, 130.

50. Ross Werland, "The Facts Behind College Kids and Debt," *Chicago Tribune*, 1 October 2000, 5.

51. Sunstein, "Behavioral Analysis of Law," 1182.

52. Eisenberg, "Limits of Cognition," 220; Daniel Kahneman and Amos Tversky, "Choices Values, and Frames," *American Psychology* 39 (1984): 341; Daniel Kahneman and Amos Tversky, "The Framing of Decisions and the Psychology of Choice," *Science* 211 (January 1981): 453–58; Kahneman and Tversky, "Prospect Theory," 263–91; Thomas Russell and Richard H. Thaler, "The Relevance of Quasi Rationality in Competitive Markets," in *Quasi Rational Economics*, ed. Richard H. Thaler (New York: Russell Sage Foundation, 1994), 240–44.

53. U. S. Senate Committee on Banking, Housing, and Urban Affairs, *Predatory Mortgage Lending Practices: Abusive Uses of Yield Spread Premiums: Hearing Before the Senate Committee on Banking, Housing, and Urban Affairs*, 107th Cong., 8 January 2002, statement of Ms. Rita Herrod.

54. Steven W. Bender, "Consumer Protection for Latinos: Overcoming Language Fraud and English Only," *American University Law*

Review 45 (1996): 1035–36; Keest and Klein, *Truth in Lending*, §
7.3.7.2; Pridgen, *Consumer Credit*, § 4.3; Marsh, "The Hard Sell,"
300; Gene A. Marsh, "Lender Liability for Consumer Fraud Practices of Retail Dealers and Home Improvement Contractors," *Alabama Law Review* 45 (1993): 1; *Brooks v. Home Cable Concepts
of Tennessee, Inc.*, 1997 U.S. Dist. LEXIS 12540, No. 96–0757-
CB-5 (S.D. Ala. July 29, 1997); *Campbell-Salva v. Direct Cable of
Mobile/Pensacola, Inc.*, U.S. Dist. LEXIS 12408, No. 96–0926
BH-M (S.D. Ala. July 14, 1997); *Johnson v. Fleet Finance, Inc.*,
785 F.Supp. 1003 (S.D. Ga. 1991).

55. Hillel J. Einhorn and Robin M. Hogarth, "Decision Making
Under Ambiguity," in *Rational Choice: The Contrast Between Eco-
nomics and Psychology*, Robin M. Hogarth and Melvin W. Reder,
eds. (Chicago: University of Chicago Press, 1987), 46–48; Hillel
J. Einhorn and Robin M. Hogarth, "Behavioral Decision Theory:
Processes of Judgment and Choice," *Annual Review of Judgment
and Psychology* 32 (1981): 53–88; Robin M. Hogarth, "Beyond
Discrete Biases: Functional and Dysfunctional Aspects of Judg-
mental Heuristics," *Psychological Bulletin* 90 (1981): 197–211;
Daniel Kahneman and Amos Tversky, "Conflict Resolution:
A Cognitive Perspective," in *Barriers to Conflict Resolution*, Ken-
neth J. Arrow, et al., eds. (New York, Norton, 1995), 54–55;
Langevoort, "Behavioral Theories of Judgement," 1504; Sun-
stein, "Behavioral Analysis of Law," 1188; Thaler, "Psychology of
Choice," 152; Amos Tversky and Daniel Kahneman, "Judgment
Under Uncertainty: Heuristics and Biases," *Science* 185 (1974):
1124–31.

56. Jonathan M. Landers and Ralph J. Rohner, "A Functional Analysis of Truth in Lending," *UCLA Law Review* 26 (1979): 715;
William C. Whitford, "The Functions of Disclosure Regulation
in Consumer Transactions," *Wisconsin Law Review* (1973): 426

57. Landers and Rohner, "Functional Analysis of Truth in Lending,"
716; Editorial, "Predatory Lenders," *The Bergen County (N.J.)*

Record, 6 May 2002, L06; Deborah Goldstein, "Protecting Consumers from Predatory Lenders: Defining the Problem and Moving Toward Workable Solutions," *Harvard Civil Rights and Civil Liberties Law Review* 35 (Winter 2000): 247.

58. Christopher Peterson, "Failed Markets, Failing Government, or Both? Learning from the Unintended Consequences of Utah Consumer Credit Law on Vulnerable Debtors," *Utah Law Review* (2001).

59. FED and HUD, *Joint Report,* 21.

60. Consumer Federation of America and Center for Economic Justice, *Credit Insurance Overcharges Hit $2.5 Billion Annually* (November 2001), 1–2; Mary Griffin and Birny Birnbaum, Consumers Union and Center for Economic Justice, *Credit Insurance: The $2 Billion A Year Rip-Off* (March 1999), 1–2; Keest and Klein, *Truth in Lending,* § 3.9.4.1; Kathleen E. Keest, *The Cost of Credit: Regulation and Legal Challenges* (Boston: National Consumer Law Center, 1995), Chapter 8; National Consumer Law Center, *Comments to the Federal Reserve Board,* n.26; Gordon Pereira, "Credit Insurance: Obtaining Relief for Post-Claim Ineligibility Determinations," *Clearinghouse Review* (December 1994): 891.

61. Consumers Union, *The $2 Billion Rip-Off,* 2–3; Consumer Federation of America, *Credit Insurance Overcharges,* 2–3; National Consumer Law Center, *Comments to the Federal Reserve Board,* n.29.

62. Consumers Union, *The $2 Billion Rip-Off,* 2–3; Consumer Federation of America, *Credit Insurance Overcharges,* 2–3; Erick Bergquist, "Single Premium Route Doesn't End Fight," *American Banker* 167 (192) (5 October 2001): 1.

63. Consumer Federation of America, *Credit Insurance Overcharges,* 3.

64. U.S.C. §§ 1011–1015.

65. Consumer Federation of America, *Credit Insurance Overcharges,* Apx. Two, p. 9, Apx. Five.

66. Marsh, "The Hard Sell," 299.

67. Consumer Federation of America, *Credit Insurance Overcharges*, 4, quoting Walter Runkle of the Consumer Credit Insurance Association in "Credit Insurance Worth It?" *Bank Rate Monitor*, 15 Feb. 1999.

68. Senate Special Committee, *Equity Predators*, statements of "Jim Dough" and Professor Gene Marsh.

69. Senate Special Committee, *Equity Predators*, testimony of Gael Carter.

70. Ibid.

71. Senate Special Committee, *Equity Predators*, testimony of "Jim Dough."

72. Marsh, "The Hard Sell," 297.

73. "FTC Files Formal Complaint Over Citigroup Lending Tactics," *Best's Review* 102 (12) (1 April 2002): 112; Bergquist, "Single-Premium Route," 1; Chris Serres, "Lender To Give Customers Refunds," *Raleigh News and Observer*, 7 September 2001, D1, statement of North Carolina Attorney General Roy Cooper; L. McNeil Chestnut, North Carolina Assistant Attorney General, *Memorandum to Hal D. Lingerfelt Commissioner of Banks Summarizing Senate Bill 1149*, 25 August 1998, available at http://www.banking.state.nc.us/bill1149.htm, viewed 14 June, 2002, § 5.

74. Keest and Klein, *Truth in Lending*, §3.9.4.1.

75. National Consumer Law Center, *Comments to the Federal Reserve Board*, n.23.

76. Richard H. McAdams, "The Origin, Development, and Regulation of Norms," *Michigan Law Review* 96 (1997): 340; Richard A. Posner, "Social Norms and the Law: An Economic Approach," *American Economic Review* 87 (1997): 365.

77. Sunstein, "Social Norms and Social Roles," 914.

78. For an introduction to recent legal commentary on social norms see: Robert Cooter, "Expressive Law and Economics," *Journal of*

Legal Studies 27 (1998): 585–608; Robert Cooter, "Normative Failure Theory of Law," *Cornell Law Review* 82 (1997): 947–79; Robert C. Ellickson, "Law and Economics Discovers Social Norms," *Journal of Legal Studies* 27 (1998): 537–54; Joseph R. Gusfield, "On Legislating Morals: The Symbolic Process of Designating Deviance," *California Law Review* 56 (1968): 54–73; Avery Katz, "Taking Private Ordering Seriously," *University of Pennsylvania Law Review* 144 (1996): 1745–63; Lawrence Lessig, "Social Meaning and Social Norms," *University of Pennsylvania Law Review* 144 (1996): 2181–89; Lawrence Lessig, "The Regulation of Social Meaning," *University of Chicago Law Review* 62 (1995): 943–1039; Lawrence Lessig, "The New Chicago School," *Journal of Legal Studies* 27 (1998): 661–91; McAdams, "Origin, Development, and Regulation of Norms," 338–433; Philip Pettit, "*Virtus Normativa*: Rational Choice Perspectives," *Ethics* 100 (July 1990): 725–55; Eric A. Posner, "The Regulation of Groups: The Influence of Legal and Nonlegal Sanctions on Collective Action," *University of Chicago Law Review* 63 (1996): 133–97; Richard A. Posner, "Social Norms, Social Meaning, and Economic Analysis of Law: A Comment," *Journal of Legal Studies* 27 (1998): 553–69; Sunstein, "Social Norms and Social Roles," 903–68; Edna Ullmann-Margalit, "Revision of Norms," *Ethics* 100 (July 1990): 756–67.

79. Robert Seidenberg, M.D., "Advertising and Drug Acculturation," in *Socialization in Drug Abuse*, Robert H. Coombs, Lincoln J. Fry, and Patricia G. Lewis, eds. (Cambridge, Mass.: Schenkman Publishing Co., 1976), 21.

80. David Caplovitz, "Consumer Credit in the Affluent Society," *Law and Contemporary Problems* 33 (1969).

81. McAdams, "Origin, Development, and Regulation of Norms," 394; Posner, "Social Norms and the Law," 367; Sunstein, "Social Norms and Social Roles," 912.

82. Galbraith, *The Affluent Society*, 170–71.

83. In this vein, Coase himself has stated presumed rational utility maximization "plays a part similar . . . to that of ether in the old physics." Coase, *The Firm, The Market, and the Law*, 2.

CHAPTER 6

1. Samuelson and Nordhaus, *Economics*, 347.
2. Ibid., 347.
3. A. C. Pigou, *The Economics of Welfare*, 4th ed. (New York: St. Martin's Press, 1960), 183–85.
4. The notion of Pareto efficiency comes from the economist Vilfredo Pareto (1848–1923) who made important advances in combining macroeconomic analysis of overall market behavior with microeconomic analysis of individual consumer and firm behavior. Wassily Leontief, "Mathematics in Economics," in *Essays in Economics: Theories and Theorizing*, vol. 1 (New York: M.E. Sharpe, 1977), 24; David Z. Rich, *The Economics of Welfare: A Contemporary Analysis* (New York: Praeger, 1989), 18, 17–21; Pigou, *Economics of Welfare*,184.
5. Marc Allen Eisner, Jeff Worsham, and Evan J. Ringquist, *Contemporary Regulatory Policy* (Boulder: Lynne Rienner Publishers, 2000), 8.
6. Robert Cooter, "Unity in Tort, Contract and Property: The Model of Precaution," *California Law Review* 73 (1985): 1–51.
7. Samuelson and Nordhaus, *Economics*, 347.
8. Ibid., 273.
9. Teresa Sullivan, Elizabeth Warren, and Jay Lawrence Westerbrook, *As We Forgive Our Debtors: Bankruptcy and Consumer Credit in America* (New Haven: Yale University Press, 1989), 316.
10. Karen Gross, *Failure and Forgiveness: Rebalancing the Bankruptcy System* (New Haven: Yale University Press, 1997), 118.
11. Elizabeth Warren, "What is a Women's Issue? Bankruptcy, Com-

mercial Law, and Other Gender-Neutral Topics," *Harvard Women's Law Journal* 25 (2002): 19 n.116.

12. Gross, *Failure and Forgiveness*, 118; Sullivan, Warren and Westerbrook, *As We Forgive Our Debtors*, 322.

13. Sullivan, Warren, and Westerbrook, *As We Forgive Our Debtors*, 311–12.

14. David Caplovitz, *Consumers in Trouble: A Study of Debtors in Default* (New York: Free Press, 1974), 233–36.

15. Edward L. Glaeser and Jose Scheinkman, "Neither a Borrower Nor a Lender Be: An Economic Analysis of Interest Restrictions and Usury Laws," *Journal of Law and Economics* 41 (1998): 27.

16. Conversely, economists point to positive externalities associated with Community Reinvestment Act lending in low- and moderate-income communities underserved by banks. Christopher A. Richardson, "The Community Reinvestment Act and the Economics of Regulatory Policy," *Fordham Urban Law Journal* 28 (2002): 1607, 1614–16.

17. Warren Bolton, "Predatory Lending Takes Money, Other Assets Out of Poor Communities," *The State (Columbia, SC)*, 21 March 2002, A14; Editorial, "Wolf At the Door: Vulnerable Need Protection Against Predatory Lenders," *Washington Post*, 10 March 2002, B10; Gloria Irwin, "Homeownership Gone Bad; Mortgage Foreclosures Hit Summit Neighborhoods Hard; High-Pressure Sales Tactics, Predatory Lenders Share Blame," *Akron Beacon Journal*, 24 February 2002, 1; Richard Newman, "A Homeowner's Nightmare: Foreclosure Rate Shows Alarming Rise in North Jersey," *The Bergen County (N.J.) Record*, 17 March 2002, B01; Bill Torpy, "Foreclosures Set One-Month Record for State," *Atlanta Journal and Constitution*, 28 March 2002, JA1; Ken Ward Jr., "Borrower Beware! Equity Lenders Taking the Homes of State Residents," *Charleston (WV) Gazette and Daily Mail*, 31 March 2002, P1A.

18. U. S. Senate Committee on Banking, Housing, and Urban Af-

fairs, *Problems in Community Development Banking, Mortgage Lending Discrimination, Reverse Redlining and Home Equity Lending Hearings*, 103d. Cong. 1ˢᵗ sess., 3, 17, 24 February 1993, 298.

19. Ibid., 301–02, statement of Chairman Donald W. Riegle Jr.

20. Ioannis N. Kallianiotis, "Saving and Investment: The Forecast Function of Interest Rates," *American Business Review*, 2(1) (1 January 2002): 50 n.17 and accompanying text.

21. U. S. House Committee on Banking and Financial Services, *Predatory Lending Practices Hearing*, 106ᵗʰ Cong., 2d sess., 24 May 2000, 106, statement of Margot Saunders.

22. Teresa A. Sullivan, Elizabeth Warren, and Jay Lawrence Westerbrook, *The Fragile Middle Class: Americans in Debt* (New Haven: Yale University Press, 2000), 173.

23. Janet Ford, *The Indebted Society: Credit and Default in the 1980s* (London: Routledge, 1988), 140–41; *Walker Bank & Trust Co. v. Jones*, 672 P.2d 73 (Utah 1983).

24. Mass Gen. Laws ch. 605 § 8 (1908); *Mutual Loan Co. v. Martell*, 222 U.S. 225, 234 (1911).

25. Ind. Adv. Legis. Serv. p. 76, § 7999.

26. *Cleveland, Cincinnati, Chicago and St. Louis Railway Company et al. v. Marshall*, 105 N.E. 570, 572 (Ind. 1914).

27. Martin Ryan, *The Last Resort, A Study of Consumer Bankrupts* (1995), 117–19.

28. R. D. Conger and G. H. Elder, *Families in Troubled Times: Adapting to Change in Rural America* (New York: Aldine de Gruyter, 1994); R.D. Conger, et al., "Linking Economic Hardship to Marital Quality and Instability," *Journal of Marriage and the Family* 52 (1990): 643–656; David Caplovitz, *Making Ends Meet: How Families Cope with Inflation and Recession* (Beverly Hills: Sage Publications, 1979), 121–22; Ford, *Indebted Society*, 108–12, 140; Sullivan, Warren, and Westerbrook, *Fragile Middle Class*, 194–96; Lynn White and Stacy Rogers, "Economic Circumstances and Family Outcomes: A Review of the 1990s," *Journal of Marriage*

and the Family 62 (4) (2000): 1035–1051; G. L. Fox and D. Chancey, "Sources of Economic Distress: Individual and Family Outcomes," *Journal of Family Issues* 19 (1998): 725–49.

29. Kathleen E. Keest, "Whither Now? Truth in Lending in Transition–Again," *Consumer Finance Law Quarterly Report* 49 (Fall 1995): 365.

30. Odette Williamson, "Protecting Elderly Homeowners from Predatory Mortgage Lenders," *Clearinghouse Review* (September–October 2000): 297; United States Senate Special Committee on Aging, *Equity Predators: Stripping, Flipping, and Packaging their Way to Profits: Hearing Before the Special Committee on Aging, United States Senate*, 105th Cong., 2d sess., 16 March 1998, testimony of "Jim Dough."

31. Edge's story appears in Dulane D. Stafford, "Lending Bill Gives Victims Legal Clout," *Atlanta Journal and Constitution*, 14 April 2002, C4.

32. Stuart's story appears in Williamson, "Protecting the Elderly," 298.

33. Johnson's story appears in Emma D. Sapong, "'Don't Borrow Trouble' Raises Awareness of Predatory Lenders," *Buffalo News*, 13 April 2002, B1.

34. Dalton Conley, *Being Black, Living in the Red: Race, Wealth, and Social Policy in America* (Berkeley: University of California Press, 1999), 2.

35. Rick Brundrett, "How Mounting Loans Devastated 87-Year-Old," *The State* (Columbia, SC), 24 February 2002, A1; Christine Dugas, "American Seniors Rack Up Debt Like Never Before: Medical Expenses Often Feed the Cycle," *USA Today*, 25 April 2002, A01; Donna Harkness, "Predatory Lending Prevention Project: Prescribing a Cure for the Home Equity Loss Ailing the Elderly," *Boston Public Interest Law Journal* 10 (2000): 1; Daniel L. Skoler, "The Elderly and Bankruptcy Relief: Problems, Protections, and Realities," *Bankruptcy Developments Journal* 6 (1989): 121.

36. Paul Mondor, "The Quasi-Law of Fair Lending," *Mortgage Banking* 57 (November 1996): 13, 14.
37. Alicia H. Munnell, et al., "Mortgage Lending in Boston: Interpreting HMDA Data," *Working Paper No. 92–7* (Boston: Federal Reserve Bank of Boston, 1992). For an introduction to the extensive debate over discrimination in mortgage lending origination see Harold A. Black, "Is There Discrimination in Mortgage Lending? What Does the Research Tell Us?" *Review of Black Political Economy* (Summer 1999): 23; Theodore E. Day and S. J. Liebowitz, "Mortgage Lending to Minorities: Where's the Bias?" *Economic Inquiry* 36 (1998), 3–28; Fred Galves, "The Discriminatory Impact of Traditional Lending Criteria: An Economic and Moral Critique," *Seton Hall Law Review* (1999): 1467; Glen W. Harrison, "Mortgage Lending in Boston: A Reconsideration of the Evidence," *Economic Inquiry* 36 (1998): 29–38; Helen F. Ladd, "Evidence on Discrimination in Mortgage Lending," *Journal of Economic Perspectives* 12 (2) (1998): 41; Stanley D. Longohfer, "Discrimination in Mortgage Lending: What Have We Learned?" *Economic Commentary* (15 August 1996), 1; Robert E. Martin and R. Carter Hill, "Loan Performance and Race," *Economic Inquiry* 38 (1) (2000): 136–50; Reynold F. Nesbia, "Racial Discrimination in Residential Lending Markets: Why Empirical Researchers Always See It and Economic Theorists Never Do," *Journal of Economic Issues* 30 (1) (1996): 51; Robert Schafer and Helen F. Ladd, *Discrimination in Mortgage Lending* (Cambridge: MIT Press, 1981); Ronald K. Schuster, "Lending Discrimination: Is the Secondary Market Helping to Make the 'American Dream' A Reality?" *Gonzaga Law Review* (2000/2001): 153; Peter P. Swire, "The Persistent Problem of Lending Discrimination: A Law and Economics Analysis," *Texas Law Review* 73 (1995): 787.
38. Melissa Allison, "Poorer Areas of Chicago Also Remain Poor in Bank Branches," *Knight Ridder/Tribune Business News*, 26 November 2001.

39. U. S. Senate Committee, *Problems in Community Development Banking*, 294–95, statement of John Long, Esq.

40. Nicole Duran, "Poll: 35 Percent Think Lenders Discriminate," *American Banker* 167(41) (1 March 2002): 3.

41. Department of Housing and Urban Development, *Unequal Burden: Income and Racial Disparities in Subprime Lending in America* (Washington, D.C.: Department of Housing and Urban Development, 2000).

42. U. S. Senate Committee, *Problems in Community Development Banking*, 87, 177.

43. Ellen Graham, "Southern Pastor Has a Mission to Deliver His Flock From Debt," *Wall Street Journal*, 12 June 2002, A1.

44. Yair Listokin, "Confronting the Barriers to Native American Homeownership on Tribal Lands: The Case of the Navajo Partnership for Housing," *Urban Lawyer* (Spring 2001): 433.

45. National Consumer Law Center, "DOJ Finds and Fines Higher Credit Prices, Loan Requirements for African Americans, Native Americans as Discriminatory," *NCLC Reports Consumer Credit and Usury Edition* 12 (March/April 1994): 42–43.

46. Ibid., 42.

47. U. S. Senate Committee, *Problems in Community Development Banking*, 186.

48. Mark Fogarty, "Home Loans Cost More for Indian Borrowers," *Indian Country Today*, 2 May 2002, available at http://www.indiancountry.com/?102018981, viewed 2 May 2002.

49. Kelsey A. Begaye, "Implementation of the Native American Housing Assistance and Self Determination Act: Testimony Before the Committee on Indian Affairs United States Senate," *Congressional Testimony by Federal Document Clearinghouse*, 13 February 2002, available at 2002 WL 2010680.

50. Editorial, "Speed Bump," *National Mortgage News* 26(25) (18 March 2002): 4.

51. Holden Lewis, "Mortgages Scarce on Native American Lands,"

Chicago Sun-Times, 2 June 2002, 11C; Richard Mize, "Predatory Lending Hits Home in State, Experts Say," *Daily Oklahoman*, 25 January 2002, 8C; "Predatory Lenders Use Courthouse," *Daily Oklahoman*, 1 June 2002, 6C.

52. TJAGSA Practice Notes, "Payday Loans: The High Cost of Borrowing Against Your Paycheck," *Army Lawyer* 27 (February 2001): 23.

53. Tom Shean, "Payday Loan Bill Draws Criticism from Military: Effort to Regulate High-Interest Loans Would Backfire, They Say," *The (Norfolk) Virginian-Pilot and Star Ledger*, 16 February 2002, D1.

54. "Senator: Borrowers Trapped by 'Payday' Loans, High Interest," *Jefferson City News Tribune Online Edition*, 28 December 1999, available at http://www.newstribune.com/stories/122899/bus_1228990024.asp (viewed: 11 January 2002).

55. Debbie Rhyne, "Aid Fund Offers Help to Military Personnel, Families," *Macon Telegraph*, 29 December 2001, 1.

56. TJAGSA Practice Notes, "The High Cost of Borrowing Against Your Paycheck," 23.

57. Martha McNeil Hamilton, "Ignorance Costs Plenty: Officials Promote Financial Literacy," *Washington Post*, 6 February 2002, E01.

58. Nadine Taub and Elizabeth M. Schneider, "Perspectives on Women's Subordination and the Law," in *The Politics of Law: A Progressive Critique*, ed. David Kairys (New York: Pantheon Books, 1982), 118; Melanie Tebbutt, *Making Ends Meet: Pawnbrokering and Working Class Credit* (New York: St. Martin's Press, 1983), 1.

59. Taub and Schneider, "Perspectives on Women's Subordination," 120; Tebbutt, *Making Ends Meet*, 1.

60. *FTC v. CITI Group/Sales Financing, Inc.*, 67 Antitrust & Trade Reg. Rep. (BNA) 252 (D.N.J. 1994); *FTC v. Ford Motor Credit Co.*, Consent Decree (E.D. Mich. 9 December 1999); *U.S. v.*

Franklin Acceptance Corp., No. 99-CV-2435, Consent Decree (E.D. Pa. 13 May 1999); Prigden, *Consumer Credit*, § 3;4

61. Warren, "What is a Women's Issue?" 19 n.41; Daniel A. Edelman, "Payday Loans: Big Interest Rates and Little Regulation," *Loyola Consumer Law Review* 11 (1999): 175; Danielle Herubin, "Some Check Cashers Charging Interest That Can Reach 520%," *Palm Beach Post*, 11 November 1998, 6B; Io Data Corporation, *Utah Consumer Lending Association: Utah Customer Study*, (Salt Lake City: Io Data Corporation, July 2001), 35; Lawrence Mishel, Jared Bernstein, and John Schmitt, *The State of Working America, 2000/2001* (Ithaca: Cornell University Press, 2001), 27–28.

62. David H. Demo and Martha J. Cox, "Families with Young Children: A Review of Research in the 1990s," *Journal of Marriage and the Family* 62(2) (2000): 876–895.

63. Jeanne Brooks-Gunn, Greg J. Duncan, and Nancy Maritato, "Poor Families, Poor Outcomes: The Well Being of Children and Youth," in *Consequences of Growing Up Poor*, Greg J. Duncan and Jeanne Brooks-Gunn, eds. (New York: Russell Sage Foundation, 1999), 2.

64. Thomas L. Hanson, Sara McLanahan, and Elizabeth Thomson, "Economic Resources, Parental Practices, and Children's Well Being," in *Consequences of Growing Up Poor*, Greg J. Duncan and Jeanne Brooks-Gunn, eds. (New York: Russell Sage Foundation, 1999), 191. R. D. Conger, et al, "A Family Process Model of Economic Hardship and Adjustment of Early Adolescent Boys," *Child Development* 63(2) (1992): 526–41; J. McLeod and M. Shanahan, "Poverty, Parenting and Children's Mental Health," *American Sociological Review* 58(3) (1993): 351–66; V. C. McLoyd, "The Impact of Economic Hardship on Black Families and Children: Psychological Distress, Parenting and Socioemotional Development," *Child Development* 61(2) (1990): 311–46; R. J. Sampson and J. H. Laub, "Urban Poverty and the Family

Context of Delinquency: A New Look at Structure and Process in a Classic Study," *Child Development* 65(2) (1994): 523–40.

65. Jeanne Brooks-Gunn, et al., "Early Intervention in Low Birth Weight, Premature Infants: Results Through Age Five Years from the Infant Health Development Program," *Journal of the American Medical Association* 272(16) (1994): 1257–62; Jeanne Brooks-Gunn, G. Guo, and F. F. Furstenberg Jr., "Who Drops Out of and Who Continues Beyond High School? A 20 Year Study of Black Youth," *Journal of Research in Adolescence* 3(37) (1993): 271–94; G. J. Duncan, Jeanne Brooks-Gunn, and Pamela K. Klebanov, "Economic Deprivation and Early-Childhood Development," *Child Development* 62(2) (1994): 296–318; Mary Corcoran and Terry Adams, "Race, Sex, and the Intergenerational Transmission of Poverty," in *Consequences of Growing Up Poor*, eds. Greg J. Duncan and Jeanne Brooks-Gunn (New York: Russell Sage Foundation, 1999), 101; R. Haveman, B. Wolfe, and J. Spaulding, "Childhood Events and Circumstances Influencing High School Completion," *Demography* 28(1) (1991): 133–157; G. J. Duncan and S. F. Hoffman, "Welfare Benefits, Economic Opportunities and the Incidence of Out-of-Wedlock Births Among Black Teenage Girls," *Demography* 27(4) (1990): 519–35.

66. Elizabeth Warren, Teresa Sullivan, and Melissa Jacoby, "Medical Problems and Bankruptcy Filings," *Harvard Law School Public Law and Legal Theory Working Paper Series*, Working Paper No. 008 (April 2000), 1.

67. N. Baydar, J. Brooks-Gunn, "Effects of Maternal Employment and Child Care Arrangements in Infancy on Preschoolers' Cognitive and Behavioral Outcomes: Evidence from the Children of the National Longitudinal Study of Youth," *Developmental Psychology* 27(6) (1991): 932–45; NICHD Early Child Care Research Network, "Poverty and Patterns of Child Care," in *Consequences of Growing Up Poor*, eds. Greg J. Duncan and

Jeanne Brooks-Gunn (New York: Russell Sage Foundation, 1999), 101.

68. Jim Abrams, "'Rapid Refunds' Really High-Cost Loans," *Miami Herald*, 24 February 2002, 7, F1; Alan Berube, et al., *The Price of Paying Taxes: How Tax Preparation and Refund Loan Fees Erode the Benefits of the EITC* (Washington, D.C.: Brookings Institution, 2002), 5; Editorial, "Preying on Arizona's Working Poor," *Arizona Daily Star*, 28 May 2002, B6; "H&R Block's Advertising Violates Prohibition Against False, Misleading Marketing," *Consumer Financial Services Law Report* 5(15) (13 February 2002): 1; *JTH Tax Inc. v. H&R Block Eastern Tax Services Inc.*, No. 01–1353, 01–1843 (4th Cir. 10 January 2002) (unpublished disposition); Damian Paletta, "Tax Refund Loans Called Predatory," *American Banker*, 1 February 2002, 5; Chi Chi Wu, Jean Ann Fox, and Elizabeth Renuart, *Tax Preparers Peddle High Priced Tax Refund Loans: Millions Skimmed From the Working Poor and the U.S. Treasury* (Washington, D.C., Boston: Consumer Federation of America & National Consumer Law Center, 31 January 2002), 4–5.

69. Official Staff Commentary, 12 CFR §226.17(c)(1)-17; *Cades v. H&R Block*, 42 F.3d 869 (4th Cir. 1994); Robert Reed, "Slamming the Brakes on Speedy Tax Refunds," *Crain's Chicago Business*, 12(11) (12 March 2002), 8; Wu, Fox, and Renuart, *Tax Preparers*, 6.

70. Wu, Fox, and Renuart, *Tax Preparers*, 7; Alan Berube and Benjamin Foreman, *Rewarding Work: The Impact of the Earned Income Tax Credit in Greater Chicago* (Washington, D.C.: Brookings Institution, November 2001); Alan Berube and Benjamin Foreman, *A Local Ladder for the Working Poor: The Impact of Earned Income Tax Credits in U.S. Metropolitan Areas* (Washington, D.C.: Brookings Institution, September 2001); Janet Kidd Steward, "Tax Credit Pumps Millions into Area," *Chicago Tribune*, 27 November 2001, 1N.

71. Berube, et al., *Price of Paying Taxes*, 1, 8–9.

72. Guido Calabresi, "Some Thoughts on Risk Distribution and the Law of Torts," *Yale Law Journal* 70 (1961): 499–553.

73. Thomas Jackson, "The Fresh-Start Policy in Bankruptcy Law," *Harvard Law Review* 98 (1985): 1393–1448.

74. U.S.C. §1–15; *Greentree Financial Corp. v. Randolph*, 121 S.Ct. 513 (2000); *Allied-Bruce Terminix v. Dobson*, 513 U.S. 265 (1995); *Carnival Cruise Lines v. Shute*, 499 U.S. 585 (1991); *Meyers v. Univest Home Loan, Inc.*, 1993 WL 307747 (N.D. Cal. 1993); *Gammaro v. Thorp Consumer Discount Co.*, 828 F.Supp. 673 (D. Minn. 1993); *Stiles v. Home Cable Concepts, Inc*, 994 F.Supp. 1410 (M.D. Ala. 1998).

75. House Report No. 97–542 (1982), reprinted in 1982 U.S.C.C.A.N. 765, 777.

76. Jean Sternlight, "As Mandatory Binding Arbitration Meets the Class Action, Will the Class Action Survive?" *William and Mary Law Review* 42 (2000): 1, 55–57.

77. Stephen K Huber, "Consumer Arbitration in the United States Supreme Court: *Greentree Financial Corporation v. Randolph*," *Journal of Texas Consumer Law* 4(3) (Spring 2001): 267; Mark E. Bunditz, "Arbitration of Disputes Between Consumers and Financial Institutions: A Serious Threat to Consumer Protection," *Ohio State Journal on Dispute Resolution* 10 (1995): 267; Thomas E. Carbonneau, "Arbitral Justice: The Demise of Due Process in American Law," *Tulane Law Review* 70 (1996):1945; Melvin Eisenberg, "The Limits of Cognition and the Limits of Contract," *Stanford Law Review* 47 (1995): 211, 240–43; Michael I. Meyerson, "The Efficient Consumer Form Contract: Law and Economics Meets the Real World," *Georgia Law Review* 24 (1990):583, 600; Jeremy Senderowicz, "Consumer Arbitration and Freedom of Contract: A Proposal to Facilitate Consumers' Informed Consent to Arbitration Clauses in Form Contracts," *Columbia Journal of Law and Social Problems* 32 (1999): 275; Shelly Smith, "Mandatory Arbitration Clauses in Consumer Contracts: Consumer Protection and the Circumvention of the Judicial System," *DePaul Law Review* 50 (2001): 1191; Jeffrey W. Stempel, "Boot-

strapping and Slouching Toward Gomorrah: Arbitral Infatuation and the Decline of Consent," *Brooklyn Law Review* 62 (1996): 1381; Jean R. Sternlight, "Panacea or Corporate Tool? Debunking the Supreme Court's Preference for Binding Arbitration," *Washington University Law Quarterly* 74 (1996): 637, 688; Patricia Sturdevant and Dwight Golaan, "Should Binding Arbitration Clauses Be Prohibited In Consumer Contracts?" *Dispute Resolution Magazine* 1 (1994): 4.

78. Senderowicz, "Consumer Arbitration and Freedom of Contract," 277–78; Ken Ward Jr., "State Court Urged to Toss One-Sided Loan Arbitration," *Charleston (WV) Gazette and Daily Mail,* 4 April 2002, 5A.

79. Haller and Alviti, "Loansharking in American Cities," 135; "Courts Coming to See Real Guilt," *The Survey* 27 (10 February 1927), 1729; Lendol Calder, *Financing the American Dream: A Cultural History of Consumer Credit* (Princeton: Princeton University Press, 1999), 119.

80. Joan Claybrook, "Mandatory Arbitration Undermines Law: More and More Businesses Use Clause to Evade Legal Obligations," *Charlotte Observer,* 1 May 2002, 17A.

81. Ronald H. Coase, "The Problem of Social Cost," reprinted in Ronald H. Coase, *The Firm, The Market, and the Law* (Chicago: University of Chicago Press, 1990), 102–103.

82. Avery Wiener Katz, *Foundations of the Economic Approach to Law* (New York: Oxford University Press, 1998), 41.

83. Coase, "Problem of Social Cost," 95–104. Following Coase, many believe because "externalities" are bargained away wherever there are no transaction costs, the concept is superfluous. This chapter retains the moniker of "externality" only because it is a descriptive word. It is equally plausible to argue the absence of an enforceable property right preventing high-cost lenders from burdening family, neighbors, or fellow citizens with confused and desperate debtors yields Pareto-dominated outcomes. Either way,

I cannot believe the underlying high-cost credit market is efficient.

84. Coase, "Problem of Social Cost," 116–17.
85. Calabresi, "Some Thoughts on Risk Distribution," 499.

CHAPTER 7

1. Jay Katz, *The Silent World of Doctor and Patient* (New York: Free Press, 1984), 1.
2. Ruth R. Faden and Tom L. Beauchamp, *A History and Theory of Informed Consent* (New York: Oxford University Press, 1986), 61.
3. Ibid., 62; Barry R. Furrow, et al., *Health Law Cases Materials and Problems*, 3d ed. (St. Paul: West Group, 1997), 398.
4. Faden and Beauchamp, *History and Theory*, 63, quoting Henri de Mondeville, "On the Morals and Etiquette of Surgeons," in *Ethics in Medicine: Historical Perspectives and Contemporary Concerns*, Stanley J. Reiser et al., eds. (Cambridge: MIT Press, 1977), 15.
5. Katz, *Silent World*, 14.
6. Furrow et al., *Health Law*, 398.
7. *Schloendorff v. Soc'y of New York Hosp.*, 105 S.E. 92, 93 (N.Y. 1914).
8. Katz, *Silent World*, 53–58; Furrow, *Health Law*, 398.
9. *Salgo v. Leland Stanford Jr. University Board of Trustees*, 317 P.2d 170, 181 (Cal. Dist. Ct. App. 1957); Faden and Beauchamp, *History and Theory*, 125; Katz, *Silent World*, 60.
10. *Salgo*, 317 P.2d at 181.
11. *Natanson v. Kline*, 350 P.2d 1093, 1100, 1106 (Kan. 1960). Katz, *Silent World*, 66.
12. Fay A. Rozovsky, *Consent to Treatment: A Practical Guide*, 2d ed. (Boston: Little, Brown, 1990), 8–9.
13. *Canterbury v. Spence*, 464 F.2d 772, 783, 786 (D.C. Cir. 1972); Katz, *Silent World*, 73.
14. George J. Annas, *Some Choice: Law, Medicine, and the Market*

(New York: Oxford University Press, 1998), *xii*; Paul S. Appelbaum et al., *Informed Consent: Legal Theory and Clinical Practice* (New York: Oxford University Press, 1987), 177; Rozovsky, *Consent to Treatment*, 82–89; Carl E. Schneider, *The Practice of Autonomy: Patients, Doctors, and Medical Decisions* (New York: Oxford University Press, 1998).

15. Mike W. Martin and Roland Schinzinger, *Ethics in Engineering* (New York: McGraw-Hill, 1983); Gordon K. Macleod, "Nuclear Power: The Case for Informed Consent," *Religious Humanism* 18 (1984): 100; Bruce Mitchell and Dianne Draper, *Relevance and Ethics in Geography* (New York: Longman, 1982); Anita M. Superson, "The Employer-Employee Relationship and the Right to Know," *Business and Professional Ethics Journal* 3 (1983): 45.

16. Arthur L. Caplan, "Can Autonomy be Saved?" in *If I Were a Rich Man Could I Buy a Pancreas? and Other Essays on the Ethics of Health Care* (Bloomington: Indiana University Press, 1992), 257. Appelbaum et al., *Informed Consent*, 56; Tom L. Beauchamp and James F. Childress, *Principles of Biomedical Ethics*, 3d ed. (New York: Oxford University Press, 1989), 76; Cathy J. Jones, "Autonomy and Informed Consent in Medical Decisionmaking: Toward a New Self-Fulfilling Prophecy," *Washington & Lee Law Review* 47 (1990): 379; Katz, *Silent World*, 79; Alan A. Meisel, "A 'Dignitary Tort' as a Bridge Between the Idea of Informed Consent and the Law of Informed Consent," *Law, Medicine and Health Care* 16 (1988): 210; Marjorie M. Schultz, "From Informed Consent to Patient Choice," *Yale Law Journal* 95 (1985): 219; Robert M. Veatch, "Abandoning Informed Consent," *Hastings Center Report* 25 (1995): 5.

17. Appelbaum et al., *Informed Consent*, 3. Clifton Perry, "Negligence in Securing Informed Consent and Medical Malpractice," *Journal of Medicine, Humanities, and Bioethics* 9 (1988): 111.

18. Rozovsky, *Consent to Treatment*, 3.

19. *Canterbury*, 464 F.2d 772, n.15 .

20. Ndiva Kofele-Kale, "The Impact of Truth-In-Lending Disclosures on Consumer Market Behavior: A Critique of the Critics of Truth-in-Lending Law," *Oklahoma City University Law Review* 9 (Spring 1984): 126; Kathleen E. Keest, "Whither Now? Truth in Lending in Transition—Again," *Consumer Finance Law Quarterly Report* 49 (Fall 1995): 366; Jonathan M. Landers, "Some Reflections on Truth in Lending," *Illinois Law Journal* (1977): 674.

21. Rozovsky, *Consent to Treatment*, 83. *Gorab v. Zook*, 943 P.2d 423 (Colo. 1997), holding duty to obtain informed consent does not extend to ongoing therapeutic treatment; Alaska Stat. § 09.55.556 (1976), dismissing requirement of disclosure for very remote risks.

22. Appelbaum et al., *Informed Consent*, 176.

23. *Sard v. Hardy*, 379 A.2d 1914 (Md. App. 1977).

24. Landers, "Reflections on Truth in Lending," 674; Jeffrey Davis, "Protecting Consumers from Overdisclosure and Gobbledygook: An Empirical Look as the Simplification of Consumer Credit Contracts," *Virginia Law Review* 407 (1977): 841, 906.

25. U.S.C. §1715z-20(f); 24 C.F.R. §205.41; John P. Caskey, *Lower Income Americans, Higher Cost Financial Services* (Madison: Filene Research Institute, 1997), 5; Department of Housing and Urban Development, *Curbing Predatory Home Mortgage Lending* (Washington, D.C.: June 2000), 60–62; Donna Harkness, "Predatory Lending Prevention Project: Prescribing a Cure for the Home Equity Loss Ailing the Elderly," *Boston Public Interest Law Journal* 10 (2000): 1, 41; Ben Jackson, "Banks in 'Literacy' Effort See Long-Term Upsides," *American Banker* 166 (186) (27 September 2001): 6.

26. Harkness, "Predatory Lending Prevention," 42.

27. Thomas Grisso and Paul S. Appelbaum, *Assessing Competence to Consent to Treatment: A Guide for Physicians and Other Health Professionals* (New York: Oxford University Press, 1998): 1.

28. American Association on Mental Deficiency, *Consent Handbook*

(Washington, D.C.: American Association on Mental Deficiency, 1977), 21–28; Grisso and Appelbaum, *Assessing Competence,* 101–26; Marshall B. Kapp and Douglas Moossman, "Measuring Decisional Capacity: Cautions on the Construction of a 'Capacimeter,'" *Psychology Public Policy and Law* (1996): 73; Roth et al., "Tests of Competency to Consent to Treatment," *American Journal of Psychiatry* 134 (1977): 910, listing five seminal tests for competency; Becky Cox White, *Competence to Consent* (Washington, D.C.: Georgetown University Press, 1994), 101.

29. White, *Competence to Consent,* 1, 3, 7.
30. David E. Ost, "The 'Right' Not to Know," *Journal of Medicine and Philosophy* 9 (1984): 301, 306–07.
31. Ga. Code Ann. §45–17–8(b)(3) (1992).
32. Nathaniel C. Nichols, "Home Alone: Home Mortgage Foreclosure Rescue Scams and the Theft of Equity," *Journal of Affordable Housing and Community Development Law* 11 (2002): 280.
33. U.S.C. §1092.
34. Jonathan M. Landers and Ralph J. Rohner, "A Functional Analysis of Truth in Lending," *UCLA Law Review* 26 (1979): 731.
35. *Brown v. Capanna,* 782 P.2d 1299 (Nev. 1989); *Kinser v. Elkadi,* 674 S.W.2d 226 (Mo. App. 1984); *Logan v. Greenwich Hospital Association,* 465 A.2d 294 (Conn. 1983).
36. *Johnson v. Kokemoor,* 545 N.W.2d 495, 497 (Wis. 1996).
37. Ibid., 507.
38. Appelbaum et al., *Informed Consent,* 54.
39. Houlton, "Consumer Behavior, Market Imperfections and Public Policy," reprinted in David A. Rice, *Consumer Transactions* (Boston: Little, Brown, 1975): 57, 63.
40. *Besta v. Beneficial Loan Co.,* 855 F.2d 532 (8th Cir. 1988); *In re Milbourne,* 108 Bankr. 552 (Bankr. E.D. Pa. 1989); Barbara Curran, *Trends in Consumer Credit Legislation* (Chicago: University of

Chicago Press, 1965), 38; Landers and Rohner, "Functional Analysis," 736 n.83; S. 2802, 95th Cong., 2d Sess. § 18(a) (1978).

41. Bankrate.com, *Mortgage Rates*, available at http://www.bankrate.com/ (viewed 31 May 2001); Online Auto Loans, *Welcome to Online Auto Loans*, available at http://online-car-auto=loan.com/ (viewed 31 May 2001); OnMortgage.com, *Mortgage Rates*, available at http://www.onmortgage.com/ (viewed 31 May 2001); Rate.net, *Credit Card Rates*, available at http://www.rate.net/ (viewed 31 May 2001).

42. See generally, http://*www.banking.state.ny.us* (updated periodically).

43. U.S.C. § 1601(a) (1993).

44. Roberta G. Ferrence: *Deadly Fashion: The Rise and Fall of Cigarette Smoking in North America* (New York: Garland, 1990): 6; Paul R. Johnson, *The Economics of the Tobacco Industry* (New York: Praeger, 1984): 4.

45. David Krogh, *Smoking: The Artificial Passion* (New York: W. H. Freeman, 1991), *xv–xvi*.

46. Ferrence, *Rise and Fall*, 6; Joseph R. Gusfield, "The Social Symbolism of Smoking and Health," in *Smoking Policy: Law, Politics, and Culture*, Robert L. Rabin and Stephen D. Sugarman, eds. (New York: Oxford University Press, 1993): 49, 50; Johnson, *Economics of the Tobacco Industry*, 4–5.

47. Gusfield, "Social Symbolism," 50–52; Johnson, *Economics of the Tobacco Industry*, 8;

48. Gusfield, "Social Symbolism," 53.

49. Kirk Davidson, *Selling Sin: The Marketing of Socially Unacceptable Products* (Westport, Conn.: Quorum Books, 1996): 17; Ferrence, *Rise and Fall*, 6; Gusfield, "Social Symbolism," 53–54; Ronald J. Troyer and Gerald Markle, *Cigarettes: The Battle Over Smoking* (New Brunswick: Rutgers University Press, 1983), 40–47; Franklin E. Zimring, "Comparing Cigarette Policy and Il-

licit Drug and Alcohol Control," in *Smoking Policy: Law, Politics, and Culture*, 95, 105, 108–09.

50. A. Lee Fritschler, *Smoking and Politics: Policymaking and the Federal Bureaucracy*, 3d ed. (Englewood Cliffs, N.J.: Prentice Hall, 1983), 20, 40–41.

51. U.S. Department of Health, Education and Welfare, *Smoking and Health: Report of the Advisory Committee to the Surgeon General of the Public Health Service* (Washington, D.C.: 1964), 29.

52. Gusfield, "Social Symbolism," 57.

53. U. S. House Interstate and Foreign Commerce Committee, *Cigarette Labeling and Advertising—1965: Hearings Before the Committee on Interstate and Foreign Commerce House of Representatives*, 89th Cong., 1965; U. S. House Interstate and Foreign Commerce Committee, *Fair Packaging and Labeling: Hearings Before the Committee on Interstate and Foreign Commerce House of Representatives—Part I & II*, 89th Cong., 1966; Rubin, "Legislative Methodology," 233.

54. House Committee, *Cigarette Labeling and Advertising—Part I*, statement of Sen. Maurine B. Neuberger.

55. Robert L. Rabin and Stephen D. Sugarman, "Overview," in *Smoking Policy: Law, Politics, and Culture*, 3, 4.

56. U.S.C. § 1333(a)(1).

57. U. S. House Committee on Energy and Commerce, Subcommittee on Health and the Environment, *Smoking Prevention Education Act: Hearings*, 98th Cong., 1983, 276; Prabhat Jha, *Curbing the Epidemic: Governments and the Economics of Tobacco Control* (Washington, D.C.: The World Bank, 1999), 47.

58. U. S. Senate Committee on Commerce, Science and Transportation, Subcommittee on the Consumer, *Alcohol Warning Labels Hearing*, 100th Cong., 1988, 2.

59. U. S. Senate Committee on Commerce, Science, and Transportation, *Comprehensive Smoking Prevention Education Act of 1981 Hearing*, 97th Cong., 1982, 5.

60. House, *Smoking Prevention Education Act Hearings–1983*, 115, 125, statement of Edwin B. Fisher Jr.

61. Jha, *Curbing the Epidemic*, 47.

62. Ibid.

63. K. E. Warner, "The Effects of the Anti-Smoking Campaign on Cigarette Consumption," *American Journal of Public Health* 67 (1977): 645.

64. Karl E. Case and Ray C. Fair, *Principles of Macroeconomics*, 4th ed. (Englewood Cliffs, N.J.: Prentice Hall, 1996), 81.

65. Robert A. Kagan and David Vogel, "The Politics of Smoking Regulation: Canada, France, and the United States," in *Smoking Policy: Law, Politics, and Culture*, 22, 25.

66. Gusfield, "Social Symbolism," 49–52. Zimring, "Comparing Cigarette Policy," 104.

67. Gusfield, "Social Symbolism," 51.

68. Fritschler, *Smoking and Politics*, 14, 72.

69. Stanton A. Glantz et al., *The Cigarette Papers* (Berkeley: University of California Press, 1996), 59.

70. Calder, *Financing the American Dream*, 293–94.

71. Elizabeth Whelan, *A Smoking Gun: How the Tobacco Industry Gets Away with Murder* (Philadelphia: George F. Stickley Co., 1984), 1.

72. Michael S. Wolgater, et al., "Organizing Theoretical Framework: A Consolidated Communication—Human Information Processing (C-HIP) Model," in *Warnings and Risk Communication*, Michael S. Wolgater et al., eds. (London: Taylor and Francis, 1999), 15, 18.

73. Michael S. Wolgater, et al., "Consumer Product Warnings: the Role of Hazard Perception," *Journal of Safety Research* 22 (1991): 71.

74. W. Kip Viscusi, *Smoking: Making the Risky Decision* (New York: Oxford University Press, 1992), 144.

75. Joseph P. Ryan, *Design of Warning Labels and Instructions* (New York: Van Nostrand Reinhold, 1991), 71.

76. U. S. Senate Committee on Banking, Housing, and Urban Development, *Predatory Mortgage Lending Practices: Abusive Uses of Yield Spread Premiums Hearing*, 107th Cong., 19 April 2002, statement of John Courson.

CHAPTER 8

1. Richard Hynes and Eric A. Posner, "The Law and Economics of Consumer Finance" *John M. Olin Law & Economics Working Paper No. 117* (2001), 2–3.

2. C.F.R. § 226.32(a)(1) (2002).

3. The Home Ownership and Equity Protection Act of 1994 was passed as Subtitle B of Title I of the Riegle Community Development and Regulatory Improvement Act, Pub. L. No. 103–325 (23 Sept.1994). Final regulations for HOEPA are found at 60 Fed. Reg. 15463 (24 March 1995).

4. For example, HOEPA does not cover open-ended home equity lines of credit. This undermines the effectiveness of the entire act because unscrupulous creditors simply structure their loans as "credit lines" in order to avoid heightened disclosure requirements. Similarly, home purchase and construction loans should not be exempted unless they fall below price thresholds. 15 U.S.C. §1602(aa)(1).

5. Cathy Lesser Mansfield, "The Road to Subprime HEL Was Paved with Good Congressional Intentions: Usury Deregulation and the Subprime Home Equity Market," *South Carolina Law Review* 51 (2000): 473, 536; National Consumer Law Center, *Comments to the Federal Reserve Board: Proposed Revisions to Regulation Z Truth in Lending Regarding Proposals to Address Predatory Mortgage Lending*, Docket No. R-100 (March 9, 2001), available at

http://www.consumerlaw.org/predatory_lending/comments_frb.
html, viewed 19 June 2001.

6. Joseph M. Kolar, et al., "Transactions Involving Real Estate and Dwellings," in Ralph J. Rohner and Fred H. Miller, *Truth in Lending*, ed. Robert A. Cook, Alvin C. Harrell, and Elizabeth Huber (Chicago: American Bar Association Section of Business Law, 2000), 457.

7. Some have recommended requiring that lenders provide a consumer rights and responsibilities pamphlet when issuing high-cost credit. Office of the North Carolina Commissioner of Banks, *Report to the General Assembly on Payday Lending*, available at <http://www.banking.state.nc.us/> (July 3, 2001); Scott Andrew Schaaf, Note, "Issues in Lending: From Checks to Cash: The Regulation of the Payday Lending Industry," *N. C. Banking Institute* 5 (April 2001): 339, 368; National Consumer Law Center, *Model Deferred Deposit Loan Act* § 7(a), available at <http://www.consumerlaw.org/> (viewed 19 June 2001). With the proposed system, this pamphlet could be integrated directly into the price disclosure document itself.

8. In 1980 Congress required the Federal Reserve Board of Governors "publish model disclosure forms and clauses for common transactions to facilitate compliance" with the Truth in Lending Act. When creditors use these model forms they are presumed to be in compliance with the act. 15 U.S.C. § 1604(b) (2001). These "safe harbor" forms have helped solve many of the original Truth in Lending compliance problems. Edward L. Rubin, "Legislative Methodology: Some Lessons form the Truth-in-Lending Act," *Georgetown Law Journal* 80 (1991): 233, 239 n.28. For a typical loan model form *see* Regulation Z, 16 C.F.R. *Appendix H—Closed-End Model forms and Clauses* Form H-2 (2000).

9. Board of Governors of the Federal Reserve System and United States Department of Housing and Urban Development, *Joint Report to Congress Concerning Reform to the Truth in Lending Act and*

the *Real Estate Settlement Procedures Act*. Washington, D.C., July 1998, 32.

10. Currently internet users are predominantly young and well off. Without government intervention, the benefits of this technology may risk exacerbating social divisions rather than closing them. Sonia Liff, "Consumer e-commerce: Potential for Social Inclusion?" *Consumer Policy Review* 10 (Sept./Oct. 2000): 162.

11. Department of Housing and Urban Development, *Curbing Predatory Home Mortgage Lending*. Washington, D.C., June 2000, 61.

12. Lendol Calder, *Financing the American Dream: A Cultural History of Consumer Credit* (Princeton: Princeton University Press, 1999), 293–94.

13. Lynn Drysdale and Kathleen Keest, "The Two-Tiered Consumer Financial Services Marketplace: The Fringe Banking System and its Challenge to Current Thinking About the Role of Usury Laws in Today's Society," *South Carolina Law Review* 51 (2000): 589, 657–59; Robin A. Morris, "Consumer Debt and Usury: A New Rationale for Usury," *Pepperdine Law Review* 15 (1988):151, 155; Vincent D. Rougeau, "Rediscovering Usury: An Argument for Legal Controls on Credit Card Interest Rates," *University of Colorado Law Review* 67(1996): 1, 9–16 ; James J. White, "The Usury Trompe l'Oeil," *South Carolina Law Review* 51 (Spring 2000): 445, 445–47.

14. Rubin, "Legislative Methodology," 252.

15. U. S. House Subcommittee on Consumer Affairs, Committee on Banking, *Consumer Credit Protection Act: Hearings on H.R. 11601*, 90th Cong., 1st sess., 1967, 387–88, statement of Hans Senholz.

16. Rubin, "Legislative Methodology," 252.

BIBLIOGRAPHY

Abbott, Barry A. and John W. Campbell. "The Truth in Lending Act After 15 Years: Its Goals and Its Limitations." *Oklahoma City Law Review* 9 (1984).

Abentrod, Susan. *The Ten Minute Guide to Beating Debt.* New York: John Wiley and Sons, 1996.

Abrams, Jim. "'Rapid Refunds' Really High-Cost Loans." *Miami Herald,* 24 February 2002, 7, F1.

Ackerman, James M. "Interest Rates and the Law: A History of Usury." *Arizona State Law Journal* (1981).

Act to Reduce the Rate of Interest. 13 Anne, c. 15 (1713). Reprinted in Katz, Avery Wiener. *Foundations of the Economic Approach to Law.* New York: Oxford University Press, 1998.

Aiyangar, K. V. Rangaswami. *Aspects of Ancient Indian Economic Thought.* Mylapore, Madras, India: The Madras Law Journal Press, 1934.

Allison, Melissa. "Area Credit Unions Not Serving All, Study Says." *Chicago Tribune,* 15 February 2002.

———. "Poorer Areas of Chicago Also Remain Poor in Bank Branches." *Knight Ridder/Tribune Business News,* 26 November 2001.

American Association on Mental Deficiency. *Consent Handbook.* Washington, D.C.: American Association on Mental Deficiency, 1977.

American Savings Education Council. "Youth and Money," 1999. Available at http://www.asec.org/youthsurvey.pdf.

Americans for Consumer Education and Competition. "Key Findings from a National Survey of High School Seniors Regarding Personal Finance Issues," 16 February 2001. Available at http://www.acecusa.org/reportcard.

Anderson, Michael H. "A Reconsideration of Rent-to-Own." *Journal of Consumer Affairs* 35(2) (1 January 2001).

Annas, George J. *Some Choice: Law, Medicine, and the Market*. New York: Oxford University Press, 1998.

Anthony, Jason and Karl Cluck. *Debt Free by 30: Practical Advice for Young, Broke, and Upwardly Mobile*. New York: Plume, 2001.

Appelbaum, Paul S. et al. *Informed Consent: Legal Theory and Clinical Practice*. New York: Oxford University Press, 1987.

Arrow, Kenneth. "Risk Perception in Psychology and Economics." *Economic Inquiry* 20 (January 1982).

Artunian, Judy. "It Can Put You in a Real Fix: Credit Repair is Just a Scam, Experts Warn." *Chicago Tribune*, 21 May 2002, 5.

Ausubel, Lawrence M. "Credit Card Defaults, Credit Card Profits, and Bankruptcy." *American Bankruptcy Law Journal* 71 (Spring 1997).

———. "The Failure of Competition in the Credit Card Market." *American Economics Review* 81 (1991).

Bainbridge, Stephen M. "Mandatory Disclosure: A Behavioral Analysis." *University of Cincinnati Law Review* 68 (2000).

Bankrate.com. *Mortgage Rates*. Available at http://www.bankrate.com/.

Bankruptcy Act of 1898. Ch. 541, §4, 30 Stat. 544–547.

Barber, James G. *Social Work with Addictions*. New York: New York University Press, 1994.

Baritz, Loren. *The Good Life: The Meaning of Success for the American Middle Class*. New York: Harper and Row, 1982.

Barr, Michael. "Access to Financial Services in the 21st Century: Five Opportunities for the Bush Administration and the 107th Congress." June 2001. Available at http://www.brook.edu.

Barty-King, Hugh. *The Worst Poverty: A History of Debt and Debtors.* London: Sutton Publishing, 1997.

Bauman, Laurie J. and Karolynn Siegel. "Misperceptions Among Gay Men of the Risk for AIDS Associated with Their Sexual Behavior." *Journal of Applied Social Psychology* 17 (1987).

Baxter, William F. "Section 85 of the National Bank Act and Consumer Welfare." *Utah Law Review* (1995).

Baydar, N. and J. Brooks-Gunn. "Effects of Maternal Employment and Child Care Arrangements in Infancy on Preschoolers' Cognitive and Behavioral Outcomes: Evidence from the Children of the National Longitudinal Study of Youth." *Developmental Psychology* 27(6) (1991).

Bears, Paul R. *Consumer Lending.* Second edition. Washington, D.C.: American Bankers Association, 1992.

Beauchamp, Tom L. and James F. Childress. *Principles of Biomedical Ethics.* Third edition. New York: Oxford University Press, 1989.

Becker, Gary. *The Economic Approach to Human Behavior.* Chicago: University of Chicago Press, 1976.

Begaye, Kelsey A. "Implementation of the Native American Housing Assistance and Self Determination Act: Testimony Before the Committee on Indian Affairs United States Senate." *Congressional Testimony by Federal Document Clearinghouse,* 13 February 2002. Available at 2002 WL 2010680.

Bell, Daniel. *Cultural Contradictions of Capitalism.* New York: Basic Books, 1976.

Bender, Steven W. "Consumer Protection for Latinos: Overcoming Language Fraud and English-Only in the Marketplace." *American University Law Review* 45 (April 1996).

———. "Rate Regulation at the Crossroads of Usury and Unconscionability: The Case for Regulating Abusive Commercial and Consumer Interest Rates Under the Unconscionability Standard." *Houston Law Review* 31(3) (Fall 1994).

Bentham, Jeremy. *An Introduction to the Principles of Morals and Legislation.* Edited by J. H. Burns and H. L. A. Hart. New York: Oxford University Press, 1996.

Bergquist, Erick. "Single Premium Route Doesn't End Fight." *American Banker* 167 (192) (5 October 2001).

Berube, Alan and Benjamin Foreman. *A Local Ladder for the Working Poor: The Impact of Earned Income Tax Credits in U.S. Metropolitan Areas*. Washington, D.C.: Brookings Institution, September 2001.

———. *Rewarding Work: The Impact of the Earned Income Tax Credit in Greater Chicago*. Washington, D.C.: Brookings Institution, November 2001.

Berube, Alan, et al. *The Price of Paying Taxes: How Tax Preparation and Refund Loan Fees Erode the Benefits of the EITC*. Washington, D.C.: The Brookings Institution, May 2002.

Bhandari, Jagdeep S. and Lawrence A. Weiss. *The Increasing Bankruptcy Filing Rate: An Historical Analysis*. American Bankruptcy Law Journal 67 (1993).

bin Haji Ghazali, Aidit. "Consumer Credit from the Islamic Viewpoint." *Journal of Consumer Policy* 17 (1994).

Birnie, Arthur. *The History and Ethics of Interest*. Glasgow: H. Hodge, 1952.

Black, Harold A. "Is There Discrimination in Mortgage Lending: What Does the Research Tell Us?" *Review of Black Political Economy* (Summer 1999).

Blackburn, Burr. "Financial Consultation Services." *Personal Finance News* 16 (1932).

Blossom, Debbie. "Pawnshops fill a niche." *Tulsa World*, 20 January 2002, 1.

Blydenburgh, Jeremiah W. *A Treatise on the Law of Usury*. New York: J. S. Voorhies, 1844.

Board of Governors of the Federal Reserve System. *Amendments Designed to Curb Predatory Lending (effective October, 1, 2002): Final Rule*, 12 CFR part 226, Docket No. A-1090. Washington D.C., 2002. Available at http://www.federalreserve.gov/regulations/regref.htm#z.

Board of Governors of the Federal Reserve System. *Federal Reserve*

Board Public Hearing on Home Equity Lending. Federal Reserve Bank of Chicago, Washington, D.C., 16 August 2000.

Board of Governors of the Federal Reserve System and the United States Department of Housing and Urban Development. *Joint Report to Congress Concerning Reform to the Truth in Lending Act and the Real Estate Settlement Procedures Act*. Washington, D.C., July 1998. Available at www.federalreserve.gov/barddocs/RptCongress/tila.pdf.

Boleat, Mark. *The Building Society Industry*. London: George Allen and Unwin, 1982.

Bolton, Warren. "Predatory Lending Takes Money, Other Assets Out of Poor Communities." *The State (Columbia, SC)*, 21 March 2002, A14.

Bongar, Bruce. *The Suicidal Patient: Clinical and Legal Standards of Care*. Washington, DC: American Psychological Association (1991).

Brack, Elliot. "Here's why pawnshops are popping up all over." *Atlanta Journal and Constitution*, 10 July 2000, JJ4.

Brandt, William K. and George S. Day. "Information Disclosure and Consumer Behavior: An Empirical Evaluation of Truth in Lending." *University of Michigan Journal of Law Reform* 7 (1974).

Brooks-Gunn, Jeanne, et al. "Early Intervention in Low Birth Weight, Premature Infants: Results Through Age Five Years from the Infant Health Development Program." *Journal of the American Medical Association* 272(16) (1994).

Brooks-Gunn, Jeanne, Greg J. Duncan, and Nancy Maritato. "Poor Families, Poor Outcomes: The Well Being of Children and Youth" *Consequences of Growing Up Poor*. Edited by Greg J. Duncan and Jeanne Brooks-Gunn. New York: Russell Sage Foundation, 1999.

Brooks-Gunn, Jeanne, G. Guo, and F. F. Furstenberg Jr. "Who Drops Out of and Who Continues Beyond High School? A 20 Year Study of Black Youth." *Journal of Research in Adolescence* 3(37) (1993).

Brundrett, Rick. "How Mounting Loans Devastated 87-Year-Old," *The State (Columbia, S.C.)*, 24 February 2002.

Bryan, Mark and Julia Cameron. *Money Drunk, Money Sober: 90 Days to Financial Freedom*. New York: Ballentine Books, 1999.

Bunditz, Mark E. "Arbitration of Disputes Between Consumers and Financial Institutions: A Serious Threat to Consumer Protection." *Ohio State Journal on Dispute Resolution* 10 (1995).

Calabresi, Guido. "Some Thoughts on Risk Distribution and the Law of Torts." *Yale Law Journal* 70.

Calder, Lendol. *Financing the American Dream: A Cultural History of Consumer Credit*. Princeton: Princeton University Press, 1999.

Camerer, Colin. "Individual Decision Making." *The Handbook of Experimental Economics*. Edited by John H. Kagel and Alvin E. Roth. Princeton: Princeton University Press, 1995.

Canner, Glenn B. "Changes in Consumer Holding and Use of Credit Cards, 1970–1986." *Journal of Retail Banking* 10 (1988).

Canner, Glenn B., Wayne Passmore, and Elizabeth Landerman. "The Role of Specialized Lenders in Extending Mortgages to Lower-Income and Minority Homebuyers." *Federal Reserve Bulletin* (November 1999).

Caplan, Arthur L. "Can Autonomy be Saved?" *If I Were a Rich Man Could I Buy a Pancreas? and Other Essays on the Ethics of Health Care*. Bloomington: Indiana University Press, 1992.

Caplovitz, David, "Consumer Credit in the Affluent Society." *Law and Contemporary Problems* 33(4) (1969).

———. *Consumers in Trouble: A Study of Debtors in Default*. New York: Free Press, 1974.

———. *Making Ends Meet: How Families Cope with Inflation and Recession*. Beverly Hills: Sage, 1979.

———. *The Poor Pay More*. New York: Free Press, 1967.

Carbonneau, Thomas, E. "Arbitral Justice: The Demise of Due Process in American Law." *Tulane Law Review* 70 (1996).

Carson, Robert B. *Economic Issues Today: Alternative Approaches*. Fifth edition. New York: St. Martin's Press, 1991.

Carson, Robert B. and Wade L. Thomas. *The American Economy: Contemporary Problems and Analysis*. New York: Macmillan, 1993.

Case, Karl E. and Ray C. Fair. *Principles of Macroeconomics*. Fourth edition. Englewood Cliffs, N.J.: Prentice Hall, 1996.

Caskey, John P. "Explaining the Boom in Check-Cashing Outlets and Pawnshops." *Consumer Finance Law Quarterly Report* (Winter 1995).

———. *Fringe Banking: Check-Cashing Outlets, Pawnshops, and the Poor*. New York: Russell Sage Foundation, 1994.

———. *Lower Income Americans, Higher Cost Financial Services*. Madison: Filene Research Institute, 1997.

Charles, Henry C. *The Credit System in France, Great Britain, and the United States*. Philadelphia: Carey, Lee and Blanchard, 1838.

Chestnut, L. McNeil, North Carolina Assistant Attorney General. *Memorandum to Hal D. Lingerfelt Commissioner of Banks Summarizing Senate Bill 1149*, 25 August 1998. Available at: http://www.banking.state.nc.us/bill1149.htm.

Clark, Evans. *Financing the Consumer*. New York: Harper and Brothers, 1930.

Claybrook, Joan. "Mandatory Arbitration Undermines the Law: More and More Businesses Use Clause to Evade Legal Obligations." *Charlotte (N.C.) Observer*, 1 May 2002, 17 A.

Coase, Ronald H. *Essays on Economics and Economists*. Chicago: University of Chicago Press, 1994.

———. *The Firm, the Market, and the Law: Essays on the Institutional Structure of Production*. Chicago: University of Chicago Press, 1988.

———. "The Nature of the Firm." *Economica* 4 (1937).

———. "The Problem of Social Cost." Reprinted in *The Firm, The Market, and the Law*. Chicago: University of Chicago Press, 1990.

Cochran, Thomas C. *Challenges to American Values: Society, Business, and Religion*. New York: Oxford University Press, 1985.

Cohen, Marcel. "Insights into consumer confusion." *Consumer Policy Review* 9 (Nov./Dec., 1999).

Coleman, James. "Efficiency, Utility, and Wealth Maximization." *Markets, Morals, and the Law*. Cambridge: Cambridge University Press, 1988.

Colemen-Lochner, Lauren. "Disease of Affluence; Easy Credit, internet Malls, and the Thrill of the Hunt All Spell Trouble for Compulsive Shoppers." *The Bergen County (N.J.) Record* 2 April 2000, B1.

Collins, Chuck and Felice Yeskel. *Economic Apartheid in America: A Primer on Economic Inequality and Insecurity.* New York: New Press, 2000.

Comment, "Syndicate Loan-Sharking Activities and New York's Usury Statute." *Columbia Law Review* (1966).

Comyn, Robert Buckley. *A Treatise on the Law of Usury.* London: T. Davison, 1817.

Conger, R. D. and G. H. Elder. *Families in Troubled Times: Adapting to Change in Rural America.* New York: Aldine de Gruyter, 1994.

Conger, R.D., et al. "A Family Process Model of Economic Hardship and Adjustment of Early Adolescent Boys." *Child Development* 63(2) (1992).

———. "Linking Economic Hardship to Marital Quality and Instability." *Journal of Marriage and the Family* 52 (1990).

Conley, Dalton. *Being Black, Living in the Red: Race, Wealth, and Social Policy in America.* Berkeley: University of California Press, 1999.

"Consumer Activists Opposing 'Rent-to-Own' Legislation." *Congress Daily*, 27 November 2001.

Consumer Federation of America. *College Student Consumer Knowledge: The Results of a Nationwide Test.* Washington, D.C.: Consumer Federation of America, 1993.

———. *High School Student Consumer Knowledge: A Nationwide Test.* Washington, D.C.: Consumer Federation of America, 1991.

———. "Large Banks Increase Charges to Americans in Credit Counseling: New Practices Will Hurt Consumers on the Brink of Bankruptcy," *Press Release*, 28 July 1999. Available at http://www.consumerfed.org/fairshare.pdf.

———. *U.S. Consumer Knowledge: The Results of a Nationwide Test.* Washington, D.C.: Consumer Federation of America, 1990.

Consumer Federation of America and Center for Economic Justice,

Credit Insurance Overcharges Hit $2.5 Billion Annually. Washington, D.C.: Consumer Federation of America, 2001.

Consumer Federation of America, et al., *Open Letter in Opposition to Industry-Supported Rent-to-Own Bill: HR 1701,* 27 November 2001. Available at http://ww.pirg.org.

Consumers Union. *Access to the Dream: Subprime and Prime Mortgage Lending in Texas.* Austin: Consumers Union, April 2000. Available at http://www.consumersunion.org.

———. *Credit Scoring Facts.* Available at http://www.consumer.org/finance/scorewc200.htm.

———. *In Over Our Heads: Predatory Lending and Fraud in Manufactured Housing.* Austin: Consumers Union, February 2002. Available at http://www.consumersunion.org.

Consumers Union and Center for Economic Justice. *The $2 Billion Rip-Off.* Washington, D.C.: Consumer Federation of America & Center for Economic Justice, March, 1999.

Conyn, John, Attorney General of Texas. "Be Wary of Payday Loans," *Ask the AG.* Available at http://www.occc.state.tx.us.

Cooter, Robert. "Expressive Law and Economics." *Journal of Legal Studies* 27 (1998).

———. "Normative Failure Theory of Law." *Cornell Law Review* 82 (1997).

———. "Unity in Tort, Contract and Property: The Model of Precaution." *California Law Review* 73 (1985).

Corcoran, Mary and Terry Adams. "Race, Sex, and the Intergenerational Transmission of Poverty." *Consequences of Growing Up Poor.* Edited by Greg J. Duncan and Jeanne Brooks-Gunn. New York: Russell Sage Foundation, 1999.

Cornell, T. J. *The Beginnings of Rome: Italy and Rome from the Bronze Age to the Punic Wars (c. 1000–264 BC).* New York: Routledge, 1995.

Countryman, Vern. "Bankruptcy and the Individual Debtor—A Modest Proposal to Return to the Seventeenth Century." *Catholic University Law Review* 32 (1983).

"Courts Coming to See Real Guilt." *The Survey* 27 (10 February 1972).

Crawford, Michael. *The Roman Republic.* Second edition. Cambridge: Harvard University Press, 1993.

"Credit Insurance Worth It?" *Bank Rate Monitor,* 15 February 1999.

Cude, Brenda J. "Estimating the Returns to Informed Decision-Making." *Journal of Consumer Affairs* 21 (1987).

Curliss, Andrew J. "Loan Tactic Targeted." *Raleigh (N.C.) News and Observer,* 12 April 2002, B3.

Curran, Barbara. *Trends in Consumer Credit Legislation.* Chicago: University of Chicago Press, 1965.

Dahl, Robert A. *A Preface to Economic Democracy.* Berkeley: University of California Press, 1985.

Danieri, Cheryl L. *Credit Where Credit is Due: The Mont-de-Piete of Paris, 1777–1851.* New York: Garland Publishing, 1991.

Dau-Schmidt, Kenneth G. "An Economic Analysis of the Criminal Law as a Preference-Shaping Policy." *Duke Law Journal* (1990).

Davidson, D. Kirk. *Selling Sin: The Marketing of Socially Unacceptable Products.* Westport, Conn.: Quorum Books, 1996.

Davis, Jeffrey. "Protecting Consumers from Overdisclosure and Gobbledygook: An Empirical Look at the Simplification of Consumer Credit Contracts." *Virginia Law Review* 63 (1977).

Dawes, Chris. "Overview of Recent Developments in Truth in Lending." *Consumers Financial Law Quarterly Report* 48 (1994).

Day, Theodore E. and S. J. Liebowitz. "Mortgage Lending to Minorities: Where's the Bias?" *Economic Inquiry* 36 (January 1998).

Debtors Anonymous. "History of Debtors Anonymous." Available at http://www.debtorsanonymous.org/about/history.htm.

Debtors Anonymous. *A Currency of Hope.* Needham, Mass: Debtors Anonymous General Service Board, 1999.

"Debts Drove Upholsterer to Kill Himself." *Northern Echo,* 30 March 2000.

Demo, David H. and Martha J. Cox. "Families with Young Children:

A Review of Research in the 1990s." *Journal of Marriage and the Family* 62(2) (2000).

Depository Institutions Deregulation and Monetary Control Act of 1980. Public Law 96–221.

DeRoover, Raymond. *Money, Banking and Credit in Mediaeval Bruges.* Cambridge, Mass.: Mediaeval Academy of America, 1948.

Dessart, W. C. A. M. and A. A. A. Kuylen. "The Nature, Extent, Causes and Consequences of Problematic Debt Situations." *Journal of Consumer Policy* 9 (1986).

Dickerson, Marla and Stuart Silverstein. "In Tough Times, Pawnshops Are Thriving Lending: The economic slowdown creates more need for quick cash, spurring new growth in an old industry." *Los Angeles Times*, 30 September 2001, C1.

Dollar, Jr., Creflo A. *No More Debt! God's Strategy for Debt Cancellation.* College Park, GA: World Changers Ministries, 2001.

Dornberg, John. "Vienna's Dorotheum: A Singular Auction House and Hockshop." *Smithsonian* 21 (Dec. 1990).

Douglas, Paul H. *In Our Time.* New York: Harcourt, Brace and World, 1968.

Driver, G. R. and John C. Miles. *The Babylonian Laws.* Oxford: Clarendon Press, 1955.

Drysdale, Lynn and Kathleen Keest. "The Two-Tiered Consumer Financial Services Marketplace: The Fringe Banking System and its Challenge to Current Thinking About the Role of Usury Laws in Today's Society." *South Carolina Law Review* 51 (Spring 2000).

Dublin, Jack. *Credit Unions: Theory and Practice.* Detroit: Wayne State University Press, 1971.

Dugas, Christine. "American Seniors Rack Up Debt Like Never Before: Medical Expenses Often Feed the Cycle." *USA Today*, 25 April 2002, A01.

Duncan, G. J. and S. F. Hoffman. "Welfare Benefits, Economic Opportunities and the Incidence of Out-of-Wedlock Births Among Black Teenage Girls." *Demography* 27(4) (1990).

Duncan, G. J., Jeanne Brooks-Gunn, and Pamela K. Klebanov. "Economic Deprivation and Early-Childhood Development," *Child Development* 62(2) (1994).

Duran, Nicole. "Poll: 35% Think Lenders Discriminate." *American Banker* 167(41) (1 March 2002).

Durkin, Thomas A. "Credit Cards: Use and Consumer Attitudes, 1970–2000." *Federal Reserve Bulletin* (September 2000).

Dyer, R. A. "Study cites complaints in mobile home sales." *Fort Worth Star-Telegram* 15 February 2002.

Eckman, Richard P. "The Delaware Consumer Credit Bank Act and 'Exporting' Interest Under Section 521 of the Depository Institutions Deregulation and Monetary Control Act of 1980." *Business Lawyer* 39 (1984).

Edelman, Daniel A. "Payday Loans: Big Interest Rates and Little Regulation." *Loyola Consumer Law Review* 11 (1999).

Editorial, "Borrowing Trouble: How Can Legislators Not Be Offended by Payday–Advance Businesses that Charge Outrageous Fees to Cash Strapped Consumers? Leaders, Step Forward." *Orlando Sentinel*, 17 April 2000, A10.

Editorial, "It was illegal when it was loansharking." *Kansas City Star*, 2 March 2001, B6.

Editorial, "Predatory Lenders." *The Bergen County (N.J.) Record*, 6 May 2002, L06.

Editorial, "Predatory Lending: A Shameful Practice That Must Be Ended." *The State (Columbia, S.C.)*, 24 February 2002.

Editorial, "Preying on Arizona's Working Poor." *Arizona Daily Star*, 28 May 2002, B6.

Editorial, "Speed Bump." *National Mortgage News* 26(25) (18 March 2002).

Editorial, "Street of Broken Dreams." *Portland Oregonian*, 3 September 2000, F04.

Editorial, "Time To Restore Loan-Sharking Laws." *Santa Fe New Mexican*, 9 April 2000, F-8.

Editorial, "What will they do? Predatory lenders are circling Florida's poor: it's up to state leaders to come to the rescue and fend off the sharks." *Orlando Sentinel*, 2 April 1999, A14.

Editorial, "Wolf At the Door: Vulnerable Need Protection Against Predatory Lenders." *Washington Post*, 10 March 2002, B10.

Einhorn, Hillel J. and Robin M. Hogarth. "Behavioral Decision Theory: Processes of Judgment and Choice." *Annual Review of Judgment and Psychology* 32 (1981).

————. "Decision Making Under Ambiguity." *Rational Choice: The Contrast Between Economics and Psychology*. Edited by Robin M. Hogarth and Melvin W. Reder. Chicago: University of Chicago Press, 1987.

Einzig, Paul. *Primitive Money In Its Ethnological, Historical and Economic Aspects*. Oxford, New York: Pergamon Press, 1966.

Eisenberg, Melvin A. "The Limits of Cognition and the Limits of Contract." *Stanford Law Review* 47 (1995).

Eisner, Marc Allen, Jeff Worsham, and Evan J. Ringquist. *Contemporary Regulatory Policy*. Boulder: Lynne Rienner Publishers, 2000.

Ellickson, Robert C. "Law and Economics Discovers Social Norms." *Journal of Legal Studies* 27 (1998).

Elliehausen, Gregory and Edward C. Lawrence. *Payday Advance Credit in America: An Analysis of Demand*. Washington, D.C.: Georgetown University, McDonough School of Business Credit Research Center, 2001.

Elliot, Richard. "Addictive Consumption: Function and Fragmentation in Postmodernity." *Journal of Consumer Policy* 17 (1994).

Elster, John. *Strong Feelings: Emotions, Addiction and Human Behavior*. Cambridge: MIT Press, 2000.

Employee Benefit Research Institute. "The Reality of Retirement Today: Lessons in Planning for Tomorrow." *EBRI Issue Brief* No. 181 (January 1997).

Eskridge, Jr., William N. "One Hundred Years of Ineptitude: The Need for Mortgage Rules Consonant with the Economic and Psychological Dynamics of the Home Sale and Loan Transaction." *Virginia Law Review* 70(6) (September 1984).

Ewen, Elizabeth. *Immigrant Women in the Land of Dollars*. New York: Monthly Review Press, 1985.

Fabritius, Manfred M. and William Borges. *Saving the Savings and Loan: The U.S. Thrift Industry and the Texas Experience, 1950–1988*. New York: Praeger, 1989.

Faden, Ruth R. and Tom L Beauchamp. *A History and Theory of Informed Consent*. New York: Oxford University Press, 1986.

Federal Reserve Board. *Official Staff Commentary*. 12 CFR §226.17(c)(1)-17.

Federal Reserve Board. *Regulatory Analysis of Revised Regulation Z*. 46 Fed. Reg. 20,941, 20,942 (1979).

Federal Trade Commission. *Credit Repair: Self Help May Be Best*. Available at http://www.ftc.gov/bcp/conline/pubs/credit/repair.htm.

Federal Trade Commission. *Consumer Information Remedies: Policy Review Session 279*. Washington, D.C., 1979.

Federal Trade Commission. *Survey of Rent-to-Own Customers 55–57, ES-4*. Washington, D.C.

Feinstein-Bartl, Beth. "Pines OKs New Ban on Flea Markets, City Ordinance Revision Also Bars Pawnshops." *Sun-Sentinel Ft. Lauderdale*, 9 January 2000, 15.

Ferguson, Charles and Donald McKillop. *The Strategic Development of Credit Unions*. New York: John Wiley and Sons, 1997.

Ferrence, Roberta G. *Deadly Fashion: The Rise and Fall of Cigarette Smoking in North America*. New York: Garland, 1990.

Finley, M. I. *Economy and Society in Ancient Greece*. London: Chatto and Windus, 1981.

Fishbein, Allen J. "The Community Reinvestment Act after Fifteen Years: It Works, But Strengthened Federal Enforcement is Needed." *Fordham Urban Law Journal* 20 (1993).

Fleishman, Sandra. "Facing Foreclosure: It's an Owner's Nightmare, but Not All Houses Go to Auction." *Washington Post*, 2 February 2002.

Fogarty, Mark. "Home Loans Cost More for Indian Borrowers." *Indian*

Country Today, 2 May 2002. Available at http://www.indiancountry.com/?102018981.

Fonseca, John R. *Consumer Credit Compliance Manual*. Second edition. Rochester, NY: Lawyers Cooperative Publishing Co., 1984 and Supp. 2000.

———. *Handling Consumer Credit Cases* 1. Third edition. Rochester, N.Y.: Lawyers Cooperative Pub. Co. 1986 and Supp. 1999.

Ford, Janet. *The Indebted Society: Credit and Default in the 1980s*. London: Routledge, 1988.

Forrester, Julia Patterson. "Constructing a New Theoretical Framework for Home Improvement Financing." *Oregon Law Review* 75 (1996).

———. "Mortgaging the American Dream: A Critical Evaluation of the Federal Government's Promotion of Home Equity Financing." *Tulane Law Review* 69(2) (December 1994).

Foust, Dean. "Easy Money: subprime lenders make a killing catering to poorer Americans. Now Wall Street is getting in on the act." *Business Week*, 24 April 2000, 107.

Fox, G. L. and D. Chancey. "Sources of Economic Distress: Individual and Family Outcomes." *Journal of Family Issues* 19 (1998).

Fox, Jean Ann. "What Does it Take To Be a Loanshark in 1998? A Report on the Payday Loan Industry." *Practicing Law Institute: Corporate Law and Practice Course Handbook Series*, 1047 (April–May 1998).

Fox, Jean Ann and Ed Mierzwinski. *Rent-A-Bank Payday Lending: How Banks Help Payday Lenders Evade State Consumer Protections*. Washington, D.C.: Consumer Federation of America & U.S. Public Interest Research Group: 2001.

———. *Show Me the Money: A Survey of Payday Lenders and Review of Payday Lender Lobbying in State Legislatures*. Washington, D.C.: State Public Interest Research Groups & Consumer Federation of America, 2000.

Frascogna, Jr., X. M. "Check Cashers: An Expanding Financial Service." *Mississippi College Law Review* 19 (Fall 1998).

Freedman, Alix M. "Peddling Dreams: A Market Giant Uses Its Sales

Prowess To Profit on Poverty." *Wall Street Journal*, 22 September 1993. Reprinted in *Merchants of Misery: How Corporate America Profits From Poverty*. Edited by Michael Hudson. Monroe, Maine: Common Courage Press.

Fried, Mark. "Grieving for a Lost Home." *The Urban Condition*. Edited by Leonard J. Duhl. New York: Basic Books, 1963.

Frierson, James G. "Changing Concepts on Usury: Ancient Times Through the Time of John Calvin." *American Business Law Journal* 7 (1969).

Fritschler, A. Lee. *Smoking and Politics: Policymaking and the Federal Bureaucracy*. Third edition. Englewood Cliffs, N.J.: Prentice Hall, 1983.

"FTC Files Formal Complaint Over Citigroup Lending Tactics." *Best's Review* 102 (12) (1 April 2002).

Fuchs, Stephen A. "Discriminatory Lending Practices: Recent Developments, Causes and Solutions." *Annual Review of Banking Law* 10 (1991).

Furrow, Barry R. *Health Law Cases Materials and Problems*. Third edition. St. Paul, MN: West Group, 1997.

Galbraith, John Kenneth. *The Affluent Society*. Second revised edition. Boston: Houghton Mifflin Co., 1969.

Gallert, David, et al. *Small Loan Legislation: A History of the Regulation of the Business of Lending Small Sums*. New York: Russell Sage Foundation, 1932.

Galves, Fred. "The Discriminatory Impact of Traditional Lending Criteria: An Economic and Moral Critique." *Seton Hall Law Review* 1999.

Gavin, Larry T. "Disproportionality and the Law of Consequential Damages: Default Theory and Cognitive Reality." *Ohio State Law Journal* 59 (1998).

Geller, Adam. "Payday Lenders Face Fiery Criticism: consumer advocates say federal law allows institutions to operate like loan sharks." *Salt Lake Tribune*, 28 January 2001, D6.

"Get Into the Pawnbrokers for Hard Times Ahead." *Sunday Business Post*, 17 June 2001.

Glaeser, Edward L. and Jose Scheinkman. "Neither a Borrower nor a Lender Be: An Economic Analysis of Interest Restrictions and Usury Laws." *Journal of Law and Economics* 41 (1998).

Glantz, Stanton A., et al. *The Cigarette Papers*. Berkeley: University of California Press, 1996.

Glenn, John M., et al., *Russell Sage Foundation 1907–1946*. Volume 1. New York: Russell Sage Foundation, 1947).

Goldberg, Kenneth J. "Lender Liability and Good Faith." *Boston University Law Review* 68 (1988).

Goldman, Lee. "My Way and the Highway: The Law and Economics of Choice of Forum Clauses in Consumer Form Contracts." *Northwestern Law Review* 86 (1992).

Goldstein, Deborah. "Protecting Consumers from Predatory Lenders: Defining the Problem and Moving Toward a Workable Solution." *Harvard Civil Rights-Civil Liberties Law Review* 35 (Winter 2000).

Graaff, J. De V. *Theoretical Welfare Economics*. First paperback edition. London: Cambridge Press, 1967.

Graham, Ellen. "Southern Pastor Has a Mission to Deliver His Flock From Debt." *Wall Street Journal*, 12 June 2002, A1.

Gramlich, Governor Edward M. "Remarks at the Federal Reserve Bank of Philadelphia Community and Consumer Affairs Department Conference on Predatory Lending." Philadelphia, Pa., 6 December 2000. Available at http://www.federalreserve.gov.

Grantham, Russell. "Predatory lenders feel the heat; Fed's reforms fall short, say critics and borrowers." *Atlanta Journal and Constitution*, 13 January 2002, C1.

Green, Frank and Mike Freeman. "The Debt Generation: Free Spending 20-Somethings Lured by Easy Credit." *San Diego Union Tribune*, 3 January 2002, A1.

Greenspan, Alan. "Economic challenges in the new century." *Remarks Before the Annual Conference of the National Community Reinvestment Coalition*. Washington, D.C., March 22, 2000. Transcript available at http://www.federalreserve.gov.

Greer, Thomas H. and Gavin Lewis. *A Brief History of the Western World*. Sixth edition. New York: Harcourt Brace Jovanovich College Publishers, 1992.

Grether, David M., Alan Schwartz, and Louis L. Wilde. "The Irrelevance of Information Overload: An Analysis of Search and Disclosure." *Southern California Law Review* 59 (January 1986).

Griffith, Elwin. "The Quest for Fair Credit Reporting and Equal Credit Opportunity in Consumer Transactions." *University of Memphis Law Review* 25 (Fall 1994).

————. "Truth in Lending—The Right of Recission Disclosure of the Finance Charge, and Itemization of the Amount Financed in Closedend Transactions." *George Mason Law Review* 6 (Winter 1998).

Grisso, Thomas and Paul S. Appelbaum. *Assessing Competence to Consent to Treatment: A Guide for Physicians and Other Health Professionals*. New York: Oxford University Press, 1998.

Gross, Karen. *Failure and Forgiveness: Rebalancing the Bankruptcy System*. New Haven: Yale University Press, 1997.

Gruver, Deb. "Pawnshop Owners in Wichita, Kan., Expect to Have Happy Holidays." *Knight Ridder/Tribune Business News*, 11 October 2001.

Guart, Al. "'Loanshark' Banks Bite Apple." *New York Post*, 7 April 2002, 23.

Gull, Nicole. "Pawn business not allowed to add check cashing." *Kansas City Star*, 30 January 2002, 14.

Gusfield, Joseph R. "On Legislating Morals: the Symbolic Process of Designating Deviance." *California Law Review* 56 (1968).

————. "The Social Symbolism of Smoking and Health." *Smoking Policy: Law, Politics, and Culture*. Edited by Robert L. Rabin and Stephen D. Sugarman. New York: Oxford University Press, 1993.

Guttentag, Jack. "Your Mortgage: Confused Borrowers Can Make Easy Prey." *Los Angeles Times*, 23 September 2001, K5.

————. "Your Mortgage: Lenders Entice Passive Borrowers." *Los Angeles Times*, 30 September 2001, K4.

"H&R Block's Advertising Violates Prohibition Against False, Misleading Marketing." *Consumer Financial Services Law Report* 5(15) (13 February 2002).

Hadfield, Gillian K., Robert Howse, and Michael J. Trebilcock. "Information-Based Principles for Rethinking Consumer Protection Policy." *Journal of Consumer Policy* 21 (1998).

Haller, Mark H. and John V. Alviti. "Loansharking in American Cities: Historical Analysis of a Marginal Enterprise." *The American Journal of Legal History* 21 (1977).

Hamilton, Martha McNeil. "Ignorance Costs Plenty: Officials Promote Financial Literacy." *The Washington Post*, 6 February 2002, E01.

Hannan, Timothy H. "Retail Fees of Depository Institutions, 1994–99." *Federal Reserve Bulletin* (January, 2001).

Hanson, Jon D. and Douglas A. Kysar. "Taking Behavioralism Seriously: the Problem of Market Manipulation." *New York University Law Review* 74 (1999).

———. "Taking Behavioralism Seriously: a Response to Market Manipulation," *Roger Williams University Law Review* 6 (2000).

———. "Taking Behavioralism Seriously: Some Evidence of Market Manipulation." *Harvard Law Review* 112 (1999).

Hanson, Thomas L., Sara McLanahan, and Elizabeth Thomson. "Economic Resources, Parental Practices, and Children's Well Being." *Consequences of Growing Up Poor*. Edited by Greg J. Duncan and Jeanne Brooks-Gunn. New York: Russell Sage Foundation, 1999.

Hardy, Charles O., et al. *Consumer Credit and its Uses*. New York: Prentice-Hall, 1938.

Harkness, Donna. "Predatory Lending Prevention Project: Prescribing a Cure for the Home Equity Loss Ailing the Elderly." *Boston Public Interest Law Journal* 10 (2000).

Harrison, Glenn W. "Mortgage Lending in Boston: A Reconsideration of the Evidence." *Economic Inquiry* 36 (January 1998).

Hausman, Daniel M. *The Inexact and Separate Science of Economics*. New York: Cambridge University Press, 1992.

Haveman, R., B. Wolfe, and J. Spaulding. "Childhood Events and Circumstances Influencing High School Completion." *Demography* 28(1) (1991).

Hays, R. Allen. *The Federal Government and Urban Housing.* Albany: State University of New York Press, 1985.

Hazard, Carol. "Payday Lending gets Warner OK." *Richmond Times-Dispatch*, 10 April 2002, B1.

Heichelheim, Fritz M. *An Ancient Economic History: From the Paleolithic Age to the Migrations of the Germanic, Slavic and Arabic Nations.* Volumes one and two. Second edition. Translated by Joyce Stevens. Leiden, A.W. Sijthoff: 1958.

Hendren, John. "More states allow triple-digit loan rates." *Tuscaloosa News* 10, January 1999, 6B.

Henretta, John. "Parental Status and Child's Home Ownership." *American Sociological Review* 49 (1984).

———. "Race Differences in Middle Class Lifestyle: The Role of Home Ownership." *Social Science Research* 8 (1979).

Henretta, John and Richard Campbell. "Net Worth as an Aspect of Status." *American Journal of Sociology* 83 (1978).

Herubin, Danielle. "Some Check Cashers Charging Interest That Can Reach 520%." *Palm Beach Post*, 11 November 1998, 6B.

Herzog, Peter W. *The Morris Plan of Industrial Banking.* Chicago: A.W. Shaw Company, 1928.

Hewitt, Janet Reilley. "Better Tools for Bigger Challenges." *Mortgage Banking* 57(5) (February 1997).

Hill, Claudia. "Electronic Filing: Does the New Wave Conceal a Dangerous Undertow?" *Tax Notes* 43 (10 April 1989).

Hitzeman, Harry. "Village gives itself option to revoke pawnshop license." *Chicago Daily Herald*, 3 March 2001, 4.

Hogarth, Jeanne M. "Financial Literacy and Consumer Sciences." *Journal of Family and Consumer Sciences* 94(1) (1 January 2002).

Hogarth, Robin M. "Beyond Discrete Biases: Functional and Dysfunctional Aspects of Judgmental Heuristics." *Psychological Bulletin* 90 (1981).

Hogarth, Robin M. and Howard Kunreuther. "Risk, Ambiguity, and Insurance." *Journal of Risk and Uncertainty* 2 (1989).

Home Ownership and Equity Protection Act. Public Law No. 103–325. 23 September 1994. 60 *Federal Register* 15,463, 24 March 1995.

Homer, Sidney and Richard Sylla. *A History of Interest Rates.* Third edition. New Brunsick: Rutgers University Press, 1996.

Houlton, Dean. "Consumer Behavior, Market Imperfections and Public Policy." Reprinted in David A. Rice. *Consumer Transactions.* Boston: Little, Brown, 1975.

How to Legalize Drugs. Edited by Jefferson M. Fish. Northvale, N.J.: Jason Aronson, 1998.

Huang, Ray. *1587: A Year of No Significance: The Ming Dynasty in Decline.* New Haven: Yale University Press, 1981.

Huber, Stephen K. "Consumer Arbitration in the United States Supreme Court: *Greentree Financial Corporation v. Randolph.*" *Journal of Texas Consumer Law* 4(3) (Spring 2001).

HUD Statement of Policy, 1999–2001. *Federal Register* 64 (1 March 1999).

Hudson, Michael. "Cashing in on Poverty: How Big Business Wins Every Time." *The Nation*, 20 May 1996.

———. "Going for Broke: How the 'Fringe Banking' Boom Cashes in on the Poor." *The Washington Post*, 10 January 1993, C01.

———. "'Signing their Lives Away'—Ford Profits from Vulnerable Consumers." *Merchants of Misery: How Corporate America Profits from Poverty.* Monroe, Maine: Common Courage Press, 1996.

Hunt, E. K. *Property and Prophets: The Evolution of Economic Institutions and Ideologies.* Seventh edition. New York: Harper and Row, 1995.

Hunt, Mary. *Debt Proof Your Holidays.* New York: St. Martin's Mass Market Paper, 1997.

Hynes, Richard and Eric A. Posner. "The Law and Economics of Consumer Finance." *John M. Olin Law & Economics Working Paper No. 117* (2001).

"In Brief: FirstMerit to Close Prefab Lending Unit." *American Banker* 167(210) (1 November 2001).

Indiana Department of Financial Institutions, "Summary of Payday Lender Examination: 7/199 Thru 9/30/99." Available at http://www.dfi.state.in.us.

Io Data Corporation. *Utah Consumer Lending Association: Utah Customer Study.* Salt Lake City: Io Data Corporation, July 2001.

Irwin, Gloria. "Homeownership Gone Bad; Mortgage Foreclosures Hit Summit Neighborhoods Hard; High-Pressure Sales Tactics, Predatory Lenders Share Blame." *Akron Beacon Journal,* 24 February 2002, 1.

Issacharoff, Samuel. "Can There Be a Behavioral Law and Economics?" *Vanderbilt Law Review* 51 (1998).

Ivins, Molly. "Feeding Off the Bottom," *Raleigh News and Observer,* 12 April 2000, A19.

Jackson, Ben. "Banks in 'Literacy' Effort See Long-Term Upsides." *American Banker* 166(186) (27 September 2001).

―――. "Federal Courts at Odds Over Payday Lending Pact." *American Banker* 167(108) (6 June 2002).

―――. "Programs Tout Financial Literacy for All Ages." *American Banker* 167 (65) (5 April 2002).

Jackson, Howell E. and Jeremy Berry. "Kickbacks or Compensation: The Case of Yield Spread Premiums." Available at http://www.law.harvard.edu/faculty/hjackson/jacksonberry0108.pdf.

Jackson, Kenneth T. *Crabgrass Frontier: The Suburbanization of the United States.* New York: Oxford University Press, 1985.

Jackson, Thomas. "The Fresh-Start Policy in Bankruptcy Law." *Harvard Law Review* 98 (1985).

James, Reggie, et al. "In Over Our Heads: Predatory Lending and Fraud in Manufactured Housing." *Consumers Union Southwest Regional Office Public Policy Series* 5(1) (February 2000).

Jaworski, Robert. "Culpepper: An Epic Battle Continues." *Consumer Finance Law Quarterly Report* (Winter 2001).

Jaworski, Robert M. "RESPA Section 8: The YSP Waiting Game Continues." *Business Lawyer* (May 2001).

Jaynes, Gerald D. *Branches Without Roots: Genesis of the Black Work-*

ing Class in the American South, 1862–1882. New York: Oxford University Press, 1985.

Jha, Prabhat. *Curbing the Epidemic Governments and the Economics of Tobacco Control*. Washington, D.C.: The World Bank, 1999.

Joch, Alan. "Can You Deal Down Debt? Professional 'Negotiators' May Promise Quick Fixes, But the Best Counselors Aim at Roots of Debt." *Christian Science Monitor*, 10 December 2001.

Johns, C. H. W. *Babylonian and Assyrian Laws, Contracts and Letters*. New York: Charles Scribner, 1904.

———. *The Oldest Code of Laws in the World: The Code of Laws Promulgated By Hammurabi, King of Babylon*. New York: Charles Scribner, 1903.

Johnson, Chris, Vice President, Urgent Money Service. "Letter to the Editor." *Greensboro News and Record*, 7 January 2002, A6.

Johnson, Paul R. *The Economics of the Tobacco Industry*. New York: Praeger, 1984.

Johnson, Stacy. *Life or Debt: A One Week Plan for a Lifetime of Financial Freedom*. New York: Ballantine Books, 2001.

Johnson-Elie, Tannette. "How to Avoid Debt: By Just Saying No." *Milwaukee Journal and Sentinel*, 4 September 2001, 01D.

Johnston, Lloyd and Patrick M. O'Malley. "Why Do the Nation's Students Use Drugs and Alcohol? Self-Reported Reasons From Nine National Surveys." *Journal of Drug Issues* 16 (1986).

Jolls, Christine. "Behavioral Economics Analysis of Redistributive Legal Rules." *Vanderbilt Law Review* 51 (1998).

Jolls, Christine, Cass R. Sunstein, and Richard H. Thaler. "Behavioral Approaches to Law and Economics." *Stanford Law Review* 50 (1998).

Jones, Cathy J. "Autonomy and Informed Consent in Medical Decisionmaking: Toward a New Self-Fulfilling Prophecy." *Washington and Lee Law Review* 47 (1990).

Jones, Owen D. "Time-Shifted Rationality and the Law of Law's Leverage: Behavioral Economics Meets Behavioral Biology." *Northwestern Law Review* 95 (2001).

Jordan, Robert L. and William D. Warren. "Disclosure of Finance Charges: A Rationale." *Michigan Law Review* 64 (1966).

Jordan, William Chester. *Women and Credit in Pre-Industrial and Developing Societies*. Philadelphia: University of Pennsylvania Press, 1993.

Julavits, Robert. "Addition by Subtraction: GreenPoint Quits Prefab." *American Banker* 167(3) (4 January 2002).

———. "Economy's Streak Cited in Slump for Prefab Homes." *American Banker* 171(166) (7 September 2000).

Kagan, Robert A. and David Vogel. "The Politics of Smoking Regulation: Canada, France, and the United States." *Smoking Policy: Law, Politics, and Culture*. Edited by Robert L. Rabin and Stephen D. Sugarman. New York: Oxford University Press, 1993.

Kahneman, Daniel and Amos Tversky. "Choices Values, and Frames." *American Psychology* 39 (1984).

———. "Conflict Resolution: A Cognitive Perspective." *Barriers to Conflict Resolution*. Edited by Kenneth J. Arrow, et al. New York: Norton, 1995.

———. "The Framing of Decisions and the Psychology of Choice." *Science* 211 (January 1981).

———. "Prospect Theory: An Analysis of Decision Under Risk." *Econometrica* 47 (March 1979).

Kahneman, Daniel, Jack L. Knetsch, and Richard H. Thaler. "Experimental Tests of the Endowment Effect and the Coase Theorem." *Journal of Political Economy* 98 (1990).

Kallianiotis, Ioannis N. "Saving and Investment: The Forecast Function of Interest Rates." *American Business Review* 2(1) (1 January 2002).

Kandarian, Paul E. "Fortune's Fleeting, Pawnshops are Forever." *Boston Globe*, 20 February 2000, 1.

Kapp, Marshall B. and Douglas Moossman. "Measuring Decisional Capacity: Cautions on the Construction of a 'Capacimeter.'" *Psychology, Public Policy and Law* (1996).

Katz, Avery Wiener. *Foundations of the Economic Approach to Law.* New York: Oxford University Press, 1998.

———. "Taking Private Ordering Seriously." *University of Pennsylvania Law Review* 144 (1996).

Katz, Jay. *The Silent World of Doctor and Patient.* New York: Free Press, 1984.

Katz, Laurence M. "Usury Laws and the Corporate Exception." *Maryland Law Review* 23 (1962).

Keest, Kathleen E. *The Cost of Credit: Regulation and Legal Challenges.* Boston: National Consumer Law Center, 1995.

———. "Stone Soup: Exploring the Boundaries Between Subprime Lending and Predatory Lending." *Practicing Law Institute Corporate Law and Practice Course Handbook Series* (April 16, 2001).

———. "Whither Now? Truth in Lending in Transition—Again." *Consumer Finance Law Quarterly Report* 49 (Fall 1995).

Keest, Kathleen E. and Gary Klein. *Truth In Lending.* Boston: National Consumer Law Center, 1995.

Keest, Kathleen E., Jeffrey I. Langer, and Michael F. Day. "Interest Rate Regulation Developments: High Cost Mortgages, Rent-to-Own Transactions, and Unconscionability." *Business Lawyer* (May 1995).

Keister, Lisa A. *Wealth in America: Trends in Wealth Inequality.* Cambridge: Cambridge University Press, 2000.

Kelso, Robert. "Social and Economic Background of the Small Loan Problem." *Law and Contemporary Problems* 8 (1941).

Kennickell, Arthur B., Martha Starr-McCluer, and Brian J. Surette. "Recent Changes in U.S. Family Finances: Results from the 1998 Survey of Consumer Finances." *Federal Reserve Bulletin,* (January 2000).

Kilborn, Peter T. "New Lenders With Huge Fees Thrive on Workers With Debts." *New York Times,* 18 June 1999, A1.

Kim, Pauline. "Bargaining with Imperfect Information: A Study of Worker Perception of Legal Protection in an At-Will World." *Cornell Law Review* 83 (1997).

King, Lawrence P. "The History and Development of the Bankruptcy Rules." *American Bankruptcy Law Journal* 70 (1996).

Klein, Gary. "Consumer Bankruptcy in the Balance: The National Bankruptcy Review Commission's Recommendations Tilt Toward Creditors." *American Bankruptcy Institute Law Review* 5 (Winter 1997).

Kleinfield, N. R. "Running the Little Man's Bank." *New York Times*, 13 August 1989, 37.

Kofele-Kale, Ndiva. "The Impact of Truth-in-Lending Disclosures on Consumer Market Behavior: A Critique of the Critics of Truth-in-Lending Law." *Oklahoma City University Law Review* 9 (Spring 1984).

Kolar, Joseph M., et al., "Transactions Involving Real Estate and Dwellings." Ralph J. Rohner and Fred H. Miller. *Truth in Lending*. Edited by Robert A. Cook, Alvin C. Harrell, and Elizabeth Huber. Chicago: American Bar Association Section of Business Law, 2000.

Korobokin, Russell. "Inertia and Preference in Contract Negotiation: The Psychological Powers of Default Rules and Form Terms." *Vanderbilt Law Review* 51 (1998).

———. "The Status Quo Bias and Contract's Default Rules." *Cornell Law Review* 83 (1998).

Korobokin, Russell and Thomas S. Ulen. "Law and Behavioral Science: Removing the Rationality Assumption from Law and Economics." *California Law Review* 88 (2000).

Kramer, Samuel Noah. *The Sumerians: Their History, Culture, and Character*. Chicago: University of Chicago Press, 1963.

Kripke, Homer. "Consumer Credit Regulation: A Creditor-Oriented Viewpoint." *Columbia Law Review* 68 (1968).

Kristof, Kathy M. "Understanding, Guarding Against Abusive Practices." *Los Angeles Times*, 10 September 2001, C5.

Krogh, David. *Smoking: The Artificial Passion*. New York: W. H. Freeman, 1991.

Kunreuther, Howard, et al. "Insurer Ambiguity and Market Failure." *Journal of Risk and Uncertainty* 7 (1993).

Labaree, Leonard W. *The Papers of Benjamin Franklin.* Volume 7. New Haven: Yale University Press, 1963.

Ladd, Helen F. "Evidence on Discrimination in Mortgage Lending." *Journal of Economic Perspectives* 12(2) (Spring 1998).

Landers, Jonathan M. "Some Reflections on Truth in Lending." *Illinois Law Journal* (1977).

Landers, Jonathan M. and Ralph J. Rohner. "A Functional Analysis of Truth in Lending." *UCLA Law Review* 26 (1979).

Lane, Robert E. *The Loss of Happiness in Market Democracies.* New Haven: Yale University Press, 2000.

Langholm, Odd. *The Aristotelian Analysis of Usury.* New York: Columbia University Press, 1984.

Langevoort, Donald C. "Behavioral Theories of Judgment and Decision Making in Legal Scholarship: A Literature Review." *Vanderbilt Law Review* 51 (1998).

———. "Selling Hope, Selling Risk: Some Lessons for Law from Behavioral Economics About Stockbrokers and Sophisticated Consumers." *California Law Review* 84 (1996).

———. "Statutory Obsolescence and the Judicial Process: The Revisionist Role of the Courts in Federal Banking Regulation." *Michigan Law Review* 85 (1987).

Larson, Jennifer and Frank Green. "Home inequity loans hallmark of 'predatory' mortgage lending include very high interest rates, unneeded credit insurance and balloon payments." *San Diego Union-Tribune,* 21 August 2001, H1.

Larson, Michael D. "It's buyer beware when you're shopping for a subprime loan." Bankrate.com, February 2, 2001. Available at http://www.bankrate.com.

Lasch, Christopher. *The Culture of Narcissism: American Life in an Age of Diminishing Expectations.* New York: Norton, 1978.

Lawrence, David B. *Handbook of Consumer Lending.* Englewood Cliffs, N.J.: Prentice Hall, 1992.

Leary, Edward G. "Report of the Commissioner of Financial Institutions." *State of Utah* 30 (June 2001).

Lee, W. A. "Fair, Isaac & Co. Taps Institutions For Credit Score Distribution." *American Banker* 167(67) (9 April 2002).

Leibsohn, Daniel. "Financial Services Innovation in Community Development." *Journal of Affordable Housing and Community Development Law* (Winter 1999).

Leontief, Wassily, "Mathematics in Economics." In *Essays in Economics: Theories and Theorizing*. Vol. 1. New York: M.E. Sharpe, 1977.

Lessig, Lawrence. "The New Chicago School." *Journal of Legal Studies* 27 (1998).

———. "The Regulation of Social Meaning." *University of Chicago Law Review* 62 (1995).

———. "Social Meaning and Social Norms." *University of Pennsylvania Law Review* 144 (1996).

Leuchtenburg, William E. *The Perils of Prosperity, 1914–1932.* Second edition. Chicago: University of Chicago Press, 1993.

Levinthal, Charles F. *Drugs, Behavior, and Modern Society.* Boston: Allyn and Bacon, 1996.

Levinthal, Louis Edward. "The Early History of Bankruptcy Law." *University of Pennsylvania Law Review* 66 (1918).

Lewis, Holden. "Mortgages Scarce on Native American Lands." *Chicago Sun-Times*, 2 June 2002, 11C.

Lewis, Jake. "Renting to Owe: Rent-to-Own Companies Prey on Low-Income Consumers." *Multinational Monitor*, 1 October 2001, 16.

Liff, Sonia. "Consumer e-commerce: potential for social inclusion?" *Consumer Policy Review* 10 (Sept./Oct. 2000).

Linforth, Ivan M. "Solon the Athenian." *Classical Philology*. Berkeley: University of California Publications, 1919.

Listokin, Yair. "Confronting the Barriers to Native American Homeownership on Tribal Lands: The Case of the Navajo Partnership for Housing." *Urban Lawyer* (Spring 2001).

Longhofer, Stanley D. "Discrimination in Mortgage Lending: What Have We Learned?" *Economic Commentary* (15 August 1996).

Loonin, Deanne and Elizabeth Renuart. "Less Than Six Degrees of Separation: Consumer Law Connections to Your Practice (Part I)." *Clearinghouse Review* (March–April 1998).

Lutton, Laura Pavlenko. "Small-Bank Lenders Feast on Surge in Prefabs." *American Banker* 164(77) (23 April 1999).

MacDonald, Scott D. and Albert L. Gastmann. *A History of Credit and Power in the Western World.* New Brunswick: Transaction Publishers, 2001.

Macleod, Gordon K. "Nuclear Power: The Case for Informed Consent." *Religious Humanism* 18 (1984).

MacPherson, James. "Carpenter believes would-be financial savior a predatory lender." *Alaska Journal of Commerce* 25(31) (5 August 2001).

Mandell, Lewis. *The Credit Card Industry: A History.* Boston: Twayne Publishers, 1990.

Manning, Robert D. *Credit Card Nation.* New York: Basic Books, 2000.

Mansfield, Cathy Lesser. "The Road to Subprime HEL Was Paved with Good Congressional Intentions: Usury Deregulation and the Subprime Home Equity Market." *South Carolina Law Review* 51 (2000).

March, James G. and Herbert A. Simon. *Organizations.* New York: Wiley, 1958.

Marisco, Richard D. "Fighting Poverty Through Community Empowerment and Economic Development: The Role of the Community Reinvestment and Home Mortgage Disclosure Acts." *New York Law School Journal of Human Rights* 12 (Spring 1995).

Marsh, Gene A. "The Hard Sell in Consumer Credit: How the Folks in Marketing Can Put You Into Court." *Consumer Finance Law Quarterly Report* 52 (Summer 1985).

———. "Lender Liability for Consumer Fraud Practices of Retail Dealers and Home Improvement Contractors." *Alabama Law Review* 45 (Fall 1993).

Marshall, Alfred. *Principles of Economics.* Eighth edition. London: Macmillan and Company, 1970.

Martin, Mike W. and R. Schinzinger. *Ethics in Engineering*. New York: McGraw-Hill, 1983.

Martin, Robert E. and Carter Hill. "Loan Performance and Race." *Economic Inquiry* 38(1) (January 2000).

Martin, Susan Lorde and Nancy White Huckins. "Consumer Advocates vs. The Rent-to-Own Industry: Reaching a Reasonable Accommodation." *American Business Law Journal* (Spring 1997).

McAdams, Richard H. "The Origin, Development, and Regulation of Norms." *Michigan Law Review* 96 (1997).

McCaul, Elizabeth, Superintendent of Banks, *Industry Letter on Payday Loans*, 13 June 2000. Available at http://www.banking.state.ny.us.

McCoid, John C. II. "Discharge: The Most Important Development in Bankruptcy History." *American Bankruptcy Law Journal* 70 (1996).

McLeod, J. and M. Shanahan. "Poverty, Parenting and Children's Mental Health." *American Sociological Review* 58(3) (1993).

McLoyd, V. C. "The Impact of Economic Hardship on Black Families and Children: Psychological Distress, Parenting and Socioemotional Development." *Child Development* 61(2) (1990).

McNeil, Martha. "Ignorance Costs Plenty: Officials Promote Financial Literacy." *Washington Post*, 6 February 2002, E01.

McNichols, Janet. "Pawnshop plan in former hardware store meets opposition." *St. Louis Post-Dispatch*, 18 June 2001, 4.

Medoff, James and Andrew Harless. *The Indebted Society: Anatomy of an Ongoing Disaster*. Boston: Little, Brown and Company, 1996.

Meisel, Alan A. "A 'Dignitary Tort' as a Bridge Between the Idea of Informed Consent and the Law of Informed Consent." *Law, Medicine and Health Care* 16 (1988).

Meyerson, Michael I. "The Efficient Consumer Form Contract: Law and Economics Meets the Real World." *Georgia Law Review* 24 (1990).

————. "The Reunification of Contract Law: The Objective Theory of Consumer Form Contracts." *University of Miami Law Review* (1993).

Mierzwinski, Ed. *Mistakes Do Happen: Credit Report Errors Mean Consumers Lose.* Washington, D.C.: U.S. Public Interest Research Group, 1998.

Miller, Carol Marbin. "'Car pawn' customers fight back." *St. Petersburg Times,* 16 July 1996, 1B.

Miller, Hilary B. "Payday Loans and Predatory Lending." *Practicing Law Institute: Corporate Law and Practice Course Handbook Series* 1242 (16 April 2001).

Miller, Richard Lawrence. *The Case for Legalizing Drugs.* New York: Preager, 1991.

Millett, Paul. *Lending and Borrowing in Ancient Athens.* Cambridge, New York: Cambridge University Press, 1991.

Minutaglio, Bill. "Prince of Pawns: With a keen appreciation for the high-return, low-risk investment, Jack Daugherty is making hock shops a hot corporate property." *Merchants of Misery: How Corporate America Profits from Poverty.* Edited by Michael Hudson. Monroe, Maine: Common Courage Press, 1996.

Mishel, Lawrence, Jared Bernstein, and John Schmitt. *The State of Working America, 2000/2001.* Ithaca, N.Y.: Cornell University Press, 2001.

Mitchell, Bruce and Dianne Draper. *Relevance and Ethics in Geography.* New York: Longman, 1982.

Mitchell, Jann. "Kicking the Shopping Habit." *Sunday Oregonian,* 25 June 2000, L13.

Mitchell, Lesley. "Credit Counselors Warn Consumers to Be Wary of Scams." *Salt Lake Tribune,* 20 May 2002, D1.

Mize, Richard. "Predatory Lending Hits Home in State, Experts Say." *Daily Oklahoman,* 25 January 2002, 8C, City Edition.

Mondeville, Henri de. "On the Morals and Etiquette of Surgeons." *Ethics in Medicine: Historical Perspectives and Contemporary Concerns.* Edited by Stanley J. Reiser et al. Cambridge: MIT Press, 1977.

Mondor, Paul. "The Quasi-Law of Fair Lending." *Mortgage Banking* 57 (November 1996).

Moore, Charlotte M. "Heeding Another Voice: What Do the People

Who Educate Homebuyers Think About Homebuyer Education?" *Mortgage Banking* 57 (September 1997).

Moore, Linda A. "Casinos, Economy, Attitudes Affect Both Sides of Pawnshop Business." *The Memphis Commercial Appeal*, 27 May 2001, C1.

Morris, Robin A. "Consumer Debt and Usury: A New Rationale For Usury." *Pepperdine Law Review* 15 (1988).

Morse, Neil J. "Coping with a wild market." *Mortgage Banking* 62(4) (1 January 2002).

Moss, David A. and Gibbs A. Johnson. "The Rise of Consumer Bankruptcy: Evolution, Revolution, or Both?" *American Bankruptcy Law Journal* 73 (Spring 1999).

Moss, Lisa Blaylock. "Modern Day Loansharking: Deferred Presentment Transactions & the Need for Regulation." *Alabama Law Review* (Summer 2000).

Munnell, Alicia H., et al. *Mortgage Lending in Boston: Interpreting HMDA Data.* Boston: Federal Reserve Board of Boston, 1992.

Murray, J. B. C. *The History of Usury from the Earliest Period to the Present Time.* Philadelphia: J.B. Lippincott, 1866.

Nader, Ralph. "Blood Money: Uncovering the Unscrupulous Practices of Creditors." *Tallahassee Democrat*, 26 May 2002, 1.

National Consumer Law Center. *Comments to the Federal Reserve Board: Proposed Revisions to Regulation Z Truth in Lending Regarding Proposals to Address Predatory Mortgage Lending*, Docket No. R-100. March 9, 2001. Available at <http://www.consumerlaw.org/predatory_lending/comments_frb.html.

National Consumer Law Center. "DOJ Finds and Fines Higher Credit Prices, Loan Requirements for African Americans, Native Americans as Discriminatory." *National Consumer Law Center Reports Consumer Credit and Usury Edition* 12 (March/April 1994).

National Consumer Law Center, *Model Deferred Deposit Loan Act* § 7(a). June 19, 2001. Available at <http://www.consumerlaw.org/>.

National Consumer Law Center. *Stop Predatory Lending: A Guide for Legal Advocates.* Boston: National Consumer Law Center, 2001.

National Consumer Law Center. "Why Yield Spread Premium Payments are 'Fees' For HOEPA purposes." *Consumer Rights Litigation Conference Manual.* Boston: National Consumer Law Center, 2001.

Nelson, Benjamin. *The Idea of Usury: From Tribal Brotherhood to Universal Otherhood.* Second edition. Princeton, New Jersey: Princeton University Press, 1949.

Nesbia, Reynold F. "Racial Discrimination in Residential Lending Markets: Why Empirical Researchers Always See it and Economic Theorists Never Do." *Journal of Economic Issues* 30(1) (March 1996).

Nesbitt, Sara. "Borrowing a better image: pawnshops cater to a new generation of bargain hunters." *The Colorado Springs Gazette,* 13 May 2001, 1.

Newman, Richard. "A Homeowner's Nightmare: Foreclosure Rate Shows Alarming Rise in North Jersey." *The Bergen County (N.J.) Record,* 17 March 2002, B01.

———. "Shark Attacks: An Encounter with Predatory Lenders Can Leave You Without Your Money—Or Your Home." *The Bergen County (N.J.) Record,* 6 January 2002, B01.

Ngyuyen, Hang. "Pawnshops hope new loans help industry in lean times." *Dallas Morning News,* 23 August 2000, 1A.

NICHD Early Child Care Research Network. "Poverty and Patterns of Child Care." *Consequences of Growing Up Poor.* Edited by Greg J. Duncan and Jeanne Brooks-Gunn. New York: Russell Sage Foundation, 1999.

Nichols, Nathaniel C. "Home Alone: Home Mortgage Foreclosure Rescue Scams and the Theft of Equity." *Journal of Affordable Housing and Community Development Law* 11 (2002).

Niefeld, M. R. *The Personal Finance Business.* New York: Harper and Brothers, 1933.

Nieman, Donald G. Introduction to *From Slavery to Sharecropping: White Land and Black Labor in the Rural South, 1865–1900.* New York: Garland, 1994.

Nixon, Ron. "Application Denied: Do Lending Institutions Overlook Hispanics?" *Hispanic* 11(11) (November 1998).

Noonan, John T. *The Scholastic Analysis of Usury.* Cambridge: Harvard University Press, 1957.

Nugent, Rolf. *Consumer Credit and Economic Stability.* New York: Russell Sage Foundation, 1939).

Obara, Patricia E. "Predatory Lending." *Banking Law Journal* (June 2001).

Oeltjen, Jaret C. "Florida Pawnbrokering: An Industry in Transition." *Florida State University Law Review* 23 (Spring 1996).

———. "Pawnbrokering on Parade." *Buffalo Law Review* 37 (1989).

Office of the North Carolina Commissioner of Banks. *Report to the General Assembly on Payday Lending.* 22 February 2001. Available at http://www.banking.state.nc.us/.

Oliver, Gordon. "Manufactured Promises: Some Buyers of Manufactured Houses Find Themselves Trapped in Bad Deals," parts 1 and 2. *Portland Oregonian,* 20 and 21 August 2000, A01.

Online Auto Loans. *Welcome to Online Auto Loans.* Available at http://www.online-car-auto=loan.com/.

OnMortgage.com. *Mortgage Rates.* Available at http://www.onmortgage.com/.

Ord, Mark. *Essays on the Law of Usury.* Third edition. Hartford, Conn.: Printed for the editor, 1809.

Ost, David E. "The 'Right' Not to Know." *Journal of Medicine and Philosophy* 9 (1984).

Osteen, Sissy R. and Tricia Auberle. "Homebuyer Education: A Doorway to Financial Literacy." *Journal of Family and Consumer Sciences* 94(1) (1 January 2002).

Paletta, Damian. "In Brief: Hawke Says Don't Overlook the 'Underbanked.'" *American Banker* 167(53) (19 March 2002).

———. "Tax Refund Loans Called Predatory." *American Banker,* 1 February 2002, 5.

Parsons, James Bunyon. *The Peasant Rebellions of the Late Ming Dynasty.* Tucson: University of Arizona Press, 1970.

"Pawnshops plug into energy crisis." *Houston Chronicle*, 29 May 2001, 9.

Pereira, Gordon. "Credit Insurance: Obtaining Relief for Post-Claim Ineligibility Determinations." *Clearinghouse Review* (December 1994).

Perin, Constance. *Everything in Its Place: Social Order and Land Use in America*. Princeton: Princeton University Press, 1977.

Perry, Clifton. "Negligence in Securing Informed Consent and Medical Malpractice." *Journal of Medicine, Humanities, and Bioethics* 9 (1988).

Peterson, Christopher. "Failed Markets, Failing Government, Or Both?: Learning from the Unintended Consequences of Utah Consumer Credit on Vulnerable Debtors." *Utah Law Review* (2001).

———. "Only Until Payday: A Primer on Utah's Growing Deferred Deposit Loan Industry." *Utah Bar Journal* 15(2) (March 2002).

Pettit, Phillip. "*Virtus Normativa*: Rational Choice Perspectives." *Ethics* 100 (July 1990).

Pigou, A.C. *The Economics of Welfare*. Fourth edition. New York: St. Martin's Press, 1960.

Plato. *The Republic*. Translated by Francis MacDonald Conford. New York: Oxford Press, 1945.

Plous, Scott. *The Psychology of Judgement and Decisionmaking*. Philadelphia: Temple University Press, 1993.

Porter, Robert. "Public and Private Debts." *North American Review* 153 (1891).

Posner, Eric A. "The Regulation of Groups: The Influence of Legal and Nonlegal Sanctions on Collective Action." *University of Chicago Law Review* 63 (1996).

Posner, Richard A. "Rational Choice, Behavioral Economics, and the Law." *Stanford Law Review* 50 (1998).

———. "Social Norms and the Law: An Economic Approach." *American Economic Review* 87 (1997).

———. "Social Norms, Social Meaning, and Economic Analysis of Law: A Comment." *Journal of Legal Studies* 27 (1998).

"Predatory Lenders Use Courthouse." *Daily Oklahoman*, 1 June 2002, 6C.

Preddy, Melissa. "Web Sites help make first steps to recovering from debt." *Gannett News Service*, 9 March 2000.

"Pressure As a Collection Tool: Turn Up the Heat to Get Paid." *Consumer Credit Collector* 5 (October 1997).

Prigden, Dee. *Consumer Credit and the Law*. West Group, 2001.

Public Law No. 96–221 Title V. Codified at 12 U.S.C. 1735f-7a.

Puckett, T.C. "Consumer Credit: A Neglected Area in Social Work Education." *Contemporary Social Work Education* 2 (1978).

Pugh, Olin S. and F. Jerry Ingram. *Credit Unions: A Movement Becomes an Industry*. Reston, Va.: Reston Publishing Co., 1984.

Quinn, Jane Bryant. "Little Loans Come at Staggering Cost." *Washington Post*, 13 June 1999, H02.

Rabin, Matthew. "Psychology and Economics." *Journal of Economic Literature* 36 (1998).

Rabin Robert L. and Stephen D. Sugarman. "Overview." *Smoking Policy: Law, Politics, and Culture*. Edited by Robert L. Rabin and Stephen D. Sugarman. New York: Oxford University Press, 1993.

Rachlinski, Jeffrey J. "A Positive Psychological Theory of Judging in Hindsight." *University of Chicago Law Review* 65 (1998).

Radigan, Mary. "Predatory Lenders Bank on Ignorance: Extra Charges and Penalties Put Homes at Risk." *Grand Rapids Press*, 5 November 2001, A8.

Ragan, Jr., James R. and Lloyd B. Thomas Jr. *Principles of Micro Economics*. Ft. Worth: Harcourt Brace Jovanovich, 1993.

Ramos, Barren E. "Materials on Residential Mortgage Litigation Preface." *Practicing Law Institute Corporate Law and Practice Course Handbook Series* 1242 (April 16, 2001).

Ransom, Roger L. and Richard Sutch. *One Kind of Freedom: The Economic Consequences of Emancipation*. Second edition. Cambridge: Cambridge University Press, 1977.

Rasmussen, Robert K. "Behavioral Economics, the Economic Analysis of Bankruptcy Law and the Pricing of Credit." *Vanderbilt Law Review* 51 (1998).

Rate.net. *Credit Card Rates.* Available at http://www.rate.net/.

Reed, Robert. "Slamming the Brakes on Speedy Tax Refunds." *Crain's Chicago Business* 12(11) (12 March 2002).

Regulation Z. Appendix H—Closed-End Model forms and Clauses Form H-2 (2000). 16 C.F.R.

"Report of the Staff to Chairman Gramm, Committee on Banking, Housing and Urban Affairs—Predatory Lending Practices: Staff Analysis of Regulators' Responses." 23 August 2000. Reprinted in *Consumer Finance Law Quarterly Report* 54 (Summer 2000).

Rhyne, Debbie. "Aid Fund Offers Help to Military Personnel, Families." *Macon Telegraph*, 29 December 2001, 1.

Rice, David. *Consumer Transactions.* Boston: Little, Brown and Co., 1975.

Rich, David. *The Economics of Welfare: A Contemporary Analysis.* New York: Praeger, 1989.

Richardson, Christopher A. "The Community Reinvestment Act and the Economics of Regulatory Policy." *Fordham Urban Law Journal* 28 (2002).

Rohner, Ralph J., ed.. *The Law of Truth in Lending.* Boston: Warren, Gorham and Lamont, 1984.

Roska, John. "How High Can the Finance Companies Go? With Interest Rates, the Sky Is the Limit." *St. Louis Post-Dispatch*, 16 July 1998.

Roth, Loren H. et al. "Tests of Competency to Consent to Treatment." *American Journal of Psychiatry* 134 (1977).

Rougeau, Vincent D. "Rediscovering Usury: An Argument for Legal Controls on Credit Card Interest Rates." *University of Colorado Law Review* 67 (1996).

Rozovsky, Fay A. *Consent to Treatment: A Practical Guide.* Second edition. Boston: Little, Brown, 1990.

Rubin, Edward L. "Legislative Methodology: Some Lessons From the Truth-in-Lending Act." *Georgetown Law Journal* 80 (1991).

Rudin, Ronald. *In Whose Interest? Quebec's Caisses Populaires 1900–1945*. Montreal: McGill-Queens' University Press, 1990.

Russell, Thomas and Richard H. Thaler. "The Relevance of Quasi Rationality in Competitive Markets." *Quasi Rational Economics*. Edited by Richard H. Thaler. New York: Russell Sage Foundation, 1994.

Ryan, Elizabeth. "Plus Ça Change: Part II (Or, Check Cashers as Lenders: The More Things Change, the Worse they Get)." *NCLC Reports—Consumer Credit and Usury Edition* 11 (1993).

Ryan, Franklin Winton. *Usury and Usury Laws*. Boston: Houghton Mifflin Company, 1942.

Ryan, Joseph P. *Design of Warning Labels and Instructions*. New York: Van Nostrand Reinhold, 1991.

Ryan, Martin. *The Last Resort, A Study of Consumer Bankrupts*. Brookfield, VT: Avebury, 1995.

S. 2802. 95th Cong., 2d sess. § 18(a), 1978.

Saggs, H. W. F. *Babylonians*. Norman: University of Oklahoma Press, 1995.

Salem, George M. and Aaron C. Clark. "Bank Credit Cards: Loan Loss Risks Are Growing." *GKM Banking Industry Report* (11 June 1996).

Sampson, R. J. and J. H. Laub. "Urban Poverty and the Family Context of Delinquency: A New Look at Structure and Process in a Classic Study." *Child Development* 65(2) (1994).

Samuelson, Paul A. and William D. Nordhaus. *Economics*. Fifteenth edition. New York: McGraw-Hill, 1995.

Sanders, Edmund. "Sub-Prime Lender Says it has Been Fair, But Activists See Examples of Predatory Lending: The Two Sides are Meeting to Resolve Their Differences." *Los Angeles Times*, 9 April 2000, C1.

Sapong, Emma D. "'Don't Borrow Trouble' Raises Awareness of Predatory Lenders." *Buffalo News*, 13 April 2002, B1.

Saunders, Margot. National Consumer Law Center, "Testimony before the Committee on Financial Services, Subcommittee on Financial Institutions & Consumer Credit regarding H.R. 1701." 12 July 2001. Available at http://ww.pirg.org.

Schaaf, Scott Andrew. "From Checks to Cash: Regulation of the Payday Lending Industry." *North Carolina Banking Institute* 5 (April 2001).

Schafer, Robert F. and Helen F. Ladd. *Discrimination in Mortgage Lending*. Cambridge: MIT Press, 1981.

Schill, Michael H. "An Economic Analysis of Mortgagor Protection Laws." *Virginia Law Review* (1991).

Schmedemann, Deborah A. "Time and Money: One State's Regulation of Check-Based Loans." *William Mitchell Law Review* 27 (2000).

Schneider, Carl E. *The Practice of Autonomy: Patients, Doctors, and Medical Decisions*. New York: Oxford University Press, 1998.

Schultz, Marjorie M. "From Informed Consent to Patient Choice." *Yale Law Journal* 95 (1985).

Schuster, Ronald K. "Lending Discrimination: Is the Secondary Market Helping to Make the 'American Dream' A Reality?" *Gonzaga Law Review* (2000/2001).

Schwartz, Alan and Louis Wilde. "Imperfection in Markets for Contract Terms." *Virginia Law Review* 69 (1983).

Seidenberg, Robert, M.D. "Advertising and Drug Acculturation." *Socialization in Drug Abuse*. Edited by Robert H. Coombs, Lincoln J. Fry, and Patricia G. Lewis. Cambridge: Schenkman Publishing Co., 1976.

Segerstrom, Susan, et al. "Optimistic Bias Among Cigarette Smokers." *Journal of Applied Social Psychology* 23 (1993).

"Senator: Borrowers Trapped by 'Payday' Loans, High Interest." *Jefferson City News Tribune Online Edition*, 28 December 1999. Available at http://www.newstribune.com/stories/122899/bus_1228990024.asp.

Senderowicz, Jeremy. "Consumer Arbitration and Freedom of Contract: A Proposal to Facilitate Consumers' Informed Consent to Arbitration Clauses in Form Contracts." *Columbia Journal of Law and Social Problems* 32 (1999).

Serres, Chris. "Lender To Give Customers Refunds." *The Raleigh News and Observer*, September 2001, D1.

"Set Deadlines to Create Urgency," *Consumer Credit Collector* 5 (October 1997).

Shean, Tom. "Payday Loan Bill Draws Criticism from Military: Effort to Regulate High-Interest Loans Would Backfire, They Say." *Norfolk Virginian-Pilot and Star Ledger*, 16 February 2002, D1.

Sheehan, Tom. "Pawnshop to Trade in Name for Downtown Delaware Home." *Columbus (Ohio) Dispatch*, 23 October 1999, 7B.

Shefrin, Hersh M. and Richard H. Thaler. "The Behavioral Life-Cycle Hypothesis." *Quasi Rational Economics*. Edited by Richard H. Thaler. New York: Russell Sage Foundation, 1994.

Sichelman, Lew. "Housing Scene: Subprime lender makes effort to address consumer concerns." *Origination News* 10(2) (24 August 2001).

Simpson, Dwayne D. and Saul B. Sells. "Effectiveness of Treatment for Drug Abuse: An Overview of the DARP Research Program." *Advances in Alcohol and Substance Abuse* 2 (1982).

Simpson, D. P. *Cassell's Latin Dictionary*. New York: MacMillan Publishing, 1959.

Skoler, Daniel L. "The Elderly and Bankruptcy Relief: Problems, Protections, and Realities." *Bankruptcy Developments Journal* 6 (1989).

Smallwood, James. "Perpetuation of Caste: Black Agricultural Workers in Reconstruction Texas." *African American Life, 1861–1900: From Slavery to Sharecropping*. Edited by Donald G. Nieman. New York: Garland, 1994.

Smith, Adam. *An Inquiry into the Nature and Causes of the Wealth of Nations*. Edited by Richard F. Teichgraeber, III. New York: Random House, 1985.

Smith, Shelly. "Mandatory Arbitration Clauses in Consumer Contracts: Consumer Protection and the Circumvention of the Judicial System." *DePaul Law Review* 50 (2001).

Sorohan, Mike. "MBA Launches Consumer Fraud Web Site." *Real*

Estate Finance Today Electronic Ed., 11 March 2002. Available on Westlaw at 2002 WL 10349754.

Squires, Gregory D. "Community Reinvestment: An Emerging Social Movement." *From Redlining to Reinvestment.* Edited by Gregory D. Squires. Philadelphia: Temple University Press, 1992.

Squires, Michael. "Short-term Loan Firms Prospering: Critics Say High Interest Rates, Easy Terms Have Led to Exploitation of Working Poor." *Las Vegas Review Journal*, 23 December 2001, 16.

Stafford, Dulan. "Lending Bill Gives Victims Legal Clout." *Atlanta Journal and Constitution*, 14 April 2002, C4.

Stempel, Jeffrey W. "Bootstrapping and Slouching Toward Gomorrah: Arbitral Infatuation and the Decline of Consent." *Brooklyn Law Review* 62 (1996).

Sterling, Hillard M. and Philip G. Schrag. "Default Judgments Against Consumers: Has the System Failed?" *Denver University Law Review* 67 (1990).

Stern, Eric. "Bill would limit 'payday' loans: Holden considers measure; interest rates up to 400 pct. drew attention of legislators." *St. Louis Post-Dispatch*, 26 June 2001, B1.

Sternlight, Jean R. "As Mandatory Binding Arbitration Meets the Class Action, Will the Class Action Survive?" *William and Mary Law Review* 42 (2000).

———. "Panacea or Corporate Tool? Debunking the Supreme Court's Preference for Binding Arbitration." *Washington University Law Quarterly* 74 (1996).

Steward, Janet Kidd. "Tax Credit Pumps Millions into Area." *Chicago Tribune*, 27 November 2001.

Stowers, Andrea and Mark Cole. "A Bankruptcy Wake-Up Call." *Mortgage Banking* 57 (February 1997).

Strauss, Steven D. and Azriela L. Jaffe. *The Complete Idiot's Guide to Beating Debt.* Alpha Books, 1999.

Stringer, Kortney. "Best of Times is Worst of Times for Pawnshops." *Wall Street Journal*, 22 August 2000, B1.

Sturdevant, Patricia and Dwight Golaan. "Should Binding Arbitration Clauses Be Prohibited In Consumer Contracts?" *Dispute Resolution Magazine* 1 (1994).

Sullivan, Charlene A. *Understanding the Consumer Credit Environment.* New York: Executive Enterprises Publications, 1989.

Sullivan, Teresa, Elizabeth Warren, and Jay Lawrence Westbrook. *As We Forgive Our Debtors: Bankruptcy and Consumer Credit in America.* New Haven: Yale University Press, 1989.

———. *The Fragile Middle Class: Americans in Debt.* New Haven: Yale University Press, 2000.

Sunstein, Cass R. "Behavioral Analysis of Law." *University of Chicago Law Review* 64 (1997).

———. "Behavioral Analysis of Law and Economics: A Progress Report." *American Law and Economic Review* 1 (1999).

———. "Legal Interference With Private Preferences." *University of Chicago Law Review* 53 (1986).

———. "Social Norms and Social Roles." *Columbia Law Review* 96 (1996).

Superson, Anita M. "The Employer-Employee Relationship and the Right to Know." *Business and Professional Ethics Journal* 3 (1983).

Swagler Roger M. and Paula Wheeler. "Rental Purchase-Agreements: A Preliminary Investigation of Consumer Attitudes and Behaviors." *Journal of Consumer Affairs* (22 June 1989).

Swire, Peter P. "The Persistent Problem of Lending Discrimination: A Law and Economic Analysis." *Texas Law Review* 73 (March 1995).

Tabb, Charles Jordan. "The History of the Bankruptcy Laws in the United States." *American Bankruptcy Institute Law Review* 3 (Spring 1995).

Tadmor, H. "The Period of the First Temple, the Babylonian Exile and the Restoration." *A History of the Jewish People.* Edited by H. H. Ben-Sasson. Cambridge: Harvard University Press, 1976.

Taub, Nadine and Elizabeth M. Schneider. "Perspectives on Women's Subordination and the Law." *The Politics of Law: A Progressive Critique.* Edited by David Kairys. New York: Pantheon Books, 1982.

Taylor, Shelley E. *Positive Illusions: Creative Self-Deception and the Healthy Mind*. New York: Basic Books, 1990.

Tebbutt, Melanie. *Making Ends Meet: Pawnbroking and Working-Class Credit*. New York: St. Martin's Press, 1983.

Thaler, Richard H. "The Psychology of Choice and the Assumption of Economics." *Quasi Rational Economics*. Edited by Richard Thaler. New York: Russell Sage Foundation, 1994.

Thornburg, Lacy H., North Carolina Attorney General. "Statement on H 1108—Representative Hackney's Rent-to-Own Bill," 9 July 1987.

Timmons, Heather. "Home Equity: Despite Potholes, Some See Gold in Prefab Lending." *American Banker* 163(148) (5 August 1998).

"Title/pawn crackdown to be delayed." *(Jacksonville) Florida Times Union*, 21 March 1997, B1.

TJAGSA Practice Notes. "Payday Loans: The High Cost of Borrowing Against Your Paycheck." *Army Lawyer* 27 (February 2001).

Tocqueville, Alexis de. *Democracy in America*. Edited by Phillips Bradley. New York: Vintage Books, 1945.

Torpy, Bill. "Foreclosures Set One-Month Record for State." *Atlanta Journal and Constitution*, 28 March 2002, JA1.

Troyer Ronald J. and Gerald Markle. *Cigarettes: The Battle Over Smoking*. New Brunswick: Rutgers University Press, 1983.

Tucker, David M. *The Decline of Thrift in America: Our Cultural Shift From Savings to Spending*. New York: Praeger, 1991.

Tversky, Amos and Daniel Kahneman. "Judgment Under Uncertainty: Heuristics and Biases." *Science* 185 (1974).

———. "Rational Choice and the Framing of Decisions." *Rational Choice: The Contrast Between Economics and Psychology*. Edited by Robin M. Hogarth and Melvin W. Reder. Chicago: University of Chicago Press, 1987.

Tversky, Amos, Shamuel Sattath, and Paul Slovic. "Contingent Weighting in Judgment and Choice," *Psychology Review* 95 (1988).

Ullmann-Margalit, Edna. "Revision of Norms." *Ethics* 100 (July 1990).

United Nations International Drug Control Programme. *World Drug Report*. Oxford: Oxford University Press, 1997.

U. S. Department of Health, Education and Welfare. *Smoking and Health: Report of the Advisory Committee to the Surgeon General of the Public Health Service*. Washington D.C., 1964.

U. S. Department of Housing and Urban Development. *Curbing Predatory Home Mortgage Lending*. Washington, D.C., June 2000. Available at http://www.huduser.org/publications/hsgfin/curbing.html.

U. S. Department of Housing and Urban Development. *Unequal Burden: Income and Racial Disparities in Subprime Lending in America*. Washington, D.C. Available at http://www.hud.gov/library/bookshelf18/pressrel/subprime.html.

U. S. House Committee on Banking and Financial Services. *Consumer Debt: Hearing Before the House of Representatives*. 104th Cong., 1996.

U. S. House Committee on Banking and Financial Services. *Predatory Lending Practices: Hearing Before the Committee on Banking and Financial Services, U.S. House of Representatives*. 106th cong., 2d sess., 24 May 2000.

U. S. House Committee on Banking, Finance, and Urban Affairs. *Discriminatory Mortgage Lending Patterns, Field Hearing*. 101st Cong., 1st sess., 1989.

U. S. House Committee on Interstate and Foreign Commerce. *Cigarette Labeling and Advertising—1965: Hearings Before the Committee on Interstate and Foreign Commerce*. 89th Cong., 1965.

U. S. House Committee on Interstate and Foreign Commerce. *Fair Packaging and Labeling: Hearings Before the Committee on Interstate and Foreign Commerce*. Part I & II, 89th Cong., 1966.

U. S. House Report No. 97–542 (1982). Reprinted in 1982 U.S.C.C.A.N. 765, 777.

U. S. House Report No. 1040, 90th Cong., 2d sess. Reprinted in 1968 U.S.C.C.A.N. 1962, 1970.

U. S. House Report No. 3899.

U. S. House Subcommittee on Consumer Affairs, Banking, and Currency. *Consumer Credit Protection Act: Hearings on H.R. 11601 Before the Subcommittee on Consumer Affairs, Banking and Currency.* 90th Cong., 1st sess., 1967.

U. S. House Subcommittee on Consumer Credit and Insurance of the Committee on Banking, Finance and Urban Affairs. *Kiddie Credit Cards: Hearing Before the House of Representatives.* 103rd Cong., 2d sess., 10 March 1994.

U. S. House Subcommittee on Consumer Credit and Insurance of the Committee on Banking, Finance and Urban Affairs. *Refund Anticipation Loans: Hearing before the House of Representatives.* 103rd Cong., 2d sess., 14 April 1994.

U. S. House Subcommittee on Government Operations. *Mortgage Delinquencies and Defaults: Hearings Before a Subcommittee of the House.* 97th Cong., 2d sess. 1, 1982.

U. S. House Subcommittee on Health and the Environment of the Committee on Energy and Commerce. *Smoking Prevention Education Act: Hearings Before the House of Representatives.* 98th Cong., 1983.

U. S. House Subcommittee on Housing and Community Opportunity of the Community on Banking and Financial Services. *The American Home Ownership Act of 1998: Hearing Before the U.S. House of Representatives.* 103rd Cong., 2d sess., July 23, 1998.

U. S. House Subcommittee on Housing and Community Opportunity of the Committee on Banking and Financial Services. *Consumer Abuses in Home Improvement Financing: Hearing before the Subcommittee of the U.S. House of Representatives.* 105th Cong., 2d sess., 30 April 1998.

U. S. House Subcommittee on Housing and Economic Opportunity of the Committee on Banking and Financial Services. *The Role of Mortgage Brokers in the Mortgage Finance Market: Hearing before the U.S. House of Representatives.* 105th Cong., 2d sess., 27 March 1998.

U. S. Senate Committee on Banking, Housing, and Urban Affairs. *Hearing on the State of Financial Literacy and Education in America.* 107th Cong., 2d sess., 5 and 6 February 2002.

U. S. Senate Committee on Banking, Housing, and Urban Affairs. *Predatory Mortgage Lending Practices: Abusive Uses of Yield Spread Premiums—Hearing Before the U.S. Senate.* 107th Cong., 2002.

U. S. Senate Committee on Banking, Housing and Urban Affairs. *Problems in Community Development Banking, Mortgage Lending Discrimination, Reverse Redlining and Home Equity Lending: Hearings Before the United States Senate.* 103d. Cong. 1st sess., 3, 17, and 24 February 1993.

U. S. Senate Committee on Banking, Housing, and Urban Affairs. *Truth in Lending Simplification and Reform Act, Hearings on S.108 Before the U.S. Senate.* 96th Cong. 1st sess., 1979.

U. S. Senate Committee on Commerce, Science, and Transportation. *Comprehensive Smoking Prevention Education Act of 1981: Hearing.* 97th Cong., 1982.

U. S. Senate Special Committee on Aging. *Equity Predators: Stripping, Flipping, and Packaging their Way to Profits: Hearing Before the Special Committee on Aging, United States Senate.* 105th Cong., 2d sess., 16 March 1998.

U. S. Senate Subcommittee on the Consumer of the Committee on Commerce, Science, and Transportation. *Alcohol Warning Labels: Hearing Before the United States Senate.* 100th Cong., 1988.

U. S. Senate Subcommittee on Consumer and Regulatory Affairs of the Committee on Banking, Housing, and Urban Affairs. *Discrimination in Home Mortgage Lending Hearing Before the U.S. Senate.* 102d Cong., 1990.

U. S. Senate Subcommittee on Consumer Affairs of the Committee on Banking, Housing, and Urban Affairs. *Simplify and Reform the Truth in Lending Act: Hearings Before the United States Senate.* 95th Cong., 1st sess., July 11, 1977.

Veatch, Robert M. "Abandoning Informed Consent." *Hastings Center Report* 25 (1995).

Vega, Sara D. *Short Term Lending Final Report.* Springfield, IL: Illinois Department of Financial Institutions, 1999.

Veverka, Amber. "Payday Lending Persists in NC: some Lenders

Keep up Practice After Linking to Out of State Banks." *Charlotte Observer,* 26 December 2001, 1A.

Vinarsky, Cynthia. "Youngstown, Ohio, Program Helps Homeowners Victimized by Predatory Lenders." *Knight Ridder Tribune Business News,* 14 April 2002. Available on Westlaw at 2002 WL 19772538.

Visa Consumer Bankruptcy Reports. *Consumer Bankruptcy: Bankruptcy Debtor Survey.* Visa, U.S.A.., Inc., July 1996.

Viscusi, W. Kip. *Smoking: Making the Risky Decision.* New York: Oxford University Press, 1992.

Waggoner, Judy. "Pawnshops in Appleton, Wisc. Area See Business Surge When Economy Slips." *Knight Ridder/Tribune Business News,* 16 December 2001.

Walden, Michael L. "The Economics of Rent-to-Own Contracts." *Journal of Consumer Affairs* (22 December 1990).

Walsh, Charles J. and Marc S. Klein. "From Dog Food to Prescription Drug Advertising: Litigating False Scientific Claims Under the Lanham Act." *Seton Hall Law Review* 22 (1992).

Ward, Jr., Ken. "Borrower Beware! Equity Lenders Taking the Homes of State Residents." *Charleston (W.V.) Gazette and Daily Mail (WV),* 31 March 2002, P1A.

———. "State Court Urged to Toss One-Sided Loan Arbitration." *Charleston (W.V.) Gazette and Daily Mail,* 4 April 2002, 5A.

Ware, Baxter. "The Lure of the Loan Shark," *Harper's Weekly* 52 (11 July 1908).

Warner, K. E. "The Effects of the Anti-Smoking Campaign on Cigarette Consumption." *American Journal of Public Health* 67 (1977).

Warren, Charles. *Bankruptcy in United States History.* Cambridge: Harvard University Press, 1935.

Warren, Elizabeth. "The Bankruptcy Crisis." *Indiana Law Journal* 73 (1998).

———. "What is a Women's Issue? Bankruptcy, Commercial Law, and Other Gender-Neutral Topics." *Harvard Women's Law Journal* 25 (2002).

Warren, Elizabeth, Teresa Sullivan, and Melissa Jacoby. "Medical

Problems and Bankruptcy Filings." *Harvard Law School Public Law and Legal Theory Working Paper Series*, Working Paper No. 008 (April 2000).

Watson, Jamal E. "Banking on a Costly Alternative: Low Earners Turn to Check Cashing Stores." *Boston Globe*, 28 February 2000, A1.

"Web Site Offers Credit Score Information." *Chicago Tribune*, 16 April 2002, 7, North Sports Final Edition.

Weinstein, Neil D. "Optimistic Biases About Personal Risks." *Science* 246 (1989).

————. "Unrealistic Optimism about Future Life Events." *Journal of Personality and Social Psychology* (1980).

————. "Unrealistic Optimism About Susceptibility to Health Problems: Conclusions From a Community-Wide Sample." *Journal of Behavioral Medicine* 10 (1987).

————. "Why It Won't Happen To Me: Perceptions of Risk Factors and Susceptibility." *Journal of Personality and Social Psychology* 39 (1980).

Weisberg, Robert. "Commercial Morality, the Merchant Character, and the History of Voidable Preference." *Stanford Law Review* 39 (November 1986).

Werland, Ross. "The Facts Behind College Kids and Debt." *Chicago Tribune*, 1 October 2000, 5.

Westen, Tracy A. "Usury in the Conflict of Laws: The Doctrine of the Lex Debitoris." *California Law Review* 55 (1967).

Westermann, William Linn. "Banking in Antiquity." *Journal of Economic and Business History* 3 (1930).

Weston, Liz Pulliam. "Get Loan Rate Based on Your Credit Score: Web Site is First to Let Consumers See How Lenders Determine Interest For Mortgage, Car Financing; Some Say it Won't Help Most Targets of Predatory Practices." *Los Angeles Times*, 6 March 2002, C6.

Wheat, Willis J. "A Study on the Status of the Pawnbroker Industry in the State of Oklahoma." *Consumer Finance Law Quarterly Report* (Winter 1998).

Whelan, Elizabeth. *A Smoking Gun: How the Tobacco Industry Gets Away with Murder.* Philadelphia: George F. Stickley Company, 1984.

White, Becky Cox. *Competence to Consent.* Washington, D.C.: Georgetown University Press, 1994.

White, James J. "The Usury Trompe l'Oeil." *South Carolina Law Review* 51 (Spring, 2000).

White, Lynn and Stacy Rogers. "Economic Circumstances and Family Outcomes: A Review of the 1990s." *Journal of Marriage and the Family* 62 (4) (2000).

White, Michelle J. "Why Don't More Households File for Bankruptcy?" *Journal of Law, Economics and Organizations* 14 (1998).

Whitford, William C. "The Functions of Disclosure Regulation in Consumer Transactions." *Wisconsin Law Review* (1973).

———. "The Ideal of Individualized Justice: Consumer Bankruptcy as Consumer Protection, and Consumer Protection Bankrutpcy." *American Bankruptcy Law Journal* 68 (1994).

Wilemon, Tom. "Pawnbrokers Question New Laws." *Biloxi (MS) Sun Herald,* 10 October 2001, A2.

Willenzik and Leymaster. "Recent Trends in Truth-in-Lending Litigation." *Business Lawyer* 35 (1980).

Williams, Christian. "Combating the Problems of Human Rights Abuses and Inadequate Organ Supply Through Presumed Donative Consent." *Case Western Reserve Journal of International Law* 26 (Spring/Summer 1994).

Williamson, Odette. "Protecting Elderly Homeowners from Predatory Mortgage Lenders." *Clearinghouse Review* (September–October 2000).

Wolgater, Michael S., et al. "Consumer Product Warnings: the Role of Hazard Perception." *Journal of Safety Resolutions* 22 (1991).

———. "Organizing Theoretical Framework: A Consolidated Communication–Human Information Processing (C-HIP) Model."

Warnings and Risk Communication. Edited by Michael S. Wolgater et al. London: Taylor and Francis, 1999.

Wu, Chi Chi, Jean Ann Fox, and Elizabeth Renuart. *Tax Preparers Peddle High Priced Tax Refund Loans: Millions Skimmed From the Working Poor and the U.S. Treasury*. Washington, D.C., Boston: Consumer Federation of America & National Consumer Law Center, 31 January 2002. Available at http://www.consumerfed.org.

Zhu, Lilan Y. and Carol B. Meeks. "Effects of Low Income Families Ability and Willingness to Use Consumer Credit on Subsequent Outstanding Credit Balances." *Journal of Consumer Affairs* 28(2) (22 December 1994).

Zimring, Franklin E. "Comparing Cigarette Policy and Illicit Drug and Alcohol Control." *Smoking Policy: Law, Politics, and Culture*. Edited by Robert L. Rabin and Stephen D. Sugarman. New York: Oxford University Press, 1993.

INDEX